Introduction to Security

FIFTH EDITION

Robert J. Fischer

Gion Green

Butterworth-Heinemann

Boston London Oxford Singapore Sydney Toronto Wellington

Library of Congress Cataloging-in-Publication Data

Fischer, Robert J.
    Introduction to security / Robert J. Fischer and Gion Green.—5th ed.
        p.   cm.
    Green's name appeared first on earlier edition.
    Includes bibliographical references and index.
    ISBN 0-7506-9191-3 (casebound : acid-free paper)
    1. Private security services.   2. Private security services—
Management.   3. Industry—Security measures.   4. Retail trade—
Security measures.   I. Green, Gion.   II. Title.
    HV8290.G74   1992
    363.2'89—dc20   91–29328
                                                                    CIP

British Library Cataloguing in Publication Data

Fischer, Robert J.
    Introduction to security.—5th ed
    I. Title   II. Green, Gion
    658.473

    ISBN 0-7506-9191-3

Butterworth–Heinemann
80 Montvale Avenue
Stoneham, MA 02180

10   9   8   7   6   5   4   3   2

Printed in the United States of America

This fifth edition is dedicated to the memory of Gion Green, a man who contributed much to the professionalism of the security field and to those who contributed their time and expertise to the revisions in this volume.

Contents

10 The Inner Defenses: Intrusion and Access Control   233

19   Security: Its Problems, Its Future   457

□ □ □
□ □ □
□ □ □

Preface and Acknowledgments, Fifth Edition

As I noted in the preface to the fourth edition of *Introduction to Security* in 1985, "[M]any changes have occurred over the past years and many more are certain to come." The same can be said of security in 1992. Keeping in mind the basic concept set out by Gion Green in his first edition of *Introduction to Security*, this edition will "cover the total picture, giving the reader a glimpse of the various, diverse components which make up the security function."

This fifth edition has been thoroughly updated and revised to bring the reader up to date with the new developments in the security field. Ironically the single, most important development since the fourth edition has been the publication of *The Hallcrest Report II, Private Security Trends 1970–2000*. When the fourth edition of *Introduction to Security* was published it was simply the *Hallcrest Report*. *Hallcrest II* notes that changes have been substantial and will continue to impact the field through the year 2000. Among the greatest changes are those involved in the relationship between private security and policing, technology, and structure of security operations. All these areas have been addressed in this edition. Other current topics such as drugs in the workplace and economic crimes appear as new material in the text. As a result of the new materials, the revised text has 19 chapters rather than 18. In order to accommodate new materials/issues associated with hiring (such as the 1989 Polygraph Act and other labor related regulations) in an organized fashion, the chapter on internal theft control has been broken into two new chapters. Furthermore the chapters on security and the law and computer security have again been extensively updated to reflect changing legal precedents and technology.

I wish to express my gratitude to Terry Magel, chair of the Computer Science Department, Eastern Kentucky University, and Wesley Eller, Corporate Security Representative, Deere and Company, for their assistance in updating the materials on computer security. I am extremely grateful for the contributions of David Steeno, professor, Ferris State University, and Julie Gilmere, associate professor, Western Illinois University, for their efforts in updating the legal chapter. Thanks also to Jon Blevins, Regional Director Loss Prevention, Walmart, for his review of the chapter on retail security and to Lawrence S. Jones, security consultant, Glendale, California; Richard Atlas, E.J. Brooks Company, and Brian Robbins, District Loss Prevention Supervisor, Walmart, for their contributions in the area of cargo security. Kevin Cassidy, vice president, Summit Security Systems Inc., Elmhurst, New York; William McCamey, Western Illinois University, and Don Bytner, assistant fire chief, Macomb, Illinois, contributed to the update on fire and safety.

I must also express much gratitude for the work of Joe Panici, Marketing and Finance Department, Western Illinois University, and Timothy D. Crowe, criminologist, Louisville, Kentucky, for their work on the insurance chapter. Without their help, this chapter would have ceased to exist. I also thank John Chuvala III for his overall review of the fourth edition and of the changes that I subsequently made. His thoughts on the revisions, especially on the futures chapter, were greatly appreciated. I also appreciate the help of the many people who reviewed the materials for Butterworth-Heinemann who remain anonymous. Their suggestions were helpful. Thanks go to all the people who took the time to comment briefly on the fourth edition and offer suggestions on the revisions.

In addition, I am grateful to Greg Franklin and Andrea Seward of Butterworth-Heinemann for their assistance during the preparation and publication of this book.

Finally I would like to give special thanks to my associates at Western Illinois University for their support, especially to Deans Rodney Fink and Mary Leach who allowed the time for me to work on the manuscript and to Provost Burton Whitthuhn and President Ralph Wagoner who approved administrative leave so that I might complete the project. Most of all, I would like to thank my wife, Kathy, and my children, Ian and Jenni, for their understanding, love, and support.

PART

I

Introduction

1

□ □ □
□ □ □
□ □ □

Origins and Development of Security

Security implies a stable, relatively predictable environment in which an individual or group may pursue its ends without disruption or harm and without fear of disturbance or injury. The concept of security in an organizational sense has evolved gradually throughout the history of western civilization, shaped by a wide variety of institutional and cultural patterns.

In examining the origins and development of security, it should be noted that security holds a mirror up, not to nature, but to society and its institutions. Thus in medieval England, there were programs to clear brush and other concealment on either side of the king's roads as a precaution against robbers, and to protect citizens from night thieves, there were night watchmen. In the United States in modern times, these rudimentary security measures find their counterparts in the cleared areas adjoining perimeter fences and buildings, in security patrols, and in intrusion alarms. Throughout history it is possible to trace the emerging concept of security as a response to, and a reflection of, a changing society, mirroring not only its social structure but also its economic conditions, its perception of law and crime, and its morality. Thus security remains a field of both tradition and dramatic change. The introduction of high-tech and computers has thus changed the nature of the job of security professional of the 1990s. Security today must be directed toward the twenty-first century, yet we cannot forget the basic foundations on which the field has developed.

Security in England

Feudalism and Security

In early England, feudalism provided a very high degree of security for both the individual and the group. The Anglo-Saxons brought with them to England a predisposition to accept mutual responsibility for civil and military protection of individuals. They also brought a strong affinity for the feudal contract whereby an overlord guaranteed the safety of persons and property and provided arms and treasures to vassals who administered the work of the serfs bound to the land.

In a world of constant warfare between men of power, security could be found in no other way. Stability lay in the system and in the power and cleverness of the lord. Group security lay in group solidarity. The formal systems of security that developed over the years of the Middle Ages were largely confirmations of those systems toward which the people of this society had gravitated naturally.

Post-Norman Reforms

Post-Norman England, beginning with King John, saw the introduction of concepts declaring the supremacy of law over the arbitrary edict, thus developing a base of confidence in the continuity of the system and its institutions. Above all, there was a formal declaration of the individual's rights and of responsibilities between the state and its subjects and among subjects themselves.

Judicial reforms during this era saw the emergence of local juries, circuit judges, coroners to restrain the power of local sheriffs, and justices of the peace appointed to hear and determine criminal cases. The movement also began that would eventually see the complete separation of courts and the exercise of the rule of law from the whims and power of the king.

Concurrently, there were measures specifically aimed at the enforcement of public order. The Statute of Winchester (also known as the Statute of Westminster) in 1285 revived and reorganized the old institutions of national police and national defense. It described the "duty of watch and ward," which enjoined every man to pursue and bring to justice felons whenever "hue and cry" was raised.

Every district was made responsible for crimes committed within its bounds; the gates of all towns were required to be closed at nightfall, and all strangers were required to give an account of themselves to the magistrates. Interestingly, one "security" practice already mentioned required brushwood and other concealments to be cleared for a space of 200 feet on either side of the king's highways to protect travelers against attack by robbers.

Attempts were made to control vice and crime at the local level, and boroughs enacted their own ordinances to that end. Since organized agencies for the enforcement of such laws were virtually nonexistent, however, these efforts had a limited success. Privately established night watches and patrols were often the citizens' only protection against direct assault.

Exploration and Change

The development of systems of protection and enforcement appeared to come with greater rapidity and sophistication from the fourteenth through the eighteenth centuries. Seeds for this development were planted during the social revolution that heralded the end of the remaining elements of the feudal structure in the latter half of the thirteenth century.

Security was one thing in a largely rural society controlled by kings and feudal barons; it was another thing entirely in a world swept by enormous changes. The voyages of exploration, which opened new markets and trade routes, created a new and increasingly important merchant class whose activities came to dominate the port cities and trading centers. Concurrently, acts of enclosure and consolidation drove displaced small tenants off the land, and they migrated to the cities in great numbers.

By 1700, the social patterns of the Middle Ages were breaking down. Increased urbanization of the population had created conditions of considerable hardship. Poverty and crime increased rapidly. No public law enforcement agencies existed that could restrain the mounting wave of crime and violence, and no agencies existed that could alleviate the causes of the problem.

Different kinds of police agencies were privately formed. Individual merchants hired men to guard their property. Merchant associations also created the *merchant police* to guard shops and warehouses. *Night watchmen* were employed to make their rounds. *Agents* were engaged to recover stolen property, and *parochial police* were hired by the people of various parishes into which the major cities were divided.

Attention then turned to the reaffirmation of laws to protect the common good. Although the Court of Star Chamber, which gave the English monarchy all control over decisions of law, had been abolished in 1641, its practices were not officially proscribed until 1689 when Parliament agreed to crown William and Mary if they would reaffirm the ancient rights and privileges of the people. They agreed, and Parliament ratified the Bill of Rights, which for all time limited the power of the king as well as affirming and protecting the inalienable rights of the individual.

The Eighteenth Century

By the eighteenth century, it is possible to discern both the shape of efforts toward communal security and the kinds of problems that would continue to plague an increasingly urban society for the next 200 years.

In 1737, for instance, a new aspect of individual rights came to be acknowledged; for the first time, tax revenues were used for the payment of a night watch. This was a significant development in security practice since it was a precedent-setting step that established for the first time the use of tax revenues for common security purposes.

Eight years later, Parliament authorized a special committee to study security problems. The study resulted in a program employing various existing private security forces to extend the scope of their protection. The resulting heterogeneous group, however, was too much at odds. It proved ineffective in providing any satisfactory level of protection.

In 1748, Henry Fielding, magistrate and author (most notably of the unforgettable *Tom Jones*), proposed a permanent, professional, and adequately paid security force. His invaluable contributions included a foot patrol to make the streets safe, a mounted patrol for the highways, the famous "Bow Street Amateur Volunteer Force" or special investigators, and police courts. Fielding is credited with conceiving the idea of *preventing* crime instead of seeking to control it.

It is interesting to note that Fielding also wrote an ironic novel called *Jonathan Wild—The Story of a Great Man*. Its hero, Jonathan Wild, was a real person in eighteenth-century London, perhaps the most notorious fence, thief, and master criminal of modern times. He was so real in fact that an account of his activities occupies eight pages of a staff report prepared in 1972 for the Select Committee on Small Business of the U.S. Senate, more than 200 years after Wild was hanged at Tyburn.

How is it that the spectre of Jonathan Wild still haunts those bodies charged with finding means to minimize crime? In many ways, Wild's career typified the problems of security—or more specifically theft control—in the eighteenth century.

For many centuries, English common law almost totally ignored the receiver of stolen goods. As the Senate committee report observes, "Because Jonathan Wild was such an extraordinary criminal, it is easy to lose sight of the fact that first he was at best a receiver and that second his whole organization was geared to facilitate that primary enterprise."[1] But mere receiving of stolen goods, even with knowledge, did not make the receiver an accessory in the eyes of the law.

Perhaps this attitude of common law can be explained in part by the relative unimportance of dealings in stolen property in the early stages of the development of criminal law. Until the seventeenth century, the amount of movable property available for theft was probably limited, and opportunities to dispose of this property, other than by personal consumption, were rather restricted. Lacking a professional police force, the attention of the community, and the law, was primarily directed toward apprehending offenders rather than tracing and recovering stolen property. The victims of property crimes were left to rely on their own ingenuity, bolstered by several shaky legal remedies, to secure the return of their plundered goods and chattels.

It was not until the late seventeenth century that Parliament moved for the first time to combat the problem of the receiver of stolen goods. In 1691, under a statute enacted during the reign of William and Mary, the receiver was made subject to prosecution, but only as an accessory after the fact. The tradition remained throughout the eighteenth and early nineteenth centuries that the receiver was an accessory rather than a principal to the crime. The weakness of the law in its attitude toward property crimes as much as the lack of effective law enforcement combined to make possible Jonathan Wild's legendary career.

The Impact of Industrial Expansion

The Industrial Revolution began to gather momentum in the latter half of the eighteenth century. By 1801, the poet William Blake, of apocalyptic vision, was writing disapprovingly of "these dark, Satanic mills." Like the migrations off the land 200 years earlier, people again flocked to the cities—not pushed this time, as they had been earlier, by enclosure and dispossession but rather lured by promises of work and wages.

The already crowded cities were choked with this new influx of wealth seekers. What they found were long hours, crippling work, and miserly wages. Men and women—even very young children—worked in unsafe factories. Disease periodically swept the crowded quarters. Family life, heretofore the root of all stability, was virtually destroyed in this environment. Thievery, crimes of violence, and juvenile delinquency were the order of the day. All the ills of such a structure, as we see in analogous situations today, overtook the emerging industrial centers.

Little was done to alleviate the growing problems. Indeed the prevailing philosophy of the time argued against doing anything. In 1776, Adam Smith gained a large and appreciative audience with his *Wealth of Nations*. In it, he contended that labor was the source of wealth and that it was by freedom of labor, by allowing the worker to pursue his own interest in his own way, that the public wealth would best be promoted. Any attempt to force labor into artificial channels, to shape by laws the course of commerce, or to promote special branches of industry in particular counties would be not only wrong to the worker and merchant but also harmful to the wealth of the state.

In this new age in which such statements of *laissez faire* were generally accepted, industrial centers became the spawning grounds for crimes of all kinds. At one time, counterfeiting was so common that it was estimated that more counterfeit than government issue money was in circulation. Over 50 false mints were found in London alone.

The backlash to such a high crime rate was inevitable and predictable. Penalties were increased to deter potential criminals. At one time, over 150 capital offenses existed, ranging from picking pockets to serious crimes of violence. Yet no visible decline in crime resulted. It was for all purposes a "society that lacked any effective means of enforcing the criminal laws in general. A Draconian code of penalties that proscribed the death penalty for a host of crimes failed to balance the absence of efficient enforcement machinery."[2]

Private citizens resorted to carrying arms for protection, and they continued to band together to hire special police to protect their homes and businesses.

Sir Robert Peel and the "Bobbies"

In 1822, Sir Robert Peel became home secretary. He had abiding interest in creating a strong, unified, professional police force. This interest had emerged earlier when, as secretary for Irish affairs, he had reformed the Irish constabulary—members of which were thereafter referred to as "Peelers." As home secretary, Peel initiated the criminal law reform bill, and he reorganized the metropolitan police force, also referred to as "Peelers" or more commonly "Bobbies." He also attempted to decentralize police efforts and to develop the responsibility of each community for its own security.

Unfortunately, not all of Sir Robert's efforts met with success. Neither the Police Act of 1835, establishing city and borough police forces; the County Act of 1839, setting up county police; nor various other acts passed in midcentury, created adequate police operations. Private guard forces continued in use to recover stolen property and to provide protection for private persons and businesses.

Nevertheless, based on Peel's thoroughgoing reforms and revisions, the metropolitan police force became a model for law enforcement agencies in years to come, not only in England but also in the United States. Modern policing, it is often said, was born with the "Bobby."

Security in the United States

Security practices in the early days of colonial America followed the patterns that colonists had been familiar with in England. The need for mutual protection in a new and alien land drew them together in groups much like those of earlier centuries.

As the settlers moved west in Massachusetts, along the Mohawk Valley in New York, and into central Pennsylvania and Virginia, the need for protection against hostile Indians and other colonists—French and Spanish—was their principal security interest. Settlements generally consisted of a central fort or stockade surrounded by the farms of the inhabitants. If hostilities threatened, an alarm was sounded and the members of the community left their homes for the protection of the fort where all able-bodied persons were involved in its defense. In such circumstances, a semimilitary flavor often characterized security measures, which included guard posts and occasional patrols.

Protection of people and property in established towns again followed English traditions. Sheriffs were elected as chief security officers in colonial Virginia and Georgia; constables were appointed in New England. Watchmen were hired to patrol the streets at night. As *Private Security: Report of the Task Force on Private Security* notes, "These watchmen remained familiar figures and constituted the primary security measures until the establishment of full-time police forces in the mid-1800's."[3]

Such watchmen, it should be pointed out, were without training, had no legal authority, were either volunteers or else paid a pittance, and were generally held in low regard—circumstances that bear a remarkable similarity to observations in *The Rand Report* on private security in 1971.[4]

Development of Private Security

The development of police and security forces seems to follow no predictable pattern other than that such development was traditionally in response to public pressure for action.

Outside of the establishment of night watch patrols in the seventeenth century, little effort to establish formal security agencies was made until the beginnings of a police department were established in New York City in 1783. Detroit followed in 1801, and Cincinnati, in 1803. Chicago established a police department in 1837; San Francisco, in 1846; Los Angeles, in 1850; Philadelphia, in 1855; and Dallas, in 1856.

New York, influenced by the recent success of the police reforms of Sir Robert Peel, adopted his general principles in 1833. By and large, however, police methods in departments across the country were rudimentary. Most

American police departments of the early nineteenth century, as a whole, were inefficient, ill-trained, and corrupt.

In addition, the slow development of public law-enforcement agencies, both state and federal, combined with the steady escalation of crime in an increasingly urban and industrialized society, created security needs that were met by what might be called the first professional private security responses in the second half of the nineteenth century.

In the 1850s Allan Pinkerton, a copper (police officers who were identified by the copper badges they wore) from Scotland and the Chicago Police Department's first detective, established what was to become one of the oldest and largest private security operations in the United States, Pinkertons. Today it has over 55,000 employees. Pinkerton's North West Police Agency, formed in 1855, provided security and conducted investigations of crimes for various railroads. Two years later the Pinkerton Protection Patrol began to offer a private watchman service for railroad yards and industrial concerns. President Lincoln recognized Pinkerton's organizational skills and hired the agency to perform intelligence duties during the Civil War. Pinkerton is also credited with hiring the first woman to become a detective in this country well before the women's suffrage movement had realized its aims.[5]

In 1850, Henry Wells and William Fargo were partners in the American Express Company, chartered to operate a freight service east of the Mississippi River; and by 1852, they had expanded their operating charter westward as Wells Fargo and Company. Freight transportation was a dangerous business, and these early companies usually had their own detectives and security personnel known as "shotgun riders."

Brinks, Inc., was founded by Washington Perry Brink in Chicago in 1859 as a freight and package delivery service. More than 30 years later in 1891, he transported his first payroll—the beginning of armored car and courier service. By 1900, Brinks had a fleet of 85 wagons in the field.[6] Brinks, Wells Fargo, and Adams Express were the first major firms to offer security for the transportation of valuables and money.

William J. Burns, a former Secret Service investigator and head of the Bureau of Investigation (forerunner of the FBI), started the William J. Burns Detective Agency in 1909. It became the sole investigating agency for the American Bankers' Association and grew to become the second largest (after Pinkerton's) contract guard and investigative service in the United States.[7] Today it has more than 30,000 employees. For all intents and purposes, Pinkerton's and Burns were the only national investigative bodies concerned with nonspecialized crimes in the country until the advent of the FBI.

Another nineteenth century pioneer in this field was Edwin Holmes, who offered the first burglar alarm service in the country in 1858. Holmes purchased an alarm system designed by Augustus Pope. Following Holmes, the American District Telegraph (ADT) was founded in 1874. Both companies installed alarms and provided response to alarm situations as well as maintaining their own equipment. Baker Industries initiated a fire control and detection equipment business in 1909.

From the 1870s, only private agencies had provided contract security services to industrial facilities across the country. In many cases, particularly around the end of the nineteenth century and during the depression of the 1930s, the services were, to say the least, controversial. Both the Battle of Homestead in 1892 during which workers striking that plant were shot and beaten by security forces and the strikes in the automobile industry in the middle 1930s are examples of excesses from overzealous security operatives in relatively recent history. With few exceptions, proprietary, or in-house, security forces hardly existed before the defense-related "plant protection" boom of the early 1940s. The impetus for modern private security effectively began in that decade with the creation of the federal Industrial Security Program (today named the Defense Industrial Security Program [DISP], a subordinate command within the Defense Investigative Service [DIS]) to improve plant security, and it came of age in the third quarter of the twentieth century. The original manual developed by the Industrial Security Program consisted of only 17 pages. Today the DIS Industrial Security Manual (ISM) is over 350 pages.

By 1955, security took a major leap forward with the formation of the American Society for Industrial Security (ASIS). For most practitioners, 1955 signifies the beginning of the modern age of security. Before 1955, there were no professional organizations of note, no certifications, no college programs, and no cohesive body to advance the interests of the field.

Today's changed climate for increased security services came as businesses undertook expanded operations that in turn needed more protection. Retail establishments, hotels, restaurants, theaters, warehouses, trucking companies, industrial companies, hospitals, and other institutional and service functions were all growing and facing a serious need to protect their property and personnel. Security guards were the first line of defense, but it was not long before that important function was being overchallenged by the increasing complexity of fraud, arson, burglary, and other areas in which more sophisticated criminal practices began to prevail. Security consulting agencies and private investigation firms were founded in increasing numbers to handle these special types of cases. From among these, another large contractor was to emerge and join the field alongside Pinkerton's, Burns, Globe, Brinks, and the others: In 1954, George R. Wackenhut formed the Wackenhut Corporation in company with three other former FBI agents, creating today's second-largest U.S. security firm.

The private sector entered security in another form during the 1960s and 1970s. Common businesses and industries created central repositories of security information deemed important to all of their common interests nationwide and made it available in various ways to their separate groups. Their purpose was to decrease loss by networking information that would prevent criminals from victimizing members of the group once anything was known that could be used to alert them.

Variously called "alliances," "bureaus," or possibly security or loss prevention "institutes," these groups became deeply entrenched as providers of valuable information and services. Their methods of dissemination vary with what is appropriate to the business for which they were founded but include circulating "hot" lists, newsletters with "wanted" pictures and descriptions of characteristic modes of operation, telephone chain calling to alert merchants within an area, and so on. Nationally available repositories of other types of industry-specific data are usually maintained also and can be accessed by members. Not only do these groups serve the private sector in its effort to survive against crime but they also make their collected intelligence available to law enforcement.

Some presently existing groups are The National Auto Theft Bureau (NATB), the Mutual Loss Research Bureau of Chicago (arson investigations), and the Jewelers Alliance of New York City. Still other groups serve similar functions by collecting records of insurance claims and spotting fraud, issuing periodic records of defaulted or dubious credit cards, and so on. It seems likely that the measures taken by these and other business associations to limit their losses and protect their members will spread to other areas in which there is today an increasing concern about excessive risk. Some of these areas could include computer and other high-tech industries, and anti-terrorism and executive protection alliances. The need for information for employment background checks has also led to the creation of information bureaus like National Employment Screening Service of Tulsa, Oklahoma. Other sources of information are listed in the *National Employment Screening Directory: A Guide to Background Investigations.*[8]

Expenditures in private security now exceed $52 billion annually, up from $20 billion in 1980. The expenditures continue to grow. Even as the anti-Vietnam War protest created a demand for additional security services during the 1970s, the threat of terrorism against U.S. business throughout the world and the kidnapping of executives assigned outside the United States by various extremist groups created a demand. With this dynamic growth have come profits, problems, and increasing professionalism. Each is a significant part of the picture of security today.[9]

Crime Trends and Security

During the 25 years roughly spanning the mid-1950s to the late 1970s, the United States became the victim of what Arthur J. Bilek, chairman of the Task Force on Private Security of the National Advisory Committee on Criminal Justice Standards and Goals, has called "a crime epidemic." The FBI's annual Uniform Crime Reports (UCR) documented the continuing steady increase in crimes of all types until 1981. Then for the first time, the UCR reflected a modest overall decrease that continued into 1984 despite an increase in rape (6 percent) and assault (1 percent).[10] The overall trends indicated first in the UCR of 1984 continued through 1989. The preliminary 1990 UCR indicates that, during the first six months of 1990, large cities (of over 1 million population) reported a 20 percent increase in murders. Overall violent crime was up 10 percent, the largest increase since 1986 when it went up 12.1 percent over 1985. The only good news reported showed that burglaries declined by 5 percent. Other crime was up including robbery, which increased by 9 percent, and car theft, which was up 6 percent. The figures prompted Senator Joseph R. Biden, Jr., chairman of the Senate Judiciary Committee, to complain that "drug dealers are battling over turf, and we are waging an anemic war to stop it." Attorney General Dick Thornburgh's office called the figures "further evidence of the need to pass a crime bill that is tough on criminals."[11] While there has been a decrease in the number of crimes reported against households, it is truly unfortunate that violent crime continues to increase.

Gallup Polls taken each year indicate that the fear of crime is an even greater problem than the crime rate itself would indicate. The consistency of survey results indicating that crime touched 25 percent of all American households during the year preceding each survey led Gallup to conclude that "the actual crime situation in this country is more serious than official governmental figures indicate." Still National Crime Survey (NCS) reports show that the percentage of households touched by crime has declined overall by 23 percent between 1975 and 1988.[12] And the most recent NCS data (for 1989) indicate that the level of crime did not change from 1988. Certain types of crimes, however, were noticeably different. Burglaries decreased by 7.3 percent; the number of household thefts increased by 6.4 percent; and motor vehicle thefts increased slightly.[13] Victimization trends over the past 16 years are graphically presented in Figure 1.1.

Although the NCS indicates a decline in the number of offenses, the cost of business crime continues to increase. *Hallcrest II* reports that business crime was estimated at $114 billion in 1990 and will increase to $200 billion by the turn of the century.

The estimated figures on the extent of crime against business, ranging from $67 billion to $320 billion, have not been adequately studied since the mid-1980s and dramatize the absence of consistent hard data indicating the exact size of the problem today. Variations of billions of dollars in estimates are the result of educated guessing, interpolation, and adjustment for inflation. Some progress has been made in the last decade, however, in coming to grips with the problem of defining the size of the problem. *Hallcrest II* re-

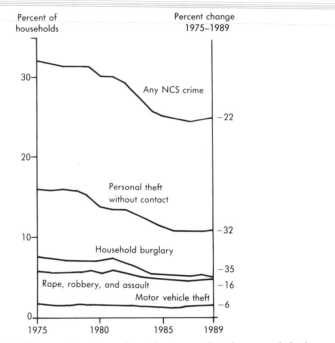

Figure 1.1 Households experiencing selected crimes of violence and theft, 1975–1989. (Modified from "A National Crime Survey Report: Crime and the Nation's Households, 1989," *Bureau of Justice Statistics Bulletin* [September 1990].)

searchers, using the best available data, the *UCR*, have estimated the total direct cost of economic crime against business to be at least $114 billion.[14]

Obviously figures vary, principally because satisfactory measures of many crimes against business and industry have not yet been found but also because much internal crime in particular is never reported to the police. Reasons for not reporting to the police are: to avoid bad publicity, because internal disciplinary action has already been taken, or to avoid embarrassing management by exposing to the public its lack of security controls. Nevertheless such questions as may exist concern only the degree, not the fact, of the dramatic escalation of crimes against business in our society.

As the brief history of security has indicated, there is always an intimate link between cultural and social change and crime as there is between crime and the security measures adopted to combat the threat. A bewildering variety of causes, both social and economic, are cited for rising crime in this era. Among them are an erosion of family and religious restraints, the trend toward permissiveness, the increasing anonymity of business at every level of commerce, the decline in feelings of worker loyalty toward the company, high unemployment, the Vietnam War and its attendant turmoil, and a general decline in morality accompanied by the pervasive attitude that there is no such thing as right and wrong but rather only what feels good.

This change in attitude and personal values has created a new problem for security managers. McDonnell Douglas Corporation recently fired 150 employees who allegedly used interest-free company loans intended for the purchase of computers to buy stereo equipment and other luxury items. A data-processing employee reportedly processed the $4000 loans by printing phony invoices for computers.[15] According to a recent study by the Josephson Institute for the Advancement of Ethics, "[a]n unprecedented proportion of today's youth lack commitment to core moral values like honesty, personal responsibility, respect for others and civic duty."[16]

It is far beyond the scope of this book to attempt to analyze or even to catalog all of the factors involved in the trend toward increasing crime even were we to restrict such a study to crimes against business and industry. What is important here is to make clear note of the fact of such increases—and of their impact on society's attempt to protect itself.

Most significant is the realization that "the sheer magnitude of crime in our society prevents the criminal justice system by itself from adequately controlling or preventing crime."[17] In spite of their steady growth, both in costs and in numbers of personnel, public law enforcement agencies have increasingly been compelled to be reactive and to concentrate more of their activities on the maintenance of public order and the apprehension of criminals. As the *Report of the Task Force on Private Security* observed as early as 1976, "U.S. Bureau of the Census statistics reflect some 12.4 million commercial and business establishments in the United States. The approximate 500,000 local law enforcement personnel in this country can not possibly provide protection for all of these establishments."[18] In the past 10 years, the federal government funded studies by the Hallcrest Corporation to study whether progress has been realized in the public/private battles against crime. Both *Hallcrest I* and *Hallcrest II* generally report the same trends. *Hallcrest II* notes a growing interest in privatization of some areas of public law enforcement to ease the burden of law enforcement and provide security where overworked police agencies cannot possibly offer services.[19] More will be said on these important reports in the following pages.

Growth of Private Security

Society has in recent times relied almost exclusively on the police and other arms of the criminal justice system to prevent and control crime. But today the sheer volume of crime and its cost, along with budget cutbacks in the public sector, have overstrained public law enforcement agencies. Private security must play a greater role in the prevention and control of crime than ever before. *Hallcrest II* reports that in 1990 there were over 1.5 million persons employed in private security with total expenditures for its products and services estimated at $52 billion.[20] This compares with police protection expenditures for federal, state, and local governments of only $30 billion.

In 1985, *Private Security and Police in America: The Hallcrest Report* estimated that total security expenditures were $35.5 billion.[21] The $16.5 billion differential indicates just how much private security has grown in little more than half a decade. Various sources, including the Hallcrest System's study of private security, *Hallcrest II*, estimate that growth in expenditures will continue to rise at an annual rate of approximately 6 percent. As is indicated in Figure 1.2, *Hallcrest II* forecasts that about 410,000 new operating personnel will have entered private security employment by the year 2000, and sales of security equipment are expected to increase greatly as is shown in Table 1.1.

Of the many forces acting to affect the business of security, the federal and state government are no longer the most significant spenders. As was mentioned above, a comparison of expenditures for crime prevention by government and the private sector shows that in 1990 the private sector spent $52 billion compared to government expenditures of $30 billion. Projections

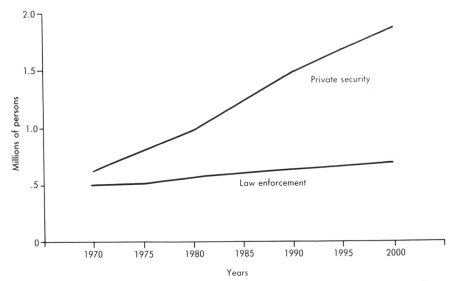

Figure 1.2 Private security and law enforcement employment. Comparison of private security and law enforcement expenditures. (From William Cunningham, J. Strauchs, Clifford W. VanMeter, *The Hallcrest Report II: Private Security Trends 1990–2000* [Boston: Butterworth-Heinemann, 1990], p. 237.)

Table 1.1 Security Services and Equipment Market (in millions of dollars)

	1987	1988	1989	1992	2000
Total security industry	15,982	17,646	19,795	28,750	91,090
Security services revenues	11,143	12,315	13,831	19,960	61,300
Central station	5,260	6,049	7,200	11,600	45,100
Corporate and VIP protection	454	490	530	700	1,510
Guard and armored car	1,112	1,200	1,250	1,660	3,690
Security guard and investigation	4,317	4,576	4,851	6,000	11,000
Electronic security equipment sales	4,839	5,331	5,964	8,790	29,790
Automatic garage door operators	455	505	553	840	2,690
Bomb detectors	39	43	49	80	290
CCTV equipment	428	478	534	810	2,660
Computer security equipment	158	181	215	350	1,400
Electronic access control equipment	419	462	516	760	2,410
Electronic article surveillance equipment	780	874	1,005	1,530	5,370
Electronic intrusion detection equipment	1,008	1,106	1,220	1,680	4,460
Electronic vehicle security systems	368	442	530	1,070	7,150
Fire detection equipment	800	822	882	1,040	1,680
Metal detectors	65	71	79	110	330
Telephone security equipment	243	263	285	370	840
X-ray devices	76	84	96	150	510

Source: Leading Edge Reports, "Security Products & Service," Cleveland Heights, Ohio, 1990.

for the year 2000 indicate that expenditures from the private sector will be twice as much at that spent by the government.[22]

Growing Pains and Government Involvement

Inevitably, the explosive growth of the security industry in the second half of this century has not been without its problems, leading to rising concern for the quality of selection, training, and performance of security personnel. Horror stories involving armed and untrained guards have drawn mass media attention. Both *The Rand Report* and *Report of the Task Force on Private Security* called attention to a serious lack of adequate training at all levels of private security. And within the industry itself, there is increasing pressure for improved standards, higher pay, and greater professionalism.

Basic to involvement at the federal level in crime prevention was the Law Enforcement Assistance Administration (LEAA), which was established to encourage cooperation among local law enforcement agencies and to promote research, development programs, and studies—generally to improve the criminal justice system.

Established by the Omnibus Act of 1968, the LEAA grew out of the President's Commission on Law Enforcement and Administration of Justice established in 1965. Its principal role was to allocate funds to state and local governments for the improvement of law enforcement procedures. In addition, it budgeted funds for the collection and dissemination of crime statistics and, through its National Institute of Law Enforcement and Criminal Justice, for development of new approaches, techniques, systems, equipment, and devices designed to improve law enforcement.

The Rand report referred to in this chapter was prepared under an LEAA grant. The five volumes of this report, generated after a 16-month study, sought to describe the nature and extent of the private security industry; to examine its problems, costs, and benefits to society; and to suggest guidelines for its future development and regulation. It was this report that first drew national attention to some of the problems of the private security industry, particularly in the areas of inadequate training and abuses of authority.

The National Advisory Committee on Criminal Justice Standards and Goals was formed by the LEAA in 1975 with the purpose of developing and publishing standards and goals for every area of the criminal justice system and crime prevention. Task forces were formed to investigate such areas of concern as the police, the courts, corrections, the juvenile justice system, organized crime, terrorism, and private security. Most relevant to our purposes is the Task Force on Private Security, chaired by Arthur J. Bilek.

The *Report of the Task Force on Private Security* was released in 1976. It represented a giant step in the articulation of uniform standards for the selection and training of personnel, for the development of a code of ethics, for research and standards in areas of physical security systems and equipment, and for improved interaction between private and public law enforcement in their common goal of crime prevention. It is through the promulgation of such uniform standards and goals, along with increased public debate, that the necessary professionalism will come to the giant new industry of private security.

The Hallcrest Reports

In order to obtain a clear, current picture of the extent and nature of private security efforts, the National Institute of Justice (NIJ), the successor to LEAA, in the mid-1980s contracted with Hallcrest Systems, Inc., to conduct research to determine:

1. The general character of the private security industry in the United States, updating previous research
2. The contribution private security makes to crime control and order maintenance (and to identify opportunities for improvement)
3. The working relationships between private security and public law enforcement agencies (and to develop recommendations for improved cooperation and coordination)

Private Security and Police in America: The Hallcrest Report was published in 1985. The publication of the report was the culmination of a 30-month project. In general, the results parallel those of *The Rand Report* and the *Report of the Task Force on Private Security*. The *Hallcrest Report*, however, differs in that it shows that the industry has made considerable progress since 1976. The field is still relatively new, but no longer an infant. The future holds a great deal of promise for improved standards, professionalism, and growth of career opportunities.

The Hallcrest Report II: Private Security Trends (1970 to 2000) was also supported by a grant from NIJ. The main purposes of this new study were to:

1. Profile the growth and changes in the private security industry over the past two decades
2. Identify emerging and continuing issues and trends in private security and its relationships with public law enforcement
3. Present recommendations and future research goals in the interest of greater cooperation between private security and law enforcement

Hallcrest II notes some improvements within the field. In particular the report notes that during the 1980s the field experienced its greatest growth ever. Despite the rapid growth in security numbers and expenditures business crime grew even faster. The report indicates that security is at a crucial point of change and that the 1990s will be a decade of change with a reduction in proprietary security staffs with a greater reliance on hybrid systems and a greater reliance on technology. Trends and issues studied by the Hallcrest group will be discussed in more detail in other chapters of this book. The changes reported indicate that security/loss prevention is truly moving toward a new professionalism.

A New Professionalism

Today private security is moving toward a new professionalism. In defining the desired professionalism, Saul Astor, President of Management Safeguards, Inc, cites the need for a code of ethics and for credentials, including education and training, experience, and membership in a professional society.

This thrust toward professionalism is observable in the proliferation of active private security professional organizations and associations. It is promoted by such organizations as the ASIS, which has a membership of more than 24,732 security managers, double the 1985 figure; the Academy of Security Educators and Trainers (ASET); the International Association for Hospital Security (IAHS); the National Association of School Security Directors (NASSD); and the Security Equipment Industry Association (SEIA). It finds its voice in the library of professional security literature—both magazines and books. And it looks to its future in the continued development of college-level courses and degree programs in security.

ASIS has adhered to a professional code of ethics, one mark of a true profession, since its inception. During the past decade, the group established the Certified Protection Professional (CPP) program that requires security managers desiring certification to be nominated by a CPP member and to complete a rigorous test. These programs will be discussed in more detail in Chapter 3.

Despite the many efforts to professionalize the field of private security, there are still many who feel that major obstacles need to be overcome. The most persistent one has to do with the training and education of the contract security guard. (A distinction between contract and proprietary guards needs to be made. Proprietary guards, those hired directly by a company, are generally better trained and paid than are their contract counterparts.) Many guards—no matter whether they are contract or proprietary—are underpaid, undertrained, undersupervised, and not regulated. Minimal standards do exist in some places, but there is still a reluctance to train, educate, and adequately compensate the guard force. Business considerations in making a product for profit can make it difficult for companies to see the need for paying for costly security programs. Thus they often opt for the lowest-priced solution no matter whether it affords real protection. Fortunately this kind of thinking is undergoing a change as industry realizes that the adage "you get what you pay for" very definitely applies to the quality of security. This realization will in turn add pressure to industry to upgrade the position of security guard. Current standards, codes of ethics, and educational courses ASIS has introduced in its CPP program are directed at security management personnel, not security guards.

One recent development in the evolution of training for line security staff is the development of the Certified Protection Officer (CPO) program, established in 1986 by the International Foundation for Protection Officers, a nonprofit organization. The CPO program is being offered at a number of colleges in the United State and Canada. Additional information on this program is presented in Chapter 3.

A New Philosophy

"A systems approach to security is appropriate today, as more and more businesses are giving the responsibility for protecting assets to the security and loss prevention department."[23] In that insightful comment, Dr. Kenneth Fauth, director of security and loss prevention at Spiegel, Inc., suggests clearly that security and loss prevention have evolved well beyond the guard at the gate. Though that post is still vital, today's business assets comprise an almost infinite variety of production needs. Moreover security increasingly includes protection against contingencies that might prevent normal company operation from continuing and from making a profit. And as the concept of risk management is further integrated into a comprehensive loss-prevention program, the security function focuses less and less on enforcement and more on anticipating and preventing loss through proactive programming. Such challenges indisputably require high-level security management and an increasingly well-credentialed group of security professionals.

A good example of the total proactive integrated approach to security/loss prevention has been developed by Doctor Norman Bottom and Professor John Kostanoski. They have applied a systems approach to the problem of assets protection. Formulated as a new way of considering security and loss prevention, and called WAECUP (an acronym for Waste, Accidents, Error, Crime, and Unethical Practices), the system replaces the traditional crime orientation in security with a multiloss orientation.[24]

The systems approach as outlined by C. West Churchman in 1968 is the process of focusing on central objectives rather than on attempting to solve individual problems within an organization. By concentrating on the central objectives, the management team can address specific problems that will lead toward the accomplishment of the central objective. In the context of WAE-CUP, the central objective is overall loss reduction. The specific problem areas include waste, accidents, error, crime, and unethical practices. Bottom and Kostanoski refer to this systems approach as a multiloss orientation since management's central objective is the reduction of losses. According to Bottom and Kostanoski, "All identified loss threats can be brought together in [this] useful model."[25]

Today, in the words of *The Hallcrest Report:*

> Citizen fear of crime and awareness that criminal justice resources alone cannot effectively control crime has led to a growing use of individual and corporate protective measures, including private security products and services and neighborhood based crime prevention. Law enforcement resources have stabilized and in some cases are declining. This mandates greater cooperation with the private sector and its private security resources to jointly forge a partnership on an equal basis for crime prevention and reduction. Law Enforcement can ill afford to continue isolating and, in some cases, ignoring this important resource. The creative use of private security human resources and technology may be the one viable option left to control crime in our communities.[26]

Hallcrest II reports progress in cooperative ventures over the past five years. The establishment of joint councils within ASIS and the International Association of Chiefs of Police (IACP) has increased communication between the public and private sectors. In addition the National Sheriffs' Association (NSA) created its Private Security Industry Committee in the mid-1980s. In 1986 with the financial support of NIJ, the Joint Council of Law Enforcement and Private Security Association was established comprised of representatives from NSA, IACP, and ASIS. These groups have developed numerous cooperative programs over the past five years of which only a few will be mentioned.

Operation Bootstrap, the development of Chief Michael Shanahan, co-chair of the IACP Private Sector Liaison Committee (PSLC), has become a very successful program with national visibility. The program is now active in 45 states providing management training and self-help programs on effective supervision, conflict resolution, group problem solving, and stress management. Participating corporations donated over $500,000 in executive training programs for over 1000 law enforcement personnel.

The National Crime Prevention Council (NCPC) has become involved with the private security sector in cooperative crime-prevention programs. The best known NCPC project is McGruff,"Take a Bite Out of Crime." The project would not be possible without the support of private donations from the Advertising Council ranging between $40 and $50 million. In addition, Southland Corporation has distributed over 20 million McGruff brochures.

These are but two of the many programs developed over the past five years. A more comprehensive discussion of programs is provided by *Hallcrest II*.[27]

Review Questions

1. What events in medieval England brought about the creation and use of private night watches and patrols?
2. What factors or conditions of the times made it possible for Jonathan Wide to become so extraordinarily successful?
3. Who was responsible for developing the concept of crime prevention?
4. How did World War II affect the growth of modern private security?
5. What was LEAA and what has been its impact on the private security industry?
6. What is WAECUP and what is its significance?
7. What is *The Hallcrest Report?*
8. What is *Hallcrest II?*
9. Discuss the extent of security's growth in this country. What are some of the reasons for the professionalization of the field of private security?

References

1. *An Analysis of Criminal Redistribution Systems and Their Economic Impact on Small Business* (Oct. 26, 1972), pp. 21–29.
2. Ibid., p. 25.
3. Clifford Van Meter, Executive Director, *Private Security: Report of the Task Force on Private Security* (Washington, D.C.: National Advisory Committee on Criminal Justice Standards and Goals, 1976), p. 30.
4. James S. Kakalik and Sorrell Wildhorn, *The Rand Report* (Santa Monica, Calif.: The Rand Corporation, 1971).
5. S. A. Levine, *Allan Pinkerton: American's First Private Eye* (New York: Dodd, Mead, 1963), p. 33.
6. Kakalik and Wildhorn, *The Rand Report*, pp. 94–95.
7. William Cunningham, John J. Strauchs, Clifford W. Van Meter, *The Hallcrest Report II: Private Security Trends 1970–2000* (Boston: Butterworth-Heinemann, 1990), p. 295.

8. Dan Backus, "Hiring Personnel: It's a Gamble," *Security Management* (September 1987), 144.

9. Cunningham et al., *The Hallcrest Report II*, p. 175.

10. Federal Bureau of Investigation, U.S. Department of Justice, *Uniform Crime Reports for the United States* (Washington, D.C.: GPO, 1985).

11. "Violent Crime Soars This Year," *Peoria Journal Star*, 22 October 1990, p. A2.

12. Cunningham et al., *The Hallcrest Report II*, p. 16.

13. *Bureau of Justice Statistics Bulletin* (October 1990), pp. 1–2.

14. Cunningham et al., *The Hallcrest Report II*, p. 30.

15. "150 Scheming Employees Fired," *Peoria Journal Star*, 27 May 1990.

16. "Study Reports Youth Lack Commitment," *Macomb Journal*, 12 October 1990, p. 14.

17. Van Meter, *Private Security*, p. 18.

18. Ibid.

19. Cunningham et al., *The Hallcrest Report II*, p. 269.

20. Ibid., p. 298.

21. William Cunningham and Todd H. Taylor, *Private Security and Police in America: The Hallcrest Report* (Portland, Ore.: Chancellor Press, 1985), p. 107.

22. Cunningham et al., *The Hallcrest Report II*, p. 234.

23. Kenneth G. Fauth as quoted in Norman R. Bottom and John Kostanoski, *Security and Loss Control* (New York: Macmillan, 1983), p. vii.

24. Bottom and Kostanoski, *Security and Loss Control*, pp. 1, 2.

25. Norman R. Botton and John Kostanoski, *Introduction to Security and Loss Control* (Englewood Cliffs, N.J.: Prentice Hall, 1990), p. 1.

26. Cunningham and Taylor, *Private Security and Police in America*, p. 275.

27. Cunningham et al., *The Hallcrest Report II*, pp. 246–65.

2 □ □ □
□ □ □
□ □ □

Career Opportunities in Loss Prevention

Today security is a major management function in American business. Where they were almost unheard of 25 or even 15 years ago, there are now vice presidents of loss prevention reporting directly to the presidents of many companies and having the same impact on management decisions as do, for example, the vice presidents of operations or distribution.

Career opportunities in different areas of business, industry, and government security vary; the perceived need for an integral and integrated security function in the management of the widest variety of enterprises can be anticipated as becoming the norm in the near future.

Factors Increasing Security Opportunities

Among the factors that tend to create inviting career paths in security, none is more significant than the explosive growth of the protection function as was briefly described in Chapter 1. The number of personnel engaged in private security will double between 1980 and 2000 to more than 1.8 million persons. Various studies place the growth rate generally for security products and services at from 12 percent to 15 percent annually, and there is no sign of slowing. Rapid advances in electronic technology create new opportunities almost daily.[1]

Other positive considerations for the future of not only jobs in security but also the changes and requirements for individual advancement or growth within the career field include:

- The increasing professionalism of security is reflected in higher standards of educational criteria and experience and correspondingly higher salaries, especially at management levels.
- The rapid growth of the loss-preventive function has created a shortage

of qualified personnel with management potential, meaning less competition and greater opportunities for advancement for those who are qualified.

- The shift in emphasis to programs of prevention and service rather than of control or law enforcement has broadened the security function within the typical organization.
- The presence of both two- and four-year degree programs as well as master's-level study in criminal justice and/or security at the college level is creating a new awareness of a rising generation of trained security personnel at the corporate management level. Many companies, especially larger corporations, are actively emphasizing the degree approach in hiring.

As in many other areas of a society that is belatedly recognizing the needs and the potential contributions of women, blacks, and other minorities, opportunities for these groups are particularly good. *Hallcrest II* points out the scarcity of good demographic information on personnel employed in the security field. Yet if the Hallcrest study of St. Louis is any indication, the number of women in private security has doubled within the last 15 years. The employment of minorities, particularly blacks, has remained at about 50 percent.[2]

The Security/Loss-Prevention Occupation

No matter whether you recognize the protection function by titles such as loss prevention, security administration, or industrial security, the basic function of modern security remains the same. Security helps prevent losses. As noted in Chapter 1, losses from crime have continued to increase despite the decline in criminal behavior reported through the National Crime Survey (NCS). For every product manufactured, someone is waiting to make an illegal profit by stealing or through manipulation of processes and records. For every security device installed, someone is determined to find a method to defeat it. Steven C. Kaverman, CPP (Certified Protection Professional), asserts that the dynamic trends of the 1990s will affect our businesses in the year 2000 and beyond. "Team management concepts, a changing work force, and educational demands are three issues that will pose a universal challenge to the flexibility of security professionals and corporate executives at every level."[3]

Much like law enforcement, security is basically a recession-proof occupation, particularly at line (guard) levels. The need for educated/trained security officers and administrators is increasing with the need to counteract terrorism, computer crime, embezzlement, employee theft, drugs in the workplace, fraud, and shoplifting. The U.S. Department of Labor has identified security as one of the fastest-growing fields of employment. Estimates indicate that for every person hired in public law enforcement, three are hired in private security. *Hallcrest II* predicts that this trend will continue through the year 2000.

Security professionals are hired by almost all kinds of organizations at all levels—line; lower, middle, and upper management; corporate; and so on. Among organizations that have security operations are banks, colleges, government agencies, hospitals, public utilities, restaurants, hotels, retail stores, insurance companies, museums, mining firms, oil companies, supermarkets, telecommunications companies, transportation companies, and office buildings. Within each of these broad areas, security personnel perform many different functions, including personnel protection, computer security, coupon security, disaster management, crime prevention, proprietary information security, white collar crime investigations, counterterrorism security, guard force management, investigations, physical security, crisis management, plant security, privacy and information management, fire prevention and safety, and drug abuse prevention and control.

The ASIS (American Society for Industrial Security) Committee on Academic Programs suggests that students seeking careers in security should pursue course work in security, computer science, electronics, business management, law, police science, personnel, and information management.[4] This suggestion is supported by security educators and practitioners in *Suggested Preparation for Careers in Security/Loss Prevention.*[5] Building on the ASIS committee statements, the editors developed a book of readings that have a common thread: the need for security/loss prevention personnel to have a broad understanding of various disciplines and specific skills for certain specialties. The editors suggest that specific skills are needed for all students of security—communication, management, and law. Other subject areas such as fire and computer security will depend on the students' interests.

Security Manager

Salaries of security directors with policymaking authority average $52,291 per year according to a 1990 survey conducted by Langer and Associates. Salaries for those with only one or two years of experience averages $31,693 while that for those with 25 or more years averages $58,779. This is an increase of 9.6 percent over the 1989 figures. Directors without policymaking authority average $40,175. The $52,291 figure is an increase of almost 75 percent over the 1984 figure of $31,300. The average 1990 security executive has 25 or more years of experience and a postgraduate degree (M.S. or Ph.D.). In addition, the CPP certificate is likely to be held by this individual. While the average salary is $52,291, many security directors make over $150,000 per year.[6] Figure 2.1 provides additional information on salaries.

Bodyguard

There were 528 terrorist incidents throughout the world in 1989.[7] With the increasing danger of kidnapping and threats from other areas—including disgruntled employees—the demand for executive protection specialists, or bodyguards, is increasing.

According to John Viggiano of Dignitary Protection and Investigative Services, New York, "Television makes it look like [bodyguards] have to be 6'3" with blond hair, blue eyes, and a California tan. That is nonsense. What they need is common sense, the ability to pay attention to detail, and patience."[8] Bodyguards should also know about laws and customs in different places (countries, states, cities), where they might be living or traveling with their principals. In a field once dominated by men, women are becoming more prominent as protection specialists. Most employers of executive protection specialists want a person who can fit into the executive's work and play schedule.

Bodyguard schools are now becoming prominent, and many of the students are former law-enforcement or military personnel. Skills taught include use of weapons and hand-to-hand combat. In addition, schools might also prepare the specialists with skills in protocol, dress, and specialized knowledge of alarm systems and closed-circuit TV (CCTV). Most bodyguards who graduate from reputable schools can expect to receive salaries ranging from $25,000 to $30,000. In addition, many receive an additional $7000 to $9000 in clothing allowances, automobiles, gas credit cards, insurance, and other perks. While the salaries and perks are generally excellent, burnout is high. Long hours and time spent away from friends and family eventually take their toll.

Private Investigator

According to information developed by INTELLISOURCE, a private security firm in the Midwest, the average agency employs three investigators and grosses between $75,000 and $100,000 per year. Starting salaries range between $18,000 and $20,000 per year.[9] In general, private investigators (PIs) are involved in locating missing persons, obtaining confidential information, and solving crimes. Many PIs work for businesses and lawyers while others work independently. Independent offices may be only one-

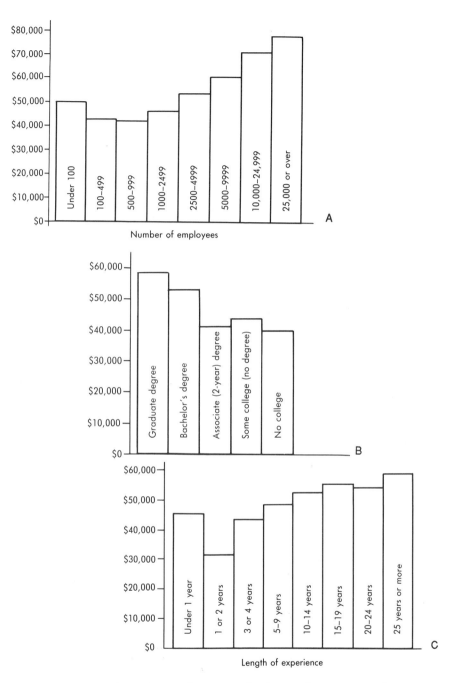

Figure 2.1 Average (mean) annual income of policy making security directors and managers by (A) size of organization, (B) level of education, and (C) length of experience. (Modified from Steven Langer, "What We Earn." Reprinted from the September 1990 issue of *Security Management*, American Society for Industrial Security, 1655 North Fort Myer Drive, Suite 1200, Arlington, VA 22209.)

person operations while others may employ several operatives or contract work to part-time investigators. These independent investigators charge from $35 to over $100 per hour. Long days and seven-day work weeks are the norm when a PI is on a case.

Good PIs develop skills that include the ability to conduct good surveillance and background checks. Some cases involve undercover investigations and require a complete understanding of a sometimes dangerous assignment, including developing a cover and dealing with people who must not know who you are. The private investigation business requires the investigator to learn the law and interviewing and investigative techniques. The best PIs also possess good verbal and written skills as well as analytical skills. Attendance at or membership in the National Association of Legal Investigators is an excellent aid to improving basic skills. Generally speaking, the outlook for jobs in this area is good. According to the bureau, the market is stable and good in all states.

A person interested in this field should consult individual state laws that vary greatly to determine what criteria must be met for licensing. Criteria vary from virtually none to extensive experience, completion of a written and/or oral examination, and interview by a state board.

Consultants

Security consultants are the specialists of the field. They generally operate as sole proprietors of a business that sells specific security expertise. Some security consultants charge more than $100 per hour and bill over $200,000 annually. Security consultants provide advice for a fee. They do not work for specific equipment companies or firms. Advice commonly purchased from the consultant consists of information from three general areas:

1. Number, quantity, and use of security personnel
2. Direction and content of security policies and procedures
3. Alternatives in security hardware

Consultants also offer training seminars on specific problem areas, for example, executive protection and disaster planning.

Security consultants are generally people who have paid their dues working in investigation or security management. Many have published articles and books. Today the completion of a Ph.D. is helpful since the title "Doctor" carries added weight if the consultant is called to testify in court. As civil litigation increases, the demand for "security experts" who can testify as credible witnesses also increases.

Opportunities in Industry

Typically the greatest opportunities in industrial security exist in larger companies that employ proprietary security forces. The career-oriented person with a certificate or degree in a recognized security or criminal justice program is actively recruited by many firms.

At one major company, the salary range for security representatives with college degrees is from $22,000 to $35,000 with potential for advancement within the company's various divisions. Someone with a B.S. or equivalent degree without experience would start at $300 to $350 per week; with experience, at $400 to $450 per week. Investigators, usually with experience either in military or law enforcement investigation, earn from $425 to $500 weekly.

The security director at one major manufacturing facility with a highly progressive security program reports being interested in hiring only those applicants with at least a B.S. in security from a recognized security or criminal justice program.

Opportunities in Retail

The retail field provides a diversity of job opportunities in security from the entry-level position of the uniformed security officer (or blazer-jacketed "host") to the shoplifting investigator. Positions are available both with retail stores and chains and with security service companies, which provide such services as undercover and shopping investigations. There are many openings for those without experience but with the education, ambition, and aptitude that might make them successful in retail security. Many companies today provide their own training for shoppers and other investigators even though the employees have no investigative experience. Alertness, resourcefulness, courage, and self-assurance are often more important than is specific experience.

There are many different types of operations in the retail industry. Security has had its impact in virtually every operation—from the discount store through the department store to the supermarket. The recognition of the importance of inventory shrinkage to the company's profit picture and the necessity for loss prevention is, or soon will be, almost universal. Those companies that do not accept this necessity, in the words of one ranking retail executive, simply will not remain in business.

The entry-level position in one company includes many students recruited from criminal justice and security programs as well as sales personnel crossing over to security. Many of these employees work part-time while they are going to school. Full-time security officers, including many of the formerly part-time students who have completed their college programs, earn between $16,000 and $24,000 per year. Investigators earn from $18,000 up.

These figures apply to a successful retail program but its success is indicative of the direction that retail security must take in the future.

Opportunities in Health Care

Hospital security officers make up the vast majority of persons employed in hospital security. According to Russell Colling, a nationally known health care security authority and author of *Hospital Security*,[10] the officer who prepares for advancement (through a combination of education beyond high school and field experience) can look to numerous supervisory, investigative, training, fire prevention, and safety positions in the field.

Hospital security officers generally earn more than do their counterparts in other industries because of the variety of duties requiring a higher-than-average amount of training. The officer must also be able to interact effectively with the medical community as well as with patients and visitors under conditions of frequent stress. Salaries, however, do vary by location.

Security directors in the health-care field earn salaries that average $41,500.[11] Such positions generally require at least four years of college preparation and considerable field experience. Like so many other areas of security, as Colling observes, hospital security is just coming into its own.

Airport and Airline Security

The airport and airline security field at the level above the line security officer is one that is still dominated by former law-enforcement personnel, particularly former special agents of the FBI. The security directors of many major airlines are former FBI agents, and this is also true of many investigators.

This situation is not unique to airlines, of course. Former agents of the bureau can be found in a great many corporate security jobs in U.S. business and industry. Both the experience and the qualifications required by the FBI have generally been highly regarded in the private sector. The ambitious, career-minded security aspirant could do far worse than consider a period of service in the FBI as a springboard to a promising position in industry, including the airline industry.

Pay for investigators with major carriers is good, starting at or near $22,500. But qualifications are also high. Almost all have college degrees. Many have law degrees and five or more years of FBI experience.

In airport security, a wide variety of entry-level positions exists for the line security officer, especially at major airports. Here again the field is relatively new, mushrooming especially since the hijacking scares that began in the late 1960s (and continue today, even with increased security standards). It seems clear that, with mandated security requirements including physical security and access controls, baggage screening, 100 percent screening of air passengers and carry-on luggage, cargo security, and other controls, the demand for personnel to fill these needs will continue to rise.

Hotel Security

The hotel and motel industry has been characterized in the past by serious neglect of many security responsibilities, an attitude that has only slowly been changing in spite of a number of very large awards by the courts in recent years against hotels or motels charged with negligent security particularly in the area of protecting guests. This neglect, however, coupled with court-mandated responsibility, has created opportunity for security professionals.

In the words of Walter J. Buzby, coauthor of *Hotel and Motel Security Management*, "[o]pportunities in the hotel industry exist in great numbers both for 'on-the-site' positions and at the corporate home office level."[12] Except at the corporate level or the management level in large hotels, however, the salary range is relatively low in relation to the security industry as a whole. On the other side of the coin, the entry level for the person with any combination of hotel experience and security education or experience can be quite good, with clear opportunities for advancement. The average salary for on-site managers as reported by Langer and Associates is $44,057.[13]

In a related area, the future of security in high-rise apartment buildings and housing complexes offers great potential for the security professional because of the growing emphasis on the concept of total environmental protection and the threat of civil suits by residents or guests who are victimized on building property.

Campus Security

John W. Powell, nationally known campus security consultant and former security director at Yale University, observes that the rapid progress of campus security during the past 20 years has created excellent opportunities for career positions in the field. Openings in many progressive and professional campus departments provide not only challenge but also good salaries and fringe benefits as well as chance for advancement. Such departments are looking for the young, career-minded individual with particular interest in those enrolled in, or graduates of, a criminal justice degree program. Interestingly—unlike many areas of modern security—campus security has generally evolved from a low visibility operation to a highly visible, police-oriented image in response to rising crime problems on campuses.

A good-sized department will include line officers, field supervisors, shift commanders, a coordinator of line operations, and a director. Many departments also have specialized positions such as investigator and training officer. While salaries vary from department to department, and from one area of the country to another, the average salary for campus officers is between $18,000 and $24,000 per year. Directors of campus security departments command salaries that average $39,200.

Banking Security

Banks must comply with minimum federal regulations on security, as promulgated in the Bank Protection Act of 1968. The act mandates that there must be a security manager. Banks comply with this requirement in a variety of ways. Small operations often delegate security responsibilities to one of the senior bank officers. Larger banks, however, hire security managers who often are former FBI agents with an understanding of federal regulations regarding currency and fraud. There is a heavy reliance on electronic technology and physical security rather than on large staffs.

Uniformed guards are reported to earn average salaries of $18,000 annually. Guard supervisors earn approximately $27,000. The bank guard may become a casualty of technological advances as many banks are finding it more cost effective to eliminate guards in favor of physical security improvements.

Security Services

In general, security personnel at the lower operational levels earn less in contract security organizations than they do in proprietary guard forces. This is not necessarily true for investigators and other personnel at higher levels.

In the words of Saul Astor, president of Management Safeguards, Inc., "Young people should seek opportunities in security service organizations since the growth of security services has been meteoric and there is no leveling off in sight. The demand for good executives is insatiable. Very high salaries are being paid by security service organizations to the young 'comers'."[14]

Because the good loss-prevention or security executive is much less a policeman than a systems expert, auditor, and teacher, Astor recommends broad-based education and experience in such areas as accounting, industrial engineering, management, personnel, law, statistics, labor relations, and report writing.

On another level, the doubling of the number of security firms in less than a decade reflects the demand for technically qualified individuals capable of providing specialized security services ranging from alarm sales, installation, and service to alarm systems consulting. Continuing changes in the application of security hardware and systems will bring an increasing demand for the services of those who can advise users on their selection and implementation.

Locksmithing

This is a classic profession requiring a lengthy apprenticeship. There are presently an estimated 70,000 locksmiths in the United States who sell, install, and repair locking devices, safes, and vaults. Some also sell and install various alarm and electronic access-control systems.[15] Positions are available in shops where apprentice locksmiths spend their time learning the trade under a master craftsperson. Much of the work is done on an emergency basis, thus the hours are often long and irregular. The best jobs involve keying new facilities or rekeying older structures such as office buildings and motels.

Technology Experts

With the growing use of electronics in security, the demand for professionals who understand the applications of alarm technology, CCTV, and other high-tech applications within security is growing. Alarm installation is an excellent skill to learn. While most positions in this business are through distributors and contract security services, there is a trend toward proprietary positions. Certification for this area of study is available through the National Alarm Association of America (NAAA).[16]

Computer Security

This is an important example of the new frontiers opening in the loss-prevention field in response to social and technological changes. John M. Carroll, a leading computer scientist, security consultant, and author of *Computer Security*, calls for a blend of education and experience in computer science and security.[17]

Today virtually all organizations have computers that need protection. In addition, many firms generate information (customer lists, research projects, and so on) from these computer operations that also need protection.

The salary ranges mentioned in Table 2.1 have been updated to reflect current market norms. According to a 1984 study by *Data Processing and Communications Security Magazine,* the average salary for a computer security manager had reached $43,000, and the computer security specialist typically earned $34,000.[18] According to David Ballew, Chairman, Computer Sciences, Western Illinois University, salaries have remained at this high level since the mid-1980s and will continue at this level.[19]

Conclusion

Although salary scales and security applications vary in different parts of the country as well as within the different areas of business and industry—or even within the same type of business or industry—it is nevertheless possible to perceive the coming of age of security throughout the 1990s and into the twenty-first century.

The aging, poorly trained, and underpaid guard portrayed by the 1968 Rand report is an exception today as observed by the 1990 *Hallcrest II* report. The latter report notes that today's guard is younger (average age is 35 compared to 42 in 1975), better paid, and better trained than was the case at the beginning of 1970. The guard is also just as likely to be black as white, and nearly 1 out of 10 guards is a black woman. The number of women in private security has doubled every 15 years. Educational levels are up from an average of 11 years of formal education in 1975 to over 85 percent with 12 or more years in 1989.[20]

Still, more universally accepted standards of training and applicant screening and higher wage scales are needed. The opportunity for vertical movement within the security structure must be both present and perceived. But even in these areas there are encouraging signs.

The use of outside investigators and security consultants will increase as security functions become more specialized. According to *Security,* the trend for the year 2000 will be toward hiring security services and consultants and keeping specialized proprietary staff at lower numbers.[21]

Review Questions

1. What factors are increasing career opportunities in security?
2. Pick one area of security that interests you and discuss the career opportunities that presently exist.
3. How important is a college education in obtaining a position as a security manager?

Table 2.1 Opportunities in Computer Security

Title	Employer	Salary	Duties	Sources	Education
EDP security coordinator (administrator)	EDP centers	$28,000	Works with conventional security forces, representatives of computer manufacturers and software houses, and local systems programmers to implement and maintain computer security systems.	Programmers or systems analysts with training in security.	Combination of education and experience in EDP equivalent to an MS in Computer Science (for example, two years Community College and six years progressive experience in general EDP; or three years Community College and four years experience; or BS in Computer Science and two years experience); and part-time or full-time training in computer security—30 classroom hours with appropriate preparation and practicum.

Table 2.1 (*Cont.*)

Title	Employer	Salary	Duties	Sources	Education
EDP security analyst	Government, large-user companies	$40,000	Prescribes, reviews and evaluates computer systems. Conducts security inspections, surveys, and threat evaluations.	EDP security coordinators or junior security analysts with larger firms.	Same as above with one to five years experience in computer security.
EDP security consultant	Government, user companies, computer manufacturers, software houses, self-employment	$60,000+	Designs and integrates computer security systems and programs. Participates in formulating EDP security policy. Develops innovative solutions.	EDP security analysts; junior consultants with larger firms; teachers or researchers in computer security.	Same as above with record of proven accomplishment.

References

1. William Cunningham, John J. Strauchs, and Clifford VanMeter, *The Hallcrest Report II: Private Security Trends 1970–2000* (Boston: Butterworth-Heinemann, 1990), p. 209.

2. Ibid., p. 139.

3. Steven Kaverman, "2000 and Beyond," *Security Management* (September 1990): 53.

4. *Career Opportunities in Security and Loss Prevention* (Washington, D.C.: ASIS Foundation), p. 1.

5. John Chuvala, III, and Robert James Fischer, eds., *Suggested Preparation for Careers in Security/Loss Prevention* (Dubuque, Iowa: Kendall/Hunt, 1991), p. iii.

6. Steven Langer, "What We Earn," *Security Management* (September 1990): 67–72; "Security Salaries: Experienced, Degreed Decision Makers Reap Highest Reward," *Security* (June 1990): 12.

7. Cunningham et al., *The Hallcrest Report II*, p. 81.

8. Toni Mack, "Looking Out for Number One," *Forbes* (31 December 1984): 126.

9. *How to Become A Successful Private Investigator* (Naperville, Ill.: IntelSource Investigations).

10. Russell L. Colling, *Hospital Security*, 2nd ed. (Stoneham, Mass.: Butterworth Publishers, 1982).

11. Langer, "What We Earn," p. 71.

12. Walter J. Buzby, *Hotel and Motel Security Management* (Stoneham, Mass.: Butterworth Publishers, 1976).

13. Ibid., p. 71.

14. Saul D. Astor, *Loss Prevention: Control and Concepts* (Stoneham, Mass.: Butterworth Publishers, 1978), p. 246.

15. Cunningham et al., *The Hallcrest Report II*, p. 130.

16. Steven R. Keller, "Technology: Unlocking The Future For Security Practitioners," in *Suggested Preparation for Careers in Security/Loss Prevention*, eds. Chuvala and Fischer, p. 102.

17. John M. Carroll, *Computer Security*, 2nd ed. (Boston: Butterworths, 1987).

18. "Security Salaries," *Data Processing and Communications Security* (November 1984): 39.

19. Interview with David Ballew, Western Illinois University, Macomb, Ill., March 1991.

20. Cunningham et al., *The Hallcrest Report II*, pp. 138–139.

21. "Exploring Security Trends," *Security* (1989): 4.

3

□ □ □
□ □ □
□ □ □

Security Education, Training, Certification, and Regulation

Until the last decade, few security officers received adequate prejob or on-the-job training to perform the tasks so often assigned to them. While the public sector had its Wickersham Commission in the 1930s; the President's Advisory Commission,*Report on Police* in 1974; and the Police Foundation report, *The Quality of Police Education* in 1980, the private security sector was not studied intensively until the past three decades.

The Task Force on Private Security published its findings on the private security industry in 1976 and substantiated an earlier study by the Rand Corporation (1968) that indicated that the private security occupation was a very open and unregulated giant and that its order-maintenance function was mistakenly overlooked. Both studies raised questions concerning the need for training of security personnel and discussed the need for academic professional preparation programs. In 1985, *The Hallcrest Report* found some progress in both areas. The 1990 update, *Hallcrest II,* further indicated a steady improvement in security services education and training. The authors of *Hallcrest II* were quick to note, however, that the major concern voiced at the International Security Conference–East (ISC–East) in August 1989 was lack of security training.[1]

An Historical Perspective

When the first National Conference on Private Security met at the University of Maryland in December 1975, it was concluded that:

Although there is no comprehensive involvement by colleges and universities to provide educational opportunities for private security personnel, it should also be recognized that there is little evidence that the security industry or government agencies encouraged their development.[2]

Since this meeting, the topic of private security companies and agencies, and in particular of security education and training, has been widely discussed. As a result of increased interest in the level of education and training of private security personnel, the Law Enforcement Assistance Administration (LEAA) funded the National Task Force on Private Security to study security from all perspectives. In 1984, the National Institute of Justice (NIJ) supported the study of the security field by funding the Hallcrest Corporation in a national study of the security field. This report resulted in the *Hallcrest Report; Private Security and Police in America,* published in 1985. Again in 1989 NIJ granted funds to Hallcrest to develop an update of the 1985 report resulting in *The Hallcrest Report II: Private Security Trends: 1970–2000* published in late 1990.

Adequacy of Private Security Training

The status of private security training has traditionally been low. A study conducted by the Private Security Advisory Council (PSAC) in 1978 for LEAA indicated that, while security training programs were being offered by law enforcement agencies, educational institutions, training facilities, and contract or proprietary security firms, the quality varied widely. The variety in the programs was simply explained by the fact that there were no uniform standards for courses—content, length, method of presentation, instructor qualifications, or student testing.[3] The report of the Task Force on Private Security found the same lack of quality programs and for the first time made specific recommendations.[4] Unfortunately, many of these recommendations have yet to be implemented, although *Hallcrest I* and *Hallcrest II* indicate that progress has been made. *Hallcrest II* notes that private security personnel in 1990 are younger and better educated than was previously reported.

To further stress the need for private security training, however, *Hallcrest II* notes that the typical security guard receives only four to six hours of preassignment training. And as was noted in the introduction to this chapter, the primary concern voiced by those surveyed at ISC–East in August 1989 was lack of adequate security training. The *Hallcrest II* authors report that one security authority feels that security training will not receive any attention until the cost of the training exceeds the cost of litigation for failure to train.[5] Although government studies both past and present have called for attention to training issues and some standardization of training, training continues to be regulated by individual states, each with its own standards.

Illinois has a rather progressive policy that sets out specific requirements for (1) private detectives and agencies, (2) private security contractors and agencies, and (3) private alarm contractors and agencies.

To be licensed as a private detective in Illinois, the applicant must meet requirements that he or she:

1. Is at least 21 years of age;
2. Is a citizen or legal resident alien of the United States;
3. Has not been convicted in any jurisdiction of any felony or 10 years shall have expired from the time of discharge from any sentence imposed therefrom;
4. Is of good moral character which shall be a continuing requirement of licensure. . . .
5. Has not been declared by any court of competent jurisdiction incompetent by reasons of mental or physical defect or disease unless a court has since declared him [or her] competent;
6. Is not suffering from habitual drunkenness or from narcotic addiction or dependence;
7. Has a minimum of 3 years experience out of the 5 years immediately preceding his [or her] application working full-time for a licensed private detective agency as a registered private detective employee or with 3 years experience of the five years immediately preceding his [or her] application employed as a full-time investigator in a law enforcement agency of a federal, state or political subdivision . . . or an applicant who has obtained a baccalaureate degree in police science or a related field, or a business degree from an accredited college or university shall be given credit for 2 of the 3 years experience required under this Section. An applicant who has obtained an associate degree in police science or related field, or in business from an accredited college or university shall be given credit for one of the 3 years experience required under this Section;
8. Has not been dishonorably discharged from the armed services of the United States;
9. Has successfully passed an examination authorized by the Department [of Education and Registration] which shall include subjects reasonably related to the activities licensed so as to provide for the protection of the health and safety of the public.
10. Has submitted evidence to the Department of general liability insurance coverage or such equivalent guarantee as approved by the Department on such form, and in principal amounts satisfactory to the Department, but not less than $100,000 for each person; $300,000 for each occurrence for bodily injury liability

and $50,000 for property damage liability. These insurance requirements are a continuing requirement for licensure.[6]

In addition to these strict standards for acquiring a license, Illinois lists a number of actions that will result in suspension or revocation of a license.

1. Fraud or material deception in the obtaining or renewing of a registration;
2. Engaging in dishonorable, unethical or unprofessional conduct of a character likely to deceive, defraud or harm the public in the course of professional activities . . .
3. Conviction of any crime which has a substantial relationship to his [or her] employment or an essential element of which is misstatement, fraud or dishonesty, or conviction in this or any other state of any crime which is a felony under the laws of Illinois, or conviction of a felony in a federal court;
4. Performing any service in a grossly negligent manner, regardless of whether actual damage or damages to the public is established;
5. Addiction to or severe dependency upon alcohol or drugs which may endanger the public by impairing the registrant's ability to work; if the Department has reasonable cause to believe that a registrant is addicted to or dependent upon alcohol or drugs, which may endanger the public, the Department may require the registrant to undergo an examination to determine such addiction or dependency;
6. Engaging in lewd conduct in connection with professional services or activities.[7]

A glance at Table 3–1 will indicate only 50 percent of the states have any imposed training standards. It thus appears that training for private security personnel is less than adequate. This may be one reason why the public law-enforcement sector has for many years held a poor opinion of the private security profession. If private security is to have the impact on crime predicted by the Task Force on Private Security, the occupation must be professionalized. Appendix 3A at the end of this chapter provides further information on the training requirements for each state.

The Role of Higher Education

In November 1978, a seminar entitled "Meeting the Changing Needs of Private Security Education and Training" was held at the University of Cincinnati as a followup to the Report of the Task Force on Private Security and the first National Conference on Private Security. The majority of

Table 3.1   Guard Licensing and Training by State

State	License	Training
Alabama	L B	N
Alaska	S G B I	Y
Arizona	S G I	Y
Arkansas	S G P I	Y
California	S G I	Y
Colorado	L G B	N
Connecticut	S G	*
Delaware	S G	*
District of Columbia	S G	*
Florida	S G I	Y
Georgia	S G I	Y
Hawaii	S G	*
Idaho	L G B	N
Illinois	S G I	Y
Indiana	S G I	N
Iowa	S G I	*
Kansas	L G B	*
Kentucky	L G B P	N
Louisana	S G I	Y
Maine	S G	N
Maryland	S G I	*
Massachusetts	S G	N
Michigan	S G I	N
Minnesota	S G P	N
Mississippi	L	N
Missouri	L	N
Montana	S G P I	*
Nebraska	L	N

participants were academics. The interest of the academic world in security education has increased in recent years, but it is certainly not new. The demand for improved training and education in the field of security has existed since 1957.[8]

The federal government was very supportive of the development of academic programs in public law enforcement education. The major mechanism

State	License	Training
Nevada	S G	*
New Hampshire	S G P	*
New Jersey	S G	*
New Mexico	S G	*
New York	S G	N
North Carolina	S G I	*
North Dakota	S G	Y
Ohio	S G I	*
Oklahoma	S G I	Y
Oregon	L	N
Pennsylvania	S G	*
Rhode Island	S G I	**
South Carolina	S G P	Y
South Dakota	L	N
Tennessee	S G P I	Y
Texas	S G I	*
Utah	S G I	Y
Vermont	S G	*
Virginia	S G I	*
Washington	L B	N
West Virginia	S G	**
Wisconsin	S G I	*
Wyoming	L	N

For Licensing: L = Local licensing requirements; S = State licensing requirements; B = Business license; G = Guard firm license; P = Proprietary security covered in some way; I = Proof of insurance.

For Training: N = No training required; Y = Training required; * = Training required if firearms carried; ** = Not in private security statute; need license to carry gun.

Source: Bill Zalud, "Law and Order and Security," *Security* (June 1990): 55.

for this change was LEAA. The LEAA was also instrumental in stimulating interest in private security education by sponsoring the Task Force on Private Security. Its 1976 report suggested that private security education and training in the 1970s were at the level of public law enforcement in the 1960s. The LEAA might have taken an active role in funding educational programs, granting scholarships, or providing technical assistance, but the 1981 cuts in spending by the federal government resulted in the elimination of the LEAA.[9] Since security deals primarily with private companies—as opposed to law enforcement, which is concerned with society as a whole—however, the question arises whether the federal government should fund such efforts or whether support for educational opportunities and funding for private security should come from the private sector. Recently education has become a major concern for many private security operations.

As more and more private security managers receive their degrees, the overall quality of private security employees will increase since college-educated people will do their best to see that the private security occupation becomes worthy of the term professional.

The Hallcrest reports recognize the tremendous impact that law-enforcement education has had on shaping education programs in security. From a review of the literature, it is apparent that educators do not share the same views on the placement of security curricula in colleges and universities. One view shows preference for equal status with law-enforcement programs since the fields are very interrelated. A second view is that security should be a completely independent major with alliances to departments of business. Yet a third view indicates that the placement of the program is not as important as is an interdisciplinary approach to the curriculum. The degree designation is of little importance. *Hallcrest II* authors indicate that, with the historic lack of scholarly output, "it is debatable whether security, in the traditional academic sense, can be considered a separate body of knowledge."[10] Their observation is moot, however, considering the number of security education programs that have developed over the last 25 years. As was noted in 1981, security education had grown to include over 150 institutions offering associate degrees, 35 offering bachelor's and 10 offering master's degrees.[11] Although many at the Associate degree level have been eliminated, according to the *Journal of Security Administration*, there were 64 programs offering associate degrees, 38 with baccalaureates, and 15 with graduate degrees in 1990.[12]

Although at least 38 institutions of varying size and administrative organization are offering degrees in security, certain generalizations can be made about security education at the baccalaureate level. In general, programs are small and are staffed by faculty who have more experience in public law-enforcement than in security. Despite the small size of programs, most institutions express support for the programs.

Despite this support, a rather negative view on the future of security education was expressed in 1986 by the *Journal of Security Administration* when it reported that the Academy of Security Educators and Trainers (ASET) noted the following trends:[13]

1. Over 60 colleges dropped their security degrees

2. Degree programs are housed within wrong departments
3. The flight of senior security educators back to industry

While much of what ASET observed is interesting and to a large degree accurate, the conclusions are open to discussion and debate. The fact is that some security programs have prospered while others have failed. It must be remembered that security education is still a relatively young discipline. The final determinant of program success or failure is the program's ability to deliver a product that is attractive to the security industry. If the graduates of a program are not of adequate quality, the program will fail. And while criticisms are many, there are programs that have been able to identify problems and develop successful degree plans. A close look at the demographics of one of the successful programs reveals a continuing development of security offerings and program direction. Responses from graduates of the program indicate that a large proportion of its majors entering the security field eventually achieve high-paying administrative or supervisory positions in security.

In September 1990, Steven Langer of Langer and Associates reported that the composite profile of the 1990 security manager was likely to be an individual with over 25 years experience with a *graduate degree* and CPP (Certified Protection Professional) certification.[14]

The future of security education is excellent when one considers the growth evident in the field. As Dr. Norman Bottom noted as early as 1982,

> People are security-conscious today, and we're seeing more security programs being offered in colleges and universities. . . . That trend is likely to continue.[15]

While this statement was challenged in 1986, it is the opinion of many security professionals that the field was simply cleaning house and that the "diploma mills" are being discarded in favor of more practically oriented academic programs. The recent involvement of the ASIS (American Society for Industrial Security) Foundation in sponsoring a master's program indicates the growing interest of professional security managers in providing graduate education in loss prevention/security for its membership.

Hallcrest II best summarizes the issue of security education. Growth in the past 10 years has been considerable, and despite the 1986 exodus of some programs, those that are firmly established will continue to flourish. As the report indicates, "many of the programs have bridged the gap between theory and practice with internship programs in business and industry." The report, however, also stressed that additional recognition of security as an academic discipline awaits the development of a private security institute. Today the ASIS tries to fill the role of a security institute. Over the past few years, the ASIS Foundation has made tremendous strides at providing innovation within the security profession. The ASIS Foundation has made 12 research grants over the past few years. Although the amount was modest in size, the 1990 budget provided $15,000 for research. Perhaps the most visible success of the ASIS Foundation has been the establishment of the *Security Journal* published jointly with Butterworth-Heinemann.[16]

Training

Development and training of security personnel must be a continuing concern of management, Indeed the lack of adequate training in the past has been the major criticism leveled against private security both within the industry and outside it. *The Rand Report* description of the typical private guard as "an aging white male, poorly educated, usually untrained and very poorly paid"[17] has been widely quoted. Five years later in 1976 the report of the Task Force on Private Security observed that "every major research project reviewed and every study conducted for this report point to a serious lack of personnel training at all levels of private security."[18] In 1985, the *Hallcrest Report* found that this stereotype had changed.[19] Today the average security guard is 31 to 35 years of age; and although most are still male, almost 25 percent are now female and over 50 percent have had some college education. Wages for contract guards, however, are still generally low and training has not improved substantially.[20]

In their site surveys, the Hallcrest researchers found that, while the majority of all guards (both proprietary and contract) had received some prejob training, in the contract area 40 percent of the guards had completed only on-the-job training. Table 3.2 reflects the results of the national survey on range of classroom and on-the-job training. In general, it is apparent that proprietary security personnel report more training than do contractual personnel. While the Private Security Task Force (Standard 2.5) recommended that contract security personnel complete a minimum of 8 hours of formal preassignment training, as well as a basic training course of at least 32 hours within 3 months of assignment, survey results indicate that this standard is far from being implemented.[21] As noted in the introduction to this chapter, *Hallcrest II* found few changes in this area.

It is clear that adequate training can and must be an important aspect of security planning in the proprietary organization. The need is as great in contract security services, of course, where the problem is compounded by competitive pressures of the marketplace. The onus for low training standards must be borne by employers whose overriding consideration in selecting security services is the lowest bid. Proficiency in security is largely a product of the combination of experience and a thorough training program designed to improve the officers' skills and knowledge and to keep them current with

Table 3.2 Comparison of Security Training Hours Reported by Managers and Employees

	Managers			Employees		
Type of Training	*National Surveys (N=)*			*Site Surveys (N=)*		
Preassignment						
Proprietary	60%	24 hrs	(646)	60%	24 hrs	(110)
Contractual	59	8	(545)	60	8	(78)
On-the-job						
Proprietary	36	40	(646)	54	80	(110)
Contractual	52	16	(545)	56	16	(78)

Source: National Survey of Proprietary and Contractual Security Managers, (1981); Site Surveys of Security Employees, Baltimore County, Maryland and Multnomah County (Portland), Oregon metropolitan areas, (1982); Hallcrest Systems, Inc. (Later research for *Hallcrest II* reports little change in these figures.)

the field. The recommendations of the Task Force on Private Security included:

1. A minimum of eight hours of formal preassignment training
2. Basic training of a minimum of 32 hours within 3 months of assignment of which a maximum of 16 hours can be supervised on-the-job training.[22]

The merits of training will be reflected in the security officer's attitude and performance, improved morale, and increased incentive. Training also provides greater opportunities for promotion and a better understanding on the part of the officers of their relationship to management and the objectives of the job.

It should not be presumed that former law-enforcement officers require no training. They do. In order for them to be successful in security, they must develop new skills and—not incidentally—forget some of their previous training.

A training program should cover a wide variety of subjects and procedures, some of them varying according to the nature of the organization being served. Among them might be:

1. Company orientation and indoctrination
2. Company and security department policies, systems, and procedures
3. Operation of each department
4. Background in applicable law (citizen's arrest, search and seizure, individual rights, rules of evidence, and such)

5. Report writing
6. General and special orders
7. Discipline
8. Self-defense
9. First aid
10. Pass and identification systems
11. Package and vehicle search
12. Communications procedures
13. Techniques of observation
14. Operation of equipment
15. Professional standards, including attitudes toward employees

A recent study indicates that contract security services see the need for more training to reduce their possible legal liability. Figure 3.1 illustrates the areas of training the companies viewed as most important.

Properly trained security personnel are cheerful, cooperative, and tolerant in their dealings within the company. They are patient and understand that they are not members of a law-enforcement agency but employees who

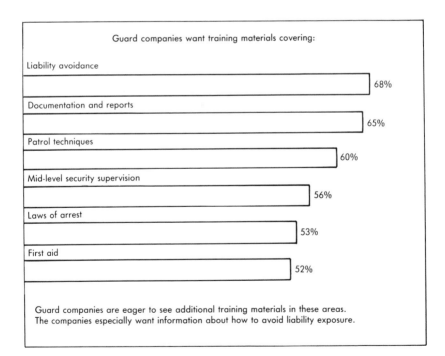

Figure 3.1 Contract guard firms call for training programs. (Modified from National Association of Private Security Industries, Inc. from *Security* magazine, Jan. 1991, p. 9, published by Cahners Publishing Company, a division of Reed Publishing USA.)

have the job of providing security. If they are good-humored, tactful, patient, and professional, their fellow employees will learn to respect them and to look to them for assistance in many ways frequently beyond the scope of their duties. They should be encouraged to provide whatever assistance they can, since this can only increase employee respect for them as individuals as well as professional security people, thereby encouraging cooperation. And employee cooperation in the security task is vital to its success.

It is distressing to note that nineteen states have no training requirement for guards. An additional nineteen require training only if firearms are carried. (See Table 3.1.)

Certification and Regulation

The authors of *Hallcrest II* reiterate the recommendations of the Task Force on Private Security in developing professional certification and applaud ASIS for the development of its CPP program. The other major recommendation noted by the authors involves certification programs for operations personnel along with mandatory minimum levels of training. This Task Force on Private Security recommendation has had little impact, and the Hallcrest authors again suggest that something be done to provide leadership in these areas. *Hallcrest I* noted, however, that the best regulator is the marketplace. The authors of that report recommended a balanced approach between industry-imposed standards and preemptive state legislation.[23] Industry-imposed standards can be successful as noted by the success of the British Security Industry Association (BSIA). BSIA industry-imposed standards reportedly cover 90 percent of Britain's security industry. The BSIA has adopted standards pertaining to personnel screening, wage levels, supervision, training liability insurance, and physical facilities.[24] If the BSIA model were followed in the United States the Hallcrest authors believe the need for governmental regulation would be minimal.

Regulation

Considering the importance of private security personnel in the anticrime effort and their quasi-law-enforcement functions, it is ironic that they receive so little training in comparison to their public-sector contemporaries. While it is ironic, the answer to why is obvious. Legislation mandates training for public law-enforcement personnel, whereas this is not the case for security personnel. A look at licensing standards for private security companies reveals that little has changed with regard to regulation of this already huge and still growing giant. (See Table 3.1.) Considering the lack of progress in establishing uniform training standards, it is difficult to support the Hallcrest contention that the "best regulator" is the marketplace. It is refreshing to see *Hallcrest II* consider the British model as an option to marketplace control. There is little indication, however, that ASIS will become involved in regulation of standards and the like as the British have done. In addition, it is doubtful that the states will provide any better guidance.

In 1987, Richter H. Moore reported on the licensing of security companies throughout the United States. In general, 8 states (Alabama, Idaho, Kentucky, Mississippi, Oklahoma, Oregon, South Dakota, and Washington) still had not enacted legislation regulating the private security industry. In the states that do have legislation, the key words that might be used to describe the composite package of legislation are "lack of uniformity." Dr. Moore reported that not only is terminology not uniform but, more importantly, there is no consensus on the degree to which the state should regulate training, licensing, and education/experience. Few states require education beyond the eighth grade, and only 13 states require examinations to determine level of ability.[25]

It is also interesting to note that, while 35 states do attempt to regulate security, only 12 include proprietary security forces in their regulatory statutes. Moore notes that this has established a double standard for in-house and contract employees performing essentially the same functions.[26]

On a positive note, Dr. Moore indicates that 33 of the 35 states have amended or added private security statutes. During the past three years, 23 states have done so.[27] These changes have not produced the control the security industry appears to need, however.

After a thorough review of the education and training currently being offered, *Hallcrest I* made the following recommendations:

1. *Standards, codes of ethics, and model licensing.* The efforts of the Task Force on Private Security and PSAC have stood the test of time, and both groups were well represented by law enforcement, business, and all facets of the security field. Statewide licensing should be required for guard and patrol, private investigation, and alarm firms. The profound effects on upgrading private security relationships with law enforcement will occur as a result of the cooperative action of the security industry, law enforcement, and state governments in implementing the measures encompassed by the Task Force on Private Security and PSAC efforts.

2. *Statewide preemptive legislation.* Although law enforcement agencies seek closer local control over private security, a proliferation of local licensing ordinances deters adoption of minimum standards and imposes an unnecessary financial burden on contract security firms with redundant licensing "paperwork" and fees. Some latitude

might be granted local law-enforcement agencies to impose tighter control on some aspects of private security operation, but the controls should not be unduly restrictive and should withstand tests and measures of cost effectiveness.

3. *Interstate licensing agency reciprocity.* Interstate operation of contract security can be unnecessarily hampered by having the same personnel comply with different personnel licensing requirements in adjacent states—and sometimes in cities and counties. The same standards of state-level licensing and regulation in all states and reciprocity (that is, recognition of other states' regulatory provisions) would facilitate more efficient delivery of security services and decrease state regulatory costs.[28]

Certification

Mention of various programs of certification was presented in Chapter 1. The growth of programs leading to certification is an indication of the professionalization of the security field. Today it is possible to receive several certification designations each of which has its special appeal. An indication of the level of heightened interest in the broad-based security professional can be seen in the results of the diligent efforts of ASIS. This society has long been interested and involved in creating standards of competence and professionalism to identify those security practitioners who have shown a willingness to devote their attention to achieving higher goals of education and training in their chosen career. As was noted earlier, the security profession has, in the past, been characterized by the transitory nature of much of its personnel. Training standards have frequently been low, and even many executives in the field were generalists without either specific work-related experience or specific training in security. Many factors have been brought to bear on this problem, and changes have been and are being made.

The ASIS program is designed to upgrade those career security persons who are willing and able to qualify for certification as CPPs. The certification board in this program was organized in 1977 and since that time has provided sufficient evidence of professional performance capability through certification to stress the importance of the CPP. "Positions available" announcements in the *Wall Street Journal*, the *Chronicle of Higher Education*, and other publications have included requirements that state: "Certification as a Protection Professional by the ASIS [is] desirable," or the candidate "must have certification as a CPP." This trend will continue as employers and the public become more aware of the CPP program.

Certification in this program is far from pro forma. Both educational and work experience are required before a candidate can be considered. If candidates meet the basic standards, they must then take an examination on both mandatory and optional subjects. It is through this program and those given by colleges and universities across the country that the goal of professionalism in the practice of security will be achieved.

Similar efforts have been made to improve the professional image of the security officer through the Certified Protection Officer (CPO) program referred to in Chapter 1. The program was founded in 1986 by the International Foundation for Protection Officers (IFPO). The first CPOs were granted in 1986, and that certification is now available through several colleges in the United States and Canada. The program is "designed to provide theoretical educational information to complement the field experience of Security Officer."[29] Topics of study include:

Introduction to security
Officer and the job
Physical security
Legal aspects
Human relations
Security as a career
First aid and CPR
Preventive security

Candidates must complete an application, obtain nominations from two security or police professionals, and complete the training program before certification is granted.

Private Security Training and Education

Other certifications are available in specific fields. The International Association for Hospital Security (IASH) offers the Certified Health Care Protection Administrator (CHCPA) designation; the United Security Professionals Association (USPA), Inc., offers the Certified Financial Security Officer (CFSO) designation; and ASET offers the Certified Security Trainer (CST) program. In 1983, the International Association of Computer Systems Security (IACSS) developed the Computer Systems Security Program (CSSP). And with the growing use of, and emphasis on, security consultants, the International Association of Professional Security Consultants (IAPSC) was founded in 1984. Of course, other groups have also developed various programs to identify competence in specific areas.

Magazines and Periodicals

Any discipline that claims to be a profession must have its own mechanism for distribution of information. In most disciplines or professions, information is distributed through professional publications. Security and loss prevention publications have changed dramatically in the last 10 years as a reflection of the growing professionalization of the field. In an article in the *Journal of Security Administration*, Norman Bottom notes that 15 years ago *Industrial Security* (now *Security Management*) and *Security World* (now *Security*) magazines were about the only publications in the security field. Bottom reports that the number of publications today have grown substantially.[30]

The use of journals and magazines in the security profession was studied by Fischer in 1981 and by Palmiotto and Travis in 1985.[31] Both studies indicated that *Security Management* and *Security World* dominated the field but that other publications were also being more widely read. Other publications that were mentioned in both the 1981 and 1985 studies include *Professional Protection, International Review, Levista Securinad, Pinkerton Focus, Campus Security*, and *Hospital Security*. The latest addition, founded in 1990, is a new publication from ASIS, *Security Journal*, adding a second academic journal to the field (the *Journal of Security Administration* was founded in 1978). Appendix 3B lists the major publications in security as well as the indexes that list articles from at least some of these publications.

Conclusion

Security education has undeniably undergone tremendous growth in the last 15 years. Academic programs in security, with a few exceptions, are relatively young. Most were established within the last 20–25 years. In general, most have been reasonably successful as the demand for college-educated security managers continues to grow. Leaders in the field, both academics and practitioners, indicate that security should seek recognition as its own distinct area of study. While some believe that the programs can find this autonomy within the criminal justice field, others believe that the field would be better off in colleges of business.

No matter what the view of security education and training might be, the reality is that the field is here to stay. As recent surveys indicate, more and more security managers are seeking or already possess degrees in the field. In addition, training standards are being mandated by a number of states, and some companies are already recognizing the financial benefits of a trained professional staff. It is apparent that security has a bright future.

Not only are security managers with degrees becoming more prevalent but line security personnel with at least associate degrees appear to be on the increase as well. The great "wash out" of security programs in the mid-1980s has proven to be a natural evolution with increases in the number of baccalaureate and graduate degrees and a decrease in associate-level programs. Security education is here to stay whether it is housed in criminal justice programs, colleges of business, or independent programs. The Hallcrest group predicted that security education would not achieve significant growth until the establishment of a security institute. While such an institute is yet to be established, security education continues to grow. Much research on various security topics is currently being produced at colleges and universities. Much of this research is academic in orientation, however, and perhaps of little value to practitioners. In this respect an institute much like the ASIS Foundation, which would support practical research, is certainly desirable.

While the status of education in security is good news, the same cannot be said for training. It is truly unfortunate that the federal government has not taken an active part in establishing minimum requirements for security personnel who often perform the same duties as do police officers. It appears obvious that the statement by Hallcrest authors that the marketplace will control private security is a "pipe dream." Even the states that now regulate the security industry in reality pay little attention to it. Considering the fact that the private police outnumber the public sector by over a two to one margin and that the field is growing at a rate of approximately 12 percent each year, it is time for the federal government to take an active role in requiring states to develop adequate legislation for security training or provide an impetus for a British model in the United States. The National Association of Private Security Industries (NAPSI), Inc., reports that 61 percent of all guard companies surveyed conduct continuing education courses for their guards and are continually looking for new training materials.[32] Let us take a lesson from the issue of police training. It was not until the establishment of LEAA and federal legislation that the states began to require adequate training for police officers. Today police officers receive an average of 320 hours of basic training. In addition, most states also have an ongoing training program once the basic course has been completed. Given the improved quality of police education and training after federal involvement, it is likely that similar results would occur in the private sector should the federal government decide to become involved in the regulation of training and education!

Review Questions

1. What role has the now-defunct LEAA played in the shaping of security education and training?

2. How does the presence of college degree programs in security enhance the field?

3. What is your view of regulation in the security field? Should the government play a role, or should the industry regulate itself?

4. How does the level of training and regulation for security personnel compare with that of the police?

5. Do you observe any differences in the level of professionalization between security management and line security officers? What are they?

References

1. William Cunningham, John J. Strauchs, Clifford W. VanMeter, *The Hallcrest Report II: Private Security Trends 1970–2000* (Boston: Butterworth-Heinemann, 1990), p. 144.

2. *Private Security: Report of the Task Force on Private Security* (Washington, D.C.: National Advisory Committee on Criminal Justice Standards and Goals, 1976), p. 270.

3. *Hallcrest Report: Model Security Guard Training Curricula, Private Security Advisory Council to LEAA, U.S. Department of Justice* (McLean, Va.: Hallcrest Press, 1978), p. 1.

4. *Private Security*, pp. 88–89.

5. Cunningham et al., *The Hallcrest Report II*, pp. 150–155.

6. *Illinois Revised Statutes, 1990*, Chapter 111, Section 14.

7. Ibid., Section 22.

8. Thomas W. Wathen, "Careers in Security—One Professional's View," *Security Management* (July 1977): 45–48.

9. "LEAA/OJARS Reorganization Plan Announced," *Justice Assistance News* (October 1980), pp. 1, 6.

10. William Cunningham and Todd H. Taylor, *Private Security and Police in America: The Hallcrest Report* (Portland, Ore.: Chancellor Press, 1985), p. 264.

11. Robert Fischer, "A Report Card on Security Education," *Security Management* (August 1983): 165–172.

12. *Journal of Security Administration*, (December 1990).

13. Norman R. Bottom, Jr., Norman Spain, Robert Fischer, Chester Quarles, "About the Security Degree—Are We Losing It? (A Discussion)," *Journal of Security Adminstration* (June 1986): 7.

14. Steve Langer, "What We Earn," *Security Management* (September 1990): 67.

15. Wayne Siatt, "Special Report: Trends in Security," *Security World* (January 1982): 27.

16. "Working For Security," *ASIS Dynamics* (January/February 1991): 8–9.

17. James S. Kakalik and Sorrell Wildhorn, *The Rand Report* (Santa Monica, Calif.: The Rand Corporation, 1971), p. 30.

18. *Private Security*, p. 87.

19. Cunningham and Taylor, *Private Security and Police in America*, p. 264.

20. Cunningham, Strauchs, and VanMeter, pp. 141–156.

21. Cunningham and Taylor, p. 264

22. *Private Security*, pp. 99–106.

23. Cunningham and Taylor, *Private Security and Police in America*, pp. 263–264.

24. Ibid., pp. 152–153.

25. Richter H. Moore, Jr., "Licensing and the Regulation of Private Security," *Journal of Security Administration* (July 1987): 22.

26. Ibid., p. 24

27. Ibid.

28. Cunningham and Taylor, *Private Security and Police in America*, p. 265.

29. *The Protection Officer: Training Manual* (Cochrane, Can.: The Protection Officer Publications, 1986).

30. Norman R. Bottom, "Periodical Literature in Security and Loss Control," *Journal of Security Administration* (June 1985): 9.

31. Michael J. Palmiotto and Lawrence F. Travis III, "Faculty Readership of Security Periodical: Use of the Literature in a New Discipline," *Journal of Security Administration* (June 1985): 30; Robert J. Fischer, "The Development of Baccalaureate Degree Programs in Private Security 1957–1980," unpublished diss. University Microfilms, Ann Arbor, Mich.

32. "Guard Companies Specify Officer Training Needs," *Security* (January 1991): 9.

3A

Security Officer Training State by State

Since there are no federal requirements for security officer training, some states have taken the initiative in instituting their own. Certain states, such as North Dakota and Oklahoma, have taken the responsibility quite seriously; others have not. Have a look and see if your state is aiding in—or neglecting—the professionalization of today's security officers. The following training requirements are reprinted with permission from The Security Letter Source Book, 1990–1991. *The* Source Book *is published by* Security Letter *and distributed by Butterworth-Heinemann, 80 Montvale Ave., Stoneham, MA 02180. The list was compiled by Robert McCrie, CPP, publisher/editor; Diane Botnick, associate editor; and Fulvia Madia, editorial assistant.*

Note: *No data is available for Alabama, Colorado, Idaho, Kansas, Mississippi, Missouri, Nebraska, Oregon, Puerto Rico, South Dakota, Washington, and Wyoming.*

Alaska

Armed and unarmed: eight-hour preassignment training on duties for temporary permit; additional 40 hours of in-service training within six months of hiring on relevant laws, fire prevention, first aid, and patrol techniques. Annual eight-hour refresher course on these topics. Armed: eight-hour preassignment training in weapons use and pertinent laws.

Source: Robert D. McCrie, Diane Botnick, Fulvia Madia, "Training—State by State," *Security Management,* Special Supplement (March 1991).

Arizona

No fixed number of hours. Guard firms' training curricula must be approved for agency license.

Arkansas

Armed and unarmed: eight-hour training course and exam on legal authority, act, and field note taking and report writing; renewal two-hour refresher course on act, two-hour course on legal authority, and exam within 60 days of expiration. Armed: four hours of firearms training on legal limitations, weapons safety, marksmanship, and range firing; minimum score of 60 percent on range. Yearly renewal—firearms training and qualification requirements as specified.

California

Armed and unarmed: 20-hour course on powers of arrest, 100 percent score on open-book exam. Armed: 14 hours of firearms training; 85 percent minimum score on written test; eight-hour range instruction.

Connecticut

Armed: seven hours of state police course and certified course for firearm permit ($25 fee for five-year permit).

Delaware

None required for unarmed. Armed: Guards must be certified by a certified instructor.

District of Columbia

Armed: four hours of classroom preassignment training; range qualification.

Florida

Armed: 16 hours of basic training at approved school. Must pass course exam with 70 percent score. Regulations detail topics, hours, and classroom space/student.

Georgia

Minimum eight hours of classroom instruction covering duties, functions, legal authority, fire prevention and control, familiarity with act, regulations, and first aid. Armed: minimum 12 hours of classroom instruction: eight hours of basic program (above) and one hour each in laws of arrest, search and seizure, mechanics of arrest, and misdemeanors and felonies. Classroom instruction on weapons use, firearm range instruction, and familiarization course for special weapons.

Hawaii

Armed: eight hours of preassignment training.

Illinois

Armed and unarmed: minimum 20 hours of basic classroom training; employer must verify successful completion. Armed: 20 hours of firearms training with practice firing on range, firearms qualification course.

Indiana

None required.

Iowa

Armed: Four-hour firearms course through county sheriff's office. On-campus requirements: successfully complete approved firearms training program, possess weapons permit, and have sworn affidavit from employer stating duties and justification. Sheriff can require additional firearms training.

Kentucky

(Special law enforcement officer only.) Eighty hours of approved program on related laws or minimum one-year, full-time employment as sworn public peace officer or successfully completed, approved exams on related subject matter. Must demonstrate proficiency in firearms safety and use and first aid. Exam fee $15; firearms exam fee $20; "reasonable fee" to cover training costs of the program.

Louisiana

Armed and unarmed: eight hours of classroom instruction within 30 days of hiring on rules, regulations, law, legal powers, first aid, general duties, and report writing. Additional eight hours within six months in approved program taught by certified instructor. Exams given after each eight-hour segment. Armed: additional eight hours of preassignment firearms course on handgun safety and firing and firing range qualification with annual four-hour refresher courses, firearms instruction, and marksmanship qualification. Must score 60 percent to qualify, 150/250 to pass course. (Detailed basic and armed training manuals available.)

Maine

None required.

Maryland

None required for unarmed. Armed: eight hours of preassignment training.

Massachusetts

None required.

Michigan

None required despite legislative attempts.

Minnesota

Bill introduced in 1989 state legislature addressed training for armed and unarmed guards and proprietary employees. No action to date.

Montana

None required for unarmed. Armed: training by approved instructor. Minimum 10 hours of training on safety, handling, liability, and statutes. Seventy percent score on firearms safety and proficiency test—written exam and combat shooting course with authorized firearm. Demonstration of reasonable competence in firearm skill as determined by certified instructor. Registration based on satisfactory completion of certified combat shooting course annually.

Nevada

None required for unarmed. Armed: six hours of classroom instruction, exam; firing range, shooting minimum of 50 rounds with 70 minimum score.

New Hampshire

None required for unarmed. Armed: four hours of classroom and range qualification; instruction to include firearms techniques, safety, and laws on use of deadly force. Minimum qualification score of 75 percent for practical police course or tactical revolver course, shotgun familiarization course if used.

New Jersey

None required for unarmed. Armed: number of hours of training not specified.

New Mexico

None required for unarmed. Armed: Minimum 20 hours—four hours of classroom training related to legal aspects of use of deadly force, 16 hours on the range. Additional four-hour shotgun qualification course if shotgun carried. Ten-hour yearly requalification course—two hours of classroom and eight hours of range instruction program specified.

New York

None required. Bills now in committee would require training for armed and unarmed guards.

North Carolina

None for unarmed guards. Armed: four hours of classroom training by certified trainer on legal limits on handgun use, knowledge of act, range firing, and procedure and safety. Must fire 70 percent score on approved target course. Annual renewal includes complete refresher course and requalification on prescribed range firing. Guard agencies or in-house departments may qualify as training institutions if programs include required courses taught by approved instructors.

North Dakota

Three levels:

Apprentice: Minimum 16 hours of classroom instruction on security services, first aid, and other training employer deems necessary for assignment. Minimum 16 hours of field training under supervision of qualified security officer before working unsupervised.

Security officer: After 1,000 hours and before 2,000 hours as active apprentice, individual applies for registration as private security officer that is contingent on training—32 hours of classroom instruction, which includes required curriculum and other training employer deems necessary.

Commissioned security officer: Requires 4,000 hours of active service as security officer and additional 80 hours of classroom instruction based on suggested curricula.

Ohio

None required for unarmed guards. Armed: as of 1986, must satisfactorily complete firearms basic training program, including 20 hours of handgun training and five hours of training in use of other firearms if used or authorized equivalent training or former peace officer training. Must requalify annually on firearms range.

Oklahoma

Private security division's motto: "Professionalism Through Training." Second only to North Dakota in length of training. Three courses of instruction:

I: Basic, 22 hours of instruction related to general private security tasks.

II: Security guard, 18 hours of instruction related to tasks of unarmed guards.

IV: Firearms, phases I and II, plus 24 hours of training in care, handling, and firing of revolvers and shotguns (eight hours of classroom, 16 hours of range).

Armed: I, II, IV—64 hours for Armed Security Guard Training Course at approved schools. Specifies student-instructor ratios of 30:1 (5:1 for range) and instructor qualifications and facilities standards (for example, 10 sq. ft./ student). During phase IV, must take Minnesota Multiphasic Personality Inventory or approved equivalent given by qualified person and evaluated by licensed psychologist chosen and paid for by student.

Pennsylvania

Armed: 40-hour basic training course; eight hours of additional training required for five-year license renewal.

Rhode Island

None required for unarmed. Armed: range test required with minimum score of 195/300.

South Carolina

Unarmed: eight hours of instruction. Armed: 12 hours of preassignment instruction, including classroom instruction.

Tennessee

Completed within 30 days of employment, basic four-hour course on general training by certified trainer. Armed: eight more hours of classroom firearm training—four hours on range and marksmanship training—with 75 percent score on silhouette target course. Renewal: four-hour refresher training, requalification in firearm use with minimum 75 percent score. Requirements given for certified trainers—contractor proprietary employee.

Texas

None required for unarmed. Armed: 30-hour basic training program, including minimum five hours on firearms.

Utah

Model programs provided in rules. Unarmed: 12 hours of training prior to application—minimum six hours of classroom instruction, six hours of on-the-job training working unarmed and accompanied by licensed guard. Armed: 12 hours of preassignment training as for unarmed guard. Twelve hours of firearms instruction with certificate as proof: four hours of classroom, eight hours of range experience with weapon to be used on duty.

Must pass range test with 70 percent score. Renewal: eight hours of in-service training and same firearm instruction as required for original license.

Vermont

None required for unarmed. Armed: 16 hours of preassignment classroom instruction program to stress safe and proper use and handling of firearms and dogs, legal responsibility for improper or negligent use of either. NRA-approved police combat or security firing course using silhouette targets. Dog handlers: 16 hours of classroom and practical exercise training, additional four hours of firearm training if armed. Training waived with proof of equivalent training elsewhere.

Virginia

At agent's discretion for unarmed guards; none required. Armed: training certification of firearm classroom training and range firing for specific weapon; two-year firearm certification $50; renewal $15. Must carry registration card while on duty.

West Virginia

None required.

Wisconsin

None required for unarmed. Armed: Wisconsin Department of Justice course prescribed with certified trainer; annual recertification.

3B

Security Journals, Magazines, and Newsletters

Domestic Security Journals and Magazines

Campus Law Enforcement Journal (bimonthly)
Data Processing and Communications Security (bimonthly)
Journal of Healthcare Protection Management (three issues)
Journal of Security Administration (biannually)
Library and Archival Security (quarterly)
Lipman Report (monthly)
Locksmith Ledger (monthly)
Polygraph (quarterly)
Protection of Assets Manual (monthly)
Security Management and Plant Protection (monthly)
Security Journal (quarterly)
Security Management (monthly)
Security Systems Digest (biweekly)
Security Systems Administration (monthly)
Security World (monthly)

Foreign Security Magazines

Brazil

Seguridad/Security (bimonthly)

Canada

Canadian Security (six issues annually)
National Loss Prevention (quarterly)
The Protection Officer (trimonthly)

Great Britain

International Security Review (bimonthly)
Security Times (quarterly)

The Netherlands

Computers and Security (three issues annually)

Italy

esse Come (bimonthly)
Seiezione Sicurrezze

Domestic and Foreign Newsletters

Comsec Letter (monthly)
Corporate Security (monthly)
Data Processing Auditing Report (monthly)
The Expert Witness Report
Foreign Intelligence Literary Scene (bimonthly)
Hospital Security and Safety Management (monthly)
Hotel/Motel Security and Safety Management (monthly)
International Cargo Crime Prevention (monthly)
The Lipman Report (monthly)
Nursing Home Security and Safety Management (monthly)
Periscope (quarterly)
Protection of Assets Bulletin (monthly)
Retail Security Management Letter (monthly)
Scientific Sleuthing Newsletter (quarterly)
Security Newsletter
Security Systems Digest (biweekly)
2600 (monthly)
Polygraph Law Reporter (quarterly)

Private Security Case Law Reporter (ten issues annually)
Security Law Newsletter (monthly)
Security and Special Police Legal Update (bimonthly)

Periodical Indexes

Criminal Justice Periodical Index (three issues annually)
International Risk Control Review (quarterly)

PART

II

The Security Function

4

Defining Security's Role

During the nineteenth and twentieth centuries, public police operated only on a local basis. They had neither the resources nor the authority to extend their investigations or pursuit of criminals beyond the sharply circumscribed boundaries in which they performed their duties. When the need arose to reach beyond these boundaries or to cut through several of these jurisdictions, law enforcement was undertaken by such private security forces as the Pinkerton Agency, railway police, or the Burns Detective Agency.

As the police sciences developed, public agencies began to assume a more significant role in the investigation of crime and, through increased cooperation among government agencies, the pursuit of suspected criminals. Concurrent with this evolution of public law enforcement, private agencies shifted their emphases away from investigation and toward crime prevention. This led to an increasing use of guard services to protect property and to maintain order. Today in terms of numbers, guard forces are by far the predominant element in private security.

But what other protective measures are available? Who provides them? Who is responsible for planning and executing these procedures? Where do the roles of private and public police overlap, and where do they diverge? What are the particular hazards for which private security is now held responsible, and how is it determined that threats are sufficient to justify the adoption of protective procedures? To answer these questions, it is necessary to define private security and its role more exactly.

What Is Private Security?

Although the term "private security" has been used in previous pages without question, there is no universal agreement on a definition or even on the suitability of the term itself. Cogent arguments have been made, for example, for substituting the term "loss prevention" for security.

The *Rand Report* defines private security to include all protective and loss-prevention activities not performed by law-enforcement agencies. Specifically,

> The terms private police and private security forces and security personnel are used generically in this report to include all types of private organizations and individuals providing all of security-related services, including investigation, guard, patrol, lie detection, alarm, and armored transportation.[1]

The Task Force on Private Security takes exception to this definition on several grounds. The task force argues that "quasi-public police" should be excluded from consideration on the grounds that they are paid out of public funds even though they may be performing what are essentially private security functions. The task force also makes the distinction that private security personnel must be employees of a "for-profit" organization or firm as opposed to a nonprofit or governmental agency. The complete task force definition states:

> Private security includes those self-employed individuals and privately funded business entities and organizations providing security-related services to specific clientele for a fee, for the individual or entity that retains or employs them, or for themselves, in order to protect their persons, private property, or interests from varied hazards.[2]

The task force argues that the profit motive and the source of profits are basic elements of private security. While this definition might be suitable for the specific purposes of the report, it hardly seems acceptable as a general definition. Many airports, hospitals, and schools, to name only three types of institutions, employ private security forces without for-profit orientation. Yet it would be difficult to contend, for example, that the members of the International Association for Hospital Security (IAHS) are not private security personnel.

The Hallcrest reports never formally defined the terms of security or loss prevention but relied on the earlier definitions of terms. These reports consider, however, the security or loss-prevention field in its broadest application and thus avoid getting bogged down in discussions of profit motive or specific tasks. The reports focus on the functional aspects of security, recognizing that the functions of security and loss prevention are performed by both the public law enforcement sector and private agencies.

The wisdom of the Hallcrest reports authors in broadly defining security on the basis of functional aspects is borne out in the data presented in *Hallcrest II*. There the authors report on the 1987 NIJ (National Institute of Justice) study, *Public Policing—Privately Provided*. This report states that several large national security companies are working with federal, state, and local governments in contracting out selected tasks or functions.[3] *The New York Times* reported in 1985 that about 36,000 of the total 1.1 million private security jobs were assigned to government contracts.[4]

Thus neither the profit nature of the organization being protected nor even the source of funds by which personnel are paid holds up as a useful distinction. A night watchman at a public school is engaged to protect a non-profit installation and is paid out of public funds. His function, however, is clearly different from that of a public law-enforcement officer. He is—and is universally accepted as—a private security guard. How then should private security be defined for the purpose of this text?

The opening lines of this text suggest that "security implies a stable, relatively predictable environment in which an individual or group may pursue its ends without disruption or harm and without fear of such disturbance or injury."

Such security can be effected by military forces, by public law-enforcement agencies, by the individual or organization concerned, or by organized private enterprises. Where the protective services are provided by personnel who are not only paid out of public funds but also charged with the *general* responsibility for the public welfare, their function is that of public police. Where the services are provided for the protection of *specific* individuals or organizations, they normally fall into the area of private security.

Security Hazards

The hazards against which private security seeks to provide protection are commonly divided into manmade and natural.

Natural hazards may include fire, windstorm, flood, earthquake, and other acts of nature that could result in building collapse, equipment failure, accidents, and safety hazards. It should be noted that fire is also quite often manmade, intentionally or unintentionally.

Manmade hazards may include crimes against the person (for example, robbery or rape) or crime against property (theft and pilferage, fraud and embezzlement). In addition, man also creates problems through espionage and sabotage, civil disturbances, bomb threats, fire (as noted above), and accidents.

The degree of exposure to specific hazards will vary for different facilities. The threat of fire or explosion is greatest in a chemical plant; the potential of loss from shoplifting or internal theft is greatest in a retail store. Each organization or facility must ideally be protected against a full range of hazards, but in practice, a particular protection system will emphasize some hazards more than others.

In some organizations, the whole area of accident prevention and safety has taken on such importance, primarily because of state and federal occupational safety and health legislation, that this responsibility has become a full-time objective in itself, in the charge of a director of safety. Security can then devote its energies to other areas of loss. Similarly some large industrial facilities have full-time fire departments. In most situations, however, both fire and accident prevention are part of the responsibility of the security department.

Security Functions

Security practices and procedures cover a broad spectrum of activities designed to eliminate or reduce the full range of potential hazards (loss, damage, or injury). These protection measures may include, but are by no means limited to:

1. Building and perimeter protection, by means of barriers, fences, walls, and gates; protected openings; lighting; and surveillance (guards)
2. Intrusion and access control, by means of door and window security, locks and keys, security containers (files, safes, and vaults), visitor and employee identification programs, package controls, parking security and traffic controls, inspections, and guard posts and patrols
3. Alarm and surveillance systems
4. Fire prevention and control, including evacuation and fire response programs, extinguishing systems, and alarm systems
5. Emergency and disaster planning
6. Prevention of theft and pilferage by means of personnel screening, background investigations, procedural controls, and polygraph and PSE (Psychological Stress Evaluator) investigations
7. Accident prevention and safety
8. Enforcement of crime- or loss-related rules, regulations, and policies.

In addition to these basic loss-prevention functions, security services in some situations might also provide armored car and armed courier service, bodyguard protection, management consulting, security consulting, and other specific types of protection.

These services may be *proprietary*, or in-house, in which case the security force is hired and controlled directly by the protected organization, or they may be *contract* security services in which case the company contracts with a specialized firm to provide designated security services for a fee. Contract security employees are actually employees of the contract security firm. Most security functions may be provided by either proprietary or contract forces or services; and in practice, it is common to find a combination of such services used.

Security Services

Security services in 1990 totaled approximately 107,000 companies doing an estimated $51 billion in business, primarily providing guard, investigative, central station alarm, and armored car and courier services. It has been said that six large, publicly owned firms dominate the industry, accounting for approximately half of all revenues generated by contract security services. According to *Hallcrest II*, however, the number of smaller firms is increasing and claiming a larger share of the total market.[5]

Many firms, particularly the smaller ones, specialize in specific types of services offered to a client. The larger the firm, the more likely it is to provide a full range of security services. The major categories of these services are guard forces, patrols, consulting services, investigative services, alarm response, and armored car delivery and courier services.

According to various sources, guard services, whether proprietary or contract, are in greater demand today than ever before. People and companies turn to guards because psychologically they feel that technology or hardware may not be enough.[6] However, *Hallcrest II* reports that the 1990s will be marked by diminishing in-house staff, redistribution of security decision making inside and outside, and an increased reliance on equipment.[7] Although some proprietary firms are relying more on technology to reduce guard-cost overhead, three basic trends are apparent. First as the number of legal problems associated with inappropriate actions of guards increases, public outrage will eventually force states to regulate training and standards. Second as the field grows, it will attract better qualified individuals. And third there will be a trend to disarm security personnel. *Hallcrest II* indicates that only 10 percent of the guard force is presently armed. It also reports that this percentage has already taken a dramatic decrease and the report predicts that the percentage will be at not more than 5 percent by the year 2000.[8]

These predictions are justified considering the changes in the demographics of security guards since 1972 when *The Rand Report* indicated that the typical security guard was "an aging white male, poorly educated averaging between 40 and 55 years of age, [and] . . . had little education beyond the ninth grade."[9] *Hallcrest I* indicated that the average guard is a young white male, age 33 with a high school diploma (85 percent) and a 45 percent chance of having at least some college education.[10] *Hallcrest II* reiterates this finding by noting that the contemporary private security guard is better educated and younger.[11]

Guard Services

Guard supply represents the major service provided in the industry today. The majority of guards work for contract security agencies, but many firms hire their own security staff (proprietary security). Only part of the guard's job is crime-related. Whenever it is possible or necessary, they are required to prevent major crimes and to report those that have been committed. But their major role may be to direct traffic, to screen persons desiring access to a facility, and generally to enforce company rules. In many modern applications, the role is less regulatory than helpful. They may direct or escort persons to their destination within a facility, act as receptionists or sources of information, or be primarily concerned with safety.

Since many guards are concerned for only a small percentage of their time with crime-related activity, there is some effort in various quarters to adjust the guards' appearance to fit their roles by outfitting them in blazers and slacks rather than in a uniform with its police or coercive connotation.

A guard is, however, a guard. Even if, in a particular assignment, she is never confronted with criminal activity, the guard is still charged with certain responsibilities in that area and is responsible in addition for protecting the interests of her employer on the employer's property.

Private guards differ from public police both in their legal status and in that they perform in areas where the public police cannot legally or practically operate. The public police have no authority to enforce private regulations, nor have they the obligation to investigate the unsubstantiated possibility of crime (such as employee theft) on private property.

The job of the private guard is to provide specific services under the direction and control of a private employer who needs to exercise controls or supervision over the company's property or goods or to provide additional services that the public police as a practical matter simply cannot provide.

Patrol Services

Private patrol services offer a periodic inspection of various premises by one or more patrols operating either on foot or in patrol cars.

The tour of such patrols may cover several locations of a single client or include several establishments owned by different clients within a limited neighborhood. Inspections of patrolled premises may be visual perusal from the outside, or they may require entering the premises for a more thorough inspection. Typically the arrangement made with a client specifies that a certain number of inspections will be made within a given period of time or with specified frequency.

The patrol differs from the guard in operating through a tour covering various locations, whereas the guard stands a fixed post or walks a limited area. The patrol service is more economical since the guard maintains a post for the full period during which a danger exists. But the patrol has the possible disadvantage of being circumvented by an intruder who knows that there will be some period of time between inspections of a given premise.

Consulting Services

Many firms that seek professional assistance in determining their vulnerabilities and risks look not to the police but to those in the private security sector who are professionally trained to assess security needs and make appropriate recommendations. As with any profession, some people emerge as experts who then sell their expertise for a fee. These people are commonly referred to as consultants since they are paid for their professional opinions. According to *Hallcrest II* the use of security consultants is expected to increase over the next 10 years. Consultant services are generally divided into four general categories: (1) engineering-related, (2) management, (3) executive protection, and (4) computer security.

Investigative Services

The private investigator is a gatherer of facts—in essence, a researcher who spends the greatest portion of the time collecting background information for preemployment checks on personnel, background checks of applicants for insurance or credit, and investigation of insurance claims. Much of this work is noncrime-related although it may involve either part- or full-time undercover investigations of employee theft or detection of shoplifting.

Investigations in divorce-related matters are declining as divorce laws become more liberal. Investigations of "significant others," however, are increasing as people become more interested in what their love interests do with their spare time. Tracing missing persons or investigating criminal matters on behalf of the accused is a very small part of a typical investigator's work. In fact, the Pinkerton Agency will not handle any matter involving the defense of persons under prosecution by public law-enforcement agencies or matters pertaining to domestic or marital investigation.

Although there are situations, such as the long-term relationship between the American Bankers Association and the Burns Agency, where private investigations are called upon to supplement the work of public police, the great majority of private investigative work is complementary to the public law enforcement effort.

A growing number of investigators are engaged in litigation investigations—that is, gathering data for defense and plaintiff law firms preparing for trial in civil court.

Alarm Response Services

Central station alarm systems consist essentially of alarm sensors located in the protected premises and a communication line from the sensors to a privately owned central station alarm board that is monitored and responded to by private security personnel (see Figure 4.1). Many city codes require that alarm systems be tied into a central station operation.

In some cases, central station systems do not dispatch personnel to re-

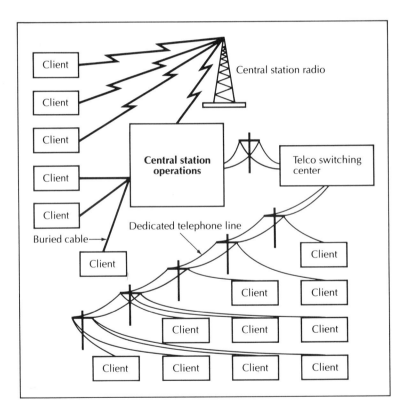

Figure 4.1 Central station operation. The initiation of certain sensors and various devices at a remote location are signaled automatically to an appropriately equipped central alarm-monitoring facility. These signals are supervised, recorded, and maintained through the services of the central station operator. Client locations can tie into the central station via dedicated telephone lines, buried cable, or radio. (From Don T. Cherry, *Total Facility Control* [Stoneham, Mass.: Butterworth Publishers, 1986], p. 34.)

spond to an alarm but rather relay the alarm received to public police head-quarters. But in most such systems, the alarm is relayed, and someone is also sent to the scene.

Alarms connected to a central station are usually designed to detect intrusion, but they can also be used to monitor industrial processes or conditions.

Certainly, central station coverage of a facility is cheaper than full-time security employees performing essentially the same function. A drawback is that the current false-alarm rate for virtually all intrusion systems is still very high, resulting in a growing resistance to the use of direct connection systems to police headquarters. Central station operators have some flexibility in checking the validity of an alarm before notifying the police, so they may to some degree reduce the incidence of false alarms demanding police response.

In cases where central station personnel actively investigate the intrusion, even take steps to apprehend a suspect before the arrival of the police, they supplement the public police effort.

Armored Delivery Services

Armored delivery services provide for the safe transfer of money, valuables, or any goods the employer may wish to move from one location to another. By far the widest use of this service is to transport cash and negotiables from a receiving point to a bank or other depository. Payrolls, cash receipts, or cash supplies for daily business are the principal traffic of the armored delivery service.

Personnel employed by such services are not concerned with the general security of the premises they serve; their responsibility is confined to the safe transport of sensitive items as directed by the customer.

Courier services perform a similar function in the safe transport of valuables. They are distinguished from armored car services principally by using means other than special armored vehicles.

Other Services

In addition to the services described, private security firms also provide such services as crowd control, canine patrol, bodyguard and escort service, executive protection, polygraph examination, psychological stress evaluation, drug testing, honesty testing, employee assistance services, and other related loss-prevention assistance to business and industry. Bodyguard service in particular has increased rapidly since the mid-1970s in response to the rising incidence of executive kidnappings and hostage situations. And during the mid-1980s, various firms have entered the area of drug testing to meet the demand for a drug-free work environment.

Contract versus Proprietary Services

Early researchers (including the authors of *The Rand Report*) perceived more rapid growth in contract security services than in proprietary security. The exception to this perception was the Task Force on Private Security that "concluded that the growth of proprietary security has paralleled that of contractual security."[12] *Hallcrest I* substantiates the earlier predictions. Although many firms are considering contract services, some existing proprietary security operations are converting to hybrids with proprietary management and contractual line services. *Hallcrest II* supports *Hallcrest I*'s observations, noting that growth in proprietary security has stabilized and is predicted to show a 2 percent drop by the year 2000. The authors believe the trend will be toward increased use of contract employees, products, and services, causing the employee numbers in the contract area to double by the year 2000.[13]

Since the various contract functions described in the preceding pages can be undertaken as proprietary (or in-house) activities, how is the choice to be made between the two types of services? The subject of contract services versus proprietary security has been debated in most of the major security periodicals for 15 years or more. Some of the conclusions are reflected in the following discussion of the relative merits of the two approaches to security services. The question of which is the most sensible approach, however, is best answered by the manager of the firm or organization contemplating security services. Her decision will rest on the particular characteristics of the company. These characteristics will include the location to be guarded, the size of the force required, its mission, the length of time the guards will be needed, and the quality of personnel required.

Advantages of Contract Services

Cost

Few experts disagree that contract guards are less expensive than is a proprietary unit. An unarmed guard will earn an average of $7.70 per hour;[14] in-house guards typically earn more because of the general wage rate of the facility employing them. In many cases, that wage level has been established by collective bargaining. Table 4.1 shows the average hourly rate in selected metropolitan areas.

Contract guards receive fewer fringe benefits, and their services can be provided more economically by large contract firms by virtue of savings in costs of hiring, training, and insurance because of volume. Short-term guard

Table 4.1 Hourly Security Officer Compensation in Selected U.S. Metropolitan Areas

Metropolitan Area	Mean	Median	Middle Range
Anaheim, CA			
Manufacturing	$10.37	$11.05	$6.88–13.56
Nonmanufacturing	5.51	5.48	4.80– 5.75
Atlanta			
Manufacturing	11.29	13.85	7.75–14.68
Nonmanufacturing	5.61	5.25	5.00– 5.75
Austin			
Manufacturing	7.31	7.54	6.76– 7.89
Nonmanufacturing	4.50	4.25	4.00– 5.00
Baltimore			
Manufacturing	11.61	12.10	9.76–13.73
Nonmanufacturing	5.17	5.40	4.00– 6.00
Boston			
Manufacturing	9.89	10.00	8.39–11.32
Nonmanufacturing	6.38	6.00	5.55– 6.75
Charleston, SC			
Manufacturing	7.85	7.53	6.81– 8.63
Nonmanufacturing	4.23	3.88	3.63– 5.00
Charlotte, NC			
Manufacturing	6.43	5.84	5.36– 6.33
Nonmanufacturing	5.69	5.00	4.20– 6.00
Chicago			
Manufacturing	9.37	8.86	6.00–12.87
Nonmanufacturing	6.01	5.25	4.80– 6.85
Cincinnati			
Manufacturing	10.53	10.80	8.85–12.84
Nonmanufacturing	4.20	4.00	3.75– 4.25
Cleveland			
Manufacturing	9.97	10.56	7.72–12.32
Nonmanufacturing	4.60	4.25	4.00– 4.75
Dallas			
Manufacturing	9.55	8.75	7.52–11.75
Nonmanufacturing	5.15	4.75	4.50– 5.50
Denver			
Manufacturing	10.67	13.30	7.05–13.38
Nonmanufacturing	4.86	4.40	4.00– 5.00
Detroit			
Manufacturing	12.48	14.39	10.86–14.39
Nonmanufacturing	6.31	4.56	4.25– 6.11
Hartford, CT			
Manufacturing	9.33	9.45	8.43–10.29
Nonmanufacturing	6.47	6.00	5.50– 7.00

Table 4.1 (Cont.)

Metropolitan Area	Mean	Median	Middle Range
Houston			
Manufacturing	9.10	8.30	7.08–10.73
Nonmanufacturing	5.50	5.10	4.70– 6.00
Huntsville, AL			
Manufacturing	5.65	5.62	4.80– 6.16
Nonmanufacturing	4.19	4.00	3.50– 4.30
Indianapolis			
Manufacturing	11.33	12.07	8.69–14.10
Nonmanufacturing	4.86	4.00	3.75– 5.12
Kansas City			
Manufacturing	11.28	11.49	10.25–11.96
Nonmanufacturing	4.56	4.00	3.65– 4.75
Los Angeles			
Manufacturing	10.54	10.35	8.50–13.56
Nonmanufacturing	5.61	5.15	4.75– 6.10
Miami			
Manufacturing	6.92	7.02	6.37– 7.64
Nonmanufacturing	5.21	5.00	4.35– 5.72
Milwaukee			
Manufacturing	13.41	14.34	14.34–14.34
Nonmanufacturing	4.67	4.25	3.90– 5.09
Minneapolis			
Manufacturing	10.90	11.06	10.28–11.18
Nonmanufacturing	5.47	5.25	4.75– 5.75
Newark			
Manufacturing	11.78	11.18	10.75–13.87
Nonmanufacturing	5.49	5.00	4.50– 6.16
New Orleans			
Manufacturing	8.00	8.22	6.76– 9.31
Nonmanufacturing	4.36	3.73	3.50– 4.20
New York			
Manufacturing	11.00	11.62	9.14–13.07
Nonmanufacturing	5.80	5.00	4.56– 6.10
Philadelphia			
Manufacturing	10.99	10.73	9.79–12.45
Nonmanufacturing	5.18	5.00	4.33– 5.50
Phoenix			
Manufacturing	8.16	8.35	6.15– 9.83
Nonmanufacturing	4.99	4.65	4.50– 5.00
Pittsburgh			
Manufacturing	10.60	10.62	8.93–11.77
Nonmanufacturing	4.73	4.27	3.75– 5.25

Metropolitan Area	Mean	Median	Middle Range
Riverside, CA			
Manufacturing	7.75	7.47	5.42– 9.63
Nonmanufacturing	4.96	4.70	4.25– 5.40
Salt Lake City			
Manufacturing	6.61	6.50	5.95– 7.20
Nonmanufacturing	4.43	4.50	3.75– 5.00
San Jose, CA			
Manufacturing	10.54	10.23	8.42–13.99
Nonmanufacturing	6.43	6.25	5.80– 7.00
St. Louis			
Manufacturing	12.12	12.76	10.31–13.85
Nonmanufacturing	4.45	4.00	3.80– 4.75
Washington, DC			
Manufacturing	8.75	7.89	7.12–10.25
Nonmanufacturing	7.02	7.25	6.13– 7.45

Notes: Mean, or average, is computed by totaling earnings of all the workers and dividing by the total number of workers. The median designates the wage at which half of the workers earn more and half earn less than the amount stated. The middle range is derived from two values: a fourth of the workers receive the same or less than the lower of these two rates and a fourth earn the same or more than the higher rate.

Source: Reprinted with permission from Security Letter Source Book 1990–1991 by Robert D. McCrie, CPP (Security Letter: New York) distributed by Butterworth-Heinemann.

service on a proprietary basis can create such large start-up costs that the effort is impractical.

Liability insurance, payroll taxes, uniforms and equipment, and the time involved in training, sick leave, and vacations are all extra cost factors that must be considered in deciding on whether to establish a proprietary force.

Administration

Establishing an in-house guard service requires the development and administration of a recruitment program, personnel screening procedures, and training programs. It will also involve the direct supervision of all guard personnel. Hiring contract guards solves the administrative problems of scheduling and substituting manpower when someone is sick or terminates employment.

There is little question that the administrative chores are substantially decreased when a contract service is employed. At the same time, the contracting customer is obliged to check the supplier's performance of contracted services on an ongoing basis including personnel screening procedures. The customer must also insist on a satisfactory level of quality at all times. To this extent, management of the client firm is not totally relieved of administrative responsibilities.

Staffing

During periods when the need for guards changes in any way, it may be necessary to lay off existing guards or take on additional staff. Such changes may come about fairly suddenly or unexpectedly.

In-house forces rarely have this flexibility in staffing. If they have extra people available for emergency use, such staff are an unnecessary expense when they are idle. Similarly if there is a temporary decrease in the need for guards, it would hardly be efficient to dismiss extra people only to rehire additional guards a short time later when the situation changed again.

Unions

Guard users in favor of nonunion guards support their position by arguing that such guards are not likely to go out on strike, they are less apt to sympathize with or support striking employees, and they can be paid less because they receive few if any fringe benefits.

Since most unionized guards are proprietary personnel, anyone subscribing to the arguments listed here would clearly favor hiring contract guards. Only a fraction of the guards employed by the three largest contract guard agencies (Pinkerton, Burns, and Wackenhut) are unionized.

Impartiality

It is often suggested that contract guards can more readily and more effectively enforce regulations than can in-house personnel. The rationale is that contract guards are paid by a different employer and because of their relatively low seniority have few opportunities to form close associations with other employees of the client. This produces a more consistently impartial performance of duty.

Expertise

When clients hire a guard service, they also hire the management of that service to guide them in their overall security program. This can prove valuable even to a firm that is already sophisticated in security administration. A different view from a competitive supplier trying to create goodwill with a client can always be illuminating.

Advantages of Proprietary Guards

Quality of Personnel

Proponents of proprietary guard systems argue that the higher pay and fringe benefits offered by employers as well as the higher status of in-house guards attracts higher quality personnel. Such employees have been more carefully screened and show a lower rate of turnover.

Control

Many managers feel that they have a much greater degree of control over personnel when they are directly on the firm's payroll. The presence of contract supervisors between guards and client management can interfere with the rapid, accurate flow of information either up or down.

An in-house force can be trained to suit the specific needs of the facility, and the progress and effectiveness of training can be better observed in this context. The individual performance of each member of the force can also be evaluated more readily.

Loyalty

In-house guards are reported to develop a keener sense of loyalty to the firm they are protecting than do contract guards. The latter, who may be shifted from one client to another and who have a high turnover rate, simply do not have the opportunity to generate any sense of loyalty to the specified—often temporary—client-employer.

Prestige

Many managers simply prefer to have their own people on the job. They feel that the firm gains prestige by building its own security force to its own specifications rather than by renting one on the outside.

Obviously in weighing the various factors on either side of this debate, prudent managers will carefully study the quality and performance of the guard firms available to service their facility. They will make sure of the standards of personnel, training, and supervision in the guard firm. They will also make a careful analysis of the comparative costs for proprietary and contract services, and will estimate both services' relative effectiveness in a particular application.

In situations where the demand for guards fluctuates considerably, a contract service is probably indicated. If a fairly large, stable guard force is required, an in-house organization might be favored.

Hallcrest II reported that, while approximately 50 percent of the respondents used contract services for the majority of their security guard needs in

1985, the number of contract guards increased to 58 percent in 1990 and that contract guards will be more than double the number of proprietary guards by the year 2000.[15] As noted earlier, the trend of the future is toward hybrid systems, with proprietary supervision and contract guards.

Deciding on a Contract Security Firm

A variety of issues must be considered when a company or organization decides to hire a contract security firm. According to Minot Dodson, vice president of Operations and Training, California Plant Protection, Inc., the following areas should be analyzed:

1. The scope of the work
2. Personnel selection procedures
3. Training programs
4. Supervision
5. Wages
6. Benefits
7. Operating procedures
8. Contractor data
9. Terms and conditions[16]

The scope of the work should include at a minimum locations, hours of coverage, patrol checkpoints, and duties. The guard firm should be aware of, and prepared to enforce, all applicable corporate security policies—particularly those dealing with access control, personnel identification, documentation procedures for removal of materials from the facility, handling customers and employees, and emergency procedures. Proprietary security objectives and priorities should be stated clearly. The proprietary firm should also include references to expansion plans and determine how the guard firm will handle the expansion. The proprietary firm should also spell out expectations for security goals (that is, a 20 percent reduction of shrinkage) and determine how the guard firm plans to meet these goals. Proprietary performance criteria should be spelled out to include such things as what and when to report.

The organization choosing a contract service should also be able to set standards for the employees who will be protecting their facility. Standards for general appearance, age, licenses needed, physical condition, educational levels, reporting skills, background, and language ability are certainly worth listing. According to Dodson, "You should check the personnel file on each prospective guard. Look for pre-employment background and police record checks, and verify application information."[17] The proprietary firm should check training records and test scores as well as psychological test results (that is, pen and pencil tests when they are available). It is even advisable in some operations not only to interview the guard company but also to interview the prospective guards. The guard company should agree to remove any guard for reasonable cause (that is, violating regulations).

Hallcrest II notes that the Task Force on Private Security has set the minimum recommended level of training for security officers at 120 hours. Lobbying efforts on the part of cost-conscious security managers, however, have reduced the generally recommended time to only 40 hours. Despite this recommendation, many guard companies still maintain only an 8-hour indoctrination period. Proprietary firms should review the guard service's training procedures to make sure they meet specific company requirements. Some areas to consider are patrol techniques, first aid, liability and powers, fire fighting, public relations, and report writing. Proprietary firms also have the right to request additional special requirements. Whether the decision is to contract or not to contract, the firm will generally get what it pays for.

Supervision of the contract is another concern. Employing firms should understand the entire chain of command in the guard company. Supervisors from the contract service should maintain regular contact with guards and make random checks on all shifts and work days. The response time of supervisors can be critical, and radio or telephone contact should be possible at all times. Direct contact with a supervisor, however, should also be available within no more than one hour.

Wages are tremendously important. The quality of personnel is often directly related to the wage level. The client company, not the guard service, should establish the minimum wage to be paid to security employees. What is a good minimum wage? The Bureau of Labor Statistics provides data on average food and transportation costs for low-income families. According to *Hallcrest II* researchers, unarmed guards who averaged $7.70 per hour in 1990 earned 50 percent less than the average income of a police officer.[18] Thus some guards may be making less than a survival wage. One implication of this is that underpaid guards might take advantage of their employment and steal from the contracting firm. Dodson suggests that guards receive $.10 to $.30/hour over the calculated minimum wage for the areas contracted, thus making the job more desirable and reducing the temptation to steal.[19] At a minimum, guards should be paid at least what semiskilled labor in the area is earning.

While fringe benefits offered by guard firms might not seem an area of much concern to the employing companies, they should be. In a field where the turnover rate of some guard services is 200 percent annually, perks become very important in retaining quality personnel. Benefits might include cash bonus plans, sick leave, health insurance, and overtime pay. Other perks might be life insurance, pension funds, and paid education and training. Per-

Table 4.2 Security Firm Evaluation Analysis

Instructions: Rate each proposal topic and other observation as follows: high = +1; average = 0; low = −1. Add all +1s and subtract all −1s in each section to obtain subtotals. Then add and subtract subtotals to obtain the overall rating.

Ratings can be ranked as: 50 to 77, excellent; 25 to 49, above average; 0 to 24, average; −1 to −34, below average; and −35 to −77, poor.

Retain this rating sheet to verify that you have done everything possible to select a competent security company.

Consideration	Score	Consideration	Score
1. *Bid package*		3. *Training*	
a. All requested information provided in proposal	____	a. Prehire classroom training (8 hours minimum)	____
b. Quality of proposal presentation	____	b. Prehire classroom training testing	____
c. Timeliness of submission of proposal	____	c. Training manual	____
Subtotal	____	d. Training manual testing	____
		e. Training film usage	____
		f. Training films testing	____
		g. Training facilities	____
		h. On-the-job training program	____
2. *Personnel*		i. On-the-job training tests	____
a. Past employment checks (preemployment)	____	j. Continuing training program	____
b. Reference checks (preemployment)	____	k. Continuing training tests	____
c. Psychological testing (preemployment)	____	l. Advanced training program	____
d. Polygraph testing (preemployment)	____	m. Advanced training tests	____
e. Prehire evaluation of personnel	____	n. State certified training school	____
f. Prehire evaluation of personnel files	____	o. College certified training/trainers	____
g. Basic qualifications	____	Subtotal	____
h. Security aptitude testing (preemployment)	____	4. *Supervision*	
i. Management quality (top level)	____	a. Selection	____
j. Management quality (mid-level)	____	b. Training and testing	____
k. Supervision (first line)	____	c. Site supervision	____
l. EEO Program	____	d. Field supervision	____
m. Average length of employee service	____	e. Visits and assistance	____
Subtotal	____	f. Employee evaluation reports	____
		g. Response capabilities	____
		Subtotal	____

Consideration	Score	Consideration	Score
5. *Employee Wages and Benefits*		b. Management response	_____
		c. Additional services ability	_____
a. Wage distribution by grade and scale	_____	d. Uniforms provided	_____
b. Longevity rewarded	_____	e. Uniform cleaning and maintenance provided	_____
c. Merit pay proposed	_____	f. Emergency response capabilities	_____
d. Health insurance	_____	g. Post orders	_____
e. Life insurance	_____	h. Client control of operations	_____
f. Holidays	_____	i. Financial stability	_____
g. Vacation	_____	j. Standard of performance for guards	_____
h. Sick pay	_____	k. Service agreement	_____
i. Bereavement Pay	_____	l. Periodic polygraph testing	_____
Subtotal	_____	Subtotal	_____
6. *Insurance*			
a. General liability	_____	8. *Cost of Service*	
b. Care, custody, and control	_____	a. Cost factor detail	_____
c. Errors and omissions	_____	b. Standard time fee	_____
d. Employee dishonesty	_____	c. Overtime fees	_____
e. Excess liability (umbrella form)	_____	d. Holiday fees	_____
f. Workmen's compensation	_____	e. Effective rate	_____
g. Automobile liability	_____	f. Equipment fee	_____
h. Policy exclusions	_____	g. Billing periods	_____
i. Policy availability	_____	Subtotal	_____
j. Cancellation notification	_____		
k. Self-insured on any portion of insurance	_____	9. *Other Considerations*	
Subtotal	_____	a.	_____
		b.	_____
7. *Operational Considerations*		c.	_____
		Subtotal	_____
a. 24-hour, 365-day operations department	_____	*Grand Total*	_____

Source: Adapted from "How to Select a Guard Company," *Security World* (November 1983), 39. Copyright 1983. A Cahners Publication.

haps the best fringe benefit for many contract guards is paid uniforms and equipment. While the cost of these perks is usually reflected in the cost to the buyer, it should not be taken out of the guard's already-meager wages.

The preceding discussion is just one way of viewing a guard service; other factors can also be considered. Howard M. Schwartz, former vice president of the Mid-Atlantic Division of Burns International Security Services, Inc., suggests evaluating:

1. The guard agency's understanding of the psychological factors that influence security's effect on business and industrial environments and the firm's ability to incorporate these tactical measures into its services
2. The agency's understanding of the essential difference between security and law enforcement
3. The agency's ability to apply creative solutions to security problems
4. The agency's ability to involve all of the client firm's employees in a positive effort supporting the overall security program
5. The agency's willingness and ability to be flexible and modify tactical approaches to meet changing needs.[20]

For one suggested format, consider the security firm evaluation analysis presented in Table 4.2.

Private Security and Public Law Enforcement

It should be noted that public and private police may, in certain circumstances, perform the same functions for the same individuals or organizations. A law-enforcement officer might in some circumstances be assigned to protect a threatened individual; a private bodyguard frequently is hired to perform the same protective function. Public police commonly perform patrol functions, which include checking the external premises of stores or manufacturing facilities. But patrol is also one of the major activities of private security. The activity itself then is not always differentiating. Private security functions are essentially client-oriented; public law enforcement functions are society- or community-oriented.

Another key distinction is the possession and exercise of police powers—that is, the power of arrest. The vast majority of private security personnel have no police powers; they act as private citizens. In some jurisdictions, "special officer" status is granted in most cases by statute or ordinance, which includes limited power of arrest in specified areas or premises. The limitations on the exercise of special police powers and the fact that their activities are client-oriented and client-controlled (as opposed to being directed primarily by public law enforcement agencies) make it reasonable to include such personnel as part of the private security industry. (This discussion omits the situation of the law enforcement officer who is moonlighting as a part-time private security guard since police powers in that situation derive from the public rather than the private role.)

For our purposes, then, private security can be defined as those individuals, organizations, and services paid through private funding sources to protect property through the prevention or investigation of crimes.

As early as 1975 the Task Force on Private Security stated that, "public law enforcement and private security agencies should work closely together, because their respective roles are complementary in the effort to control crime. Indeed, the magnitude of the nation's crime problem should preclude any form of competition between the two."[21] As noted in the previous section, however, even though the roles of the two groups are similar (in fact overlapping in many areas), they are not identical. The roles should be complementary, but in reality the two groups interrelate and interact. Most contact between public and private agencies is spontaneous and cooperative, but far too often the contact is negative, to the detriment of both groups.

According to experts in the field, the relationship between the two groups is strained (although personal contacts may be warm) because of several key issues.

1. Lack of mutual respect
2. Lack of communication
3. Lack of law enforcement knowledge of private security
4. Perceived competition
5. Lack of standards for private security personnel
6. Perceived corruption of police
7. Jurisdictional conflict especially when private problems (that is, corporate theft, arson) are involved
8. Confusion of identity and the issues flowing from it such as arming and training of private police
9. Mutual image and communications problems
10. Provision of services in borderline or overlapping areas of responsibility and interest (that is, provision of security during strikes, traffic control, shared use of municipal and private firefighting personnel)
11. Moonlighting policies for public police and issues stemming from these policies
12. Difference in legal powers, which can lead to concerns about abuse of power, and so on (that is, police officers working off duty may now be private citizens subject to rules of citizen's arrest)

13. False alarm rates (police resent responding to false alarms), which in some communities are over 90 percent.

Historically, public police have often accused the private sector of mishandling cases, breaking the law to make cases, being poorly trained, and generally being composed of those who could not meet the standards for police officers. The private security sector often views the public sector as being self-centered and arrogant. Moreover public law-enforcement officers often moonlight thereby taking work away from the private security sector. Even today the private sector is still considered by public police as only somewhat effective in reducing direct-dollar crime loss; and its contributions to reducing the volume of crime, apprehending criminal suspects, and maintaining order are judged ineffective. In fact, according to the results of *Hallcrest II*, public law enforcement gave private security low ratings in 10 areas, including quality of personnel, training, and knowledge of legal authority. The feelings about the lack of training may be justified; only 50 percent of the states presently have provisions for licensing and training security officers.

On the other hand, the employment of 150,000 police officers as private security personnel during their off-duty hours has also caused much criticism.[22] Some say that moonlighting police are only "hired guns," and that such police officers take jobs away from security firms. Other problems include the question of who is liable for the officer's actions. Is the employer of the off-duty officer liable, or does the liability stay with the police department who trained the officer?

Another source of conflict is the high rate of false alarms. When an alarm sounds, an alarm company employee may respond, or the police department may be called. In some jurisdictions, police report that up to 10–12 percent of all calls for police service are from false alarms. *Hallcrest II* indicates that 95 percent to 99 percent of all alarms are false.[23] Some police departments have reacted to this high rate by fining alarm companies or businesses.

Yet much of the conflict between private and public agencies is the result of misconception. There is a general misunderstanding of the roles played by the respective agencies. Perhaps this is understandable since even within their own areas police and private security officers often fail to understand the common goals of other agencies.

Complementary Roles

Despite the misconception that working together for a common goal is difficult to achieve, police departments and private security agencies are beginning to work together at times unknowingly. The idea that public property is protected only by the public police is another such misconception. The federal government has over 10,000 contract security guards patrolling federal offices and buildings. In many cities, police departments have turned to private agencies to protect courts, city buildings, airports, and museums. In other areas, it is generally accepted that the protection of private property is the responsibility of the owner. When a crime occurs, however, it is the local police who are usually called.

A third misconception is that the private security sector is primarily concerned with crime prevention and deterrence rather than with investigation and apprehension. In reality, store detectives in many major cities make more arrests each year than do local police officers. In addition, certain types of crime are no longer investigated by local police departments but have instead become the job of private security personnel; these include credit card fraud, single bogus checks, and some thefts.

Since some degree of complementary activity already exists, what can be done to improve the perceptions the two areas have of each other and to foster cooperative efforts? According to *Hallcrest II*, a variety of methods could improve cooperation between the two areas. The study notes the formation of joint private and public sector task forces to study major crime issues and recommend strategies to offset losses. Another recommendation is that data files from both sectors should be more freely exchanged. Private security personnel are often not allowed access to information on criminal cases even as a follow-up on data originally entered by them. Third, joint seminars on business crime have been developed to help the two areas better understand their respective roles. Operation Bootstrap is an excellent example of a cooperative venture in sharing information and experience and in understanding respective roles.[24]

As *Hallcrest II* reports, it appears that the private sector will become increasingly involved in the crime prevention area; public law enforcement will then be free to concentrate more heavily on violent crimes and crime response. *Hallcrest I* and *II* found that most security managers were willing to accept more responsibility for minor criminal acts within their jurisdictions. The new activities most likely include burglar alarm response, investigation of misdemeanors, and many preliminary investigations of other criminal offenses. The public sector is also willing to give up some areas of responsibility because it is "potentially more cost effectively performed by private security."[25] Some of these areas include building security, parking enforcement, and court security.

Yet other areas of conflict remain that may take some time to resolve. Often security managers do not report many criminal offenses. This is a source of concern for many police managers. Security managers may fail to report crimes for any of the following reasons: lax charging policies of prosecutors, administrative delays in prosecution, court proceedings that might reveal more about their organizations than management wants known, and a perception that courts are unsympathetic to business losses.

Just how effective private security can be depends to a large degree on whether public law-enforcement and private sector professionals are able to form a close partnership. *Hallcrest II* recommends:

1. Upgrading private security. Statewide regulatory statutes are needed for background checks, training, codes of ethics, and licensing.
2. Increasing police knowledge of private security.
3. Expanding interaction. Joint task forces are needed, and both groups should share investigative information and specialized equipment.
4. Experimenting with the transfer of police functions.[26]

Hallcrest II reported some progress in each of these areas and recommended continued work. As *Hallcrest II* concluded:

> In just the past few years, the forging of cooperative crime and fear reduction ventures between the public and private sectors has begun—albeit slowly. The number of partnerships and the diversity of programs undertaken is evidence of the desire and need for enhanced communication and cooperation between the law enforcement, private security and business communities.[27]

Review Questions

1. What does the term "private security" mean?
2. What are the differences between proprietary and contractual guard services?
3. What are the basic services typically performed by contractual security personnel?
4. What are the advantages and disadvantages of using contractual security services?
5. What are the advantages and disadvantages of using proprietary security services?
6. What factors should be considered when deciding on a guard firm?
7. Describe the relationship between public law enforcement and private security. What are the major problems?

References

1. James S. Kakalik and Sorrell Wildhorn, *The Rand Report* (Santa Monica, Calif.: The Rand Corporation, 1971), p. 3.
2. *Private Security: Report of the Task Force on Private Security* (Washing-

ton, D.C.: National Advisory Committee on Criminal Justice Standards and Goals, 1976), p. 4.

3. William C. Cunningham, John J. Strauchs, Clifford W. VanMeter, *The Hallcrest Report II: Private Security Trends 1970–2000* (Boston: Butterworth-Heinemann, 1990), p. 276.

4. Martin Tolchin, "Private Guards Get New Role in Public Law Enforcement," *The New York Times*, 29 November 1985, p. 1.

5. Cunningham, et al., pp. 17, 181.

6. Wayne Siatt and Sally Matteson, "Special Report: Trends in Security," *Security World* (January 1982): 25.

7. Bill Zalud, "What's Happening To Security," *Security* (September 1990): 42.

8. Cunningham, et al., p. 139.

9. Kakalik and Wildhorn, *The Rand Report*, p. 67.

10. William Cunningham and Todd H. Taylor, *Private Security and Police in America: The Hallcrest Report* (Portland, Ore.: Chancellor Press, 1985), p. 89.

11. Cunningham, et al., p. 136.

12. *Private Security*, pp. 32–33.

13. Zalud, p. 44.

14. Cunningham, et al., p. 156.

15. Ibid., p. 181.

16. Thomas J. Serb, "How to Select a Guard Company," *Security World* (November 1983): p. 33.

17. Ibid.

18. Cunningham, et al., p. 156.

19. Serb, p. 33.

20. Ibid., p. 38.

21. *Private Security*, p. 19.

22. Cunningham, et al., p. 290.

23. Ibid., p. 282.

24. Ibid., pp. 243–266.

25. Ibid.

26. Cunningham and Taylor, p. 275.

27. Ibid., p. 266.

5

□ □ □
□ □ □
□ □ □

The Proprietary
Security Organization

Security problems become apparent in virtually every area of a given company's activities. The need to deal forcefully and systematically with these problems has become increasingly evident to the industrial and commercial community, and steps have been taken by greater and greater numbers of these organizations to create a security effort as an organic element of the corporate structure rather than turning to outside (contract) security services or to minimal efforts at physical security. The trend as predicted by *Hallcrest II* is toward security operations that are controlled by an in-house staff with specific services provided by technology and contract guard operations.

Where and how the in-house or proprietary security department operates within the organizational framework and how this relates to the total security system of individual concerns depends on the needs of that organization. General principles will apply throughout much of the business community, but specific applications must be tailored to the problems faced by each enterprise. Our concern here then is with those considerations that have broad application in the organization of the security function.

Determining the Need

In evaluating the need to install or expand the company security function, the immediate urgency for increased security must be considered along with the status, growth, and prior performance of the current security effort if any. The peculiarities of the company in the context of intracompany relationships, whether by design or natural evolution, must be a factor. The potential for growth of the company and the attendant growth of staff activities should also be considered.

Ultimately management will have to determine the costs and the projected effectiveness of the security function. The growing trend is for management to make this determination with the assistance and guidance of a professional consultant. This trend has caused a growth in the number of security consultants, particularly independent consultants who do not have a vested interest in the outcome of their recommendations. Determining costs and effectiveness is only the first step. Having done this, management will then have to face the important question of whether security can be truly and totally integrated into the organization. If on analysis it is found that the existing structure would in some way suffer from the addition of new organizational functions, alternatives to the integrated proprietary security department must be sought.

These alternatives usually consist only of the application and supervision of physical security measures. This inevitably results in the fragmentation of protective systems in the areas requiring security. These alternatives are sometimes effective, however, especially in those firms whose overall risk and vulnerability are low. But as crime against business continues to climb and as criminal methods of attack and the underground network of distribution continue to become more sophisticated, anything less than total integration will become increasingly inadequate.

Once management has recognized that existing problems—real or potential—make the introduction or enlargement of security a necessity for continued effective operation, it will be obliged to exert every effort to create an atmosphere in which security can exert its full efforts to accomplish stated company objectives. Any equivocation by management at this point can only serve to weaken or to ultimately undermine the security effectiveness that might be obtained by a clearer statement of total support and directives resulting in intracompany cooperation with security efforts.

Security's Place in the Organization

The degree and nature of the authority vested in the security manager become matters of the greatest importance when such a function is fully integrated into the organization. Any evaluation of the scope of authority required by security to perform effectively must consider a variety of factors—both formal and informal—that exist in the structure. Figures 5.1 and 5.2 are organization charts showing security's position in two hypothetical corporations.

Since the economic slowdown of the early 1990s and the tightening of company budgets, there seems to be a trend toward downsizing security departments and consolidating a number of related responsibilities under one broader department. Figure 5.3 suggests growing linkages among security, risk management, facilities management, safety, operations administration, human resources, and internal audit.[1] One way of consolidating various re-

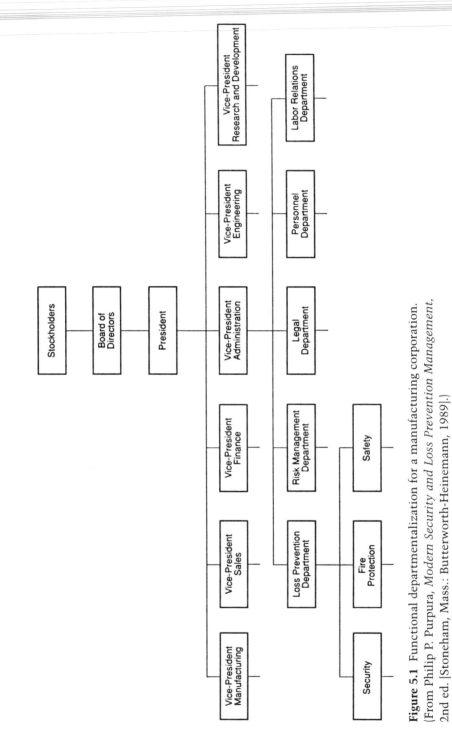

Figure 5.1 Functional departmentalization for a manufacturing corporation. (From Philip P. Purpura, *Modern Security and Loss Prevention Management,* 2nd ed. [Stoneham, Mass.: Butterworth-Heinemann, 1989].)

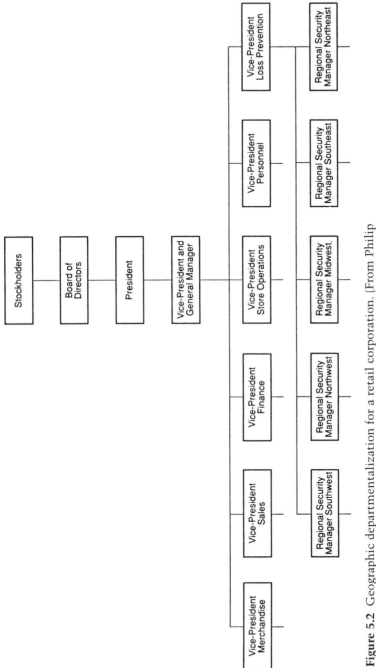

Figure 5.2 Geographic departmentalization for a retail corporation. (From Philip P. Purpura, *Modern Security and Loss Prevention Management*, 2nd ed. [Stoneham, Mass.: Butterworth-Heinemann, 1989].)

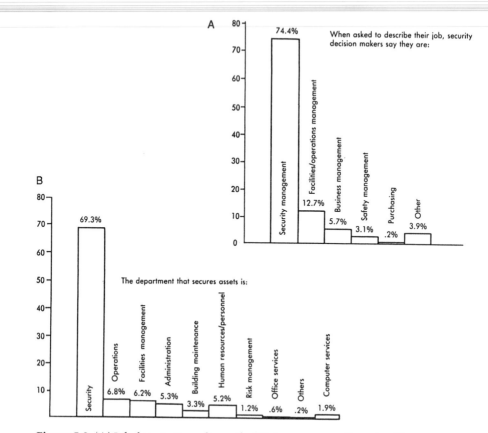

Figure 5.3 (A) Job descriptions diversify, (B) departments diversity (From *Security 1990 Profile Study* published by Cahners Publishing Company, a division of Reed Publishing USA.)

lated security functions is to create an assets protection department that can include the functions of security, information management, internal audit, and risk management (see Figure 5.4).

However the security/assets protection department is constructed, there are certain distinguishing features that should characterize it. It should:

- Champion asset protection
- Solve more complex issues with less staff
- Identify risk for the company
- Develop programs to manage risk
- Quantify results to the bottom line
- Develop pilot asset protection programs
- Provide business solutions to security problems
- Reduce insurance premiums

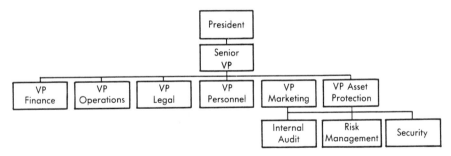

Figure 5.4 Possible security organization due to downsizing. (From *Security* magazine, May 1991, p. 25. Published by Cahners Publishing Company, a division of Reed Publishing USA.)

- Use shared resources to manage costs
- Establish common objectives with risk management, internal audit, and information management[2]

Definition of Authority

It is management's responsibility to establish the level of authority at which security may operate in order to accomplish its mission. It must have authority to deal with the establishment of security systems, be able to conduct inspections of performance in many areas of the company, and be in a position to evaluate performance and risk throughout the company.

All such authority relationships, of course, should be clearly established in order to facilitate the transmission of directives and the necessary responses to them. It should be noted, however, that these relationships take many forms in any company, not infrequently including the assumption of a role by a member of the organization who becomes accepted as a designated executive simply by past compliance and by custom. In such cases, where management does not move to curtail or redefine this authority, the executive continues in such a posture indefinitely regardless of formal status. It is management's responsibility to reassess the chains of authority continually in the interest of efficient operation.

Organizational structure generally distinguishes between line and staff relationships. Line executives are those who are delegated authority in the direct chain of command to accomplish specific organizational objectives. Staff personnel generally provide an advisory or service function to a line executive.

In general, the security managers can be considered to serve a staff function. Traditionally this means that, as heads of specialized operations, they are responsible to a senior executive or (in the fully integrated organization) to the president of the company. Their role is that of advisor. Theoretically it is the president who implements the activities suggested by advisors.

This is not always the practice. By the very nature of their expertise, security managers have authority delegated by the senior executive to whom they report. In effect, they are granted a part of the authority of their line superior. This is known as functional authority.

Such authority appears on a table of organization, but it is often delegated and can be modified or withdrawn by a superior. In the case of security, this functional authority may consist of advising operating personnel on security matters, or it may (and should) develop into more complete functional responsibility to formulate policies and issue directives prescribing procedures to be followed in any area affecting the security of the company.

Most department managers cooperate with security directives readily since they lack the specialized knowledge required of upper-echelon security personnel and are generally unfamiliar with the requirements of effective supervision of security systems and procedures. It is nonetheless important that the security manager operate with the utmost tact and diplomacy in matters that may have an effect, however small, on the conduct of personnel or procedures in other departments. Every effort should be made to consult with the executive in charge of any such affected department before issuing instructions that implement security procedures.

Levels of Authority

Obviously there are many mixtures of levels of authority at which security managers operate.

Their functional authority may encompass a relatively limited area, prescribed by broad outlines of basic company policy.

In matters of investigation, they may be limited to staff functions in which they may advise and recommend or even assist in conducting the investigation, but they might not have direct control or command over the routines of employees.

It is customary for security managers to exercise line authority over preventive activities of the company. In this situation, they command the guards who in turn command the employees in all matters over which security managers have jurisdiction.

Security managers will, of course, have full line authority over the conduct of their own departments within which they will have staff personnel as well as those to whom they have delegated functional authority.

Reduced Losses and Net Profit

Although security is a staff function, it could be viewed as a line operation—and one day may be. By reducing losses, an effective security program, intelligently managed, can maximize profits as surely as can a merchandising or a production function.

With soaring crime rates that currently cost business approximately $114 billion annually, every business is targeted for losses. And all of these losses come off the net profit.

Many managers, particularly those in retail establishments, push as hard as possible for new records in gross sales. They frequently brush aside words of caution about inventory loss from internal and external theft. Unfortunately there are companies that generate millions of dollars in gross sales that have filed for bankruptcy.

It is the net profit that keeps business and industry alive. The gross income may be a splashy figure, and it may provide some excitement for the proud manager. But the net profit is the bottom line: Anything that eats away at that lifeline seriously endangers the organization.

An effective security operation could cut losses by as much as 75 percent. The savings between the investment in security and the additional earnings realized from reduced losses are net profit. In this light, security can be seen as a vital contributor to the profit of any company. Any security operation that can minimize losses and maximize net profits should clearly take its place as an independent organizational function, reporting to the highest level of executive authority.

Nonintegrated Structures

In spite of the obvious advantages of integrating security into the organization as an organic function (an independent, basic unit of the firm like accounting or engineering), many firms continue to relegate this operation to a reporting activity of some totally unrelated department (for example, engineering). Since in many cases the operation grew out of a security need that arose in a particular area, that area tends to assume administrative control over security and to maintain that control long after security has begun to extend its operational activities beyond departmental lines into other spheres of the company.

In this way, security was traditionally attached to the financial function of the organization since financial control was usually the most urgent need in a company otherwise unprepared to provide internal security. The disadvantages of such an arrangement are severe enough to endanger the effectiveness of security's efforts.

Functional authority cannot be delegated beyond the authority of the delegant. What this means is that, when the security manager gets authority from the comptroller, it cannot extend past the comptroller's area of responsibility. If the comptroller can extend the role of security by dispensation of the chief executive, the line of authority becomes clouded and cumbersome.

Most business experts agree that functional authority should not be used to direct the activities of anyone more than one level down from the delegate in order to preserve the integrity of line functions. Clearly the assignment of security under the financial officer is a clumsy arrangement representing bad management practices.

Relation to Other Departments

Every effort should be made to incorporate security into the organizational functions. It must be recognized, however, that by so doing management creates a new function that, like personnel and finance among others, cuts across departmental lines and enters into every activity of the company.

Security considerations should ideally be as much a presence in every decision at every level as are cost decisions. This will not mean that security factors will always take precedence over matters of production or merchandising, for example, any more than that specific price factors will always take precedence over other decisions in these same areas. But security should always be considered. If its recommendations are overridden from time to time—sometimes a wise decision where the cost of disruption involved in overcoming certain risks is greater than is the risk itself—this will be done with full knowledge of the risks involved.

Obviously the management of the security function and its goals must be compatible with the aims of the organization, This means that security must provide for continued protection of the organization without significant interference with its essential activities. Security must preserve the atmosphere in which the company's activities are carried on by developing systems that will protect those activities in much their existing condition rather than attempting to alter them to conform to certain abstract standards of security. When the overall objectives of any organization are bent and shaped to accommodate the efforts of any of the particular functions designed to help achieve those aims, the total corporate effort inevitably becomes distorted and suffers accordingly.

Organizationally, the relationship between security and other departments should present no difficulty. The interface serves to solve potentially disruptive or damaging problems shared by both functions. The company's goals are achieved by the elimination of all such problems. In practice, however, this harmony is not always found. Resentment and a sense of loss of authority can interfere with the cooperative intradepartmental relationships that are so vital to a company's progress. Such conflicts will be minimized where security's authority is clearly defined and understood.

The Security Manager's Role

Directing our attention to the generalization of the security operation and the manager's role in it, we can find many common elements that are significant. In its organizational functions, security encompasses four basic activities with varying degrees of emphasis:

1. Managerial, which includes those classic management functions common to managers of all departments within any organization. Among these are planning, organizing, employing, leading, supervising, and innovating
2. Administrative, which involves budget and fiscal supervision, office administration, establishment of policies governing security matters and development of systems and procedures, development of training programs for security personnel and security education of all other employees, and provision of communication and liaison between departments in security related matters
3. Preventive, which includes supervision of guards; patrols; fire and safety personnel; inspection of restricted areas; regular audits of performance, appearance, understanding, and competence of security personnel; control of traffic; and condition of all security equipment such as alarms, lights, fences, doors, windows, locks, barriers, safes, and communication equipment
4. Investigative, which involves security clearances, investigation of all losses or violations of company regulations, inspections, audits, liaison with public police and fire agencies, and classified documents

It is important to remember that the last three functions must be carried out to further the organizational needs of security. It follows that in order to perform effectively the security manager must be thoroughly conversant with all of the techniques and technologies inherent in such functions. But in order to achieve the stated goals or the projected ends of the organization the security manager must be sufficiently skilled in managerial duties to effectively plan, guide, and control the performance of the department.

The security manager cannot remain, as has been true so often in the past, merely a "security expert," a technician with a high enough degree of empirical or pragmatic information to qualify for certain basic preventive or investigative tasks. The more this manager is personally involved in such jobs, the more he will neglect the managerial functions. Security's role in the operation will suffer accordingly.

The company that recognizes the need for, and the efficiency of, incorporating security as an organic part of its enterprise has begun creating a new organizational function. Along with such traditional functions as marketing, production, finance, and personnel, security will play a significant role in the daily as well as the projected destiny of the company.

In this light, it is clear that the security manager is an indispensable member of the staff with a role that extends far beyond the limited, time-honored position of principal in charge of burglar alarms and package inspections. This is not to suggest that there is any trend toward establishing a power base for security management, but rather that many enlightened, modern company managers have assigned a higher priority to integrated security systems in an effort to encourage the growth of this essential element of the firm's survival.

Ron D. Davis, Director of Security, General Dynamics Space Systems Division, says:

> A successful manager will need to develop certain skills. Among these are planning, motivation techniques, public speaking, personnel management, and budgeting. These areas will not only help in preparing the manager for the future but make them more effective in their current employment.[3]

Organizing the Security Function

Although the organization and administration of the security department is a subject in itself beyond the scope of this general introduction to security, it is nevertheless important to get an overview of the security organization by looking briefly at both its function and at the staff required to implement it. From a management point of view, organizing the security effort involves:

1. Planning
2. Establishing controls
3. Organizing the security department
4. Hiring personnel
5. Training
6. Supervising
7. Implementing security

8. Departmental reviewing and evaluating
9. Acting as security/loss prevention advisor to top management

Planning

An extraordinarily common mistake in security planning is to put the cart before the horse—that is, to create a department, hire personnel, and then look for something for the department to do on the premise that crime is rising, losses almost certainly exist, and therefore something must be done.

In reality, need comes first. A hazard must exist before it becomes practical to establish an organized effort to prevent or minimize it. The first step in security planning is a detailed analysis of potential areas of loss, their probability, and their gravity in terms of corporate goals. Only then can the specific objectives of the security function be defined.

This relationship of corporate goals to security planning is suggested in Figure 5.5. To express this relationship in a simplified way: If a company's goal is higher profits and if the widespread prevalence of employee theft is eating away those profits, a primary objective of the security function should be to reduce employee theft and thus to contribute to the corporate goal of increased profits.

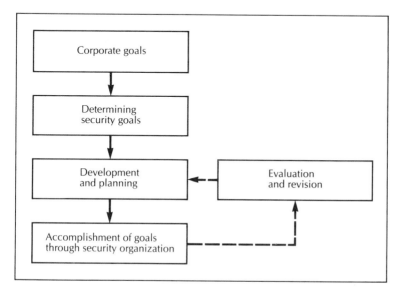

Figure 5.5 Establishing objectives in security planning.

Analyzing risk is discussed in detail in Chapter 7. In addition to threat assessment, planning involves establishing objectives, allocating resources within prescribed or authorized budgetary limitations, and determining what should be done, how it should be done, and how soon it should be set into operation.

Establishing Controls

Security planning, including threat assessment, will result in determining the degree of security required in all areas of a company. Decisions must also be made as to the means by which such security can be most efficiently, effectively, and economically achieved. New policies and procedures may be formulated, physical aids to security ordered, and the size and deployment of security personnel determined. All of these factors must be balanced when one is considering the protection of the facility in order to arrive at a formula that provides the most protection at the least expense.

Controls must be established over procedures such as shipping, receiving, warehousing, inventory, cash handling, auditing, and accounting. The most effective and efficient method of implementing such controls is to present a control or accountability system to the relevant department managers and to allow them to express their views and make counter suggestions. In this way, a totally satisfactory control procedure can be mutually agreed on. With the current use of computers for many of these operations, the ability to audit is enhanced. Along with benefits, however, the computer offers additional security challenges. Only when established controls break down or prove to be inadequate should the security manager or the deputy step in to handle the matter directly.

As will be discussed in later chapters, loss-prevention controls also cover all physical protection devices, including interior and exterior barriers, alarm and surveillance systems, and communication systems. Loss prevention also incorporates the principles of risk management that will be discussed in Chapter 7. Identification and traffic flow patterns are other necessary controls. Identification implies the recognition of authorized versus unauthorized personnel, visitors, vehicles, goods, and materials.

Organizing the Security Department

An organization, as such, is people, so in considering the organizational structure of a security department, we are referring to the assignment of duties and responsibilities to people in a command relationship in order to achieve defined goals.

It is necessary first to identify tasks and then to develop the organization required to discharge them. To put this another way, the goals or objectives of the department are divided into practical work units, and within those units, specific jobs are defined.

A simplified table of organization for a small industrial security department of 20 persons might take the form charted in Figure 5.6. Even such a small organization requires a careful description of specific duties and responsibilities from the manager down to the guard on patrol with clearly defined report command. In this example, the security manager would have more extensive line duties than would be the case in a larger department. He would be more directly involved in day-to-day operations (such as investigations), whereas in a larger department he might be occupied entirely with planning, advising, communications, public relations, and other administrative duties, leaving operations to subordinates.

The security organization, like any other organizational structure, must be designed to meet particular needs. For this reason, it is impossible to suggest a model organization for an individual security department even within the same type of enterprise (such as manufacturing or retail). The specific risks, the size of the company, the physical environment, and the budget all affect and to a great extent dictate the nature of the security response and thus of the organization needed to carry it out. One company's ideal organizational structure will not fit another's except by chance.

This does not mean that the individual manager cannot benefit from the practices of others; he should not try to adopt any other security package,

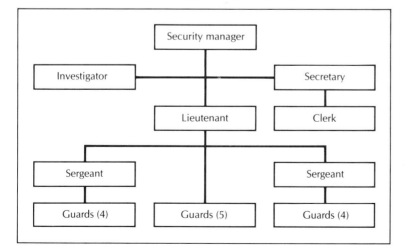

Figure 5.6 The organization of a small industrial security department.

however. Instead he must adapt standard practices to suit the particular situation.

Some common matters of concern in any organizational structure are delegation of authority, span of control, and the question of how many personnel are required.

Delegation of authority is necessary in any organization containing more than a handful of people. Delegation separates the ultimate and the operating responsibility. In Figure 5.6, the security manager delegates responsibility for supervising guard-force operations to the lieutenant who in turn delegates the operating responsibility to the sergeants on the first and third shifts since the lieutenant obviously cannot work three full shifts.

For delegation of authority to work, the responsibility must be truly delegated: It cannot be given and then routinely overridden. Once the manager has determined that the lieutenant is capable of supervising the guard function in the example, he should allow the lieutenant to exercise that responsibility. And at each stage of the organizational ladder, the subordinate to whom authority is delegated must accept that responsibility; otherwise the entire command structure breaks down.

The degree to which a manager or supervisor is able to delegate responsibility rather than trying to do everything personally is a good measure of managerial ability. Conversely it has been said that the single most common management failing—in all organizations, not just security—is the inability or unwillingness to delegate responsibility and the authority necessary to carry necessary tasks out. The result is inevitably a bottleneck at the managerial level where one person must do or approve everything. The corollary result is a weakening of the entire chain of command below the managerial level.

Span of control refers to the number of personnel over which any individual can exercise direct supervision effectively. In the small security department illustrated in Figure 5.6, there is a sergeant over 4 guards on both the first and third shifts. The lieutenant supervises the 5 guards on the second shift. Many would regard this as a relatively ideal situation. Giving a supervisor too little to do, however, can sometimes be as damaging as giving him too much. The effective span of control for a given situation will depend on the complexity of duties, the number of problems, the geographical area, and many other factors. In some situations, especially where duties are routine and of a similar nature, it would be satisfactory to have one supervisor over 10 or 12 guards. Beyond that number, however, the span of control becomes so wide as to be seriously questioned. Figure 5.7 shows a narrow span of control versus a wide span of control situation.

How many security personnel are required is generally proportional to the size of the facility expressed both in terms of square footage or acreage and the number of employees involved. Small businesses of 20 or 30 employ-

Narrow Span of Management   Wide Span of Management

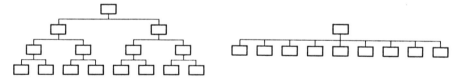

Figure 5.7 Span of control. (From Philip P. Purpura, *Modern Security and Loss Prevention Management,* 2nd ed. [Stoneham, Mass.: Butterworth-Heinemann, 1989].)

ees rarely require and even more rarely can afford the luxury of a security service of any size. At some point, however, as we consider larger and larger facilities, there is a need for such personnel. This can only be determined by the individual needs of a particular firm as demonstrated by a survey and as permitted by the funds available.

Where the security needs of a firm indicate the use of security personnel, they can be the single most important element in the security program. Since they are also the largest single item of expense, they must be used with the greatest efficiency possible. Only careful individual analysis of the needs of each facility will determine the optimum number and use of security personnel. For example, premises with inadequate perimeter barriers would need a larger security force than would those with effective barriers. In determining security needs, therefore, it is important that all protective elements be considered as a supportive whole.

One rule of thumb that deserves mention concerns the number of personnel required to cover a single post around the clock, providing coverage for three eight-hour shifts. The number is not three but rather four and a half or five persons to allow for vacation time, sick leave, termination, and/or training. In the larger organization, there is greater flexibility in the deployment of manpower, and four and a half persons might provide sufficient coverage. In the small organization, five guards would be needed as a minimum to cover that single post 24 hours a day on an ongoing basis.

Hiring Security Personnel

The selection of security personnel must be preceded by a careful analysis of personnel needs to implement plans previously drawn. Job descriptions must be developed, and labor markets must be explored.

Whatever specifications are arrived at, it is important that security personnel be emotionally mature and stable people who can, in addition to their other skills and training, relate to people under many conditions, including those of stress. It is also important to look for those persons whose potential is such that they may be expected to advance into the managerial ranks.

In considering the selection of personnel, it is useful to examine briefly the kinds of responsibilities they may be expected to assume.

Duties of Security Personnel

The duties of security officers are many and varied, but among them are common elements that can serve as a guide to every security manager.

1. They protect the buildings and grounds to which they are assigned, including the contents, occupants, and visitors.
2. They enforce rules and regulations governing the facility.
3. They direct traffic—both foot and vehicular.
4. They maintain order on their posts and help people who require assistance or information.
5. They familiarize themselves with all special and general orders and carry them out to the letter.
6. They supervise and enforce applicable systems of identifying personnel and vehicles, conduct package and vehicle inspection, and apprehend people entering or leaving the facility without the required authorization.
7. They conduct periodic prescribed inspections of all areas at designated times to ascertain their security and safety.
8. They act for management in maintaining order and report any incidents that disrupt such order.
9. They report incidents of employees engaged in horseplay, loitering, or violation of clearly stated policies. They report all sickness or accidents involving employees.
10. They instantly sound the alarm and respond to fires.
11. They log and turn in lost or unclaimed property. In the event that any property is reported stolen, they check the recovered property log before proceeding in the matter.
12. They make full reports to supervisors on all unusual circumstances.
13. They may be responsible for emergency planning and medical emergencies.

Because of the growing number of lawsuits filed against firms for negligent security the selection and training of security personnel has become a critical issue for security managers. Issues surrounding training are discussed in detail in Chapter 3, and liability issues are presented in Chapter 6.

Posts and Patrols

Security personnel may be assigned to a variety of posts, but these fall into just a few categories. Personnel may be assigned to a fixed post, to a patrol detail, or to reserve.

Fixed posts may be gate houses, building lobbies, or any particularly sensitive or dangerous location. Patrol duty involves walking or riding a given route to observe the condition of the facility. The perimeter is an important patrol as are warehouse areas and open yard storage areas. Reserves are people standing by in the event that assistance is needed by security personnel on fixed posts or patrol duty. The scope of their special orders varies from company to company, but a list of the things that might be required will give the flavor of the tour of duty in an industrial facility.

Security personnel on patrol will make their tours on routes or in areas assigned by the supervisor in charge. They must be fully aware of all policies and procedures governing their tour as well as those that govern the area patrolled.

1. Make sure that the area is secure from intrusion and that all gates and other entrances are closed and locked as prescribed. In interior spaces, check to see that all doors, windows, skylights, and vents are locked and secure against intrusion as well as possible damage from the weather as prescribed.
2. Turn off lights, fans, heaters, and other electrical equipment when their operation is not indicated.
3. Check for unusual conditions, including accumulation of trash or refuse, blocking of fire exits, lack of access to firefighting equipment. Any such conditions, if not immediately correctable, must be reported immediately.
4. Check for unusual sounds, and investigate their source. Such sounds might indicate an attempted entry, the movement of unauthorized personnel, the malfunctioning of machinery, or any other potentially disruptive problem.
5. Check any unusual odors and report them immediately if the source is not readily discovered. Such odors frequently indicate leakage or fire.
6. Check for damage to doors, tracks, or weight guards. In cases where doors have been held open by wedges, tiebacks, or other devices, these should be removed and their presence reported at the end of the tour of duty.
7. Check for running water in all areas, including wash rooms.
8. Check that all firefighting equipment is in its proper place and that access to it is in no way obstructed.

9. Check whether all processes in the area of the patrol are operating as prescribed.
10. Check the storage of all highly flammable substances such as gasoline, kerosene, and volatile cleaning fluids to assure that they are properly covered and secured against ignition.
11. Check for cigar or cigarette butts. Report the presence of such butts in no smoking areas.
12. Report the discovery of damage or any hazardous conditions no matter whether they can be corrected.
13. Exercise responsible control over watchman and fire-alarm keys and keys to those spaces as may be issued.
14. Report all conditions that are the result of violations of security or safety policy. Repeated violations of such policies will require investigation and correction.

To carry out such assignments, it is essential that security personnel meet high standards of character and loyalty. They must be in good enough physical condition to undergo arduous exertion in the performance of their duties. They must have adequate eyesight and hearing and have full and effective use of their limbs. In some circumstances exceptions may be made, but these would be for assignments to posts requiring little or no physical exertion or dexterity. They must be of stable character and should be capable of good judgment and resourcefulness.

All applicants for such positions must be carefully investigated. Since they will frequently handle confidential material as well as items of value and since they will in general occupy positions of great trust, they must be of the highest character. Each applicant should be fingerprinted and checked through local and federal agencies where it is legally permissible. Background investigations of the applicants' habits and associates should also be conducted. Signs of instability or patterns of irresponsibility should disqualify them.

All of these recommendations set high standards for the security officer, but nothing less will satisfy the emerging professionalism of the security function.

Supervision

In addition to planning, establishing controls, organizing a department, hiring personnel, and training, the security manager's responsibilities include supervision of security. And it is in the handling of this function that the entire security program will prove either effective or inadequate.

Security managers must maintain close supervision over communications within their own departmental structures. It is essential that they communicate downward in expressing departmental directives and policies. It is equally important that they receive regular communication up the organizational ladder from their subordinates. They must regularly study and analyze the channels of communication to be certain that the input they receive is accurate, relevant, timely, concise, and informative.

In addition, security managers must set up a system of supervision of all departmental personnel to establish means for reviewing performance and instituting corrective action when it is necessary.

They must above all lead. Their qualities of leadership will in and of themselves prove ultimately to be the most effective supervisory approach.

Security personnel are in many respects the most effective security devices available. They rarely turn in false alarms. They can react to irregular occurrences. They can follow and arrest a thief. They can detect and respond. They can prevent accidents and put out fires. In short, they are human and can perform as no machine can. But, as humans, they are subject to human failure. Security personnel must be adequately supervised in the performance of their duties. It is important to be sure that policy is followed, that each member of the security force is thoroughly familiar with policy, and that the training and indoctrination program is adequate to communicate all the necessary information to each member of the security staff. Guards must be disciplined for violations of policy, and at the same time, management must see to it that they now know the policy that was violated.

All of these elements must be regularly reviewed. It must be remembered that well-trained, well-supervised security personnel may be the best possible protection available, but badly selected, badly supervised guards are not an asset at all and, worse, could themselves be a danger to security. They can, after all, succumb to temptation like any other individuals. Their opportunities for theft are far greater than those of the average employee.

Issuance and use of keys to stockrooms, security storage, and other repositories of valuable merchandise or materials must be limited and their use strictly accounted for. Fire protection not otherwise covered by sensors or sprinkler systems is not often a major problem in such spaces, and in the event a fire were to threaten, the door could be broken or a guardhouse key could be used to enter the endangered area.

Although all security personnel have been subjected to thorough background investigation before assignment and have been closely observed during the early period of employment, they may still yield to the heavy pressure of temptation and opportunity presented when they have free and unlimited access to all of the firm's goods. Although it is not sound personnel practice to show distrust or lack of faith in the sincerity of security personnel, it is risky to fail to adequately supervise these personnel. After all, we are all human! We are all subject to temptation and may succumb to anger. Such problems can only be dealt with through enlightened leadership and supervision.

Leadership

A security manager is expected to be a leader and expert on security issues within the organization. Leadership is difficult for even the experts to define, and in this limited space, little can be said about this vital trait. Leadership, however, is more easily understood in comparison to "followership." The person who has the most influence in a group and carries out most of the leadership functions is designated a leader. While leadership is difficult to define, it is easier to identify skills necessary to be a successful leader. The most widely accepted classification of skills was proposed by Katz[4] and later by Mann.[5] The skills are depicted in Figure 5.8. Just as skills for leaders have been identified in broad categories, so have roles. Mintzberg[6] identified ten.

1. Figurehead
2. Leader
3. Liaison
4. Monitor
5. Disseminator
6. Spokesperson
7. Entrepreneur
8. Disturbance handler
9. Resource allocator
10. Negotiator

Implementation of Security

The next element with which the security manager must deal is the image or representation of the security function. In order for security to be effective in any organization, it must have the implied approval and confidence of that organization. Every time a guard is overbearing or a system cumbersome and inefficient is installed, the image of security suffers.

It is the task of the security manager to undertake a regular program of indoctrination to define the role of security and of security personnel clearly within the organization. Since employee participation and cooperation are essential to the success of any security effort, it is extremely important that a thorough indoctrination program eliminate any tendency to alienate these important allies by overbearing or bullying attitudes on the part of security personnel. Such a program must also impress on all security people the im-

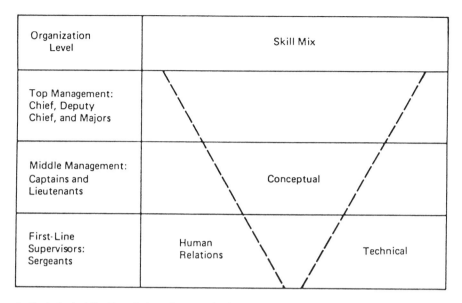

Organization Level	Skill Mix		
Top Management: Chief, Deputy Chief, and Majors			
Middle Management: Captains and Lieutenants		Conceptual	
First-Line Supervisors: Sergeants	Human Relations		Technical

1. Technical skills: Knowledge about methods, processes, procedures, and techniques for conducting a specialized activity, and the ability to use tools and operate equipment related to that activity.

2. Human relations skills: Knowledge about human behavior and interpersonal processes, ability to understand the feelings, attitudes, and motives of others from what they say and do (empathy, social sensitivity), ability to communicate clearly and effectively (speech fluency, persuasiveness), and ability to establish effective and cooperative relationships (tact, diplomacy, knowledge about acceptable social behavior).

3. Conceptual skills: General analytical ability, logical thinking, proficiency in concept formation and conceptualization of complex and ambiguous relationships, creativity in idea generation and problem solving, ability to analyze events and perceive trends, anticipate changes, and recognize opportunities and potential problems.

Figure 5.8 Skill mix: conceptual, human relations, and technical. (From Gary A. Yukl, *Leadership in Organizations* [Englewood Cliffs, N.J.: Prentice-Hall, 1981], pp. 85–86.)

portance of their roles in public relations, both as employees of the company and as members of the security department.

No matter how well the department is organized, it cannot be effective without the full support of the people in the organization it serves. To achieve this support, the department must be educated in attitudes, duties, and demeanor and proper supervision must ensure that these attitudes are maintained. The very fact that security personnel are controlling the movement and conduct of other members of their community suggests that they must themselves be carefully controlled to avoid giving rise to feelings of resentment and hostility. The entire organization can suffer great harm as a result of general animosity directed at only one member of the security department who has acted improperly or unwisely.

Departmental Evaluation

Regular departmental evaluations should try to determine whether security policies and procedures are being properly followed and whether such existing policies and procedures are still desirable in their present form or should be modified to better achieve predetermined goals. These evaluations should also review all manpower and equipment needs and the efficiency of their current use in the conduct of the security program.

Since security concerns itself with prevention of damage, disruption, or loss, its effectiveness is never easy to evaluate. The absence of events is not in itself revealing unless there are accurate accounts of actual crimes against the organization during some prior, analogous period to provide a standard of measurement.

Even such a comparison is of dubious value as the basis for a thorough, ongoing, objective analysis of security effectiveness. Circumstances change; personnel terminate; motivating elements alter or disappear. And there is always the haunting uneasiness created by the possibility that security procedures might be so ineffective that crimes against the company have gone virtually undetected in which case the reduction or absence of detected crime presents a totally misleading picture of the company's position.

Personnel Review

In reviewing departmental performance, all records of individual personnel performance should be examined. The degree of familiarity of employees with their duties, the extent of their authority, and their departmental and organizational goals should be examined. Corrective indoctrination should be required as indicated. The health, appearance, and general morale of each staff member should be noted.

Equipment Review

The state of all security equipment should be reviewed regularly with an eye to its current condition and the possible need for replacement, repair or substitution. This review should cover all space assigned for use by security personnel on or off duty, uniforms, arms (if any), communication and surveillance equipment (vehicles, keys, and report forms). Carelessness or inadequate maintenance of such gear should be corrected immediately.

Procedures Review

A review of security department procedures is essential to the continued efficacy of the department. All personnel should be examined periodically for their compliance with directives governing their area of responsibility. Familiarity with department policies should be evaluated and corrective action taken where it proves necessary. At the same time, the very usefulness of prescribed procedures should be reviewed, and changes should be initiated where they are deemed advisable.

Review Questions

1. Discuss the statement: In general, the security manager can be considered to be serving a staff function.
2. Why is functional authority important to the security manager?
3. What categories of concern should be reviewed during a security department evaluation?
4. What are the key tasks involved in organizing the security function? Explain the importance of each.
5. Describe the duties of the security officer on patrol.

References

1. Bill Zalud, "Vanishing Jobs Mark Security Mid-Life Crisis," *The Zalud Report* (November 1990): 3.
2. Edward J. Flynn, "Revolutionary Call For Asset Protection Management," *Security* (May 1991): 25.
3. Ronald Davis, "The Importance of Management Skills in the Security Profession," in *Suggested Preparation for Careers in Security/Loss Prevention*, John Chuvala, III and Robert Fischer, eds. (Dubuque, Ia.: Kendall Hunt, 1991), p. 51.
4. R. L. Katz, "Skills of an Effective Administrator," *Harvard Business Review* (January/February 1955): 33–42.
5. F. C. Mann, "Toward an Understanding of the Leadership Role in Foreman Organization," in *Leadership and Productivity*, R. Dubin, G. C. Homans, F. C. Mann, and D. C. Miller, eds. (San Francisco: Chandler, 1965).
6. H. Mintzberg, *The Nature of Managerial Work* (New York: Harper & Row, 1973).

6

□ □ □
□ □ □
□ □ □

Security and the Law

Whereas public police and protection services derive their authority to act from a variety of statutes, ordinances, and orders enacted at various levels of government, private police function essentially as private citizens. Their authority to so function is no more than the exercise of the right of all citizens to protect their own property. Every citizen has common law and statutory powers that include arrest, search, and seizure. The security officer has these same rights, both as a citizen and as an extension of an employee's right to protect her employer's property. Similarly, this common law recognition of the right of defense of self and property is the legal underpinning for the right of every citizen to employ the services of others to protect property against any kind of incursion by others.

The broad statement of such rights, however, in no way suggests the full legal complexities that surround the question. In common law, case law, and state statutes as well as in the basic authority of the U.S. Constitution, privileges and restrictions further defining these rights abound. The body of law covering the complex question of individual rights of defense of person and property contains many apparent contradictions and much ambiguity. In their efforts to create a perfect balance between the rights of individuals and the needs of society, the courts and the legislatures have had to walk a narrow path. As the perception of society's needs changed or as the need for the protection of the individual became more prominent, a swing in the attitudes of the courts and the legislatures became apparent. This led to some confusion especially among those with little or no knowledge of the law.

It is of enormous value, therefore, for everyone engaged in security to pursue the study of both civil and criminal law. Such a study is aimed neither at acquiring a law degree nor certainly at developing the skills to practice law. It is directed toward developing a background in those principles and rules of law that will be useful in the performance of the complex job of security.

Without some knowledge of the law, security officers frequently cannot serve their clients' interests. They may subject themselves or their employers to ruinous lawsuits through well-meaning but misguided conduct. In cases that must eventually go to court, handling of evidence, reports, and interrogations may be critical to the case; without an understanding of legal processes and how they operate, the cases could be lost.

In short, the pursuit of security itself involves contact with others. In each such contact, there is a delicate consideration of conflicting rights. Without an appreciation of the elements involved, the security officer cannot perform properly.

Since for the purposes of this book we are primarily interested in civil and criminal law—both have major implications for the security officer and for the industry—it is useful to distinguish between them. Criminal law deals with offenses against society (corporations are of course part of society and can be either criminals or victims). Every state has its criminal code that classifies and defines criminal offenses. Criminal law is the result of a jurisdiction either using common law, which was adopted from English traditions, or passing specific legislation called statutory law. (In some jurisdictions both are used.) When criminal offenses are brought into court, the state takes an active part, considering itself to be the offended party.

Civil law, on the other hand, has more to do with the personal relations and conflicts between individuals, corporations, and government agencies. Broken agreements, sales that leave a customer dissatisfied, outstanding debts, disputes with a government agency, accidental injuries, and marital breakup all fall under the purview of civil law. In these cases, private citizens, companies, or government agencies are the offended parties, and the party found at fault is required to directly compensate the other party.

This chapter is intended as a guide to some of the intricacies of criminal and civil law with primary emphasis on civil actions. It is aimed at those subjects with which a security officer would most likely be confronted. It will deal with substantive law (statutes and codes) or that portion of the law that concerns the rights, duties, and penalties of individuals in their relationships with each other. Procedural law is the other of the two divisions of the law. It deals with the rules of court procedure and the mechanics of the legal machine.

Security, Public Police, and the U.S. Constitution

The framers of the U.S. Constitution with their grievances against England uppermost in mind when they were creating a new government were primarily concerned with the manner in which the powerless citizen was or could be abused by the enormous power of government. The document they created was concerned, therefore, not with the rights of citizens against each other but rather with those rights with respect to federal or state action.

Breaking and entering by one citizen on another may be criminal and subject to tort action (a civil wrong not involving a breach of contract), but it is not a violation of any constitutional right. Similar action by public police is a clear violation of Fourth Amendment rights and, as such, is expressly forbidden by the Constitution.

The public police have substantially greater powers than do security personnel to arrest, detain, search, and interrogate. Where security people are, as a rule, limited to the premises of their employer, public police operate in a much wider jurisdiction.

At the same time, the public police are limited by various restrictions imposed by the Constitution. Although the issue is not entirely clear, private police are not as a rule touched by these same restrictions.

Public police are limited by federal statutes that make it a crime for officials to deny others their constitutional rights. The Fourth and Fourteenth Amendments are most frequently invoked as the cornerstones of citizen protection against arbitrary police action. The exclusion of evidence from court action is one penalty paid by public police for violation of the search provision of the Fourth Amendment. For the most part private police are not affected by these restrictions.

Sources of Law

All law, whether civil or criminal, has its source in either common law, statutory law, or case law (judge made). The following discussion can be applied to either civil or criminal law as it has developed over the past century. Although today's criminal law is primarily statutory, civil law particularly tort law is essentially judge-made and created in response to changing social conditions.

Common Law

At one time, the principal source of law in the United States was English common law. Although common law may also refer to judge-made (as opposed to legislature-made) law, to law that originated in England and grew from everchanging custom, or to written Christian law, the term is most commonly used to refer to the English common law that has been changed to reflect specific U.S. customs.

Some states have preserved the status of common law offenses, while others have abolished common law and written most of the common law principles into statutes. Some states are still using both common and statutory law, whichever is appropriate.

Case Law

When a case goes to court, it is usually preceded by numerous cases of similar nature. Those preceding cases have usually been resolved in such a way as to put to rest any doubts as to the meaning of the governing statutes as well as to clarify the attitude of the courts regarding the violation involved. Each of these cases has established a precedent that will guide the court in subsequent cases based on the same essential facts. Since the facts in any two cases are rarely precisely the same, opposing attorneys cite prior cases whose facts more readily conform to their own theory or argument in the case at hand. They, too, build their case on precedents or case law already established. It is up to the court to choose one of the two sides or to establish its own theory. This is a very significant source of our law in addition to the common law.

Since society is in a constant state of change, it is essential that the law adapt to these changes. At the same time, there must be a stability in the law if it is to guide behavior. People must know that the law as it appears today will be the same tomorrow, that they will not be punished tomorrow for behavior that was permitted today. They need to know that each decision represents a settled statement of the law and that they can conduct their affairs accordingly. So the published decisions of the appellate courts become guides to the meaning of the law and in effect become the law itself. Their judgments flesh out legislative enactments to give them clear outlines. Such interpretations based on precedents are never regarded lightly and in legal terms are *"stare decisis"* or "let the decision stand."

This does not mean that each decided case locks the courts forever into automatic compliance. Conditions that created the climate of the earlier decision may have changed, rendering the precedent invalid. And there are cases decided in such a narrow way that they cannot be applied beyond that case. Further there is nothing that prevents review of a decision at the time of a later case. If the court agrees that the earlier case was in error, it will not be influenced by a faulty precedent.

So it can be seen that case law is an important source of the law; it provides a climate of legal stability without closing the law to responsiveness to changing needs.

Statutory Law

Federal and state legislatures are empowered to enact laws that describe additional crimes. The authority to do so emanates from the U.S. Constitution and from the individual state constitutions. These constitutions do not specifically establish a body of criminal law. In general, they are more concerned with setting forth the limitations of governmental power over the rights of individuals. But they do provide both for the authority of legislative action in establishing criminal law and for a court system to handle these as well as civil matters.

Much criminal law is, in fact, the creation of the legislatures. The legislatures are exclusively responsible for making and defining laws. The courts may find some laws unconstitutional or vague and thus set them aside, but they may not create laws. Only the legislatures are empowered to do that.

The Power of Security Personnel

Security personnel are generally limited to the exercise of powers possessed by every citizen. There is no legal area where the position of a security officer as such confers any greater rights, powers, or privileges than those possessed by every other citizen. A few states go contrary to this norm—for example, Michigan—and confer additional arrest powers for security personnel after the completion of a designated number of hours of training.[1] As a practical matter if officers are uniformed they will very likely find that in most cases people will comply with their requests. Many people are aware neither of their own rights nor of the limitations of the powers of a security officer. Thus security officers can obtain compliance to directives that may be if not illegal beyond their power to command. In cases where security officers have unwisely taken liberties with their authority, the officers and their employers may be subject to the penalties of civil action. The litigation involved in suing security officers and their employers for a tort is slow and expensive, which may make such recourse impossible for the poor and for those unfamiliar with their rights. But the judgments that have been awarded have had a generally sobering effect on security professionals and have probably served to reduce the number of such incidents. Criminal law also regulates security activities. Major crimes such as battery, manslaughter, kidnapping, and breaking and entering—any one of which might be encountered in the course of security activities—are substantially deterred by criminal sanctions.

Further limitations may be imposed on the authority of a security force by licensing laws, administrative regulations, and specific statutes directed at security activities. Operating contracts between employers and security firms may also specify limits on the activities of the contracted personnel.

Classes of Crimes

A crime has been defined as a voluntary and intentional violation by a legally competent person of a legal duty that commands or prohibits an act for the protection of society.[2]

Since such a definition encompasses violations from the most trivial to the most disruptive and repugnant, efforts have long been made to classify crimes in some way. In common law, crimes are classified according to seriousness from treason (the most serious) to misdemeanors (the least serious). Crimes in most states do not list treason separately and deal with felonies as the most serious crimes and misdemeanors as the next in seriousness, with different approaches to the least serious crimes, those known as infractions in some jurisdictions, less than misdemeanors in others, and petty offenses in still others. It will become apparent why security specialists should understand the nature of a given crime and its classification since such considerations will be important in determining their right to arrest, to use force in making the arrest, and to search and various other considerations that must be determined under possibly difficult circumstances and without delay. Serious crimes like murder, rape, arson, armed robbery, and aggravated assault are felonies. Misdemeanors include charges such as disorderly conduct and criminal damage to property.

Felonies

From the time of Henry II of England, there has been a general understanding that felonies comprised the more serious crimes. This is true in modern U.S. law as far as it goes, but clearly the definition of felony must be pinned down more precisely than that if it is to be used as a classification of crime and if courts are to respond differently to felons than they would to another type of law breaker. The definition of a felony is by no means standard throughout the United States. In some jurisdictions, there is no distinction between felonies and misdemeanors.

The federal definition of a felony is an offense punishable by death or by imprisonment for a term exceeding one year. The test, then, for a felony is the length of time that punishment is imposed on the convicted person.

A number of states follow the federal definition. In those states, felony is a crime punishable by more than a year's imprisonment. The act remains a felony whatever the ultimate sentence may actually be. The crime is classified as a felony because it could be punished by a sentence of more than a year. Other states provide that, "[a] felony is a crime punishable with death or by imprisonment in the state prison." This definition hinges on the place of confinement rather than, as in the federal description, the length of confinement.

Some states bestow broad discretionary powers on the judge by providing that certain acts may be considered either a felony or a misdemeanor depending on the sentence. The penalty clauses in the statutes thus involved specifically state that if the judge should sentence the defendant to a state prison, the act for which he was convicted shall be a felony (under the state definition of a felony) but if the sentence be less than such confinement the crime shall be a misdemeanor.

The distinction can be very important in that in most states where arrest by private citizens (for example, security personnel) is covered by statute, it is clear that arrests for crimes that are less than felonies may be made only where the offense is committed in the presence of the arrester. In the case of arrest for a felony, the felony must in fact have been committed (though not necessarily in the presence of the arrester), and there must be reasonable grounds to believe the person arrested committed it. In other words, security employees, unlike police officers, act at their own peril.

> A police officer has the right to arrest without a warrant where he reasonably believes that a felony has been committed and that the person arrested is guilty, even if, in fact, no felony has occurred. A private citizen, on the other hand, is privileged to make an arrest only when he has reasonable grounds for believing in the guilt of the person arrested and a felony has in fact been committed.[3]

Some states, however, do allow for citizen arrest in public order misdemeanors. Making a citizen's arrest, which must be recognized as the only kind of arrest that can be made by a security officer, is a privilege not a right and as such is carefully limited by law. Such limitation is enforced by the ever-present potential for either criminal prosecution or tort action against the unwise or uninformed action of a security professional.

Private Security Powers

Arrest

Arresting a person is a legal step that should not be taken lightly. A citizen's power to arrest another is granted by common law and in many jurisdictions by statutory law. In most cases, it is best to make an arrest only after an arrest warrant has been issued. Most citizen's arrests occur, however, when the immediacy of a situation requires arrest without a warrant. The exact extent of citizen's arrest power varies, depending on the type of crime, the jurisdiction (laws), whether the crime was committed in the presence of the arrester, or the status of the citizen (strictly a private citizen or a commissioned officer).

In most states warrantless arrests by private citizens are allowed when a felony has been committed and reasonable grounds exist for believing that the person arrested committed it. Reasonable grounds means that the arrester acted as would any average citizen who, having observed the same facts, would draw the same conclusion. In some jurisdictions, a private citizen may arrest without reasonable grounds as long as a felony was committed.

Most states allow citizen's arrest for misdemeanors committed in the arrester's presence. A minority of states, however, adhere closely to the common-law practice of allowing misdemeanor arrests only for offenses that constitute a breach of the peace and that occur in the arrester's presence (see Table 6.1.)

Although the power of citizen's arrest is very significant in the private sector because it allows security officers to protect their employer's property, there is little room for errors of judgment. The public police officer is protected from civil liability for false arrest if the officer has probable cause to believe a crime was committed, but the private officer (citizen) is liable if a crime was not committed regardless of the reasonableness of the belief. This liability is because a citizen's arrest generally can be made only if a crime has definitely been committed.

This distinction is illustrated by the case *Cervantez v. J.C. Penney Company*.[4] In this case, an off-duty police officer, moonlighting as a store detective for J.C. Penney Company, made a warrantless arrest of two individuals for misdemeanor theft. Later they were released because of lack of evidence. The plaintiffs sued the company and the officer for false arrest, imprisonment, malicious prosecution, assault and battery, intentional infliction of emotional distress, and negligence in the selection of its employee. The primary issue in the Cervantez case was whether the officer could rely on the probable cause defense. The court's decision rested on whether the officer acted as a police officer in California or as a private citizen.

The store and officer argued that the probable cause defense was sound because the detective was an off-duty police officer and thus could arrest on the basis of probable cause. The plaintiffs argued that the store detective should be governed by the rules of arrest applied to private citizens and that the officer was therefore liable for his actions because no crime had been proven. The plaintiffs contended that the officer was employed as a private security officer, and thus his arrest powers were only those of a private citizen.

Table 6.1 Statutory Arrest Authority of Private Citizen

	Minor Offense									
	Type of Minor Offense						*Type of Knowledge Required*			
	Crime	*Misdemeanor Amounting to a Breach of the Peace*	*Breach of the Peace*	*Public Offense*	*Offense*	*Offense Other Than an Ordinance*	*Indictable Offense*	*Presence*	*Immediate Knowledge*	*View*	*Upon Reasonable Grounds That Is Being Committed*
---	---	---	---	---	---	---	---	---	---	---	---
Alabama				•				•			
Alaska	•							•			
Arizona		•						•			
Arkansas											
California				•				•			
Colorado	•							•			
Georgia						•		•	•		
Hawaii	•							•			
Idaho				•				•			
Illinois						•					•
Iowa				•				•			
Kentucky											
Louisiana											
Michigan											
Minnesota				•				•			
Mississippi			•				•	•			
Montana					•			•			
Nebraska											
Nevada				•				•			
New York					•			•			
N. Carolina[a]			•								
N. Dakota				•				•			
Ohio											
Oklahoma				•				•			
Oregon			•					•			
S. Carolina				•				•			
S. Dakota				•				•			
Tennessee				•				•			
Texas			•					•		•	
Utah				•				•			
Wyoming											

Source: Charles Schnabolk, *Physical Security: Practices and Technology* (Stoneham, Mass.: Butterworth Publishers, 1983), pp. 64–65.

[a] Statute eliminates use of word *arrest* and replaces it with *detention*.

State	Felony	Larceny	Petit Larceny	Crime Involving Physical Injury to Another	Crime	Crime Involving Theft or Destruction of Property	Committed in Presence	Information a Felony Has Been Committed	View	Reasonable Grounds to Believe Being Committed	That Felony Has Been Committed in Fact	In Escaping or Attempting	Summoned by Peace Officer to Assist in Arrest	Is In the Act of Committing	Reasonable Grounds to Believe Person Arrested Committed	Probable Cause
	Type of Major Offense						*Type of Knowledge Required*					*Certainty of Correct Arrest*				
Alabama	●										●				●	
Alaska	●										●				●	
Arizona	●										●				●	
Arkansas	●									●					●	
California	●										●				●	
Colorado				●			●									
Georgia	●												●		●	
Hawaii				●			●							●		
Idaho	●										●				●	
Illinois	●									●						
Iowa	●										●				●	
Kentucky	●										●				●	
Louisiana	●										●					
Michigan	●							●			●			●		
Minnesota	●										●				●	
Mississippi	●										●				●	
Montana	●										●				●	
Nebraska	●		●								●				●	
Nevada	●										●				●	
New York	●										●					
N. Carolina[a]	●			●		●							●			●
N. Dakota	●										●				●	
Ohio	●								●						●	
Oklahoma	●										●				●	
Oregon					●		●									●
S. Carolina	●	●							●	●						
S. Dakota	●										●				●	
Tennessee	●										●				●	
Texas	●							●	●						●	
Utah	●										●				●	
Wyoming	●		●								●				●	

The California Supreme Court ruled that the laws governing the type of arrest to be applied depend on the arrester's employer at the time of the arrest. Since the officer was acting as a store detective when he made the arrest, his arrest powers were no greater than those of a private citizen. Thus probable cause could not be used as a defense against false arrest.

Some states have avoided the problem of the Cervantez case by extending the probable cause defense to private citizens. The most common extension involves shoplifting arrests. Many states have a mercantile privilege rule that allows the probable cause defense for detentions but not for arrests. The law permits a private citizen or his employees to detain in a reasonable manner and for a reasonable time a person who is believed to have stolen merchandise so that the merchant can recover the merchandise or summon a police officer to make an arrest. Some states have extended this merchant clause to cover public employees in libraries, museums, or archival institutions.

The exact extent of the protection afforded to merchants and their employees or agents depends on the individual state's statutes. Some states offer protection against liability for false arrest, false imprisonment, and defamation; others offer protection against false imprisonment but not against false arrest. It is interesting to note that very few states allow a merchant to search a detainee. The private citizen's authority to search is unclear and will be discussed later in this chapter.

Detention

Detention is a concept that has grown largely in response to the difficulties faced by merchants in protecting their property from shoplifters and the problems and dangers they face when they make an arrest. Generally detention differs from arrest in that it permits a merchant to detain a suspected shoplifter briefly without turning the suspect over to the police. An arrest requires that the arrestee be turned over to the authorities as soon as practicable and in any event without unreasonable delay.

All the shoplifting statutes refer to "detain," not to "arrest," a terminology probably derived from the thought that a distinction could be made between the two. The distinction is based on the fact that an arrest is for the purpose of delivering the suspect to the authorities and of exercising strict physical control over that person until the authorities arrive. A detention, or temporary delay, would not be termed an arrest as commonly defined. The distinction is difficult to defend but the statutes are clear. In Illinois, for example:

> Any merchant who has reasonable grounds to believe that a person has committed retail theft may detain such person, on or off the premises of

a retail mecantile establishment, in a reasonable manner and for a reasonable length of time for all or any of the following purposes:

a. To request identification;
b. To verify such identification;
c. To make reasonable inquiry as to whether such person has in his possession unpurchased merchandise and, to make reasonable investigation of the ownership of such merchandise;
d. To inform a peace officer of the detention of the person and surrender that person to the custody of a peace officer.[5]

California was one of the first states to establish merchant immunity in a 1936 Supreme Court decision; in *Collyer v. S.H. Kress Co.*,[6] the court upheld the right of a department store official to detain a suspected shoplifter for 20 minutes.

Most statutes include the merchant, employee, agent, private police, and peace officer as authorized to detain suspects, but they do not include citizens at large such as another shopper. Most of the statutes also describe the purposes of detention and the manner in which they may be conducted. These purposes are to search, to interrogate, to investigate suspicious behavior, to recover goods, and to await a peace officer.

The manner in which the detention is to be conducted is generally described as "reasonable" and for "a reasonable period of time."

The privilege of detention is, however, subject to some problems. There must be probable cause to believe theft already has taken place, or is about to take place, before a merchant may detain anyone. Probable cause is an elusive concept and one which has undergone many different interpretations by the courts. It is frequently difficult to predict how the court will rule on a given set of circumstances that may at the time clearly indicate probable cause to detain. Secondly reasonableness must exist both in time and manner of the detention or the privilege will be lost.

Interrogation

No law prohibits a private person from engaging in conversation with a willing participant. Should the conversation become an interrogation, the information may not be admissible in a court of law. The standard is whether the statements were made voluntarily.

A statement made under duress is not regarded as trustworthy and is therefore inadmissible in court. This principle applies equally to police officers and private citizens. A confession obtained from an employee by threatening loss of job or physical harm would be inadmissible and would also make the interrogator liable for civil and criminal prosecution.

The classic cases involving interrogation, generally applied to only public law enforcement officers, are *Escobedo v. State of Illinois*[7] and *Miranda v. Arizona.*[8] Today the Miranda case has become the leading case recognized by most American citizens in reference to "their rights." On March 13, 1963, Ernesto Miranda was arrested at his home and taken to a Phoenix police station. There he was questioned by two police officers who during Miranda's trial admitted that they had not advised him that he could have a lawyer present. After two hours of interrogation, the officers emerged with a confession. According to the statement, Miranda had made the confession "with full knowledge of my legal right, understanding any statement I make may be used against me." His confession was admitted into evidence over defense objections during his trial. He was convicted of kidnapping and rape. On appeal, the Arizona Supreme Court upheld the conviction indicating that Miranda did not specifically request counsel. The U.S. Supreme Court reversed the decision based on the fact that Miranda had not been informed of his right to an attorney, nor was his right not to be compelled to incriminate himself effectively protected.

Although the principle behind the *Miranda v. Arizona* decision was the removal of compulsion from custodial questioning (questioning initiated by law enforcement officers after a person has been taken into custody or otherwise deprived of freedom), it generally only applies to public law enforcement officers. The police officer must show that statements made by the accused were given after the accused was informed of the facts that speaking was not necessary, that the statements might be used in court, that an attorney could be present, and that if the accused could not afford an attorney, one would be appointed for the accused prior to questioning. These Miranda warnings are not necessary unless the person is in custody or is deprived of freedom. Based on this distinction, most courts agree that private persons are not generally required to use Miranda warnings because they are not public law-enforcement officers.

In the case, *In re Deborah C.,*[9] the California Supreme Court upheld the principle that private citizens are not required to use Miranda warnings and that statements made by the accused in citizen's arrests are admissible in a court of law. The court felt that the Miranda rationale did not apply to the retail store environment because store detectives lack the psychological edge that police officers have when the latter are questioning someone at a police station.

A few states require citizens to use a modified form of Miranda before questioning, and some—a definite minority—prohibit questioning. Wisconsin law states, "[t]he detained person must be promptly informed of the purpose of the detention and be permitted to make phone calls, but shall not be interrogated or searched against his will before the arrival of a peace officer who may conduct a lawful interrogation of the accused person."[10]

In 1987, the case of *State of West Virginia v. William H. Muegge*,[11] expanded the Miranda concept to private citizens. In this case, Muegge was detained by a store security guard who observed Muegge place several items of merchandise in his pockets and proceed through the checkout aisle without paying for those items. The security guard approached Muegge, identified herself, and asked him to return to the store office to discuss the problem. The officer ordered Muegee to empty his pockets, which contained several unpaid-for items valued at a total of $10.65. The officer next read Muegge his "constitutional rights" and asked him to sign a waiver of rights. Muegee refused and asked for the assistance of a lawyer. The officer refused the request and indicated that she would call the state police. At some time either prior to the arrival or after the arrival of the state trooper, the defendant signed the waiver and completed a questionnaire that contained various incriminating statements. At the trial, the unpaid-for items were admitted without objection and the questionnaire was read aloud over the defendant's objection. Although the court felt that the specific Miranda warnings were not necessary, it ruled that whenever a person is in custodial control mandated by state statute (that is, merchant clauses) the safeguards protecting the constitutional right not to be compelled to be a witness against oneself in a criminal case apply.

Search and Seizure

A search may be defined as an examination of persons and/or their property for the purpose of discovering evidence of guilt in relation to some specific offense. The observation of items in plain view is not a search as long as the observer is legally entitled to be in the place where the observation is made. This includes public property and private property that is normally open to the public, for example, shopping malls, retail stores, hotel lobbies, and so on.

Common law says little about searches by private persons and is inconclusive. Searches by private persons, however, have been upheld by the courts where consent to search was given and where searches were made as part of a legal citizen's arrest. The best practice to follow is to contact police officials who can then ask for a search warrant or search as part of an arrest. Since searches often need to be conducted on short notice without the aid of a police officer, however, it is important to understand several factors.

First, in a consent search, the searcher must be able to show that the consent was given voluntarily. Second the search cannot extend beyond the area for which consent to search was given. It is advisable to secure a written agreement of the consent to search. Third the consent must be given by the person who possesses the item. Possession, not ownership, is the criterion for determining whether a search was valid. Although many firms issue waivers to search lockers and other work areas, an officer must remember that the consent to search may be withdrawn at any time. If the consent is withdrawn, continuing a search might make the officer and the company liable for invasion of privacy. Some companies have solved this problem by retaining control over lockers in work areas. In this situation, workers are told that the lockers are not private and may be searched at any time.

A search made as a part of an arrest is supported by case law. In general, the principle of searching the arrestee and the immediate surroundings, defined as the area within which one could lunge and reach a weapon or destroy evidence, has been repeatedly held as constitutional. The verdict on searches incident to arrest is still mixed. In *People v. Zelinski*,[12] the California court disapproved of searches made incident to an arrest but did approve of searches for weapons for protective reasons. New York courts tend to support searches, indicating that private officers, like their public counterparts, have a right to searches incident to an arrest. In general, it appears that unless the security officer fears that a weapon may be hidden on the arrestee, the officer should wait until the police arrive to conduct a search unless permission is given for such a search.

Even in the statutes governing retail shoplifting, the area of search is limited. Some states neither forbid nor condone searches; rather, they allow security personnel to investigate or make reasonable inquiries as to whether a person possesses unpurchased merchandise. In other states, searches are strictly forbidden, except looking for objects carried by the suspected shoplifter. Courts, however, generally favor protective searches where officers fear for their own safety.

Exclusionary Rule

In a historic decision, the Supreme Court ruled that any and all evidence uncovered by public law enforcement agents in violation of the Fourth Amendment will be excluded from consideration. That means all evidence, no matter how trustworthy or indicative of guilt, will be inadmissible if it is illegally obtained. This landmark case (*Mapp v. Ohio*),[13] was the most important case that contributed to the development of the "exclusionary rule," which states that illegally seized evidence (and its fruits) are inadmissible in any state or federal proceedings. *Weeks v. United States*[14] set the stage for the later, all-inclusive decision in Mapp by holding that evidence acquired by officials of the federal government in violation of the Fourth Amendment must be excluded in a federal prosecution.

The Mapp case is clear in its application of the exclusionary rule to state and federal prosecutions. The question is, does the exclusionary rule apply to private parties? The determining case in this area is *Burdeau v. McDowell*.[15]

Unlike illegal searches conducted by public law-enforcement officers, evidence secured by a private security officer conducting an illegal search is still admissible in either criminal or civil proceedings. In *Burdeau v. McDowell*, the U.S. Supreme Court said, "[i]t is manifest that there was no invasion of the security afforded by the Fourth Amendment against unreasonable searches and seizures, as whatever wrong was done was the act of individuals in taking property of another." If such evidence is admissible, why should private sector employees concern themselves with the legality of searches? Even though the evidence is admissible, security officers who conduct illegal searches may be subject to liability for other actions, including battery and invasion of privacy.

There is considerable controversy over the Burdeau case because some people fear that constitutional guarantees are threatened by the acceptance of evidence illegally obtained by private security personnel. It is clear that any involvement by government officials constitutes "state action" or an action "under color of law" and is limited by the constitutional restrictions that apply to public police actions. In *State v. Scrotsky*,[16] the court excluded evidence obtained when a police detective accompanied a theft victim to the defendant's apartment to identify and recover stolen goods. The court held that "[t]he search and seizure by one served the purpose of both and must be deemed to have been participated in by both." The exclusionary rule is applied in this case, as in many others, to discourage government officials from conducting improper searches and from using private individuals to conduct them.[17]

In cases where private parties act independent of government involvement, the courts have not been so clear. In a significant case, *People v. Randazzo*,[18] the court admitted evidence obtained by a merchant in a shoplifting case. The court did not deal with any questions of Fourth Amendment violation since there was no state action involved. The court held that redress for the victim of an unreasonable search conducted by a private individual not under color of law is a tort action, and thus the exclusionary rule does not apply. In *Thacker v. Commonwealth*,[19] the court held that a private party acts for the state when that party makes an arrest in accordance with the state's arrest statute and thus would be subject to the exclusionary rule. On the other hand, following the Burdeau precedent, a federal district court found no state action in a case where the plaintiff alleged she was wrongfully detained, slapped, beaten, harassed, and searched by the manager and an employee of the store.[20] The plaintiff sued, alleging among other things that the employee, a security officer, was acting "under color of law" because he was licensed under the Pennsylvania Private Detective Act. The court rejected this argument and found that the Pennsylvania law "invests the licensee with no authority of state law."

In summary although public police are clearly limited by constitutional restrictions, generally private security personnel are not so limited. Provided that they act as private parties and are in no way involved with public officials, they are limited by criminal and civil sanctions but are not bound at this time by most constitutional restrictions.

Use of Force

On occasion, security personnel must use force to protect someone or to accomplish legitimate purposes. In general, force may be used to protect oneself or others, to defend property, and to prevent the commission of a criminal act. The extent to which force may be used is restricted; no more force may be used than is reasonable under the circumstances. This means that deadly force or force likely to create great bodily harm will not be allowable unless the force being used by the assailant is also deadly force or force likely to create great bodily harm. If the force exceeds what is deemed reasonable, officers and their employers are liable for the use of excessive force, which can range from assault and battery to homicide. This is the same degree of power extended to the ordinary citizen.

Self-defense

In general people may use reasonable force to protect themselves. The amount of force may be equal to, but not greater than, the force being used against them. In most states, a person can protect herself, except when that person was the initial aggressor. Most states allow that self-defense is a defense against the criminal offense of battery.

Defense of Others

Security officers may protect others just as they protect themselves. However, two different approaches to defense of others are evident. In the first approach, the officer must try to identify with the attacked person. In this position, the officer is entitled to use whatever force would be appropriate if she were the person being attacked. If the officer happens to protect the wrong person—that is, the aggressor—the officer is liable regardless of her good intentions. In the second approach, the defender may use force when it is reasonable to believe that such force is necessary. In this case, the defender is protected from liability as long as she acted in a reasonable manner.

Defense of Property

In defense of property, force may be applied, but it must be short of deadly force, which is generally allowable only in cases involving felonious attacks on property during which loss of life is likely. As noted by Schnabolk, "one may use deadly force to protect a home against an arsonist but the use of deadly force against a mere trespasser would not be permitted."[21] Security officers acting in the place of their employers are empowered to use the same force that their employers are entitled to use.

Force Used during Arrest or Detention

Like the police, the private citizen security officer has the right to use reasonable force in detaining or arresting someone. Many states still follow the common-law principles that allow deadly force in the case of fleeing felons, but many others have restricted the use of deadly force. This restriction allows the use of deadly force only in cases where the felony is both violent *and* the felon is immediately fleeing.

Prevention of Crimes

To determine the amount of force a security officer may use to prevent crimes, the courts have considered the circumstances, the seriousness of the crime prevented, and the possibility of preventing the crime by other means. Under common law a person can use force to prevent a crime. The courts have ruled, however, that the use of force is limited to situations involving felonies or a breach of the peace and that nonviolent misdemeanors do not warrant the use of force. Deadly force is justifiable in preventing a crime only if it is necessary to protect a person from harm. Some states have broadened this concept to permit the use of deadly force to prevent any felony.

Use of Firearms

Most states regulate the carrying of firearms by private citizens. Almost all states prohibit the carrying of concealed weapons while only half of them prohibit carrying an exposed handgun. Although all states excuse police officers from these restrictions, some states also exempt private security officers. Even in states that prohibit carrying concealed or exposed handguns, there are provisions for procuring a license to carry weapons in this manner.

Civil Law: The Controller for Private Security

Tort Law: Source of Power and Limits

A tort is a civil action based on the principle that one individual can expect certain behavior from another individual. When the actions of one of the parties do not meet reasonable expectations, a tort action may result. In security applications, a guard may take some action to interfere with the free movement of some person. There is a basis for a suit no matter whether the guard knows those actions are wrong or is unaware that the actions are wrong but acts in a negligent manner.

Thus tort law may be invoked for either an intentional or negligent act. In some cases, tort law may be imposed even though an individual is not directly at fault. Such a legal obligation is called "strict liability," and does not generally affect the security officer. Vicarious liability, however, is of concern to enterprises that contract or employ security services. Strict liability applies to the seller who is liable for any and all defective or hazardous products that unduly threaten a consumer's personal safety. Vicarious liability is an indirect legal responsibility; for example, the liability of an employer for the actions of an employee.

Negligence

The Restatement of Torts[22] states that "[it] is negligence to use an instrumentality, whether a human being or a thing, which the actor knows, or should know, to be incompetent, inappropriate or defective and that its use involves an unreasonable risk of harm to others." This statement has particular importance to security employers and supervisors in four areas: (1) negligent hiring, (2) negligent supervision of employees, (3) negligent training, and (4) supervisory negligence. Security officers have been held liable for negligent use of firearms and force.

In all cases of negligence, the plaintiff (the person who brings an action, the party who complains or sues) must prove the case by a preponderance of the evidence (more than 50 percent or "more likely than not") in all of the following areas:

1. An act or failure to act (an omission) by the defendant
2. A legal duty owed to the plaintiff by the defendant, the person defending or denying, and/or the party against whom relief or recovery is sought
3. A breach of duty by the defendant
4. A foreseeable injury to plaintiff
5. Harm or injury

A relatively new concept in the area of negligence is comparative fault. This concept accepts the fact that the plaintiff may have contributed to her own injury such as being in a restricted area or creating a disturbance or some hazard. In the past, the theory of contributory negligence prevented the plaintiff from collecting for injuries and so forth if she contributed somehow to her own injury. In comparative negligence, the relative negligence of the parties involved is compared, and the plaintiff who may have contributed to the injury may get some award for part of the injury for which she is not responsible. There are three types of comparative negligence statutes: (1) pure approach, (2) the 50/50 rule, and (3) the 51 percent rule. In the pure approach, the plaintiff may collect something for injuries even if she was primarily responsible for her injuries. In theory, the jury could award the plaintiff 1 percent of the damages if she is found to have contributed 99 percent to the injury. In the 50/50 rule situation the plaintiff can collect for damages if she was responsible for no more than 50 percent of the negligence. In the 51 percent situation, the plaintiff must not have contributed to more than 49 percent of the situation in order to collect damages. Regardless of the rule followed, the degree to which the plaintiff is responsible for the end result is considered before judgments are pronounced. One example of the 50/50 rule is the Illinois statute:

> In all actions on account of bodily injury or death or physical damage to property, based on negligence . . . the plaintiff shall be barred from recovering damages if the trier of fact find that the contributory fault on the part of the plaintiff is more than 50% of the proximate cause of the injury or damage for which recovery is sought. The plaintiff shall not be barred from recovering damages if the trier of fact finds that the contributory fault on the part of the plaintiff is not more than 50% of the proximate cause of the injury or damage for which recovery is sought, but any damages allowed shall be diminished in the proportion to the amount of fault attributable to the plaintiff.[23]

Table 6.2 presents the various forms of comparative liability as of 1982. An update of this chart is needed but is not yet available.

Cases involving negligence in providing adequate security on the part of firms have been increasing. Recent cases have resulted in awards to plaintiffs in individual cases of over $1 million. More will be said about this issue later in the chapter.

Intentional Torts

An intentional tort occurs when the person who committed the act was able to foresee that the action would result in certain damages. The actor intended the consequences of the actions or at least intended to commit

Table 6.2 Forms of Comparative Negligence

Pure Form	New Hampshire/50-50	Arkansas Model - 51 Percent
(Plaintiff can be at any percentage of fault.)	(Plaintiff cannot be more negligent than the defendant.)	(Plaintiff must be less negligent than the defendant.)
Alaska	Connecticut	Arkansas
California	Hawaii	Colorado
Florida	Montana	Idaho
Illinois	Massachusetts	Kansas
Louisiana	Nevada	Maine
Michigan	New Hampshire	Minnesota
Mississippi	New Jersey	North Dakota
New Mexico	Ohio	Utah
New York	Oklahoma	West Virginia
Rhode Island	Oregon	Wyoming
Washington	Pennsylvania	
	Texas	
Other	Vermont	
Georgia (Unique)	Wisconsin	
Nebraska (Slight/gross)		
South Dakota (Slight/gross)		

Chart shows the states that currently have a pure form or New Hampshire or Arkansas model of comparative liability. States with special conditions are listed separately.

Prepared by David Steeno. From *Security World* (February 1982).

the action that resulted in damages to the plaintiff. In general, the law punishes such acts by punitive measures that exceed those awarded in common negligence cases.

The most common intentional torts are:

Assault: Intentionally causing fear of harmful or offensive touching but without touching or physical contact. In most cases, courts have ruled that words alone are not sufficient to place a person in fear of harm and that the danger is imminent.

Battery: Intentionally harmful or otherwise offensive touching of another person. The touching does not have to be direct physical contact but may instead be through an instrument such as a cane or rock. In addition, the courts have found battery to exist if "something" closely connected to the body, but not actually a part of the body, is struck.[24] In this case (*Fisher v. Carrousel Motor Hotel, Inc.*), the plaintiff was attending a conference that included a luncheon. The luncheon was a buffet, and while Fisher was in line, one of the defendant's employees snatched the plate from his hand and shouted that no Negro could be served in the club. The court of appeals held that a battery can occur even though the subject is not struck. They ruled that, so long as there is contact with clothing or an object closely identified with the body, a battery can occur. From a security point of view, the contact must be nonconsensual and not privileged. Privileged contact is generally granted to merchants who need to recover merchandise; privilege is generally a defense against charges of battery if the merchant's actions were reasonable. If the touching were unreasonable, however, the plaintiff would have a case for battery. The same argument holds for searches: If a search is performed after consent has been given, no battery has occurred. If consent is not given, however, the search is illegal, and a battery has probably occurred.

False imprisonment or false arrest: Intentionally confining or restricting the movement or freedom of another. The confinement may be the result of physical restraint or intimidation. False imprisonment implies that the confinement is for personal advantage rather than to bring the plaintiff to court. This is one of the torts most frequently filed against security personnel.

Defamation: Injuring the reputation of another by publicly making untrue statements. Slander is oral defamation, while libel is defamation through the written word. The classic case of a security officer yelling "Stop thief!" in a crowded store has all the necessary elements for slander if the accused is not a thief. Although it is generally true that truth is an absolute defense in defamation issues, the courts may also look at the motivation. True statements published with malicious intent can be prosecuted in some jurisdictions. In this age of high technology, the courts have now included statements made on television or other broadcasts in the libel category. It is apparent that the courts view these types of statements as being more permanent and as reaching broad audiences.

Malicious prosecution: Groundlessly instituting criminal proceedings against another person. To prove malice, the plaintiff must show that the primary motive in bringing about criminal proceedings was not to bring the defendant to justice. Classic cases include proceedings brought about to extort money or to force performance on contracts. Although there is no liability for reporting facts to the police

or other components of the criminal justice system if the prosecution resulted from biased statements of fact, incomplete reports, or
the defendant's persuasion (political, sexual, religious, and so on), liability for malicious prosecution might be proved.

Invasion of privacy: Intruding on another person's physical solitude,
disclosing private information about another person, or publicly
placing someone in a false light. Four distinct actions fall into this
category: (1) misappropriation of the plaintiff's name or picture for
commercial advantage, (2) placing the plaintiff in a false light, (3)
public disclosure of private facts, and (4) intrusion into the seclu-
sion of another. For security purposes, invasion of privacy generally
occurs during a search or during observation of an individual. If
signs outside fitting rooms advise customers that they may be observed, some legal observers believe that shoppers should not expect privacy and thus cannot legitimately complain of invasion of
privacy. Concern over liability for invasion of privacy is increasing;
this liability may be the result of reference checks, background investigations, or the use of truth detection devices.

Trespass and conversion: Trespass is the unauthorized physical invasion of property or remaining on property after permission has been
rescinded. Conversion means taking personal property in such a
way that the plaintiff's use or right of possession of chattel is restricted. In simpler terms, conversion is depriving someone of the
use of personal property.

Intentional infliction of mental distress: Intentionally causing mental
or emotional distress to another person. The distress may be either
mental or physical and may result from highly aggravating words or
conduct.

Security and Liability

In the past few years, the number of suits filed against security
officers and companies has increased dramatically. Predictions for the next
10 years indicate that the increase will cease but that the number of suits
will continue at the present levels. One possible reason for the leveling off of
suits is that security management has a better understanding of the problems
associated with liability situations today. The earlier increase may be partly
attributed to the growth of the security industry and to the public's demand
for accountability and professionalism in the security area. Most of the cases
filed against private security officers and operations belong in the tort category as was mentioned earlier in this chapter. The individual who commits
a tort is called a tortfeasor, while the accuser is called the plaintiff. The plain-

tiff may be a person, a corporation, or an association. Torts are classified as either intentional, negligent, or strict liability. An intentional tort is a wrong perpetrated by someone who intends to break the law. In contrast, a negligent tort is a wrong perpetrated by someone who fails to exercise sufficient care in doing what is otherwise permissible. A strict, or willful, tort combines intentional and negligent torts; it involves elements of intent and malice or ill will. Malice or ill will may be attributed to someone who is aware of danger to others but who is indifferent to their safety or fails to use ordinary care to avoid injury.

In most cases of negligence, the jury considers awarding damages to compensate the plaintiff. The awards generally take into account the physical, mental, and emotional suffering of the plaintiff, and future medical payments may be allowed for.

Punitive damages are also possible but are more likely to be awarded in cases of intentional liability. Punitive damages are designed to punish the tortfeasor and to deter future inappropriate behavior. Punitive damages are also possible in negligence cases where the actions of the tortfeasor were in total disregard for the safety of others.

Foreseeability/Duty to Protect

The area of civil liability is of great importance to the security industry since the courts have been more willing to hold the industry legally responsible for protection in this area than in others. This trend is particularly noticeable in the hotel and motel industry where owners are liable for failure to adequately protect guests from foreseeable criminal activity. In some circumstances, a landlord or hotel or motel owner might be held accountable for failure to provide adequate protection from criminal actions. In *Klein v. 1500 Massachusetts Avenue Apartment Corporation*,[25] a tenant who was criminally assaulted sued the corporation. The decision centered on the issue that the landlord had prior notice of criminal activity (including burglary and assault) against his tenants and property. In addition, the landlord was aware of conditions that made it likely that criminal activities would continue. The court ruled that the landlord had failed in an obligation to provide adequate security and was thus liable. A similar case was made against Howard Johnson's by the actress, Connie Frances.[26] Frances alleged that the hotel had failed to provide adequate locks on the doors. The jury awarded Frances over $1 million.

Recent decisions *(Philip Aaron Banks, et al. v. Hyatt Corporation and Refco Poydras Hotel Joint Venture* and *Allen B. Morrison, et al. v. MGM Grand Hotel, et al.)* have followed earlier landmark cases.[27] In the Banks case, the court held the hotel liable for foreseeable events that led to the murder of Banks by a third party. Banks was shot only four feet from the hotel door. The suit alleged that the hotel failed to provide adequate security and to warn Banks of the danger of criminal activity near the hotel entrance. The jury awarded the plaintiffs $975,000, even though evidence was introduced that showed that the hotel had made reasonable efforts to provide additional protection in the area. The court stated that "the owner or operator of a business owes a duty to invitees to exercise reasonable care to protect them from injury," noting that "the duty of a business to protect invitees can extend to adjacent property, particularly entrances to the business premises, if the business is aware of a dangerous condition on the adjacent property and fails to warn its invitees or to take some other reasonable preventive action." In the Morrison case, a robber followed Morrison from the hotel desk into the elevator after Morrison had cashed in his chips and withdrew his jewelry and cash from the hotel's safe. The robber took Morrison's property at gun point and then knocked him unconscious. Morrison brought suit against the hotel for failing to provide adequate security, noting that a similar robbery had recently occurred. The appellate court supported Morrison's contention saying, "a landowner must exercise ordinary care and prudence to render the premises reasonably safe for the visit of a person invited on his premises for business purposes." In *McCarty v. Pheasant Run, Inc.*,[28] however, the court recognized that invitees who fail to take basic security precautions may not have cause for action against the hotel.

The foreseeability issue has been applied to other areas of business in recent years. In *Sharpe v. Peter Pan Bus Lines*,[29] the court awarded $550,000 for a wrongful death attributed to negligent security in a bus terminal. The same basic concept of foreseeability was applied in *Nelson v. Church's Fried Chicken*.[30] In fact, the concept of foreseeability has been expanded beyond the narrow opinion that foreseeability is implied in failure to provide security for specific criminal behavior. This concept implies that, since certain attacks have occurred in or near the company, the company should reasonably be expected to foresee potential security problems and provide adequate security. In a recent Iowa Supreme Court decision, the court abolished the need for prior violent acts to establish foreseeability. In *Galloway v. Bankers Trust Company and Trustee Midlands Mall*,[31] the court ruled foreseeability could be established by "all facts and circumstances," not just prior violent acts. Therefore prior thefts may be sufficient to establish foreseeability since these offenses could lead to violence. In another case, *Polly Suzanne Paterson v. Kent C. Deeb, Transamerica Insurance Co., W. Fenton Langston, and Hartford Accident & Indemnity Co.*,[32] a Florida court held that the plaintiff may recover for a sexual assault without proof of prior similar incidents on the premises.

Nondelegable Duty

Another legal trend is to prevent corporations from divesting themselves of liability by assigning protection services to a contractor. Under the principle of agency law, such an assignment transferred the liability for the service from the contractee to the contractor. The courts, however, have held that some obligations cannot be entirely transferred. This principle is called "nondelegable duty." Based on this principle, contractual provisions that shift liability to the subcontractors have not been recognized by the courts. These contractual provisions are commonly called "hold harmless" clauses.

Take for example, *Dupree v. Piggly Wiggly Shop Rite Foods Inc.* The court decided that:

[p]ublic policy requires [that] one may not employ or contract with a special agency or detective firm to ferret out the irregularities or his customers or employees and then escape liability for the malicious prosecution or false arrest on the ground that the agency and/or its employees are independent contractors.[33]

Imputed Negligence

Imputed negligence simply means that, "by reason of some relation existing between A and B, the negligence of A is to be charged against B, although B has played no part in it, has done nothing whatever to aid or encourage it, or indeed has done all that he possibly can to prevent it. This is commonly called 'imputed contributory negligence.'"[34]

Vicarious Liability

One form of imputed negligence is "vicarious liability." The concept of vicarious, or imputed, liability arises from agency law in which one party has the power to control the actions of another party involved in the contract or relationship. The principal is thus responsible for the actions of a servant or agent. In legal terms, this responsibility is called *respondeat superior.* In short, employers are liable for the actions of their employees while they are employed on the firms' business. Employers are liable for the actions of their agents even if the employers do nothing to cause the actions directly. The master is held liable for any intentional tort committed by the servant where its purpose, however misguided, is wholly or partially to further the master's business. Employers may even be liable for some of the actions of their employees when the employees are neither at work nor engaged in company business. For example, consider the position of an employer who issues a firearm to an employee. The employee, at home and therefore off duty, plays with the firearm, which discharges and injures a neighbor. The neighbor may sue the employer for negligently entrusting a dangerous instrument to an employee or for the negligence in selecting a careless employee. The principle of *respondeat superior* (let the master respond) is well established in common law. It is not in itself the subject of any substantial dispute, and at those times when it becomes an issue in a dispute, the area of contention is factual rather than the doctrine itself. As was noted earlier, in the doctrine of *respondeat superior*, "[a] servant is a person employed by a master to perform service in his affairs, whose physical conduct in the performance of the service is controlled or is subject to the right of control by the master. This court has stated that the right of control and not necessarily the exercise of that right is the test of the relationship of master and servant. Basically, it is distinction between a person who is subject to orders as to how he does his work and one who agrees only to do the work in his own way."[35] There is no question that an employer (master) is liable for injuries caused by employees (servants) who are acting within the scope of their employment. This is not to say that the employees are relieved of all liability. They are in fact the principal in any action, but since the employee rarely has the financial resources to satisfy a third-party suit, an injured person will look beyond the employee to the employer for compensation for damages.

Clearly the relationship between master and servant under *respondeat superior* needs definition. Under the terms of the *Graalum v. Radisson Ramp* ruling, in-house security officers are servants whereas contract security personnel may not be. In the latter case, as discussed previously, contract personnel are employees of the supplying agency, and in most cases, the hiring company will not be held liable for their acts. The relationship is a complex one, however.

If security officers are acting within the scope of their employment and commit a wrongful act, the employer is liable for the actions. The matter then turns on the scope of the officer's employment and the employer-employee relationship. One court described the scope of employment as depending on:

1. The act of being of the kind the offender is employed to perform;
2. It occurring substantially within the authorized time and space limits of the employment, and
3. The offender being motivated, at least in part, by a purpose to serve the master.[36]

This is further refined in another case in which the court or in pursuit of some purpose of his own, the defendant is not bound by his conduct, but if, while acting within the general scope of his employment, he simply disregards his master's orders or exceeds his powers, the master will be reasonable for his conduct.[37]

Liability then is a function of the control exercised or permitted in the relationship between the security officer and the hiring company. If the hiring company maintains a totally hands-off posture with respect to personnel supplied by the agency, it may well avoid liability for wrongful acts performed by such personnel. On the other hand, there is some precedent for considering the hiring company as sharing some liability simply by virtue of its underlying rights of control over its own premises, no matter how it wishes to exercise that control. Many hiring companies are, however, motivated to contractually reject any control of security personnel on their premises in order to avoid liability. This, as was pointed out in *Private Police*, works to discourage hiring companies from regulating the activity of security employees and

> the company that exercises controls, e.g. carefully examines the credentials of the guard, carefully determines the procedures the guard will follow, and pays close attention to all his activities, may still be substantially increasing its risk of liability to any third persons who are, in fact, injured by an act of the guard.[38]

It is further suggested in this excellent study that there may be an expansion of certain nondelegable duty rules into consideration of the responsibilities for the actions of security personnel. As was discussed previously, the concept of the nondelegable duty provides that there are certain duties and responsibilities that are imposed on an individual and for which that individual remains responsible even though an independent contractor is hired to implement them. Such duties currently encompass keeping the workplace safe and the premises reasonably safe for business visitors. It is also possible that the courts may find negligence in cases where the hiring companies, in an effort to avoid liability, have neglected to exercise any control over the selection and training of personnel, and they may further find that such negligence on the part of the hiring company has led to injury to third-party victims.

Vicarious liability requires a direct employer-employee relationship; it does not apply to cases in which an independent contractor is working for a firm. This is because the employer has no way of controlling the way an independent contractor performs the work. There are many exceptions to this rule, however. For example, the employer may be liable for the negligent selection of the contractor, or the employer may have exercised some day-to-day control over the employee.

Criminal Liability

Criminal liability is most frequently used against private security personnel in cases of assault, battery, manslaughter, and murder. Other common charges include burglary, trespass, criminal defamation, false arrest, unlawful use of weapons, disorderly conduct, extortion, eavesdropping, theft, perjury, and kidnapping. Security officers charged with criminal liability have several options in defending their actions. First they might try to show that they were entitled to use force in self-defense or that they made a reasonable mistake, which would negate criminal intent. Other defenses include entrapment, intoxication, insanity, consent (the parties involved concurred with the actions), and compulsion (the officer was forced or compelled to commit the act). As has been already noted in previous discussions, a corporation or an association could be charged with criminal liability as well as an individual officer.

The reporting of crime is an area in which security officers are liable for criminal prosecution. In general, private citizens are no longer obliged to report crime or to prevent it. But some jurisdictions still recognize the concept of misprision of felony—that is, concealing knowledge of a felony. Such legislation makes it a crime to not report a felony. To be guilty of misprision of felony, the prosecution must prove beyond a reasonable doubt that (1) the principal committed and completed the alleged felony, (2) the defendant had full knowledge of that fact, (3) the defendant failed to notify the authorities, and (4) the defendant took affirmative steps to conceal the crime of the principal.

Security officers may also be liable for failure to perform jobs they have been contracted or employed to perform. If guards fail to act in a situation in which they have the ability and obligation to act, the courts suggest that they could be criminally liable for failure to perform their duties. Another issue in security work involves undercover operations. Many times security operatives are accused of soliciting an illegal act. Where security officers clearly intended for crimes to be committed, they may be charged with solicitation of an illegal act or conspiracy in an illegal act. This is in contrast to the public sector, where most police officers are protected by statute from crimes they commit in the performance of their duty. Thus only the private citizen may be charged with such an offense, and the only issue that can be contested is the defendant's intent.

Entrapment, which is solicitation by police officers, is another charge that may be leveled against security officers. While entrapment does not generally apply to private citizens, (the case of *State v. Farns*[39] is frequently cited to prove that entrapment does not apply to private citizens), several states have passed legislation that extends entrapment statutes to cover private persons as well as police officers. Until the issue is resolved in the courts in the next few years, security officers involved in undercover operations should be careful to avoid actions that might lead to entrapment charges.

The Courts

The process of adjudication varies between civil and criminal courts. The differences occur in that the civil courts have no accused; rather there are plaintiffs and defendants who believe that there is a cause for action rather than a violation of the law. The courts operate on many of the same rules, but the verdict in a civil case is by the preponderance of the evidence rather than by proof beyond a shadow of a doubt.

The Procedure

In the event of an arrest, the accused must by law be taken without unnecessary delay before the nearest judge or magistrate. The court may proceed with the trial in the case of a misdemeanor charge unless the accused demands a jury trial or requests a continuance, and such is ordered by the court. In a civil case, the speed toward a trial is determined by the litigants. This trial, whether civil or criminal and whether held immediately or delayed, is conducted in trial court or a court of primary jurisdiction.

If the charge is a felony, the judge or magistrate conducts a preliminary hearing, an informal process designed to determine if reasonable grounds exist for believing that the accused committed the offense as charged. If such grounds do not appear, the accused will be discharged.

If the judge finds that there are reasonable grounds for believing that the accused may have committed the offense as charged, she will "bind the accused over" for the action of the grand jury. The accused will be held in jail in the interim unless bond is paid, if the offense is bailable.

The grand jury is required by many states to consider the evidence in any felonious matter. Grand juries, usually consisting of 23 citizens of whom 16 constitute a quorum, do not conduct a trial. They hear only the state's evidence. The accused may not be accompanied by an attorney into the hearing room and may not, in most cases, offer evidence in their own behalf. Misdemeanors are not handled by grand jury action but are usually prosecuted on an "information," a document filed by the prosecuting attorney on receipt of a sworn complaint of the victim or a witness or other person who is personally informed about the circumstances of the alleged incident.

For a felony charge, the jury proceedings must result in a vote of at least 12 members for the accused to be indicted, and an indictment must be obtained in those jurisdictions that require it even if it is determined that there is reasonable grounds for prosecution at the preliminary hearing. This procedure was instituted as a constitutional guarantee in federal cases as a safeguard against arbitrary prosecutorial action. Those states that have the same requirement are also motivated to provide protection at the state and municipal level.

If an indictment (also known as a "true bill") is voted, the next step is the appearance of the accused before a judge who is empowered to try felony cases. At this time, the accused is confronted with the charges and is asked to plead. If the plea is guilty, the accused may be sentenced without further court action; if the plea is not guilty, the trial is set for some future date.

The Trial

The Sixth Amendment to the U.S. Constitution states explicitly:

> In all criminal prosecutions, the accused shall enjoy the right to a
> speedy and public trial by an impartial jury of the State and district
> wherein the crime shall have been committed, which district shall have
> been previously ascertained by law, and to be informed of the nature
> and cause of the accusation; to be confronted with the witnesses
> against him; to have compulsory process for obtaining witnesses in his
> favor, and to have assistance of counsel for his defence.

Most states have statutes specifying what constitutes a speedy trial, and the accused must be released and be thereafter immune from prosecution for that offense if not prosecuted within the time and provisions of the statutes. The accused, though entitled to be tried by an impartial jury, may waive that right and be tried by a judge alone. In that case, the judge is solely responsible for matters of fact usually determined by a jury as well as matters of law which the judge would adjudicate at all trials. If the case is heard by a jury, it will determine the validity of the facts presented and ultimately determine whether the accused is guilty as charged or not.

The jury is usually composed of 12 citizens who have as a rule been impanelled by random selection from the voter rolls. It is not constitutionally necessary to have a jury composed of 12 persons and some states have fewer people. In addition in order to broaden the base from which jurors are chosen, some courts have added driver's license and property lists to the voter registration rosters.[40] In determining the jurors who will hear any given case, the prosecuting attorney and the defense attorney will individually question a large panel of prospective jurors. Each attorney has a fixed number of peremptory challenges by which any juror the attorney feels may be unsympathetic may be unseated. After the peremptory challenges are exhausted, either attorney may challenge with cause in which case the judge must agree that the juror in question would not render a fair and impartial judgment before that juror can be dismissed. The purpose of this sometimes lengthy process of selection is to obtain a truly impartial jury that will weigh without prejudice the evidence presented by both the accused and the prosecution.

After the attorneys for both sides have presented their opening statements in which they outline the cases they are about to present, the prosecuting attorney presents the case "for the people." She presents evidence, calls witnesses, and elicits testimony. It is the prosecuting attorney's job to prove a case beyond any reasonable doubt. During this phase of the trial, witnesses are summoned for the purpose of presenting the state's case. The defense counsel may cross-examine but may not at this time initiate a new line of questioning.

After the prosecution has presented all the elements of its case, the defense may ask the court for a directed verdict of not guilty on the grounds that the prosecution has failed to present a case against the accused that would persuade reasonable jurors of the defendent's guilt. If the court is not so persuaded, the defense may present evidence refuting the prosecution's case. The roles are reversed when the defense presents its case in that the prosecution may now cross-examine defense witnesses but it may not present its own witnesses nor may its questions be other than relative to the line of questioning already undertaken by the defense. In cross-examination, opposing attorneys may seek to discredit the witness or they may try to shake the witness's testimony by showing confusion, uncertainty, or bias, but they may not launch into new areas of investigation in their cross-examinations.

The accused is not obliged to testify at any point in the trial pursuant to the protection against being "compelled in any criminal case to be a witness against himself" as guaranteed by the Fifth Amendment. If the accused chooses not to appear, the prosecutor may not comment on that fact to the jury nor in any way suggest that, by making use of this constitutional right, the accused has in some way acknowledged guilt in the matter charged.

After the defense has rested or completed the presentation of its case, the prosecution or plaintiff may rebut the defense case with additional evidence. Usually evidence ends after the prosecution or plaintiff rebuttal. At this point, the defense may again ask for a directed verdict of not guilty based on a number of factors but chiefly on the failure of the prosecution to present a substantial case against the accused.

It is important to stress that the accused are not obliged to defend themselves in any way. It is the burden of the prosecution or plaintiff to present what is known as a prima facie case against the defendant. A prima facie case is one that is proved "on the face of it." It means that the case in itself establishes the probability of guilt or culpability beyond a reasonable doubt in a criminal case or by a preponderance of the evidence in a civil case. Such a case at this point is proved "on the face of it." The defense may then destroy that case by testimony explaining away otherwise damaging evidence. The defense may elect to present no case at all, confident that the jury will not convict on the case the prosecution has presented. In most cases, however, the prosecution or plaintiff has a case, and the defense feels obliged to defend against it.

After both prosecution or plaintiff and defense have rested their cases, they make closing arguments in which they analyze the weaknesses of the opposition and the strengths of their own case in order to sway the jurors to their point of view.

Following the closing arguments, the judge instructs the jury on what points of law may be applicable. It is the jury's function to determine what it believes the facts to be, and it does so in private in the jury room. In most states, the jury must reach a unanimous decision as to the guilt or culpability of the accused. If the jury is unable to arrive at a unanimous decision as to the guilt (culpability) or innocence of the defendant and if the judge is satisfied that its deliberations have explored every possibility of arriving at such a decision and that further deliberation would be fruitless, the judge will dismiss what is referred to as the "hung jury" and declare a mistrial. The prosecution or plaintiff will then determine whether it wishes to bring the case to court again or whether it will drop the charges.

If the jury reaches a verdict of not guilty or no culpability, the defendant will be freed immediately and the matter is forever dismissed. If on the other hand the verdict is that of guilt or culpability, the defendant is then subject to sentence or disposition. In most states, the sentence or dispostion is determined by the judge with the jury functioning to determine the guilt (culpability) or innocence, except in cases dealing with murder or rape. In such cases, most states place the sentencing responsibility on the jury. The jury decides whether the penalty is to be death or imprisonment and even how many years are to be served in prison if that is the penalty.

Appeal

If the accused are convicted in the criminal trial court, they may appeal their cases to higher courts. In a civil case, either party may appeal the results of the court of record. The higher, or appellate, courts usually consist of several judges, together or "en banc," who will consider the appeal from a lower court. In such an appeal, no new evidence or testimony is presented to the court. There is no jury to determine guilt or culpability. The court examines the stenographic record of the trial court and considers the arguments, both written and oral, of defense and prosecution. The court then considers, as a matter of law, whether the trial was properly conducted; whether matters prejudicial to the rights of the accused (plaintiff or defendant) were introduced in the trial proceedings; whether the evidence provided to the jury was legally obtained, properly presented, sufficient for a jury to be entitled to return a guilty verdict or find culpability. Any of a number of errors that might appear in the trial proceedings could be sufficient grounds for overturning the original judgment. On consideration of the matters presented, the reviewing court will render a written decision that either affirms or reverses the trial court's conviction. If the original judgment is affirmed, the decision of the trial court stands; if it is reversed, the conviction is set aside and the accused is freed. If the appellate court rules that the original judgment is "reversed and remanded," it means that the conviction is nullified because of some error in the proceedings, but that the defendant may be tried again by the trial court.

Much of the law or more accurately its interpretation and hence its application comes from the continuing judgments of the courts in cases all over the country. Most of the hundreds of cases heard daily are routine and, however significant they are to the participants, represent no particularly startling legal principle nor any significant upheaval in the day-to-day conduct either of the courts or of the average person. Patterns in jurisprudence emerge, however, and landmark cases that may have routine beginnings do appear.

It is essential for a lawyer to keep up with this flood of information because legal practice is being constantly reshaped by events in courtrooms around the country. Even the casual student with only a sporadic interest in the dynamics of the legal world should have some way of researching areas of immediate concern.

Legal Research

Many sources of information are available to the researcher: legal encyclopedias, dictionaries, legal periodicals, and code books setting forth the statutes. The encyclopedias focus on legal principles and theories along with cases in which such principles predominate. There are also digests that index cases.

Reporters

Perhaps the most useful sources are the bound volumes of reported cases called "reporters" that list the decisions of the appellate court.

These decisions establish the precedents that are the cornerstone of the judicial system. Despite the large amount of available information, legal research is only as effective as the resources in the library or those obtainable through interlibrary loan. Legal research generally involves locating (1) the applicable statute, (2) the applicable case law, and (3) related articles in professional journals. Once the issue has been narrowed, the search for statute law begins. Annotated criminal codes contain not only the statute but also brief notes and citations on court decisions that will be valuable in interpreting legal decisions. Federal statutes related to criminal law are found in *The United States Code Annotated (USCA), Title 18, Crimes and Criminal Procedures.*[41]

Case Reports

In legal writing, cases are frequently cited to show how a legal principle was applied by a court. Each such citation is followed by certain figures and abbreviations that are simply a convenient way to indicate the location of a description of the elements of the case in a reporter. Cases are arranged with volumes for cases in each state. In addition to state reporters, a private publisher (West Publishing, St. Paul, Minnesota) has established what is termed the "national reporter system" in which blocks of states by geographical area are combined in various volumes. For example, appellate decisions from courts in Illinois, Massachusetts, Indiana, Ohio, and New York contained in the *Northeastern Reporter (N.E.). United States Reports* are the official case reports of the United States Supreme Court and contain full transcripts of the majority opinions as well as other concurring or dissenting opinions in the court's cases. The specifics of cases are summarized, and lists of the principals involved are given.

For a certain 1966 wiretapping case in Illinois, the citation is *"People v. Kurth,* 34 Ill. 2d 387, 216 N.E. 2d 154." Translated this means that the decision of the appellate court in the case of *People v.* (versus or against) *Kurth* can be found in the *Illinois Reporter,* second series, volume 34 on page 387; this same decision can be found in volume 216 of the *Northeastern Reporter,* second series, on page 154.

The reported decision indicates the contending parties, a synopsis of the case up to the time it appeared before the reviewing court, the decision of the court, the relevant points of law considered and decided by the court (in the opinion of the legal experts employed by the publisher), the majority opinion, and the minority opinion if there is one included. Other information includes dates, names of justices and contending attorneys, and even citations of the case if it has passed through prior appeals before the current one.

For this wealth of information, the reporters are invaluable aids to any re-search of points of law and of the cases in which they are found.

Digests and Summaries

Another useful set of sources in researching legal issues are the digests and summaries. One of the most helpful is *Shepard's Acts and Cases by Popular Names*,[42] a digest that gives the references and citations necessary to find the legislation or court decisions. Another source is *Corpus Juris Secundum*,[43] an encyclopedic compilation of criminal law based on reported cases. The *Criminal Law Digest*[44] is a one-volume digest of leading court decisions. Each volume is cumulative from 1965 when the digest was first published. The Digest indexes the *Criminal Law Bulletin (CLB)*,[45] which gives specific information on cases. Still another source is the *Criminal Law Reporter*,[46] which has an alphabetical index of cases by subject matter and a straight alphabetical listing.

Once a case has been found, it is easy to find other related cases using *Shepard's Citations*.[47] This publication allows researchers to gather all the case citations that relate to issues in the known case. The legal road is filled with bumps and potholes. There is no easy way to deal with it. Alert security managers will keep abreast of the climate in their jurisdictions and of the latest developments. There are rewards for the knowledgeable professional with an acquaintance with the law and its changes. For the unwary or uncaring, the road can be troublesome indeed.

Liability costs, while remaining relatively high, will continue the downward trend that began in 1986. As was noted earlier, the downward trend may be attributable to better prepared security officers and managers, particularly to security management, which is learning the value of risk management and making good use of proper training.

Review Questions

1. Why is a practical knowledge of the law important to the security officer and the security manager?
2. What impact does tort law have on the private security industry?
3. What makes an arrest different from a detention?
4. What are the major legal differences between public police and private security officers?
5. Why is the legal term *"respondeat superior"* important to the contract security industry?

6. What is the difference between criminal and civil law?
7. The private security industry may enforce criminal law but it is restricted by civil law. How is this possible?

References

1. Michigan Revised Statutes, Section 338.1051–338.1083.
2. Robert D. Pursley, *Introduction to Criminal Justice*, 5th ed. (New York: Macmillan, 1991), p. 35.
3. *U.S. v. Hillsman*, 522 F. 2d 454, 461 (7 Cir. 1975).
4. *Cervantez v. J.C. Penney Company*, 156 Cal. Rptr. 198 (1978).
5. *Illinois Revised Statutes*, 1985, ch. 38, par. 16A-5.
6. 5 Cal. 2d 175, 54 p. 2d 20 (1936).
7. *Escobedo v. State of Illinois*, (378 U.S. 478, 32 Ohio Op 92d) 31, 84 S.Ct. 1758 12 L.Ed(2d)977 (1964).
8. *Miranda v. Arizona*, 384 U.S., 436 86 S.Ct 1602, 16L.Ed.2d.691.
9. In re Deborah C., 1977 Cal. Rptr. 852 (1981).
10. *Wisconsin Statutes Annotated*, Section 943.50.
11. *West Virginia v. William H. Muegge*, 360 SE, 2d. 216 (1987).
12. *People v. Zelinski*, 594 P 2d 1000 (1979).
13. *Mapp v. Ohio*, 367 U.S. 643 (1961).
14. *Weeks v. United States*, 232 U.S. 383 (1914).
15. *Burdeau v. McDowell*, 256 U.S. 465 (1921).
16. *State v. Scrotsky*, 39 NJ 410, 416 189 A.2d 23 (1963).
17. *People v. Jones*, 393 NE 2d. 443 (1979).
18. *People v. Randazzo*, 220 Cal. 2d 268, 34 Cal. Rptr. 65 (1963).
19. *Thacker v. Commonwealth*, 310 Ky. 701, 221 SW 2d 682 (1949).
20. *Weyandt v. Mason Stores, Inc.*, 279 F. Supp. 283, 287 (W.D. Pa. 1968).
21. Charles Schnabolk, *Physical Security: Practices and Technology* (Stoneham, Mass.: Butterworth Publishers, 1983), p. 74.
22. Restatement of Torts, Second Section 307.
23. *Illinois Revised Statutes*, ch. 110, sections 2-116.
24. *Fisher v. Carrousel Motor Hotel, Inc.*, 424 SW2d 627 (Texas 1976).
25. *Klein v. 1500 Massachusetts Avenue Apartment Corporation*, 439 F 2d 477 DC Cir (1970).
26. *Garzilli v. Howard Johnson's Motor Lodge, Inc.*, 419 F Supp. 1210 U.S. DCT EDNY (1976).
27. *Philip Aaron Banks, et al. v. Hyatt Corporation and Refco Poydras Hotel Joint Venture*, 722 F.2d. 214 (1984); and *Allen B. Morrison, et al. v. MGM Grand Hotel, et al.*, 570 F. Supp. 1449 (1983).
28. *McCarthy v. Pheasant Run, Inc.*, F.2d 1554 (1987).
29. *Sharpe v. Peter Pan Bus Lines*, No. 49694, Suffolk County, MA.

30. *Nelson v. Church's Fried Chicken*, 31 ATLA L. Rep 84 (1987).

31. *Galloway v. Bankers Trust Company and Trustee Midlands Mall*, No. 63/86-1879 Iowa Supreme Court (1988).

32. *Polly Suzanne Paterson v. Kent C. Deeb, Transamerica Insurance Co., W. Fenton Langston, and Hartford Accident & Indemnity Co.*, 472 S. 2d 1210.

33. *Dupree v. Piggly Wiggly Shop Rite Foods Inc.*, 542 S.W. 2d 882 (Texas 1976).

34. William L. Prosser, *Handbook of the Law of Torts* 4th ed., Hornbook Series (St. Paul, Minn.: West, 1970), p. 458.

35. *Graalum v. Radisson Ramp*, 245 Minn. 54, 71 NW 2d 904, 908 (1955).

36. *Fornier v. Churchill Downs-Latonia*, 292 Ky. 215, 166 SW 2d 38 (1942).

37. *Hayes v. Sears, Roebuck Co.*, 209 P. 2d 468, 478 (1949).

38. James S. Kakalik and Sorrel Wildhurn, *The Private Police* (New York: Crane, Russak & Co., 1977).

39. *State v. Farns*, 542 P.2d 725 Kan. (1975).

40. David Neubauer, *America's Courts and the Criminal Justice System* (Pacific Grove, Calif.: Brooks/Cole, 1988).

41. *U.S. Code Annotated, Title 18 Crimes and Procedures* (St. Paul: West), 50 vols, updated annually.

42. *Shepard's Acts and Cases by Popular Names* (Colorado Springs, Col.: Shepard's/McGraw-Hill), updated annually.

43. *Corpus Juris Secundum* (New York: American Law Book Co.), 101 vols, updated annually.

44. James A. Douglas and Donald S. Benton, *Criminal Law Digest* (Boston: Warren, Gorham & Lamont), updated annually.

45. *Criminal Law Bulletin* is published by Warren, Gorham & Lamont, Boston.

46. *Criminal Law Reporter* is published by the U.S. Bureau of National Affairs, Washington, D.C.

47. *Shepard's Citations* (Colorado Springs, Col.: Shepard's/McGraw-Hill), updated annually.

PART

III

Basics of Defense

7

□ □ □
□ □ □
□ □ □

Risk Analysis and the Security Survey

Once security goals and responsibilities have been defined and an organization has been created to carry them out, the ongoing task of security management is to identify potential areas of loss and to develop and install appropriate security countermeasures. This process of study is called "risk analysis." Implicit in this approach is the concept of security as a comprehensive, integrated function of the organization. One part of this comprehensive, integrated job is the security survey, which is used to identify potential problem areas. More will be said about the survey later in this chapter.

This comprehensive view of the loss prevention function might be contrasted with more limited security responses such as:

- *One-dimensional security*, which relies on a single deterrent, such as guards
- *Piecemeal security* in which ingredients are added to the loss-prevention function piece-by-piece as the need arises without a comprehensive plan
- *Reactive security*, which responds only to specific loss events
- *Packaged security*, which installs standard security systems (equipment, personnel, or both), without relation to specific threats, either because "everybody's doing it" or on the theory that packaged systems will take care of any problems that might arise. This is akin to prescribing a remedy without diagnosing the illness—like a broad-spectrum antibiotic that will kill any virus the patient may have.

An integrated or systems approach to security is not always the desired solution. A small business, particularly one with minimal loss potential or relative ease of defense, might adequately be served (as many are) by a good lock on the door and an alarm system or by a contract guard patrol. But as the areas of loss increase and become more complex and as the ability to protect a growing company against those losses with one dimensional responses decreases, it becomes increasingly necessary to adopt a more comprehensive security program. If security is not to be one-dimensional, piecemeal, reactive, or prepackaged, it must be based on analysis of the total risk potential. In order to set up defenses against losses from crime, accidents, or natural disasters in other words, there must first be a means of identification and evaluation of the risks.

Risk Management

The first step in risk analysis involves recognizing the threats. It costs a company great sums of money to erect buildings and protect assets and personnel. But compared to putting money into research and development, which is investing in the companies' future, putting money into preventing a loss is only spending money to prevent something undesirable from happening. Although both investments involve risks, spending money on a product is dynamic and speculative and thus is a more interesting risk to take. Risks to property are generally overlooked or considered a necessary evil. Even when the risk is recognized, managers prefer to operate under the calculated risk theory. What is often overlooked in this process is the word "risk." Recently, however, businesses have been forced to come to terms with the potential consequences of taking security risks. The two alternative solutions, which should be complementary, are: (1) investment in loss-prevention techniques and (2) insurance.

Today the progressive manager recognizes that property risks are formidable and that they must be managed. Risk management may thus be defined as making the most efficient before-the-loss arrangement for an after-the-loss continuation of business. As a consequence, good insurance programs and security or loss-prevention programs are in demand. The concept of *risk management* presents a sensible approach to this complicated problem: It allows risks to be handled in a logical manner, using long-held management principles. Insurance in and of itself is no longer able to meet the security challenges faced by major corporations. To meet this challenge, insurance companies have found loss-prevention techniques and programs invaluable. A good risk management program involves four basic steps:

1. Identification of risks or specific vulnerabilities
2. Analysis and study of risks, which includes the likelihood and degree of danger of an event
3. Optimization of risk management alternatives
   a. Risk avoidance
   b. Risk reduction
   c. Risk spreading

    d. Risk transfer

    e. Self-assumption of risk

    f. Any combination of the above

  4. Ongoing study of security programs

The approach must be total; there can be no shortcuts.

Threat Assessment

    The first step in risk analysis is identifying the threats and vulnerabilities. Many threats to business are important to security, but some are more obvious than others. The key is to consider the specific vulnerabilities in a given situation. Each individual firm has problems and threats that are unique. For example, a retailing company may be less concerned about fire hazards than is a manufacturing firm that operates a foundry. A retailer will be concerned with shoplifting while a manufacturer of horseshoes may not be concerned about this problem if the horseshoes are not sold directly to the public. Employee theft, on the other hand, may be a big problem. Today it appears that drug use and abuse may be a problem found to some extent in all organizations. More will be presented on these and other topics in later chapters.

    Specific threats are not always obvious. Although it seems to be common sense to check doors, locks, and gates to control access, accessibility through walls made of inferior materials or through a poorly constructed door or door frame is a less obvious consideration. Awareness of all the possibilities is the mark of a good security manager. The best manager can think like a thief and thus is able to consider policies to reduce the vulnerability of company property. Therefore a manager must develop the ability to analyze vulnerabilities. A thorough analysis is comprehensive and accurate and leads to effective countermeasures. Once it has been completed, a vulnerability analysis—also called a security survey or audit—should be repeated on a regular basis.

The Security Survey

    In the process of risk analysis that proceeds from threat assessment (identifying risk) to threat evaluation (determining the criticality and dollar cost of that risk) to the selection of security countermeasures designed to contain or prevent that risk, one of management's most valuable tools is the security survey (see Table 7.1).

    A security survey is essentially an exhaustive physical examination of the premises and a thorough inspection of all operational systems and procedures. Such an examination or survey has as its overall objective the anal-

Table 7.1 Security Vulnerability Survey

Facility _____   Survey date _____
Address _____   Facility manager _____
                                     Telephone no. _____

I. GENERAL FUNCTION   Leased
                           Owned
_____

No. employees assnd. _____

Operating Hours:	Weekdays	Saturday	Sunday
	Opens _____	Opens _____	Opens _____
	Closes _____	Closes _____	Closes _____

Address & phone of police jurisdiction: _____

Area evaluation: _____

II. BUILDING & PERIMETER

____ 1. Type of construction?

____ 2. Door construction (hinges, hinge pins, solid core, etc.)?

____ 3. Total number of perimeter entrances?

____ 4. Are all exits & entrances supervised?
        If not, how controlled?

____ 5. Are there perimeter fences?
        Type?
        Height?
        Distance from bldg.?
        Cleared areas?
        Barbed wire top?
        Roof or wall areas close to fence?

____ 6. Are there any overpasses or subterranean passageways?

____ 7. Height of windows from ground?
        Adequately protected?

____ 8. Any roof openings or entries?

____ 9. Any floor grates, ventilation openings?

____ 10. Any materials stored outside bldg.?
         How controlled?

____ 11. Adjacent occupancy?

        Comments:

III. VEHICULAR MOVEMENT

____ 1. Is employee parking within perimeter fence?

____ 2. Are cars parked abutting interior fences?

____ 3. Are cars parked adjacent to loading docks, bldg. entrances, etc.?

____ 4. Do employees have access to cars during work hours?

____ 5. Vehicle passes or decals?

____ 6. Are guards involved in traffic control?

        Comments.

IV. LIGHTING

____ 1. Is perimeter lighting provided?
        Adequate?

____ 2. Is there an emergency lighting system?

____ 3. Are all doorways sufficiently lighted?

____ 4. Is lighting in use during all night hours?

____ 5. Is lighting directed toward perimeter?

____ 6. Is lighting adequate for parking area?

____ 7. How is lighting checked?

____ 8. Is interior night lighting adequate for surveillance by night guards (or by municipal law enforcement agents)?

____ 9. Are guard posts properly illuminated?

        Comments:

V. LOCKING CONTROLS

____ 1. Does the facility have adequate control and records for all keys?

____ 2. Is a master key system in use?

____ 3. How many master keys are issued?

____ 4. Are all extra keys secured in a locked container?

____ 5. Total number of safes?

____ 6. Last time combination(s) changed?

____ 7. If combination is recorded, where is it stored?

____ 8. Total number of employees possessing combination?

____ 9. Review procedures for securing sensitive items, i.e., monies, precious metals, high dollar value items, narcotics, etc.?

____ 10. Who performs locksmithing function for the facility?

____ 11. Is a key inventory periodically taken?

____ 12. Are locks changed when keys are lost?

        Comments:

VI. ALARMS

____ 1. Does this facility utilize any alarm devices?
        Total number of alarms?

Type	Location	Manufacturer	Remarks

____ 2. Are alarms of central station type connected to police department or outside guard service?

____ 3. Is authorization list of personnel authorized to "open & close" alarmed premises up to date?

____ 4. Are local alarms used on exit doors?

____ 5. Review procedure established on receipt of alarm?

____ 6. Is closed circuit TV utilized?

        Comments:

VII. GUARDS/SECURITY CONTROLS

____ 1. Is a guard service employed to protect this facility?

        If yes. Name: _____ No. of guards ____ No. of posts ____

____ 2. Are after hours security checks conducted to assure proper storage of classified reports, key controls, monies, checks, etc.?

____ 3. Is a property pass system utilized?

____ 4. Are items of company property clearly identified with a distinguishing mark that cannot be removed?

____ 5. Review guard patrols & frequency?

____ 6. Are yard areas and perimeter areas included in guard coverage?

_____ 7. Are all guard tours recorded?

_____ 8. Are package controls exercised re packages brought on or off premises?

_____ 9. Does facility have written instructions for guards?

_____ 10. What type of training do guards receive?

_____ 11. Are personnel last leaving building charged with checking doors, windows, cabinets, etc.?
Record of identity?

_____ 12. Are adequate security procedures followed during lunch hours?

Comments:

VIII. EMPLOYEE AND VISITOR CONTROLS

_____ 1. Is a daily visitors register maintained?

_____ 2. Is there a control to prevent visitors from wandering in the plant?

_____ 3. Do employees use identification badge?

_____ 4. Are visitors issued identification passes?

_____ 5. What type of visitors are on premises during down hours and weekends?

_____ 6. Does any company's employees other than _____ have access to facility?
List Company Names   Type Service Performed

_____ 7. Are controls over temporary help adequate?

Comments:

IX. PRODUCT CONTROLS (Shipping and Receiving)

_____ 1. Are all thefts or shortages or other possible problems, i.e., anonymous letters, crank calls, etc. reported immediately?

_____ 2. Inspect and review controls for shipping area.

_____ 3. Inspect and review controls for receiving area.

_____ 4. Supervision in attendance at all times?

_____ 5. Are truck drivers allowed to wander about the area?
Is there a waiting area segregated from product area?
Are there toilet facilities nearby?
Water cooler?
Pay telephone?

_____ 6. Are shipping or receiving doors used by employees to enter or leave facility?

_____ 7. What protection is afforded loaded trucks awaiting shipment?

_____ 8. Are all trailers secured by seals?

_____ 9. Are seal numbers checked for correctness against shipping papers? "In" and "Out"

_____ 10. Are kingpin locks utilized on trailers?

_____ 11. Is a separate storage location utilized for overages, shortages, damages?

_____ 12. Is parking (employees and visitor vehicles) prohibited from areas adjacent to loading docks or emergency exit doors?

_____ 13. Is any material stored in exterior of building?
If so how protected?

_____ 14. Are trailers or shipments received after closing hours?
If so how protected?

_____ 15. Are all loaded trucks or trailers parked within fenced area?

_____ 16. Review facility's product inventory control.
Loss   Breakage   Returns

Average
Monthly

_____ 17. Review controls over breakage.

Comments:

X. MONEY CONTROLS

_____ 1. How much cash in maintained on the premises?

_____ 2. What is the location and type of repository?

_____ 3. Review cashier function.

_____ 4. What protective measures are taken for money deliveries to facility?
To bank?

_____ 5. If armored car service utilized, list name and address.

_____

_____ 6. Does facility have procedure to control cashing of personal checks?

_____ 7. Are checks immediately stamped with restricted endorsement?

_____ 8. Are employee payroll checks properly accounted for and stored in a locked container (including lunch hours) until distributed to the employee or his supervisor?

Comments:

XI. PROPRIETARY INFORMATION

_____ 1. What type of proprietary information is possessed at this facility?

_____ 2. How is it protected?

_____ 3. Is "_____ Restricted" marking used?

_____ 4. Are safeguards followed for paper waste, its collection and destruction?

_____ 5. Are desk and cabinet tops cleared at end of day?

_____ 6. Is management aware of need for protecting proprietary information?

Comments:

XII. OTHER VULNERABILITIES

_____ 1. Trash pick ups. (Hours of pick ups, control of contractor, physical controls).

_____ 2. Scrap operations. (Physical controls of material and area, control over scrap pick ups, etc.).

_____ 3. Other.

Comments:

XIII. PERSONNEL SECURITY

_____ 1. Are background investigations conducted on employees handling products?
Handling cash?
Engaged in other sensitive duties?
Supervisory position?
All employees?

_____ 2. If so, who conducts background investigation?

_____ 3. Are new employees given any security or other type of orientation?

_____ 4. Do newly hired employees execute a corporate briefing form for inclusion in their personnel file?

_____ 5. Are exit interviews conducted of terminating employees?

_____ 6. Is a program followed to insure return of keys, credit cards, I.D. cards, manuals, and other company property?

GENERAL COMMENTS

From Charles A. Sennewold, *Effective Security Management* (Los Angeles: Security World Publishing, 1978).

ysis of a facility to determine the existing state of its security, to locate weaknesses in its defenses, to determine the degree of protection required, and ultimately to lead to recommendations for establishing a total security program.

Motivation setting the survey in motion should come from top management to insure that adequate funds for the undertaking are available and to guarantee the cooperation of all personnel in the facility. Since a thorough survey will require an examination of procedures and routines in regular operation and an inspection of the physical plant and its environs, management's interest in the project is of the highest priority.

The survey may be conducted by staff security personnel or by qualified security specialists employed for this purpose. Some experts suggest that outside security people could approach the job with more objectivity and would have less of a tendency to take certain areas or practices for granted, thus providing a more complete appraisal of existing conditions.

Whoever undertakes the survey should have training in the field and should also have achieved a high level of ability. It is also important that at least some members of the survey team be totally familiar with the facility and its operation. Without such familiarity, it would be difficult to formulate the survey plan, and the survey itself must be planned in advance to make the best use of personnel and to study the operation in every phase.

Part of the plan may come from previous studies and recommendations. These should be studied for any useful information they might offer. Another part of the survey plan will include a checklist made up by the survey team in preparation for the actual inspection. This list will serve as a guide and reminder of areas that must be examined and, once it has been drawn up, it should be followed systematically. In the event that some area or procedure has been omitted in the preparation of the original checklist, it should be included in the inspection and its disposition noted in the evaluation and recommendation.

Since no two facilities are alike—not even those in the same business— no checklist exists that could universally apply for survey purposes. The following discussion is intended only to indicate those areas where a risk may exist. It should be considered as merely a guide to the kinds of questions or specific problems that might be dealt with.

The Facility

When analyzing security risks, the security manager should look at a number of aspects of the company, giving consideration as potential security problems to:

- The perimeter. Check fencing, gates, culverts, drains, lighting (including standby lights and power), and overhangs and concealing areas. Can vehicles drive up to the fence?
- The parking lot. Are employees' automobiles adequately protected from theft or vandalism? How? Is the lot sufficiently isolated from the plant or office to prevent unsupervised back-and-forth traffic? Are there gates or turnstiles for the inspection of traffic, if that is necessary? Are these inspection points properly lighted? Can packages be thrown over or pushed through the fence into or out of the parking lot?
- All adjacent building windows and roof tops. Are spaces near these adjacencies accessible to them? Are they properly secured? How?
- All doors and windows less than 18 feet above ground level. How are these openings secured?
- The roof. What means are employed to prevent access of the roof?
- The issuance of main entrance keys to all tenants in a building. How often are entrance locks changed? What is building procedure when keys are lost or not returned? How many tenants are in the building? What businesses are they in?
- Any shared occupancy, as in office buildings. Does the building have a properly supervised sign-in log for off-hours? Do elevators switch to manual, and can floors be locked against access outside of business hours? When are they so switched? By whom can they then be operated? Who collects the trash, and how and when is it removed from the building? Are lobbies and hallways adequately lighted? What guard protection does the building have? How can guards be reached? Are washrooms open to the public? Are equipment rooms locked? Is a master key system in use? How are keys controlled and secured? Is there a receptionist or guard in the lobby? Can the building be accessed by stair or elevator from basement parking facilities?
- All areas containing valuables. Do safes, vaults, or rooms containing valuables have adequate alarms? What alarms are in place to protect against burglary, fire, robbery, or surreptitious entry?
- The off-hours when the facility is not in operation and all nighttime hours. How many guards are on duty at various times of day? Are guards alert and efficient? How are guards equipped? How many patrols are there, and how often do they make their rounds? What is their tour? What is the guard communication system?
- The control and supervision of entry into the facility. What method is used to identify employees? How are applicants screened before they are employed? How are visitors (including salespeople, vendors, and customers) controlled? How are privately owned vehicles controlled? Who delivers the morning mail and when? How are empty mail sacks han-

dled? Do you authorize salespeople or solicitors for charity in the facility? How are they controlled? Are their credentials checked? Who does the cleaning? Do they have keys? Who is responsible for these keys? Are they bonded? Who does maintenance or service work? Are their tool boxes inspected when they leave? Are their credentials checked? By whom? Are alarm and telephone company people allowed unlimited access? Is the call for their service verified? By whom? How is furniture or equipment moved in or out? What security is provided when this takes place at night or on weekends? Are messengers permitted to deliver directly to the addressee? How are they controlled? Which areas have the heaviest traffic? Are visitors claiming official status, such as building or fire inspectors, permitted free access? Are their credentials checked? By whom?

- Keys and key control. Are keys properly secured when they are not in use? Are locks replaced or recorded when a key is lost? Are locks and locking devices adequate for their purpose? Are all keys accounted for and logged? What system is used for the control of master and submaster keys?
- Fire. Are there sufficient fire boxes throughout the facility? Are they properly located? Is the type and number of fire extinguishers adequate? Are they frequently inspected? How far is the nearest public fire department? Have they ever been invited to inspect the facility? Does the building have automatic sprinklers and automatic fire alarms? Are there adequate fire barriers in the building? Is there an employee fire brigade? Are fire doors adequate? Are "no smoking" signs enforced? Are flammable substances properly stored? Is there a program of fire prevention education? Are fire drills conducted on a regular basis?
- Computer access. What is the potential for loss of equipment? Which services will be denied if the computer is inoperable? What information is stored in the computer that could cause the organization loss of profits if it was compromised?

For all its seeming length, this list contains only a sample of the kinds of questions that must be asked when conducting a survey of any facility. The list is only a general overview of some of the aspects to be covered.

General Departmental Evaluations

Each department in the organization should be evaluated separately in terms of its potential for loss. These departmental evaluations will eventually be consolidated into the master survey for final recommendations and action. Basic questions might be:

- Is the departmental function such that it is vulnerable to embezzlement?
- Does the department have cash funds or negotiable instruments on hand?
- Does the department house confidential records?
- What equipment, tools, supplies, or merchandise can be stolen from the department?
- Does the department have heavy external and/or internal traffic?
- Does the department have target items in it such as drugs, jewelry, or furs? What is the special fire hazard in the department or from adjacent areas?

These are questions that may serve to guide the survey in focusing on particular areas of risk in each department examined. Where particular risks predominate, special attention must be paid to providing some counteraction to remove them.

Personnel Department

Particular security problems are associated with personnel departments. Such concerns include:

- Can the department area be locked off from the rest of the floor and/or building after hours?
- How are door and file keys secured?
- Are files kept locked during the day when they are not in use?
- What system is followed with regard to the payroll department when employees are hired or terminated?
- What are the relationships between personnel and payroll staff?
- What are the employment procedures? How are applicants screened?
- How closely does personnel work with security on personnel employment procedures?
- Are new employees given a security briefing? By whom?
- Does the company have an incident reporting system? Are employees aware of the program? Does the company have a followup security awareness training program?

Security of personnel files is of extreme importance. Normally these files contain information on every employee, past and present, from the president on down. This information is highly confidential and must be handled that way. There can be no exceptions to this firm policy.

Accounting

The accounting department has total supervision over the firm's money and will generally be the area most vulnerable to major loss due to crime. Certainly protective systems have been in operation in this area from the company's founding, but these systems must be reevaluated regularly in light of ongoing experience to find ways of improving both their efficiency and security.

Cashier

Considerations relevant to the cashier's function include:

- How accessible is the cash operation to hallways, stairs, and elevators?
- Do posted signs clearly announce the location and operating hours of the cashier?
- Is there generally sufficient cash on hand to invite an employee to abscond with it? To attract an attempted burglary or armed robbery?
- What are the present systems of audit and controls? What forms are used?
- What are the controls put on cashier embezzlement?
- What are the opportunities for collusion in this operation?
- Is the security adequate to the risk?
- Is the cashier's office equipped with a hold-up alarm? Bullet proof glazing? Other physical protection? Hold-up instructions?

Accounts Receivable

In evaluating the frauds to which accounts receivable is vulnerable, it will be necessary to consider from experience all the possibilities and in this light to examine every step of the procedures currently in operation from billing advice through billing to crediting the account. All flow of information and action documents must be studied minutely to find if any flaw or weakness could be exploited for criminal purposes.

- Consider the billing procedure with particular attention to the forms used and the authorizations required.
- Try to determine how difficult it might be to cash a check payable to the company.
- What are the opportunities for destroying billing records and for keeping and cashing a check?
- What are the possibilities of altering invoices to show a lesser amount payable?

Accounts Payable

Accounts payable as a disbursing entity invites more attention from thieves than do most other areas. It is particularly susceptible to internal attack in a number of ways. The most common is the dummy invoice by which forged authorizations permit payment to a nonexistent account. This is relatively easy to overcome, however, by an alert staff working within a system that provides reasonable security.

- Examine all forms and systems on a step-by-step basis.
- How is the authenticity of new accounts established?

Payroll

Questions that need to be considered in relation to the payroll system include:

- What system is used to introduce a new employee into the payroll?
- Do the records in personnel and in payroll correspond? Are these cross-checked? How? By whom?
- Could an employee in personnel conspire with an employee in payroll to introduce fictitious employees into the records? What would prevent this?

Company Bank Accounts

Considerations relevant to company bank accounts are:

- Can one person transfer unlimited funds?
- Is there a ceiling limiting withdrawal of company funds?
- What instructions have been given to the bank? By whom? Who can change these instructions?
- Who audits company bank accounts? How often?
- Could the treasurer or controller leave with the company bank account?

It is well to remember here, especially when it appears that questions concerning the probity of company officers are posed, that the job of the security survey is not to make judgments on whether a criminal act is likely to occur but rather on whether it could. A survey of this nature in no way implies that treasurers are apt or in any way inclined to abscond with company funds. It simply asks whether the procedures are such that they could. If the survey finds this possible, the recommendation would surely suggest that safeguards such as countersignatures be set up so that current or future treasurers could not perform what they very likely would not perform in any event.

Data Processing

Computer-related security problems are becoming more important as companies increase their use of electronic data processing. In fact, it is rare for companies to have no major computer operations in today's competitive environment. The security manager should consider:

- Are adequate auditing procedures in effect on all programs?
- How are printouts of confidential information handled?
- What is the off-site storage procedure? How are such tapes updated?
- What is the system governing program access?
- How is computer use logged? How is the accuracy of this record verified?
- Who has keys to the computer spaces? How often is the list of authorized key holders evaluated?
- What controls are exercised over access? How often is the list of those authorized to enter updated?
- What fire prevention and fire protection procedures are in effect? What training is given employees in fire prevention and protection? What is the number, location, and condition of fire extinguishers and the basic extinguishing system?
- Is there off-site backup hardware? How is it secured?

Purchasing

This is an area subject to many temptations. Graft is often freely offered in the form of cash, expensive gifts, lavish entertainment, and luxurious vacations—all in the name of seeking the good will of the purchasing agent. Generally speaking, this is not a security matter unless the agent succumbs to the extent of paying for goods never delivered or paying invoices twice. If all the attention from vendors causes a purchasing agent to buy unwisely, that is a management concern in which security plays no role.

There are, however, some areas in the purchasing function in which security might be involved.

- What are the procedures preventing double payment of invoices? Fraudulent invoices? Invoices for goods never received? How often is this area audited?
- Are competitive bids invited for all purchases? Must the lowest bid be awarded the contract?
- What forms are used for ordering? For authorizing payment? How are they routed?

- Since purchasing is frequently responsible for the sale of scrap, waste paper, and other recoverable items, who verifies the amount actually trucked away? Who negotiates the sale of waste or scrap material? Are several prospective buyers invited to bid? How is old equipment or furniture sold? What records are kept of such sales? Is the system audited? What controls are placed on the authority of the seller?

Shipping and Receiving

Freight and merchandise handling areas are particularly troublesome as there is a great potential for theft in these areas. Close attention must be paid to current operations and efforts must continually be directed to their improvement.

- What inspections are made of employees entering or leaving such areas?
- How is traffic in and to such areas controlled? Are these areas separated from the rest of the facility by a fence or barrier?
- Where is merchandise stored after receipt or before shipment? What is the security of such areas? What is the nature of supervision in these areas?
- What is the system for accountability of shipments and receipts?
- Is the area guarded?
- What losses are being experienced in these areas? What is the profile of such loss (type, average amount, time of day)?
- Is merchandise left unattended in these areas?
- Are truck drivers provided with restroom facilities separate from those of dock personnel? Are they isolated from them at all times to prevent collusion?
- How many people are authorized in security storage areas, and who are they?

Miscellaneous

Other general security concerns include:

- What records are kept of postage meter usage? What controls are established over meter usage?
- How is the use of supplies and materials controlled?
- How are forms controlled?

Report of the Survey

After the survey has documented the full scope of its examination, a report should be prepared indicating those areas that are weak in security and recommending measures that might reasonably bring the security of the facility up to acceptable standards. On the basis of the status in the survey and considering the recommendations made, a security plan can now be drawn up.

In some cases, compromises may have to be made. The siting of the facility or the area involved, for example, may make an ideal security program with full coverage of all contingencies too costly to be practical. In such cases, the plan must be restudied to find the best approach for achieving acceptable security standards within these limitations.

It must be understood that security directors will rarely get all of what they want. As in every department, they must work within the framework of the possible. Where they are denied extra personnel, they must find hardware that will help to replace people. Where a request for more coverage by closed circuit television (CCTV) is turned down, they must develop inspection procedures or barriers that may serve a similar purpose. If at any point they feel that security costs have been cut to a point where the stated objective cannot be achieved, they are obliged to communicate that opinion to management who will then determine whether to diminish the original objective or to authorize more money. It is important, however, that security directors exhaust every alternative method of coverage before going to management with an opinion that requires this kind of decision.

Operational Audits and Programmed Supervision

The mechanism by which the security survey is administered is as important as is the survey form itself. A security survey may focus on physical security measures or procedures and is conducted on a periodic basis; an operational audit considers all aspects of the security operation on a continuing basis. The operational audit (OA) is a methodical examination, or audit, of operations. The purpose of the examination is threefold: (1) to find deviations from established security standards and practices, (2) to find loopholes in security controls, and (3) to consider means of improving the efficiency or control of the operation without reducing security.

Because the audit is an ongoing process achieved through program supervision, it is relatively inexpensive. An OA is based on the concept of programmed supervision without which the audit would become nothing more than a simple security survey. Programmed supervision (PS) is a means of making sure that a supervisor or other employees go through a prescribed series of inspections that will ascertain that functions or procedures for which they are responsible are being properly executed. Supervisors are thus conducting OAs by evaluating their areas of responsibility on an ongoing basis. A truly successful OA requires the supervisor to make the necessary inspection and to record specific recheckable findings, not just to record a simple checkmark as "yes" or "no". For example, a supervisor in a loading dock area should be required to check all steps in the shipping/receiving area. Where are truck drivers authorized to be during the loading/unloading of the truck? What procedures are followed to determine that the load count is accurate? How are broken parcels handled? The supervisor must answer each of these questions carefully and fully. As noted, the supervisor cannot simply respond with a "yes" or "no". The aggregate of several area OAs results in a divisional OA, and divisional OAs considered in aggregate are an entire company's OA.

The OA should be distinguished from its simpler sister, the security survey. A security survey begins by developing a checklist of items that the security team feels are important. For example: Are there adequate locks, alarms, and guard patrols? Do security breaches (that is, doors and windows) have adequate protection, and are they built of substantial materials? Although some security surveys involve a check of procedures, many do not. For example, it would be wise to ensure that check-in procedures at the warehouse are being followed.

The OA builds on the security survey. For many operations, a security survey may be conducted once a year, or even less frequently. The OA, however, is conducted regularly and frequently. Once the OA begins, it continues until someone in a position of authority decides that it is no longer necessary. The audit, through the process of PS, requires that supervisors regularly report whether procedures are being followed and if those procedures are adequate. Some procedures might need to be amended as the work changes to meet new demands. The OA also requires supervisors to report physical conditions regularly (such as whether the doors are locked regularly as specified).

While the security survey is better than nothing, the OA goes beyond an occasional survey. The security survey relies heavily on either the proprietary security force or on a contractor. The OA uses the management resources of the company.

Using the information gained from vulnerability analysis, security surveys, and OAs, the security manager can develop a comprehensive security plan.

Probability

Once vulnerabilities have been identified through the use of the security survey or OA, it is essential to determine the probability of loss. For example, suppose that one vulnerability involves the theft of trade secrets. Within the area of trade secrets, subcategories of vulnerabilities are identified, including the loss of information from research and development through employee turnover or negligence. Should security dollars be spent to reduce the potential for such a loss? It is not possible to say until the probability has been assessed. Will a loss certainly occur if nothing is changed, or is the occurrence improbable? When security managers are confronted with a series of problems, they must determine which problems need immediate attention. Probability is a mathematical statement concerning the possibility of an event occurring. Is it possible to reduce security risks to a mathematical equation that can be used to determine probability? Unfortunately such mathematical precision must wait until various subjective security measures can be turned into numerical values. This has not yet occurred.

The best that can be done today is to make subjective decisions about probability. Such decisions should be based on data like the physical aspects of the vulnerability being studied—for example, spatial relationships, location, and composition of the structure. Procedural considerations must also be studied. What policies exist? The history associated with the industry is of great importance, particularly the vulnerability being studied. Has the product been a target before? What is the current state of the art of thieving? Later in this book various physical security devices will be discussed. Each has its advantages, but the reality is that criminals, depending on their own education and level of determination, may find methods of overcoming each security device. How aware are potential thieves of the technology to defeat existing security devices?

Criticality

Probability cannot stand alone when the security manager analyzes which security problem to address first. For example, a certainty that someone will steal money from the company cafeteria may not warrant attention as immediate as the possibility that someone might tamper with the software used to maintain company inventory, purchasing, and order information even when the probability of such tampering is only moderately probable. To help separate the vulnerabilities into still finer categories, security managers use the principle of criticality. The term has been defined to mean the impact of a loss as measured in dollars. The concept has also been expanded to include how important the area, practice, or whatever is to the existence of the organization. The dollar loss is not simply the cost of the items lost, but also includes:

1. Replacement cost
2. Temporary replacement
3. "Down time"
4. Discounted cash
5. Insurance rate changes
6. Loss of marketplace advantage

Criticality is an extremely important concept for security managers to understand. In general, company executives who usually think in terms of cost-benefit analysis will not be interested in spending money for security if the cost is greater than the potential loss of money. Unfortunately, many security directors fail to explain that criticality is far more than just the direct cost of the items lost. Replacement costs include the new purchase price, the costs of delivery, installation costs, any additional materials needed during the installation, and other indirect costs.

A second major cost may be temporary replacement. Consider an attack on an electronic data processing (EDP) unit. If the main computer is damaged by sabotage or fire, the company will most likely need to process its data by leasing EDP equipment or through a time-sharing arrangement with a computer firm or another company. The cost of these temporary measures should be taken into consideration.

A third possible cost is "down time," the cost associated with not being able to continue business while the computer is inoperable. One possible cost in this category, depending on various company policies and union contracts, may be the wages for employees who are idled.

A fourth cost factor, discounted cash, is money lost when invested funds must be withdrawn from time certificates or other investments to pay for any of the above costs. For example, consider the loss of income on a $10,000 certificate of deposit, held at 12.9 percent interest, if the certificate is cashed early to pay delivery and installation costs.

A fifth cost involves the possible increase in insurance premiums associated with loss problems. Insurance rates will increase as losses go up.

Yet a sixth cost is the potential loss of marketplace advantage created by the loss of product markets due to sabatoge, work slowdowns, and so forth. If the product is not available when consumers want to buy it, they will turn to alternatives. In some cases, they will stay with the competitor's product.

All six factors need to be added into the criticality cost. Many security managers are surprised to find that the criticality cost can be double the cost of an item. Likewise company managers often fail to consider these indirect costs.

The Probability/Criticality/ Vulnerability Matrix

Criticality, much like probability, is a subjective measure, but it can be placed on a continuum. Consider the continuum for criticality and probability in Table 7.2.

By using the rankings generated for probability and criticality and by devising a matrix system for the various vulnerabilities, it is possible to quantify security risks somewhat and to determine which vulnerabilities merit immediate attention. Although some areas of importance may be obvious, some security executives may be surprised to find that other areas are more critical than they first surmised. For example, consider the cash theft vulnerability matrix shown in Table 7.3. Cash theft has been chosen since it is simple to calculate criticality costs for it. By considering the gross sales of the firm and its current assets, the impact of the loss of cash from each of the areas listed can be determined. In addition by considering the history of loss and the number and quality of security devices present, it is possible to estimate the probability of a cash theft. Using the system presented in Table 7.2, alphabetical and numerical values can be assigned to each vulnerability area. For example, the manager's office might be categorized as A4, which indicates that the loss of $200,000 in a company with total current assets of $300,000 could be "fatal" and that the probability of the loss occurring is "probable" based on the amount of money tempting the thief and the level of security present. Each area may be classified in the same fashion. Then it is usually possible to rank the importance of attacking each area using criticality as the most important variable. For example: A1, A5, B3, B4, C1, D4, E2. See Table 7.4. The only exception to this order of ranking occurs in the cases of F (criticality unknown) and 6 (probability unknown). If the security director cannot assign a probability or criticality to a certain item, the criti-

Table 7.2   The Probability/Criticality Matrix

Probability	*Criticality*
1. Virtually certain	A. Fatal
2. Highly probable	B. Very serious
3. Moderately probable	C. Moderately serious
4. Probable	D. Serious
5. Improbable	E. Relatively unimportant
6. Probability unknown	F. Criticality unknown

Adapted from Richard J. Healy and Timothy J. Walsh, *Industrial Security Management* (New York: American Management Association, 1971), p. 17.

Table 7.3 Cash Theft Vulnerability Matrix

Building Location	Amount of On-Hand Dollars		Account- ability Records		Area Has Physical Bounds		Area Locked		Positive Control on Admittance		Alarm Protection		Surveillance Devices		Cash in Storage Container		Bait Money Kept		History of Cash Loss	
	NBH	OT	NBH	OT	NBH	OT	NBH	OT	NBH	OT	NBH	OT	NBH	OT	NBH	OT	NBH	OT	NBH	OT
Manager's office	200,000	40,000	Y	Y	Y	Y	N	Y	N	Y	Y	Y	N	Y	Y	Y	Y	Y	N	N
Manager's secretary	300	300	Y	Y	N	N	N	Y	Y	N	N	N	N	N	Y	Y	N	N	Y	Y
Cafeteria	2,000	0	N	Y	Y	Y	N	N	N	N	N	N	N	N	N	—	N	—	Y	N
Loading dock	1,500	500	Y	Y	Y	Y	N	N	N	N	N	N	N	Y	Y	Y	N	N	Y	N
Visitor reception	100	100	N	N	N	N	N	N	N	N	N	N	N	N	N	Y	N	Y	N	Y

Data for a company with gross sales per year of $310,000 and total current assets of $300,000.

NBH = normal business hours

OT = other times

Y = yes

N = no

Table 7.4 Probability/Criticality Assessment and Ranking

	Criticality		Probability	
	NBH	OT	NBH	OT
Manager's office	A	B	2	4
Manager's secretary	D	D	2	2
Cafeteria	C	—	1	—
Loading dock	C	D	1	2
Visitor reception	D	D	2	1

Suggested Rank Order	
Manager's office NBH	A2
Manager's office OT	B4
Cafeteria NBH	C1
Loading dock NBH	C1
Visitor reception OT	D1
Visitor reception NBH	D2
Loading dock OT	D2
Manager's secretary NBH	D2
Manager's secretary OT	D2

cality should be assumed to be fatal and the probability virtually certain. To do otherwise is suicidal!

If a decision has to be made, criticality should take precedence over probability. The security director, however, should implement measures to reduce the threat to the improbable level whenever the measures are cost effective.

Alternatives for Optimizing Risk Management

Once the security probability and criticality analysis has been completed and the security problems have been identified and ranked in importance, the security manager in cooperation with company executives must decide how to proceed. As was noted earlier, there are several risk-management alternatives: risk avoidance, risk reduction, risk spreading, risk transfer, self-assumption of risk.

Risk avoidance is removing the problem by eliminating the risk. This can be accomplished by transferring responsibility to another area. For example, the manufacturing of a small transistor by company M may be a security problem. To avoid the risk, company M decides to subcontract the manufacturing process to another firm that is better suited to handling this type of product's security. Thus the risk for company M is avoided.

Risk reduction is decreasing the potential ill effects of safety and security problems when it is impossible to avoid them. For example as a result of a security survey and vulnerability analysis, the security manager has determined that company N has a high risk of money loss in the central budget office because there are no positive admittance controls and no alarms. The risk can be reduced by creating a policy for positive admittance and the installation of proximity alarm devices. The risk is never totally eliminated since the old adage "where there's a will there's a way" applies to employees and outsiders who want to steal money.

Risk spreading is decentralizing a procedure or operation so that a security or safety problem at one location will not cause a complete loss. Suppose that company M is producing a microchip at a high risk of loss. It can spread its production risk by subcontracting some of the components to other companies or by producing the components at other sites owned by company M.

Risk transfer generally means removing the risk to the company by paying for the protection of an insurance policy.

Self-assumption of risk involves planning for an eventual loss without benefit of insurance.

In all procedures to minimize risks, insurance should be considered as a valuable addition to safety and security procedures.

The Cost Effectiveness of Security

It is unlikely that any evaluation will ever absolutely determine the cost effectiveness of any security operation. A low rate of crime—whether compared to past experience, to like concerns, or to neighboring businesses—is an indication that the security department is performing effectively. But how much is being protected that would otherwise be damaged, stolen, or destroyed? This can be any figure from the total exposure of the entire organization to some more refined estimate based on the incidence of criminal attack locally or nationally, the average losses suffered by the industry in general, or the reduction in losses by the organization over a given period.

An estimate based on such figures might well serve as a practical guide to the usefulness of the security function. On the other hand, if a security operation costing $400,000 annually were estimated, by some formula using a mix of the data referred to, to have saved a potential in theft and vandalism of $300,000, would it be deemed advisable to reduce the department's operating budget by $100,000 or more? Obviously not. This would be roughly analogous to reducing or canceling insurance because damage or loss and subsequent insurance recovery for a specific period or incident were less than the cost of the premium. Security can be considered as insurance against unacceptable risks.

Studies on the role of security and related investments as part of corporate costs of risk conducted by the Risk and Insurance Management Society (RIMS) and Risk Planning Group, Inc., show that the share of the total cost for risk control in these areas has risen.[1] The rise in percentage indicates a growing awareness by management of the role security can and must play in the total package of risk control.

Cost-effectiveness studies must be made, however, as part of a periodic review of protection systems even though such studies cannot be used as a general rule in devising a magic formula for computing the cost-per-$1000 actually saved in cash or goods that would otherwise have been lost. Such a review would consider, for example, the savings that could result from the substitution of functionally equivalent electronic or other gear for manpower (the most expensive deterrent) and the feasibility of taking such a step.

Periodic Review

Even after the security plan is formulated, it is essential that the survey process be continued. A security plan to be effective must be dynamic. It must change regularly in various details to accommodate changing circumstances in a given facility. Only regular inspections can provide a basis for the ongoing evaluation of the security status of the company. Exposure and vulnerability change constantly. What may appear to be a minor alteration in operational routines may have a profound effect on the security of the entire facility.

Security Files

The survey and its resultant report are also valuable in the building of security files. From this evaluation emerges a detailed current profile of the firm's regular activities. With such a file, the security department can operate with increased effectiveness, but it should by inspections and additional surveys be kept current.

Such a database could be augmented by texts, periodicals, official papers, and articles in the general press related to security matters. Special attention should be paid to subjects of local significance. Although national crime statistics are significant and help to build familiarity with a complex subject, local conditions have more immediate import to the security of the company.

As these files are broadened, they will become increasingly useful to the security operation. Patterns may emerge, seasons may become significant, and/or economic conditions may predict events to be alert to. For example:

- Certain days or seasons may emerge as those on which problems occur.
- Targets for crime may become evident as more data is amassed. This may enable the security director to reassign priorities.
- A profile of the types and incidences of crimes—possibly even of the criminal—may emerge.
- Patterns of crime and their modus operandi on payday or holiday weekends may become evident.
- Criminal assaults on company property may take a definable or predictable shape or description, again enabling the security director to shape countermeasures better.

The careful collection and use of data concerning crime in a given facility can be an invaluable tool for the conscientious security officer. It can add an important dimension to the regular reexamination of the status of crime in the company.

Given the present atmosphere of litigation for failure to provide adequate security, the files showing an efficient security operation can be invaluable. On the other hand, poorly keep files can be as great a liability as can well-kept files on a poorly designed security plan or poorly operated security organization.

Review Questions

1. What is the difference between vulnerability to loss and loss probability?
2. What is meant by criticality of loss?
3. If a security countermeasure costs as much as, or more than, the loss being protected against for a given period, does it follow that the security measure should be discontinued because it is not cost effective?
4. Why should accounting procedures be a part of a security survey? Why are security files significant in protection planning?
5. List four typical limited loss-prevention responses.
6. What are the steps involved in a good risk-management program?
7. What is an operational audit?

Reference

1. Philip P. Purpura, *Modern Security & Loss Prevention Management*, (Boston: Butterworths, 1989), p 202.

8

□ □ □
□ □ □
□ □ □

The Outer Defenses: Building and Perimeter Protection

The cause of security can be furthered simply by making it more difficult (or to be more accurate, less easy) for criminals to get into the premises being protected. And these premises should then be further protected from criminal attack by denying ready access to interior spaces in the event that exterior barriers are surmounted by a determined intruder. This must be the first concern in security planning.

True, every security program must be an integrated whole, and each element must grow out of the specific needs dictated by the circumstances affecting the facility to be protected. But the first and basic defense is still the physical protection of the facility. Planning this defense is neither difficult nor complicated, but it requires meticulous attention to detail.

Whereas the development of antiembezzlement systems or even the establishing of shipping and receiving safeguards requires particularized sophistication and expertise, the implementation of an effective program of physical security is the product of common sense and a lot of leg work expended in the inspection of the area.

Physical security concerns itself with those means by which a given facility protects itself against theft, vandalism, sabotage, unauthorized entry, fires, accidents, and natural disasters. And in this context, a facility is a plant, building, office, institution, or any commercial or industrial structure or complex with all the attendant structures and functions that are part of an integrated operation. An international manufacturing operation, for example, might have many facilities within its total organization.

Physical security planning includes protection of (1) the grounds around the building, (2) the building's perimeter, (3) the building's interior, and (4) its contents. Figure 8.1 illustrates these four lines of protection.

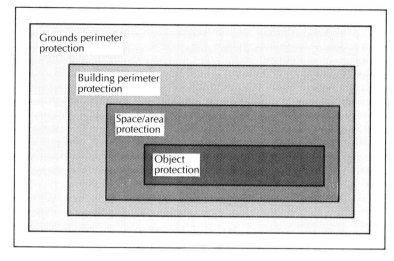

Figure 8.1 The four lines of production. (From Don T. Cherry, *Total Facility Control* [Stoneham, Mass.: Butterworth-Heinemann, 1986], p. 100.)

Barriers, Fences, and Walls

A facility's perimeter will usually be determined by the function and location of the facility itself. An urban office building or retail enterprise will frequently occupy all the real estate where it is located. In such a case, the perimeter may well be the walls of the building itself. Most industrial operations, however, require yard space and warehousing even in urban areas. In that case, the perimeter is the boundary of the property owned by the company. But in either case, the defense begins at the perimeter—the first line that must be crossed by an intruder.

Barriers

Natural and structural barriers are the elements by which boundaries are defined and penetration is deterred.

Natural barriers comprise the topographical features that assist in impeding or denying access to an area. They may consist of rivers, cliffs, canyons, dense growth, or any other terrain or feature that is difficult to overcome. Structural barriers are permanent or temporary devices such as fences, walls, grilles, doors, roadblocks, screens, or any other construction that will serve as a deterrent to unauthorized entry.

It is important to remember that structural barriers rarely if ever prevent penetration. Fences can be climbed, walls can be scaled, and locked doors and grilled windows can eventually be bypassed by a resolute assault.

The same is generally true of natural barriers. They almost never constitute a positive prevention of intrusion. Ultimately all such barriers must be supported by additional security, and most natural barriers should be further strengthened by structural barriers of some kind. It is a mistake to suppose that a high, steep cliff, for example, is by itself protection against unauthorized entry.

Fences

The most common type of fencing normally used for the protection of a facility is chain link, although barbed wire is useful in certain permanent applications, and concertina barbed wire is occasionally used in temporary or emergency situations.

Chain Link

Chain-link fencing should meet the specifications developed by the U.S. Department of Defense in order to be fully effective. (See Table 8.1 for common characteristics of chain-link fences.) It should be constructed of a nine-gauge or heavier wire with twisted and barbed selvage top and bottom. The fence itself should be at least seven feet tall and should begin no more than two inches from the ground. The bottom of the fence can be stabilized against crawling under or lifting by tying it to rigid metal poles or concrete sills. The sills are usually precast with AWF #9 wires for ties. If the soil is

Table 8.1   Common Chain Link Fence Characteristics

Characteristic	Options
Gauge	#9 (3.8 mm), #11 (3.0 mm)
Mesh	2 in. (50 mm), 1.6 in. (40 mm), 2.4 in. (60 mm)
Coating	vinyl, galvanized
Tension wires	wire, rail, cable (attached at top or bottom)
Support posts	metal posts (see Federal Specifications RR-F-191H/GEN and RR-F-191/33)
Height	6 ft. (1.8 meters), 7 ft. (2.1 meters), 8 ft. (2.4 meters)
Fabric tie downs	buried, encased in concrete, staked
Pole reinforcement	buried, encased in concrete
Gate opening	swing, slide, lift, turnstile

Source: Gary R. Cook, "The Facts on the Fence," *Security Management* (June 1990): 86.

sandy or subject to erosion, the bottom edge of the fence should be installed below ground level. The fence should be stretched and fastened to rigid metal posts set in concrete with such additional bracing as necessary at corners and gate openings. Mesh openings should be no more than two inches square. The fence should in addition be augmented by a top guard or overhang of three strands of stretched barbed wire angled at 45 degrees away from the protected property. (See Figure 8.2.) This overhang should extend out and up far enough to increase the height of the fence by at least one foot to an overall height of eight feet or more.

To protect the fence from washouts or channeling under it, culverts or troughs should be provided at natural drainage points. If any of these drainage openings are larger than 96 square inches, they too should be provided with physical barriers that will protect the perimeter without, however, impeding the drainage.

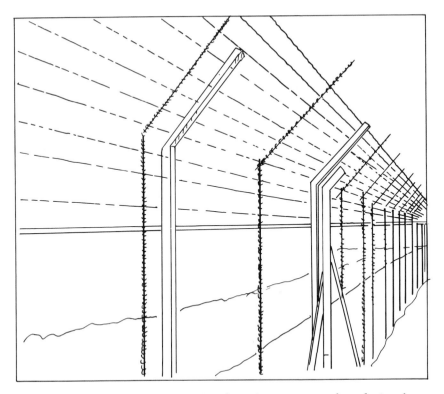

Figure 8.2 D.T.R. taut wire intrusion detection systems—the solution for airport security and high-risk facilities. (Courtesy of Safeguards Technology Inc.)

If buildings, trees, hillocks, or other vertical features are within ten feet of the fence, it should be heightened or protected with a Y-shaped top guard.

Barbed Wire

When a fence consists of barbed wire, a 12-gauge, twisted double strand with four-point barbs four inches apart is generally used. These fences, like chain-link fences, should also be at least seven feet high and they should in addition carry a top guard. Posts should be metal and spaced no more than six feet apart. Vertical distance between strands should be no more than six inches, preferably less.

Concertina Wire

Concertina wire is a coil of steel wire clipped together at intervals to form a cylinder (see Figure 8.3). When it is opened, it forms a barrier 50 feet long and either 12 or 60 inches high. Developed by the military for rapid laying, it can be used in multiple coils. It can be used either with one roll atop another or in a pyramid with two rolls along the bottom and one on the top. Ends should be fastened together, and the base wires should be staked to the ground. Concertina wire is probably the most difficult fence to penetrate, but it is unsightly and is rarely used except in a temporary application.

With the exception of concertina wire, most fencing is largely a psychological deterrent and a boundary marker rather than a barrier because in most cases such fences can be rather easily penetrated unless added security mea-

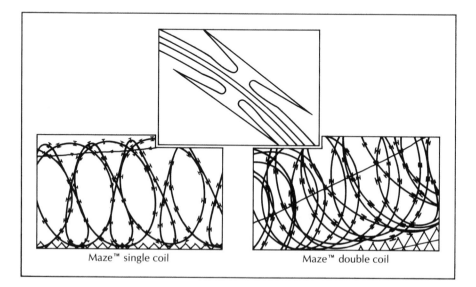

Maze™ single coil   Maze™ double coil

Figure 8.3 Concertina wire. (Courtesy of American Security Fence Corporation).

sures are taken to enhance the security of the fence. Fences may deter the undetermined, but they will only delay the determined.

Walls

In some instances, masonry, stone, brick, or block walls may be used to form all or part of the perimeter barrier. Such walls may be constructed for aesthetic reasons to replace the less decorative barriers within that part of the facility.

In those areas where masonry walls are used, they should be at least seven feet high with a top guard of three or four strands of barbed wire as in the case of chain-link fences.

Since concealment of the inside activity must be paid for by also cutting off the view of any activity outside the wall, extra efforts must be made to prevent scaling the wall. Ideally, the perimeter line should also be staggered in a way that permits observation of the area in front of the wall from a position or positions inside the perimeter.

Gates and Other Barrier Breaches

Every opening in the perimeter barrier is a potential security hazard. The more gates, the more security personnel must be deployed to supervise the traffic through them. Obviously, these openings must be kept to a minimum.

During shift changes, there may be more gates open and in use than at other times of the day when the smallest practical number of such gates are in operation. Certainly there must be enough gates in use at any time to facilitate the efficient movement of necessary traffic. The number can only be determined by a careful analysis of needs at various times of day, but every effort must be made to reduce the number of operating gates to the minimum consistent with safety and efficiency.

If some gates are not necessary to the operation of the facility or if they can be eliminated by changing traffic patterns, the openings should be sealed off and retired from use.

Padlocking

Gates used only at peak periods or emergency gates should be padlocked and secured. If it is possible, the lock used should be distinctive and immediately identifiable. It is common for thieves to cut off the plant padlock and substitute their own padlock so they can work at collecting their loot without an alarm being given by a passing patrol that has spotted an otherwise missing lock. A lock of distinctive color or design could compromise this ploy.

It is important that all locked gates be checked frequently. This is especially important where, as is usually the case, these gates are out of the current traffic pattern and are remote from the general activity of the facility.

Personnel and Vehicle Gates

Personnel gates are usually from four to seven feet wide to permit single-line entry or exit. It is important that they not be so wide that control of personnel is lost. Vehicular gates, on the other hand, must be wide enough to handle the type of traffic typical of the facility. They may handle two-way traffic, or if the need for control is particularly pressing, they may be limited to one-way traffic at any given time.

A drop or railroad crossing type of barrier is normally used to cut off traffic in either direction when the need arises. The gate itself might be single or double swing, rolling or overhead. It could be a manual or an electrical operation. Railroad gates should be secured in the same manner as other gates on the perimeter except during those times when cars are being hauled through it. At these times, the operation should be under inspection by a security guard.

Miscellaneous Openings

Virtually every facility has a number of miscellaneous openings that penetrate the perimeter. All too frequently these are overlooked in security planning, but they must be taken into account because they are frequently the most effective ways of gaining entrance into the facility without being observed.

These openings or barrier breaches consist of sewers, culverts, drain pipes, utility tunnels, exhaust conduits, air intake pipes, manhole covers, coal chutes, and sidewalk elevators. All must be accounted for in the security plan.

Any one of these openings having a cross section area of 96 square inches or more must be protected by bars, grillwork, barbed wire, or doors with adequate locking devices. Sidewalk elevators and manhole covers must be secured from below to prevent their unauthorized use. Storm sewers must be fitted with deterrents that can be removed for inspection of the sewer after a rain.

Barrier Protection

In order for the barrier to be most effective in preventing intrusion, it must be patrolled and inspected regularly. Any fence or wall can be scaled, and unless these barriers are kept under observation, they will be neutralizing the security effectiveness of the structure.

Clear Zone

A clear zone should be maintained on both sides of the barrier to make any approach to the barrier from the outside or any movement from the barrier to areas inside the perimeter immediately visible. Anything outside the barrier, such as refuse piles, weed patches, heavy undergrowth or anything else that might conceal someone's approach, should be eliminated. Inside the perimeter, everything should be cleared away from the barrier to create as wide a clear zone as possible.

Unfortunately it is frequently impossible to achieve an uninterrupted clear zone. Most perimeter barriers are indeed on the perimeter of the property line, which means that there is no opportunity to control the area outside the barrier. The size of the facility and the amount of space needed for its operation will determine how much space can be given up to the creation of a clear zone inside the barrier. It is important, however, to create some kind of clear zone, however small it might be.

In situations where the clear zone is necessarily so small as to endanger the effectiveness of the barrier, thought should be given to increasing the barrier height in critical areas or to the installation of an intrusion detection device to give due and timely warning of an intrusion to an alert guard force.

Inspection

Having established the perimeter defense and the clear zones to the maximum possible and practical, it is essential that a regular inspection routine be set up. Gates should be examined carefully to determine whether locks or hinges have been tampered with; fence lines should be observed for any signs of forced entry or tunneling; walls should be checked for marks that might indicate they have been scaled or that such an attempt has been made; top guards must be examined for their effectiveness; miscellaneous service penetrations must be examined for any signs of attack; brush and weeds must be cleared away; erosion areas must be filled in; and any potential scaling devices such as ladders, ropes, oildrums, or stacks of pallets must be cleared out of the area. Any condition that could even in the smallest degree compromise the integrity of the perimeter must be both reported and corrected. Such an inspection should be undertaken no less than weekly and possibly more often if conditions so indicate.

Hydraulic Defenses

One of the latest additions used to protect gates are hydraulic defenses (barricades). These devices are designed to deploy in 1 to 3 seconds and can stop a 15,000-lb vehicle moving at 50 mph. In most cases the devices are installed in the roadway where they are unobtrusive except for the outline of the top of the barrier, which is level with the surface into which it is installed.

Fence Protection Devices

In recent years, various devices have been designed to protect the integrity of fences. The earliest systems used electrification. Since those early days, the introduction of sensors to alert security staff of the presence of intruders has supplemented the use of fencing and in some cases replaced it. The most commonly used external intruder detection sensors are:

Fluid Pressure

In this system, a fluid pressure sensor (a small diameter tube sealed at one end and filled with fluid) is placed in the barrier. If a load is applied to the barrier, the tubes compress, placing force on the monitored fluid. This is useful in detection of persons crossing open ground and is commonly used in military installations and tank farms.

Electromagnetic Cable

This sensing device operates on the principle of electromagnetic capacitance. In simple terms, the cable creates an electromagnetic field that is constant in output. If the field is interrupted by cutting or pressure on the cable, it can be sensed and reported. The cable is normally mounted on inner chain-link or mesh fences.

Fibre Optic Cable

A beam of pulsed light is transmitted through the cable, and this is sensed at the other end. If the cable is cut or interfered with, the pulsing stops and there are changes in amplitude. The application of the cable is similar to the electromagnetic cable. Some manufacturers of high security fences, however, have incorporated the cable into the hollow strand of their normal fence material, making it impossible to detect.

Capacitive Field Effect

This sensor operates on the same principles as do the electro-magnetic systems but uses electrical rather than magnetic fields. These systems are extremely sensitive and can be affected by snow and ice. Weeds and paper debris contacting the sensor wire will also give rise to false alarms.

Active Infrared System (AIRS)

While more will be said about this system in Chapter 9, the basic premise behind it is a beam of infrared light sent to a sensor. If the beam is interrupted, the alarm sounds.

External Microwave

Whether used internally or externally this system relies on sending microwaves and on the Doppler effect. When the sensor receives an unfamiliar return of waves, an alarm condition is noted. Most external systems, however, rely on the transmission of a microwave beam to a receiver. If the beam is interrupted or changed, an alarm sounds. More will be said about microwave sensors used internally in Chapter 10.

Taut Wire

This sensor, which is placed on the wires of a fence, relies on a pendulum that is in the off position until tension on the taut wire forces the pendulum to swing into the on position, tripping the alarm.[1]

Inside the Perimeter

Unroofed or outside areas within the perimeter must be considered a second line of defense since these areas can usually be observed from the outside so that targets can be selected before an assault is made.

In an area where materials and equipment are stored in a helter-skelter manner, it is difficult for guards to determine if anything has been disturbed in any way. On the other hand, neat, uniform, and symmetrical storage can be readily observed, and any disarray can be detected at a glance.

Discarded machinery, scrap lumber, and junk of all kinds haphazardly thrown about the area create safety hazards as well as providing cover for any intruder. Such conditions must never be permitted to develop. Efficient housekeeping is basic security.

Parking

The parking of privately owned vehicles within the perimeter barrier should never be allowed. There should be no exceptions to this rule.

Facilities that cannot or will not establish parking lots outside the perimeter barrier are almost invariably plagued by a high incidence of pilferage because of the ease with which employees can conceal goods in their cars at any point during the day.

In cases where the perimeter barrier encompasses the employee and visitor parking areas, additional fencing should be constructed to create new barriers that exclude the parking areas. Appropriate guarded pedestrian gates must, of course, be installed to accommodate the movement of employees to and from their cars.

The parking lot itself should be fenced and patrolled to protect against car thieves and vandals. Few things are more damaging to morale than the insecurity that an unprotected parking area in a crime-ridden neighborhood can create.

Company cars and trucks—especially loaded or partially loaded vehicles—should be parked within the perimeter for added security. This inside parking area should be well lighted and regularly patrolled or kept under constant surveillance.

Loaded or partially loaded trucks and trailers should be sealed or padlocked and should further be parked close enough together and close enough to a building wall (or even back to back) so that neither their side doors nor rear doors can be opened without actually moving the vehicles.

Surveillance

The entire outside area within the security barrier must be kept under surveillance at all times, particularly at night. Since goods stored in this area are particularly vulnerable to theft or pilferage, this is the area most likely to attract the thief's first attention. With planning and study in cooperation with production personnel, it will undoubtedly be possible to lay out this yard area so that there are long, uninterrupted sight lines that permit inspection of the entire area with a minimum of movement. (Surveillance is discussed in detail in Chapter 9.)

Lighting

Depending on the nature of the facility, protective lighting will be designed either to emphasize the illumination of the perimeter barrier and the outside approaches to it or to concentrate on the area and the buildings within the perimeter. In either case, it must produce sufficient light to create a psychological deterrent to intrusion in addition to making detection virtually certain in the event an entry is made. The *Code of Federal Regulations*[2] lists a specific requirement of 0.2 footcandles for lighting of protected areas within a perimeter. A footcandle is a unit for measuring the intensity of illumination equal to 1 lumen per square foot or the amount of light a single candle provides over 1 square foot (see Figure 8.4).

While light must provide a specified level of illumination, it must also avoid glare that will reduce the visibility of security personnel while creating glare to deter intruders. It must also avoid casting annoying or dangerous light into neighboring areas. This is particularly important where the facility abuts streets, highways, or navigable waterways.

The system must be reliable and designed with overlapping illumination to avoid creating unprotected areas in the event of individual light failures. It must be easy to maintain and service, and it must be secured against attack. Poles should be within the barrier, power lines should be buried, and the switch box or boxes should be secure.

There should be a backup power supply in the event of power failure. Supplementary lighting, including searchlights and portable lights, should also be a part of the system. These lights are provided for special or emergency situations, and although they should not be used with any regularity, they must be available to the security force.

The system could be operated automatically by a photoelectric cell that responds to the amount of light to which it is subjected. Such an arrangement allows for lights to be turned on at dusk and extinguished at daylight. This can be set up to activate individual lamps or to turn on the entire system at once.

Other controls are timed, which simply means that lights are switched on and off by a clock. Such a system must be adjusted regularly to coincide with the changing hours of sunset and sunrise. The lights may also be operated manually.

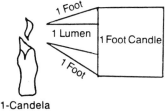

1 Square Foot

1 Foot

1 Lumen 1 Foot Candle

1 Foot

1-Candela
Light Source

Figure 8.4 Footcandle. (From Richard Gigliotti and Ronald Jason, *Security Design for Maximum Protection* [Stoneham, Mass.: Butterworth-Heinemann, 1984].)

Types of Lighting

Lamps used in protective lighting are either incandescent, fluorescent, metal halide, mercury vapor, quartz, or high- or low-pressure sodium. Each type has special characteristics suitable for specific assignments.

Incandescent

These are common lightbulbs of the type found in the home. They have the advantage of providing instant illumination when the switch is thrown and are thus the most commonly used in protective lighting systems. Some incandescents are manufactured with interior coatings that reflect the light and with a built-in lens to focus or diffuse the light. Regular high-wattage incandescents can be enclosed in a fixture that will give much the same result.

Fluorescent

These are generally of a mercury vapor type that are highly efficient, giving off approximately 62 lumens per watt. Most fluorescent lamps are temperature sensitive and thus have limited value for outdoor use in colder climates. In addition, the common flickering effect created by these lamps can have a disorienting effect of both security personnel and intruders. In addition, fluorescent lamps often interfere with radio reception.

Mercury Vapor Lamps

These common security lamps give out a strong light with a bluish cast. They are more efficient than are incandescents because of a considerably longer lamp life. In general, these lamps can tolerate power dips of up to 50 percent. Lighting time, however, is considerable.

Metal Halide

These lamps are also very tolerant of power dips. As with mercury vapor lamps the start-up time is long. A power outage of only one-twentieth of a second is enough to knock this lamp off-line.

Sodium Vapor Lights

Both the high- and low-pressure lamps give out a soft yellow light and are even more efficient than are mercury vapor lamps. They are widely used in areas where fog is a frequent problem since yellow penetrates the mist more readily than does white light. They are frequently found on highways and bridges.

Quartz Lamps

These lamps emit a very bright white light and snap on almost as rapidly as do incandescent bulbs. They are frequently used at very high wattage—1500 to 2000 watts is not uncommon in protective systems—and they are excellent for use along the perimeter barrier and in troublesome areas (see Table 8.2).

Types of Equipment

No one type of lighting is applicable to every need in a protective lighting system although manufacturers are continually working to develop just such a fixture.

Amid the great profusion of equipment in the market, there are four basic types that are in general use in security applications: floodlights, searchlights, fresnel lenses, and streetlights (see Figure 8.5). (The first three of these might in the strictest sense be considered as a single type since they are all basically reflection units in which a parabolic mirror directs the light in various ways. We will, however, deal with them separately.)

Streetlights are pendant lighting units that are built as either symmetrical or asymmetrical. The symmetrical units distribute light evenly. These units are used where a large area is to be lighted without the need for highlighting particular spots. They are normally centrally located in the area to be illuminated.

Asymmetrical units direct the light by reflection in the direction where light is required. They are used in situations where the lamp must be placed some distance from the target area. Since these are not highly focused units, they do not create a glare problem.

Streetlights are rated by wattage or even more frequently by lumens and in protective lighting applications may vary from 4000 to 10,000 lumens, depending on their use.

Floodlights

Floodlights are fabricated to form a beam so that light can be concentrated and directed to specific areas. They can create considerable glare.

Although many floodlights specify beam width in degrees, they are generally referred to as wide, medium, or narrow, and the lamp is described in wattage. Lamps run from 300 to 1000 watts in most protective applications. But there is a wide latitude in this, and the choice of one will depend on a study of its mission.

Table 8.2 Types of Luminaire Lamps Found in a Maximum Security Environment

Lamp Type	Mean Lumens per Watt	Start	Restrike	Nominal Life of Lamp (hrs.)	Percent Lumen Maintenance at Rated Life	Color Discrimination
Incandescent	4 (21) 22*	Instant	Instant	750–1,000	85–90	Excellent
Fluorescent	35 (62) 100	Rapid	Rapid/Instant†	7500–10,000	70–90	Excellent
Metal halide	68 (80) 100	3–5 min.	10–20 min.	10,000–15,000	65–75	Excellent
Mercury vapor	20 (48) 63	3–7 min.	3–6 min.	16,000–24,000	50–75	Good
High-pressure sodium	95 (127) 140	4–7 min.	Instant‡	16,000–24,000	75–85	Fair
Low-pressure sodium	131 (183) 183	8–10 min.	Instant‡	16,000–24,000	Basically constant§	Poor
Xenon ARC	||	Rapid/Instant	Instant	1500	—	Excellent

*4 (21)22 (4) = minimum mean; (21) = nominal rating for most protective lighting applications; 22 = maximum mean.

†Low-temperature ballast must be considered.

‡Instant for most lamps if less than one minute of power interruption but at a reduced lumen output.

§Current increases until end of lamp life to keep lumen output consistent.

||Use for searchlights only.

Source: Richard Gigliotti and Ronald Jason, *Security Design for Maximum Protection* (Stoneham, Mass.: Butterworth-Heinemann, 1984), p. 138.

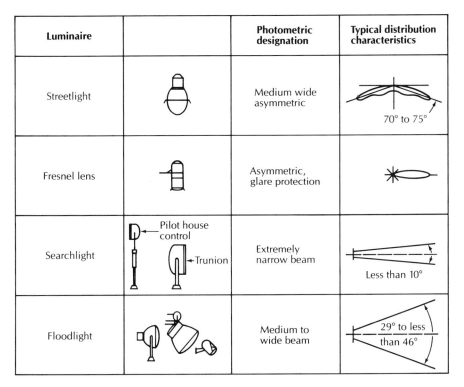

Luminaire		Photometric designation	Typical distribution characteristics
Streetlight		Medium wide asymmetric	70° to 75°
Fresnel lens		Asymmetric, glare protection	
Searchlight	Pilot house control / Trunion	Extremely narrow beam	Less than 10°
Floodlight		Medium to wide beam	29° to less than 46°

Figure 8.5 Typical equipment for protective lighting.

Fresnel Lenses

Fresnel lenses are wide-beam units, primarily used to extend the illumination in long, horizontal strips to protect the approaches to the perimeter barrier. Unlike floodlights and searchlights, which project a focused round beam, Fresnel lenses project a narrow, horizontal beam that is approximately 180° in the horizontal plane and from 18° to 30° in the vertical plane.

These units are especially good for creating a glare for the intruder while the facility remains in comparative darkness. They are normally equipped with a 300- to 500-watt lamp.

Searchlights

Searchlights are highly focused incandescent lamps that are used to pinpoint potential trouble spots. They can be directed to any location inside or outside the property, and although they can be automated, they are normally controlled manually.

They are rated according to wattage, which may range from 250 to 3000 watts, and to the diameter of the reflector, which may range from 6 inches to 2 feet (the average is around 18 inches). The beam width is from 3° to 10°, although this may vary in adjustable or focusing models.

Maintenance

As with every other element of a security system, electrical circuits and fixtures must be inspected regularly to replace worn parts, verify connections, repair worn insulation, check for corrosion in weatherproof fixtures, and clean reflecting surfaces and lenses. Lamps should be logged as to their operational hours and replaced at between 80 and 90 percent of their rated life.

Perimeter Lighting

Every effort should be made to locate lighting units far enough inside the fence and high enough to illuminate areas both inside and outside the boundary. The farther outside the boundary the lighted areas extend, the more readily guards will be able to detect the approach of an intruder.

Light should be directed down and away from the protected area. The location of light units should be such that they avoid throwing a glare into the eyes of the guard, do not create shadow areas, and create instead a glare problem for anyone approaching the boundary.

Fixtures used in barrier and approach lighting should be located inside the barrier. As a rule of thumb, they should be around 30 feet within the perimeter, spaced 150 feet apart, and about 30 feet high. These figures are, of course, approximations and will not apply to every installation. Local conditions will always dictate placement.

Floodlights or Fresnel lenses are indicated in illuminating isolated or semi-isolated fence boundaries where some glare is called for. In either case, it is important to light from 20 feet inside the fence to as far into the approach as is practical. In the case of the isolated fence, this could be as much as 250 feet. Semi-isolated and nonisolated fence lines cannot be lighted as far into the approach since such lighting is restricted by streets, highways, and other occupancies.

Since glare cannot be employed in illuminating a nonisolated fence line, streetlights are recommended.

Where a building of the facility is near the perimeter or is itself part of the perimeter, lights can be mounted directly on it. Doorways of such buildings should be individually lighted to eliminate shadows cast by other illumination.

In areas where the property line is on a body of water, lighting should be designed to eliminate shaded areas on or near the water or along the shoreline. This is especially true for piers and docks where both land and water approaches must be either lighted or capable of being lighted on demand. Before finalizing any plans for protective lighting in the vicinity of navigable waters, however, the U.S. Coast Guard must be consulted.

Gates and Thoroughfares

It is important that the lighting at all gates and along all interior thoroughfares be sufficient for the operation of the facility.

Since both pedestrian and vehicular gates are normally manned by guards inspecting credentials as well as checking for contraband or stolen property, it is critical that the areas be lighted to at least two footcandles (fc). Pedestrian gates should be lighted to about 25 feet on either side of the gate if possible, and the range for vehicular gates should be twice that distance. Streetlighting is recommended in these applications, but floodlights can also be used if glare is strictly controlled.

Thoroughfares used for pedestrians, vehicles, or forklifts should be lighted to 0.10 fc for security purposes. Much more light may be required for operational efficiency, but this level should be maintained as a minimum, no matter what the conditions of traffic may be.

Other Areas

Open or unroofed areas within the perimeter but not directly connected to it require an overall intensity of illumination of about 0.05 fc (up to 0.10 fc in areas of higher sensitivity). These areas, when they are non-operational, are usually used for material storage or for parking. Particularly vulnerable installations in the area should not, according to many experts, be lighted at all, but the approaches to them should be well lighted for at least 20 feet to aid in the observation of any movement.

Searchlights may be indicated in some facilities, especially in remote mountainous areas or in waterfront locations where small boats could readily approach the facility.

General

A well-thought-out plan of lighting along the security barrier and the approaches to it; an adequate overall level of light in storage, parking, and other nonoperational areas within the perimeter; and reasonable lighting along all thoroughfares are essential to any basic security program. The lighting required in operational areas will usually be much higher than the minimums required for security and will, therefore, serve a security purpose as well.

New lighting systems have proven effective in deterring crime. In San Diego, California, the installation of new security lighting in Spring Valley Park paid for the $17,250 investment in just six months by reducing burglaries at the community center that added up to a saving of over $25,000. Other communities reported similar results with sodium systems: In Swampscott, Massachusetts, the Clark School (K–6) replaced its old incandescent security system with a low-pressure sodium system in hopes of reducing vandalism. The cost of the old system ran only $625 per year. The new system cost $1,725 to install. It paid for itself in just a little over a year, however, by saving the school $1400 annually in vandalism-related costs.[3]

Can better lighting be sold to security management on the basis of cost effectiveness? The preceding examples are indications of just how effective

Table 8.3   Six Basic Lamp Families

Type of Lamp	Wattage Range	Initial Lumens per Watt Including Ballast Losses	Average Rated Life (Hours)
Low-pressure sodium	18–180	62–150	12,000–18,000
High-pressure sodium	35–1,000	51–130	7,500–24,000†
Metal halide	70–2,000	69–115	5,000–20,000
Mercury vapor			
Standard	40–1,000	24–60	12,000–24,000†
Self-ballasted	160–1,250	14–25	12,000–20,000
Fluorescent	4–215	14–95	6,000–20,000†
Incandescent	15–1,500	8–24	750–3,500

Data are based on the more commonly used lamps and are provided for comparison purposes only. Actual results to be derived depend on factors unique to the specific products and installation involved. Consult manufacturers for guidance.

Lumens (of light output) per watt (of power input) is a common measure of lamp efficiency. Initial lumens-per-watt data are based on the light output of lamps when new. The light output of most lamps declines with use. The actual efficiency to be derived from a lamp depends on factors unique to an installation. The actual efficiency of a lighting system depends on far more than the efficiency of lamps or lamps/ballasts alone. More than efficiency should be considered when evaluating a lighting system.

Source: John P. Bachner, "The Myths and Realities Behind Security Lighting," Security Management (August 1990): 109.

better lighting can be. In addition, high-pressure sodium lighting uses about 50 percent less energy to produce the same light as older, incandescent streetlights. Sodium systems have an efficiency per watt per lumens five or six times that of incandescent lighting and produce 106 percent more light than do the most common mercury streetlights but use about 14 percent less electricity. Table 8.3 compares wattage ranges, lumens, and rated life for six basic lamp families.

Planning Security

No business exists without a security problem of some kind, and no building housing a business is without security risk. Yet few such buildings are ever designed with any thought given to the steps that must eventually be taken to protect them from criminal assault.

A building must be many things in order for it to satisfy its occupant. It must be functional and efficient, achieve certain aesthetic standards, be properly located and accessible to the markets served by the occupant, and provide security from interference, interruption, and attack. Most of these elements are provided by the architect, but all too frequently the important element of security is overlooked.

Good security requires thought and planning of a carefully integrated system. Most security problems arise simply because no one has thought about them.

This is especially true where a company building is concerned. Since few architects have any training or knowledge in security matters, they design buildings that assist burglars or vandals by doing nothing to deter them. Because the architects' clients seldom consider security in the planning stages, buildings are erected that provide needless opportunities for crime.

Review Questions

1. What four lines of protection should be included in physical security planning?
2. How can the various openings in a perimeter be effectively protected and secured?
3. Why should parking not be allowed inside the controlled perimeter?
4. Discuss the different security applications for the various types of lighting equipment.
5. What considerations must be taken into account when installing a security lighting system?

References

1. Neil Cumming, *Security: The Comprehensive Guide To Equipment Selection and Installation* (London: Architectural Press, 1987), pp. 70–109.
2. *Code of Federal Regulations Title 10* (Washington, D.C.: GPO, 1981).
3. John P. Bachner, "The Myths and Realities Behind Security Lighting," *Security Management* (August 1990): 109–110.

9

□ □ □
□ □ □
□ □ □

Interior and Exterior Security Concerns

Besides the clearcut concerns for the perimeter and exterior security, other security vulnerabilities for the facility might be either a part of the perimeter, part of the interior or both. This chapter deals with security concerns that could be either interior or exterior problems depending upon the type of facility. For example, a freestanding retail outlet store has problems of perimeter security that include windows, doors, and roof. The same store located within the confines of a mall may not be as concerned with the windows and doors as the mall is a buffer or with perimeter defense that must be overcome before the attacker can concentrate on the store.

Buildings on or as the Perimeter

When the building forms part of the perimeter barrier or when as in some urban situations the building walls are the entire perimeter of the facility, it should be viewed in the same light as the rest of the barrier or it should be evaluated in the same way as the outer structural barrier. It must be evaluated in terms of its strength, and all openings must be properly secured.

In cases of a fence joining the building as a continuation of the perimeter, there should be no more than two inches between the two structures. Depending on the placement of windows, ledges, or setbacks, it might be wise to double the fence height gradually to the point where it joins the building. In such a case, the higher section of the fence should extend six to eight feet out from the building.

Windows and Doors

Windows and other openings larger than 96 square inches should be protected by grilles, metal bars, or heavy screening when they are less than 18 feet from the ground or when they are less than 14 feet from structures outside the barrier (that is, trees and other buildings).

Doors that penetrate the perimeter walls must be of heavy construction and fitted with strong locks.

Since both the law and good sense require that there be adequate emergency exits in the event of fire or other danger, provision must be made for such eventualities. Doors created for emergency purposes only should have exterior hardware removed so that they cannot be opened from the outside. They can be secured by a remotely operated electromagnetic holding device, or they can be fitted with alarms so that their use from inside will be substantially reduced or eliminated.

Windows

It is axiomatic that windows should be protected. Since the ease with which most windows can be entered makes them ready targets for intruders, they must be viewed as potential weak spots in any building's defenses. Most forced break-ins are through window glass—whether such glass is installed in doors or windows.

In most industrial facilities, windows should be protected with grillwork, heavy screening, or chain link fencing. In some cases, however, caution dictates that they may be needed as emergency exits beyond strict requirements of fire laws. Or where they might be needed to lead in fire hoses, consideration should be given to hinging and padlocking protective coverings for easy removal.

Burglary-Resistant Glass

In applications such as prominent administration and office buildings, where architectural considerations preclude the use of such relatively clumsy installations as mesh or industrial screen, the windows can be immeasurably strengthened by the use of either UL-listed (which means that the material or item so designated has met the standards of Underwriter's Laboratories) burglary-resistant glass or one of the brands of UL-listed polycarbonate glazing material. Both of these products are considerably more expensive than is plate glass and are generally used only in those areas where attack can be expected or where a reduction in insurance premium would justify the added expense.

Standard plate glass can be given some measure of resistance if it is covered with a four to six mil cover of mylar. This is a low-cost operation, but the mylar needs to be replaced every five years. As little as a two mil cover of mylar can keep glass from fragmenting. Thus the mylar cover is good protection from flying shards associated with bombings.

As opposed to tempered glass, which is designed to protect people from the danger of flying shards in the event of breakage, UL-listed burglary-resistant glass (frequently referred to as "safety glass") resists heat, flame, cold, picks, rocks, and most other paraphernalia from the intruder's arsenal. It is a useful security glazing material because it is durable, weathers well, and is noncombustible. On the other hand, it is heavy, difficult to install, and expensive.

The plastic glazing sold under various trade names is optically clear, thin, and easy to install.

Acrylicglazing material that appears as Plexiglas generally does not meet UL standards for burglar-resistant material; it is much stronger than ordinary glass, however, and has many useful applications in window security applications. It is also lighter in weight and cheaper than either safety glass or plastic glazings and at one and a quarter inches thick is UL approved as a bullet-resistant barrier.

All these materials have the appearance of ordinary glass. Obviously, any window so hardened against entry must be securely locked from the inside to protect against intrusion from the outside. This implies a strong window frame and supporting construction.

"Smash and Grab" Attacks

Burglary-resistant glass is used to a considerable degree in banks and retail stores where there has been a very real need to prevent "smash and grab" raids on window displays and showcases.

It should be noted that UL-listed burglary-resistant glass is a laminate of two sheets of flat glass (usually 3/16 inches thick) held together by a 1/16-inch layer of polyvinyl butyral, a soft transparent material. In this thickness, laminated glass is virtually indistinguishable from ordinary glass, hence burglars may try with a hammer or iron bar to break what they suppose to be a plate glass window. It is only after they have made a few unsuccessful tries that they realize the material is not penetrable.

Even though such attackers may flee empty-handed, the owners in such situations are left with windows with webs of cracks over the surface of the outer layer of glass, making replacement of the entire pane necessary in applications where appearance is important. Insurers in many cases require that laminated glass be clearly identified to discourage what would be a futile but damaging assault by the "smash and grab" attacker.

Screening

It can also be important to screen windows. First this might protect their use as a means by which employees can temporarily dispose of goods for later recovery. The smaller the goods being manufactured or available on the premises, the smaller the mesh in the screen must be to protect against this kind of pilferage.

Second as was noted earlier, any windows less than 18 feet from the ground or less than 14 feet from trees, poles, or adjoining buildings should receive some protective treatment unless they are well within the perimeter barrier and open directly onto an area outside the building that is particularly well secured.

Doors

Every door, whether exterior or interior, must be carefully examined to determine the degree of security required. Such an examination will also determine the type of construction as well as the locking system to be used on each door.

The required security measures at any specific door will be determined by the operations in progress within the facility or by the value of the assets stored or available in the various areas. The need for adequate security cannot be overemphasized, but it must be provided as part of an overall plan for the safe and efficient conduct of the business.

When this balance is lost, the business may suffer. Either the security function will be downgraded in favor of a more immediate convenience, or the smooth flow of business will be impeded to conform to obtrusive security standards. Either of these conditions is intolerable in any business, and it is a management responsibility to determine the balance required in establishing systems that will recognize and accommodate production and security needs.

Door Construction and Hardware

Doors are frequently much weaker than is the surface into which they are positioned. Panels may be thin, easily broken wood or glass. Locks may be old and ineffective. The door frame may be so constructed that a lever or a plastic card can be inserted between the door and jamb to disengage the bolt in the lock. Even with a properly hung door, if the jamb is of soft material (unreinforced aluminum or light pine), it can be peeled or ripped away from the bolt. This technique is referred to as "spreading." The locking bolt must throw at least an inch into the jamb for security applications. Heavy wood or metal doors with reinforced jambs can go a long way in reducing the potential for spreading.

In some cases, doors are entered by "pulling," a technique whereby the lock cylinder is ripped from the door and the locking mechanism is operated through the opening left in its face. The installation of a special, hardened steel key cylinder guard can overcome this kind of assault. Or cylinders

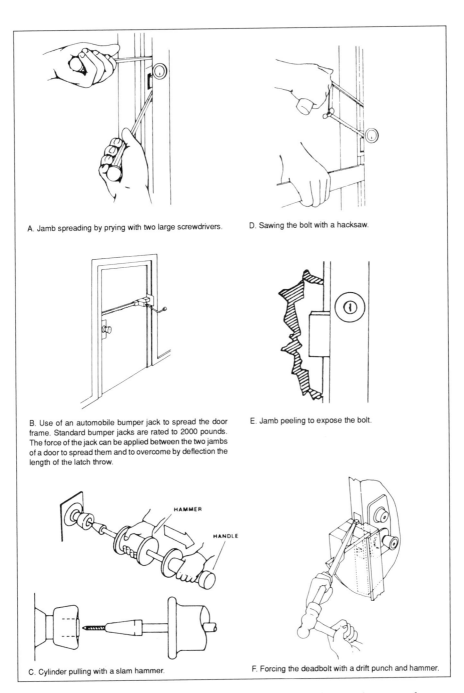

A. Jamb spreading by prying with two large screwdrivers.

D. Sawing the bolt with a hacksaw.

B. Use of an automobile bumper jack to spread the door frame. Standard bumper jacks are rated to 2000 pounds. The force of the jack can be applied between the two jambs of a door to spread them and to overcome by deflection the length of the latch throw.

E. Jamb peeling to expose the bolt.

HAMMER

HANDLE

C. Cylinder pulling with a slam hammer.

F. Forcing the deadbolt with a drift punch and hammer.

Figure 9.1 Common attack methods on doors and door frames. (Reprinted with permission of National Crime Prevention Institute, School of Justice Administration, University of Louisville, from Edgar et al., *The Use of Locks*, Butterworth-Heinemann, 1987, pp 72–76.)

should be flush or inset to prevent their being wrenched out or "popped." Figure 9.1 illustrates common techniques of attacking doors and door frames.

Door hinges may also contribute to a door's weakness. Surface-mounted hinges with mounting screws or hinge pins exposed on the exterior side of the door can be removed and entrance gained on the hinge side. To complicate the matter, the door can be replaced on its hinges after the intruder has finished, and in most cases, the intrusion will never be detected. Without any visible sign of forced entry, very few insurance policies would pay off on the stolen merchandise.

To prevent this unhappy chain of events, hinges should be installed with the screws concealed and with the hinge pins either welded or flanged to prevent removal.

Locks and Keys

Attacks against Locks

Although direct forcible assault is the method generally used to gain entry, more highly skilled burglars may concentrate on the locks. This may be their only practical means of ingress if the door and the jamb are well designed in security terms and essentially impervious to forcible attack.

Picking the lock or making a key by impression are the methods generally used. Both require a degree of expertise. In the former method, metal picks are used to align the levers or tumblers as an authorized key would, thus enabling the lock to operate. Making a key by taking impressions is a technique requiring even greater skill since it is a delicate, painstaking operation requiring repeated trials.

Because both of these techniques are apt to take time, they are customarily used to attack those doors where the intruder may work undisturbed and unobserved for adequate periods of time. The picked lock rarely shows any signs of illegal entry, and often insurance is uncollectible.

Locks as Delaying Devices

The best defense against lock-picking and making keys by impression is the installation of special pick-resistant, impression-resistant lock cylinders. They are more expensive than standard cylinders but in many applications may well be worth the added cost. Generally speaking in fact, locks are the cheapest security investment that can be made. Cost cutting in their purchase is usually a poor economy since a lock of poor quality is virtually useless and effectively no lock at all.

The elementary but often overlooked fact of locking devices is that in the first place they are simply mechanisms that extend the door or window into the wall that holds them. If, therefore, the wall or the door itself is weak or easily destroyed, the lock cannot be effective.

In the second place, it must be recognized that any lock will eventually yield to an attack. They must be thought of only as delaying devices. But this delay is of primary importance. The longer an intruder is stalled in an exposed position while he works at gaining entry, the greater are the chances of discovery. Since many types of locks in general use today provide no appreciable delay to even the unskilled prowler, they have no place in security applications.

Even the highest quality locking devices are only one part of door and entrance security. Locks, cylinders, door and frame construction, and key control are inseparable elements; all must be equally effective. If any one element is weak, the system breaks down.

All locks are essentially composed of three parts: the operating mechanism, the keying device, and the latch or bolt. Any number of combinations may be involved in any lock, and to understand a lock, one must understand the variety of items that exist in each of the essential parts.

Latches and Bolts

The simplest latch is the spring lock. Its value as a security device is negligible. Spring locks as shown in Figure 9.2 are designed primarily as latching devices to hold a door closed for privacy. Since the latch is spring loaded and has a tapered side so it will slide smoothly over the strike plate, it can easily be opened with a plastic or celluloid strip or a credit card.

The next type of latch is the dead latch. This latching device combines the advantages of the spring lock with a means of protecting the latch from carding. As can be seen in Figure 9.2, the dead latch is a simple device that holds the spring latch in position when the door is closed. When the door is unlocked, the device is in an open position to allow the latch to operate as a simple spring latch. But when the door is locked, the device is depressed by the strike plate so that the spring latch becomes "dead": It will no longer move unless it is manipulated by the operating device. The basic problem with the dead latch as a security device is that the overall length of the latch is still not long enough to keep the door from being forced open by prying between the door frame and the door.

To overcome the problem of springing doors, a dead bolt lock is needed (see Figure 9.3). The dead bolt gets its name from the fact that it does not have a tapered side and is dead in the door whether it is open or closed. The

Figure 9.2 Spring lock. The spring lock (sometimes referred to as the "key in the knob" lock) is the most convenient type of lock. It does not, however, offer a high degree of security. The spring lock shown here includes a dead latch that adds a small degree of additional security. (Courtesy of Schlage Lock Company.)

only way to manipulate a dead bolt is with an operating mechanism (key, electric switch, and so on). Dead bolts are generally long enough to overcome the problem of springing the door. Some intruders have attacked dead bolts with hacksaws, however, and cut their way through the brass alloy. To overcome this problem, the better dead bolts have a case-hardened pin in the center of the dead bolt to frustrate the use of a hacksaw.

Keying Devices and Systems

Keying devices (which include lock and key) and the mechanisms they operate are many and varied in usage and style. A brief review of the types of keying and locking devices in general use and of their characteristics follows.

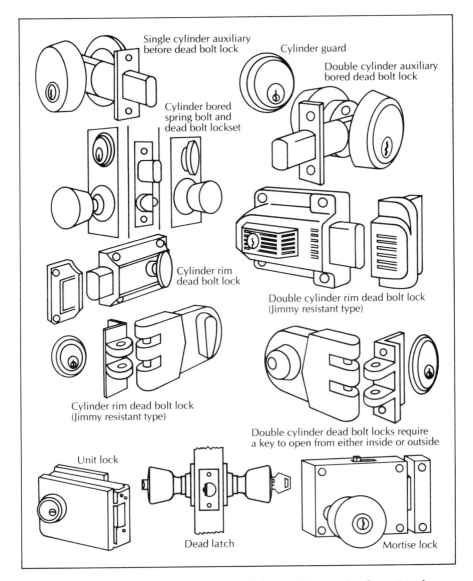

Figure 9.3 Common dead bolt locks. The bolt should extend at least 1 inch beyond the door edge. Other locks, however, that use an interlocking principle (for example, jimmy-resistant rim locks) also offer good security. If glass is within 40 inches of the lock, a double cylinder dead bolt (with keys needed for opening both sides) should be installed. This makes it impossible for a criminal to break the glass and reach inside to unlock the door. Be certain to have the key readily available so that fast exits are possible in the event of an emergency.

Warded locks are generally found in pre-World War II construction in which the keyway is open and can be seen through. These are also recognized by the single plate that includes the doorknob and the keyway. The security value of these locks is nil.

Disc tumbler locks, initially designed for use in the automobile industry, have been replaced in that industry with pin locks. Because this lock is easy and cheap to manufacture, however, its use has expanded to other areas such as desks, files, and padlocks. The life of these locks is limited because of their soft metal construction. Although these locks provide more security than do warded locks, they cannot be considered very effective. The delay afforded is approximately three minutes.

Pin tumbler locks are in wide use in industry as well as in residences (see Figure 9.4). They can be recognized by the keyway, which is irregular in shape, and the key, which is grooved on both sides. Such locks can be master keyed in a number of ways, a feature which recommends them to a wide variety of industrial applications, although the delay factor is ten minutes or less.

Lever locks are difficult to define in terms of security since they vary greatly in effectiveness. The best lever locks are used in safe deposit boxes and are for all practical purposes pick-proof. The least of these locks are used in desks, lockers, and cabinets and are generally less secure than are pin tumbler locks. The best of this variety are rarely used in common applications, such as doors, because they are bulky and expensive.

Removable Cores

In facilities that require a number of keys to be issued, the loss or theft of keys is an ever-present possibility. In such situations, it might be well to consider removable cores on all locks. These devices are made to be removed if necessary with a core key, allowing a new core to be inserted. Since the core is the lock, this has the effect of rekeying without the necessity of changing the entire device as would be the case with fixed cylinder mechanisms.

Keying Systems

Keys are generally divided into change, submaster, master, and occasionally grand master keys.

1. *The change key*—one key to a single lock within a master-keyed system.

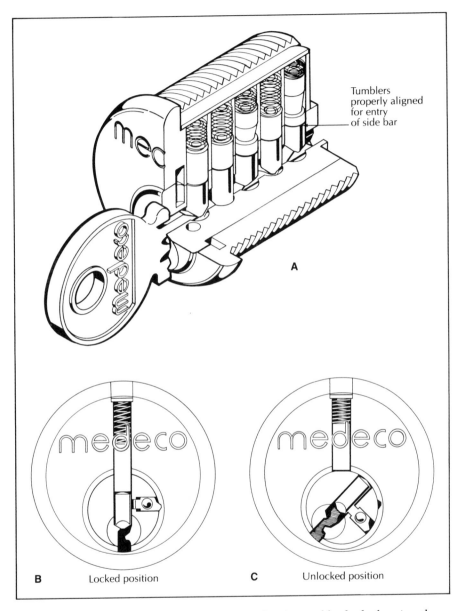

Tumblers
properly aligned
for entry
of side bar

A

B   Locked position   **C**   Unlocked position

Figure 9.4 Pin tumbler lock. (A) A cutaway of a pin tumbler lock showing the springs and tumblers. When the correct key is inserted into the lock, it will align all of the tumblers in a straight line to allow the plug to turn and operate the locking mechanism. (B) Locked position. Notice how the spring is forcing the tumbler to project partway into the inner core (plug) of the lock, making it impossible for the plug to rotate. (C) Unlocked position. The tumbler is not outside the plug, thereby allowing it to be rotated. (Courtesy of Medeco Security Locks, Inc.)

2. *The submaster key*—will open all the locks within a particular area or grouping in a given facility. In an office, a submaster might open all doors in the accounting department; in an industrial facility, it might open all locks in the loading dock area. Typically, such groupings concern themselves with a common function, or they may simply be located in the same area even if they are not otherwise related.

3. *The master key*—Where two or more submaster systems exist, a master key system is established. Such a key would open any of the systems.

4. *The grand master key*—one that will open everything in a system involving two or more master key groups. This system is relatively rare but might be used by a multipremise operation in which each location was master keyed while the grand master would function on any premise.

Obviously master and submaster keys must be treated with the greatest care. If a master key is lost, the entire system is threatened. Rekeying is the only really secure thing that can be considered, but the cost of such an effort can be enormous.

Any master key system is vulnerable. Beyond the danger of loss of the master itself and the subsequent staggering cost of rekeying—or, even more unfortunate, of the use of such a key by enterprising criminals to loot the facility—there is the problem that it necessarily serves a lesser lock. Locks in such a system are neither pick-resistant nor resistant to making a key by impression.

On the other hand, relative security coupled with convenience may make such a system preferable in some applications but not in others. Only the most careful evaluation of the particular circumstances of a given facility will determine the most efficient and effective keying system.

Rekeying

In any sizable facility, rekeying can be very expensive, but there are methods of lessening the disruption and staggering cost that can be involved in rekeying. Outer or perimeter locks can be changed first, and the old locks can be moved to interior spaces requiring a lower level of security. After an evaluation, a determination of priorities can be made and rekeying can be accomplished over a period of time, rather than requiring one huge capital outlay all at once.

Of prime importance is securing keys so that such problems do not arise.

Key Control

Every effort should be exerted to develop ways whereby keys remain in the hands of security or management personnel. In those cases where this is not possible or practical, there must be a system of inventory and accountability. In any event, keys should be issued only to those demonstrably responsible persons who have compelling need for them. Though possession of keys is frequently a status symbol in many companies, management must never issue them on that basis.

Keys should never be issued on a long-term basis to outside janitorial personnel. The high employee turnover rate in this field would suggest that this could be a dangerous practice. Employees of this service should be admitted by guards or other building employees and issued interior keys that they must return before leaving the building.

By the same token, it is bad practice to issue entrance keys to tenants of an office building. If this is done, control of this vital security point is lost. A guard or building employee should control entry and exit before and after regular building hours. If keys must be issued to tenants, however, the lock cylinder in the entrance should be changed every few months and new keys issued to authorized tenants.

A careful, strictly supervised record of all keys issued must be maintained by the security department. This record should indicate the name and department of the person to whom the key was issued as well as the date of issue.

A key depository for securing keys during nonworking hours should be centrally located, locked, and kept under supervision of security personnel. Keys issued on a daily basis or those issued for a specific, one-time purpose should be accounted for daily. Keys should be counted and signed for by the security supervisor at the beginning of each working day.

When a key is lost, the circumstances should be investigated and set forth in writing. In some instances if the lost key provides access to sensitive areas, locks should be changed. All keys issued should be physically inspected periodically to ensure that they have not been lost, though unreported as such.

Master keys should be kept to a minimum. If possible, submasters should be used, and they should be issued only to a limited list of personnel especially selected by management. Careful records should be kept of such issuance. The list should be reviewed periodically to determine whether all those authorized should continue to hold such keys.

Before a decision can be reached with respect to the master and submaster key systems and how such keys should be issued, there must be a careful survey of existing and proposed security plans, along with a study of current and planned locking devices. Where security plans have been developed with operational needs of the facility in mind, the composition of the various keying systems can be readily developed.

Locking Schedules

Door-locking schedules and responsibilities must be established and supervised vigorously. The system must be set up in such a way that a procedure for altering the routine to fit immediate needs is possible, but in all respects the schedule, whether the master or the temporary plan, must be adhered to in every detail. A breakdown in such a system, especially in large offices, institutions, or industrial facilities, could represent just the opportunity an alert criminal is waiting for.

Other Operating Mechanisms for Access Control

Besides the traditional key and lock, other mechanisms have been developed for access control purposes. The following are commonly used in security applications.

1. *Combination locks* are difficult to defeat since they cannot be picked and few experts can so manipulate the device as to discover the combination. Most of these locks have three dials that must be aligned in the proper order before the lock will open. Some such locks may have four dials for greater security. Many also have the capability of having the combination changed quickly.

2. *Code-operated locks* are combination locks in that no keys are used. They are opened by pressing a series of numbered buttons in the proper sequence. Some of them are equipped to sound an alarm if the wrong sequence is pressed. The combination of these locks can be changed readily. These are high-security locking devices. Because this type of lock can be compromised by "tailgating" (more than one person entering on an authorized opening), it should never be used as a substitute for a guard or receptionist.

3. *Card-operated locks* are electrical or, more usually, electromagnetic. Coded cards are about the size of a credit card. These frequently are fitted with a recording device that registers time of use and identity of the user. The cards serving as keys also serve as company identification cards. As with code-operated locks, tailgating can occur with this lock as well. In addition, the readers identify the card, not the individual. There are several types of card-operated systems on the market.

a. *Magnetic coded cards* are of two basic designs. The first contains a flexible magnetic sheet sealed between two sheets of plastic. The second contains a magnetic strip along one edge of the card. The code is created by magnetizing spots on the sheet or strip. The code can be erased if it is exposed to a strong magnetic field. It is possible to duplicate the magnetic pattern and create false cards.

b. *Wiegan Effect cards* rely on short-length magnetic wires embedded within the card. Cards contain up to 26 wire bits, which make millions of code combinations possible. The card is immune to demagnetization and difficult to copy.

c. *Optical coded cards* contain bar codes similar to those found on products in most grocery stores. Early cards used the visible bar codes and were easy to duplicate. Today's product contains bar codes visible only under ultraviolet or infrared light.

d. *Proximity cards* do not need to be inserted into a reader or scanned. These cards send a code to a receiver via magnetic, optical, or ultrasonic pulses.

4. *Biometric systems* are designed to recognize biological features of the individual before access is granted. These systems are in fact identity verification systems that use personnel characteristics to verify identity. While these systems bring the James Bond gadgetry to real systems, they are also currently handicapped with problems relating to the fact that physical characteristics of people do change with physical injuries, stress, and fatigue. There are several types of this "state-of-the-art" technology.

a. *Fingerprint recognition systems* optically scan a chosen fingerprint area and compare the scanned area with the file of the person to be admitted.

b. *Signature recognition systems* rely on the fact that no two people write with the same motion or pressure. Although forgers can duplicate the appearance of the signature, the amount of pressure and motions used in creating the signature will differ.

c. *Hand geometry recognition systems* use the geometry of the hand. The system basically measures finger lengths and compares them with the authorized files.

d. *Speaker verification systems* use the uniqueness of voice patterns to determine identification and control admittance. The system uses soundproof booths and requires that the person to be identified repeat a simple phrase usually four words in length.

e. *Eye retina recognition systems* analyze the blood vessel pattern in the retina of the eye. These patterns vary widely even between identical twins. The chance of false identification using this system is one in a million (see Figure 9.5).

5. *Padlocks* are detachable, portable locks that have a shackle adapted to be opened for engagement through a hasp or chain. Padlocks should be hardened and strong enough to resist prying. The shackle should be close enough to the body to prevent the insertion of a tool to force it. No lock that will be used for security purposes should have fewer than five pins in the cylinder. Padlocks can be supplied with a function that prevents the withdrawal of a key until the lock is closed.

It is important to establish a procedure requiring that all padlocks be locked at all times even when they are not securing an area. This will prevent the possibility of the lock being replaced by another to which a thief has the key.

The hardware used in conjunction with the padlock is as important as is the lock itself. It should be of hardened steel, without accessible screws or rivets, and bolted through the door to the inside, preferably through a backing plate. Shackles should be forged of hardened steel, 3/8" in both the heel and toe. The bolt ends should be burred.

6. *High security locks.* Virtually every lock manufacturer makes some kind of special high-security lock that is operated by nonduplicable keys. A reliable locksmith or various manufacturers should be consulted in cases of such need.

Figure 9.5 EyeDentify 8.5. (Courtesy of EyeDentify, Inc.)

Locking Devices

In the previous list we have considered the types of locks that are generally available. It must be remembered, however, that locks must work in conjunction with other hardware that effects the actual closure. These devices may be fitted with locks of varying degrees of security and may themselves provide security to various levels. In a security locking system, both of these factors must be taken into consideration before determining which system will be most effective for specific needs.

Electromagnetic locking devices hold doors closed by magnetism. These electrical units consist of an electromagnet and a metal holding plate. When the power is on and the door secured, they will resist a pressure of up to 1000 pounds. A high frequency of mechanical failures with this type of lock can create problems. Inconvenienced employees will often block the door open or jam the door bolting mechanism so that the lock no longer operates. Quality equipment, preventive maintenance, frequent inspections, and quick response to problems will minimize these problems.

Double cylinder locking devices are installed in doors that must be secured from both sides, requiring a key to open them from either side. Their most common application is in doors with glass panels that might otherwise be broken to allow an intruder to reach in and open the door from the other side. Such devices cannot be used in interior fire stairwell doors since firemen break the glass to unlock the door from the inside in this case.

Emergency exit locking devices are panic-bar installations allowing exit without use of a key. This device locks the door against entrance. Since such devices frequently provide an alarm feature that sounds when exit is made, they are fitted with a lock that allows exit without setting of the alarm when a key is used.

Recording devices provide for a printout of door use by time of day and by the key used.

Vertical throw devices lock into the jamb vertically instead of the usual horizontal bolt. Some versions lock into both jamb and lintel. A variation of this device is the police lock, which consists of a bar angled to a well in the floor. The end of the bar contacting the door is curved so that when it is unlocked it will slide up the door, allowing the door to open. When it is locked, it is secured to the door at one end and set in the floor at the other. A door locked in this manner is virtually impossible to force.

Electric locking devices are installed in the same manner as are other locks. They are activated remotely by an electric current which releases the strike and thus, permits entrance. Many of these devices provide minimal security since the engaging mechanisms frequently offer no security feature not offered by standard hardware. The electric feature provides a convenient method of opening the door. It does not in itself offer locking security. Since such doors are usually intended for remote operation, they should be fitted with a closing device.

Sequence locking devices are designed to insure that all doors covered by the system are locked. The doors must be closed and locked in a predetermined order. No door can be locked until its designated predecessor has been locked. Exit is made through the final door in the sequence, and entry can be made only through that same door.

Roofs and Common Walls

An important though often overlooked part of the perimeter is the roof of the building. In urban shopping centers or even in small, freestanding commercial situations where the building walls are the perimeter, entry through the roof is common. Entry can be made through skylights or by chopping through the roof—an activity rarely detected by passersby or even by patrols.

Buildings sharing a common wall have also frequently been entered by breaking through the wall from a poorly secured neighboring occupancy. All of these means of entry circumvent normal perimeter alarm systems and can therefore be particularly damaging.

Surveillance Devices

Surveillance of a facility both internally and externally is normally conducted by patrolling security personnel who watch for any signs of criminal activity. If they spot any trouble, they are in a position to take such action as necessary. Patrols cannot be everywhere, however, and with the present emphasis on cost effectiveness, other methods must be introduced to supplement patrols. A wide variety of surveillance devices, including motion picture cameras, sequence cameras, and closed circuit television (CCTV) monitors with video cameras, are being used.

Effective surveillance systems are expected to produce two possible end results. First a good system should produce an identifiable image of persons engaging in criminal behavior or in violating company policy. Second the system should also serve as a deterrent. Although there is no way to determine how many attempts are discouraged because of the presence of the system, one definite advantage is that surveillance systems generally mean lower insurance rates.

The major factor limiting the use of surveillance devices is the cost of installation and maintenance. In addition, some companies worry about the possible negative impact of these systems on employee morale.

Sequence cameras record still pictures at regular intervals or they can, by switch control, take a prearranged number of pictures in rapid succession. The time interval between pictures can be adjusted. Pictures can be taken in almost total darkness with infrared sensitive film and in infrared emission. Such systems can use almost any type of camera, from 8 to 70mm, depending on the application. Sequence cameras are often installed in operations where checks are handled since the quality of the camera's prints is excellent.

Motion picture cameras using high-speed 16mm film and fast shutter speeds can be set up to take pictures in normal light. These cameras can be activated automatically by an alarm set off by an intruder or manually by a switch. The coverage of events is limited by the amount of film in the camera. This is not a totally satisfactory device since cameras of this kind are never completely silent and need at least normal room light levels to record legibly. The quality of picture is much poorer than those taken by the sequence camera and generally the cost is higher.

CCTV systems are the state-of-the-art surveillance devices and in most cases have replaced still and motion picture systems. The CCTV systems coupled with video cassette recording equipment are exceptionally flexible (see Figures 9.6 and 9.7). The tapes can be erased and reused, a definite cost savings in comparison to other systems.

Planning for a Surveillance System

Once a decision has been made to purchase a system, careful planning must precede the purchase. Poor planning generally means wasted funds and a system that does not do the required job. Several questions should be asked before any purchase, among them:

Is the camera to be visible and used as a deterrent to crime or hidden and used in civil or criminal prosecutions? Most businesses would rather prevent a crime than go to the effort and expense of prosecution and therefore prefer visible camera locations. In addition, hidden camera sites cost more, since there is not only the investment in the camera, but also expenses for hiding the camera.

What effect, if any, will the sun have on the operation of the system? Sunlight is variable in intensity, and good light conditions may de-

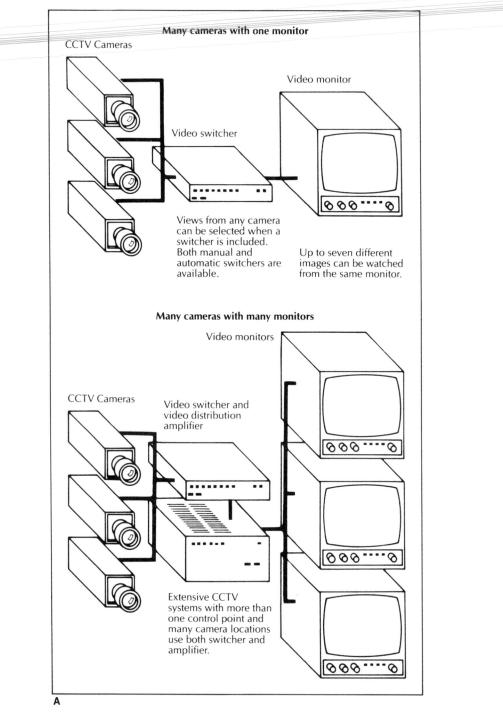

Many cameras with one monitor

CCTV Cameras

Video monitor

Video switcher

Views from any camera can be selected when a switcher is included. Both manual and automatic switchers are available.

Up to seven different images can be watched from the same monitor.

Many cameras with many monitors

Video monitors

CCTV Cameras

Video switcher and video distribution amplifier

Extensive CCTV systems with more than one control point and many camera locations use both switcher and amplifier.

A

Figure 9.6 CCTV Systems. (A) Many cameras with one monitor. (B) One camera with one monitor. CCTV Systems. (Courtesy of Chubb Security.)

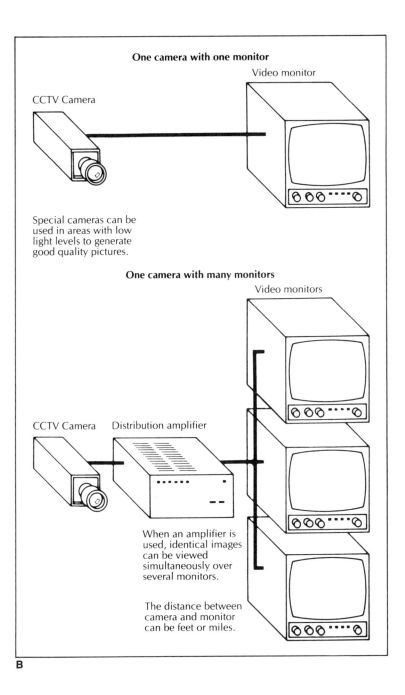

One camera with one monitor

Video monitor

CCTV Camera

Special cameras can be used in areas with low light levels to generate good quality pictures.

One camera with many monitors

Video monitors

CCTV Camera   Distribution amplifier

When an amplifier is used, identical images can be viewed simultaneously over several monitors.

The distance between camera and monitor can be feet or miles.

B

227

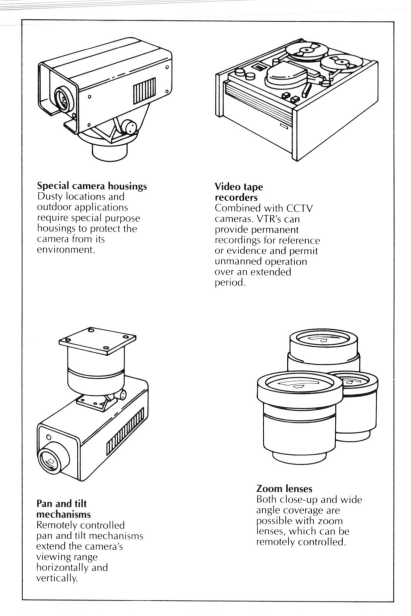

Special camera housings
Dusty locations and outdoor applications require special purpose housings to protect the camera from its environment.

Video tape recorders
Combined with CCTV cameras. VTR's can provide permanent recordings for reference or evidence and permit unmanned operation over an extended period.

Pan and tilt mechanisms
Remotely controlled pan and tilt mechanisms extend the camera's viewing range horizontally and vertically.

Zoom lenses
Both close-up and wide angle coverage are possible with zoom lenses, which can be remotely controlled.

Figure 9.7 Options that expand CCTV capabilities. (Courtesy of Chubb Security.)

teriorate as the day progresses into dusk. In addition, sunlight can cause glare. A CCTV system may allow for changes in the setting of the recording cameras to help adjust for changes in light intensity.

Where is the best location for a camera? In banks, for instance, placement might be where customers do not immediately notice the camera. In many cases, this is accomplished by placing the camera over the exits. This permits narrow-angle coverage of an area where the subject must approach the camera directly at a time when he may be comparatively off-guard (for example, you might catch a bank robber removing his disguise). In these cases, the teller does not have to signal the camera until the robber is on the way out of the bank. When the camera is placed to photograph the teller/cashier area, the employee may be endangered by attempting to trigger the camera manually.

Should the placement of the camera be high? High placement is not as efficient as it is often thought to be. Persons photographed from high locations may not be recognizable. A good spot is just high enough to see over obstacles and to protect the camera from curious observers.

A site survey is essential to effective planning. This survey is generally presented in the form of a diagram with the areas to be protected drawn to scale. The diagram should include blind spots, areas of high loss potential, exits, windows, cash registers, electrical outlets, and other data significant to the site. Lighting requirements can be determined by using an illumination meter. Record the information on the diagram, and measure illumination at both the brightest and the darkest times of the day. Levels of light should generally not be below 20–40 or above 250 footcandles (fc). If the level falls below 20 fc, you will need additional lighting or other camera equipment; if it falls above 250 fc, you will need special filters. Study the traffic flow to discover the greatest usage.

Old Construction

Older buildings—particularly, though certainly not exclusively, office buildings—present a host of different and difficult security problems. Exterior fire escapes, old and frequently badly worn locks, common walls, roof access from neighboring buildings, unused and forgotten connecting doors—all increase the exposure to burglary.

It is vital that all such openings be surveyed and plans be made for securing them. Those windows not designated as emergency exits must be barred or screened. Where windows lead to a fire escape or are accessible to adjacent fire escapes, their essential security must be accomplished within the regulations of the local fire codes. Fire safety must be a primary consideration. In cases where prudence or the law (or both) dictate that locks would be a hazard to safety, windows should be alarmed and the interior areas to which these windows provide access must be further secured. Here, security can be likened to any army retreating to secondary or tertiary lines of defense to establish a strong and defensible position.

It is also well to consider the danger of attack from neighboring occupancies in shared space where entry might be made from a low-risk, badly secured premise into a higher-risk area that might otherwise be well protected against a more direct attack.

New Construction

Modern urban buildings, though security conscious in varying degrees, present their own problems. Most interior construction is standardized. Fire and building codes are such that corridor doors can resist most attacks if the hardware is adequate. Corridor ceilings are fixed, and entrances to individual offices usually offer a fairly high degree of security.

On the other hand, modern construction creates offices that are essentially open-top boxes. They have solid exterior walls (though interior walls are frequently plaster board) and a concrete floor. But nothing of any security value protects the top. The ceiling is simply a layer of acoustical tiles lying loose on runners suspended between partition walls. In the space above these tiles—between them and the concrete slab above—are vital air conditioning ducts, and wiring for power and telephones.

In effect, any given floor of a building has a crawlspace that runs from exterior wall to exterior wall. This may not be literally so in every case, but the net result stands. It means that virtually every room and every office is accessible through this space. Once this crawlspace is reached from any occupancy, the remaining offices on that floor are accessible.

Extending dividing walls up to the next floor will not solve the problem, since this drywall construction is easily broken through and, in any case, it must be breached to allow passage of all utilities. Alarms of various kinds, which are discussed later in this book, are recommended to overcome this problem.

Security at the Building Design Stage

Once a building has been constructed, the damage has been done. Security weaknesses begin to manifest themselves, but it is far too expensive to make basic structural changes to correct them. Guard services and protective devices that might not otherwise have been necessary must be instituted. In any event, there will be some considerable expense for protection that could easily have been incorporated into the design of the building before construction began. This kind of oversight can be very expensive indeed.

Unfortunately we have not yet arrived at the point where the need for security from criminal acts is as automatic a consideration as is the need for efficiency or profits. Architects' interest in design for protection of buildings and grounds is usually minimal. They traditionally leave such demands to their clients, who usually are unaware of the availability of protective hardware and who are rarely competent to deal in the problems of protective design.

The crime rate and the growing awareness of the problem have, however, directed more attention toward the important role that building design can play in security. There have been some efforts on the part of the federal government to accentuate the architect's role in security.

Under the umbrella of environment security, concepts of crime prevention through environment design (CPTED) have received added attention in recent years. Early work in this field concentrated on residential security, particularly in public housing, with Oscar Newman's major study of "defensible space" being a pioneering work.[1] The LEAA also funded studies and provided the funds for CPTED projects in residential, commercial, and school modes.

This approach to crime prevention through environmental design has important implications for private security. It seeks to bring together many disciplines—among them urban planning, architectural design, public law enforcement, and private security—to create an improved quality of urban life through crime prevention. And in particular it encourages awareness of crime prevention techniques through physical design.

Security Principles in Design

Certain principles should always be considered in planning any building. Without them, it can be dangerously vulnerable. Some areas of consideration are:

1. The number of perimeter and building openings should be kept to a minimum consistent with safety codes.
2. Perimeter protection should be planned as part of the overall design.
3. Exterior windows, if they are less than 14 feet above ground level,

should be constructed of glass brick, laminated glass, or plastic materials, or they should be shielded with heavy screening or steel grilles.

4. Points of possible access or escape that breach the exterior of the building or the perimeter protection should be protected. Points to be considered are skylights, air conditioning vents, sewer ducts, manholes, or any opening larger than 96 square inches.

5. High-quality locks with readily changeable cylinders should be employed on all exterior and restricted area doors for protection and quick-change capability in the event of key loss.

6. Protective lighting should be installed.

7. Shipping and receiving areas should be widely separated.

8. Exterior doors intended for emergency use only should be fitted with alarms.

9. Exterior service doors should lead directly into the service area so that nonemployee traffic is restricted in its movement.

10. Dock areas should be designed so drivers can report to shipping or receiving clerks without moving through storage areas.

11. Employment offices should be located so that applicants either enter directly from outside or move through as little of the building as possible.

12. Employee entrances should be located directly off the gate to the parking lot.

13. Employee locker rooms should be located by employee entrance and exit doors.

14. Doors in remote areas should be fitted with alarms.

Review Questions

1. What factors need to be considered when you are purchasing and installing locking devices for security purposes?

2. Describe the basic principles of an effective key control plan.

3. What are the two end results of an effective surveillance system?

Reference

1. Oscar Newman, *Defensible Space: Crime Prevention Through Urban Design* (New York: Macmillan, 1973).

10

The Inner Defenses: Intrusion and Access Control

Once the facility's perimeter is secured, the next step in physical security planning is to minimize or control access to the facility's or the building's interior. The extent of this control will depend on the nature and function of the facility; the controls must not interfere with the facility's operation. It is theoretically possible to seal off access to a given operation completely, but it would be difficult to imagine how useful the operation would be in such an atmosphere.

Certainly no commercial establishment can be open for business while it is closed to the public. A steady stream of outsiders, from customers to service personnel, is essential to its economic health. In such cases, the security problem is to control this traffic without interfering with the function of the business being protected. Isolated manufacturing facilities must also provide for the traffic created by the delivery of raw materials, the shipping of fabricated goods, the provision of services, and of course the labor force, which may be operating in several shifts.

All such traffic tends to compromise the physical security of the facility. But security must be provided, and it must be provided appropriately for the operation of the facility being served.

Within any building no matter whether it is located inside a perimeter barrier or is a part of the perimeter wall, it is necessary to consider the need to protect against the internal thief as well as the potential intruder. Whereas the boundary fence is primarily designed to keep out unwanted visitors (not altogether forgetting its function in the control of movement of authorized personnel), interior security must provide some protection against the free movement of employees and others bent on pilferage as well as establishing a second line of defense against the unannounced intruder.

Since every building is used differently and has its own unique traffic composition and flow, each building presents a different security problem. Each must be examined and analyzed in great detail before an effective security program can be developed.

It cannot be overemphasized that such a program must be implemented without in any way interfering with the orderly and efficient operation of the facility to be protected. It must not be obtrusive, and yet it must provide a predetermined level of protection against criminal attack from outside or inside.

The first points of examination must be the doors and windows of buildings within the perimeter. These must be considered in terms of effectiveness no matter whether the building walls form a part of or constitute in themselves the perimeter barrier (as we have already discussed in Chapter 9) or they are a true second defense line where the building under examination is completely within the protection of a barrier.

Doors to Sensitive Areas

Doors to telephone equipment rooms, computer installations, research and development, and other sensitive areas should be equipped with automatic door-closing devices and fitted with strong dead bolts and heavy latches.

In cases where an area is under heavy security but has any degree of traffic, it might be well to consider the installation of an electric *strike* to secure the operation and control the traffic. This kind of unit is a locking device controlled remotely by a security person, permitting entry of a recognized, authorized person only when a button is pressed to release the lock. Since it requires someone on hand at all times for its operation, this system can be expensive. It must be examined with the cost-versus-security cost equation in mind.

Supply room and tool room doors should be secured whenever those rooms are not actually in use. Even when they are in use, entrance into these areas must be restricted. The usual construction of such restraints consists of either a dutch door in which the bottom half is secured or a counter that can be closed off by heavy screening, chain-link fencing material, or reinforced shutters.

Special care should be taken in the storage of small items of value. Such merchandise or material is highly pilferable by virtue of its value for resale or personal use combined with the ease with which it can be stolen. Although such items may be stored in a facility of any construction capable of providing security, it has been the experience of many firms that uniformly stacked rows, piles, or pallets of such items within a cage-type construction that provides instant eyeball inventory is the best protection. Such precautions will vary from business to business, but they must be carefully systematized to control this potentially troublesome area of loss.

Office Area Doors

Doors between production and office areas or between heavily trafficked areas and office spaces must be examined for the likelihood of their use for criminal purposes. Their construction and locking hardware will be determined by such a survey. In most cases, these passages will be minimum security areas during regular working hours since there is usually a need for movement between these areas. When there is little or no use of the office area, these doors should be secured.

Traffic Patterns

Doors must be analyzed for their function in laying out the security plan. In some cases, they may serve a dual purpose as, for example, fire doors, which are designed to close automatically in the event of a fire. These doors, which may remain open at the discretion of management, must be fitted to form an effective and automatic barrier to the spread of fire. They may be desirable when fire doors separate a production area from a warehouse or storage area. During those times when the production area is in operation but the warehouse is not, such fire doors can perform a security function by remaining closed.

In other cases, doors must be examined in an effort to establish a schedule for their use. Employee entrances that are the authorized points of passage for all employees may be staffed by security personnel, depending on whether the control point is established there or farther out on the perimeter. These doors could be secured once the employees have entered, thus denying entrance to unauthorized visitors as well as preventing any employees from wandering out to the fence or the parking lot or any other location where they might cache contraband for later pickup or transport.

It is axiomatic, however, that any door used as an entrance will in a time of emergency be used as an exit by some employees. This is true in apartments and office buildings and even in industrial facilities where the employees are thoroughly familiar with the premises. No matter what or how many designated emergency exits or procedures there may be, some individuals in a time of tension or near panic will seek out the door with which they are most familiar.

The entrance then must always be considered an emergency exit, and it should be equipped with panic hardware. To protect against surreptitious use, it should also be fitted with at least a local alarm.

The same, of course, is true of the designated emergency exits. These doors should, in addition, be stripped of all exterior hardware on the outside since they are not intended for operational use at any time.

Personnel doors leading to and from the dock area must be carefully controlled and supervised at all times when the dock is in use. These and dock doors must be secured when the area is no longer operational.

Fire doors in office buildings should be fitted with alarms to prevent surreptitious use and access to the interior. Public stairwells should be prohibited or discouraged unless doors from them open into reception areas.

Traffic Control

Controlling traffic in and out and within a facility is essential to the facility's security program. Perimeter barriers, locked doors, and screened windows prevent or deter the entry of unauthorized visitors. But since some traffic is essential to every operation no matter how highly classified it may be, provision must be made for the control of this movement.

Specific solutions will depend on the nature of the business. Obviously retail establishments, which encourage high volume traffic and regularly handle a great deal of merchandise both in and out, have a problem of a different dimension from that of the industrial operation working on a highly classified government project. Both, however, must work from the same general principles toward providing the greatest possible security within the efficient and effective operation of the job at hand.

Controlling traffic includes the identification of employees and visitors and directing or limiting their movements and the control of all incoming and outgoing packages and of trucks and private cars.

Visitors

All visitors to any facility should be required to identify themselves. When they are allowed to enter after they have established themselves as being on an authorized call, they should be limited to predetermined, unrestricted areas. The obvious exception is in firms where the public have free access to the facility, that is, retail stores.

If possible, sales, service, and trade personnel should receive clearance in advance on making an appointment with the person responsible for their being there. Although this is not always possible, most businesses deal with such visitors on an appointment basis and a system of notifying the security personnel can be established in a majority of cases.

Businesses regularly called on unannounced—by salesmen or other tradespeople—should set aside a waiting room that can be reached without passing through sensitive areas. In some cases, it may be advisable to issue passes that clearly designate them as visitors. If they will be escorted to and from their destination, a pass system is probably unnecessary.

Ideally, all traffic patterns involving visitors should be short, physically confined to keep them from straying, and capable of being observed at all points along the route. In spread-out industrial facilities, they should take the shortest, most direct route that will not pass through restricted, sensitive, or dangerous areas and will pass from one reception area to another.

To achieve security objectives without alienating visitors and without in any way interfering with the operation of the business, any effective control system must be simple and understandable. It must incorporate certain specific elements in order to accomplish its aims. It must limit entry to those people who are authorized to be there and be able to identify such people. It must have a procedure by which persons may be identified as being authorized to be in certain areas and prevent theft, pilferage, or damage to the assets of the installation. And it must prevent injury to the visitor.

Employee Identification

Small industrial facilities and most offices find that personal identification of employees by guards or receptionists is adequate protection against intruders entering under the guise of employees. In plants of over 50 employees per shift or in high-turnover businesses, this type of identification is inadequate. The opportunity for error is simply too great.

The most practical and generally accepted system is the use of badges or identification cards. Generally speaking, this system should designate when, where, how, and to whom passes should be displayed; what is to be done in case of loss of the pass; procedures for retrieving badges from terminating employees; and a system for cancellation and reissue of all passes, either as a security review or when a significant and specific number of badges have been reported lost or stolen.

To be effective, badges must be tamper-resistant, which means that they should be printed or embossed on a distinctive stock that is worked with a series of designs difficult to reproduce. They should contain a clear and recent photograph of the bearer, preferably in color. The photograph should be at least one inch square and should be updated every two or three years or when there is any significant change in facial appearance such as the growing or removal of a beard or moustache. It should, in addition, contain vital statistics such as date of birth, height, weight, color of hair and eyes, sex, and both thumbprints. It should be laminated and of sturdy construction. In cases where there are areas set off or restricted to general employee traffic, it might be color coded to indicate those areas to which the bearer has authorized access.

If a badge system is established, it will only be as effective as is its enforcement. Facility guards are responsible to see that the system is adhered to, but they must have the cooperation of the majority of the employees and the full support of management. If the system is simply a pro forma exercise, it becomes a useless annoyance and would better be dispensed with.

Pass Systems

As we have just noted, all employees entering or leaving a facility or area should be identified and their authorizations to be there should be checked. This can be achieved through one of many badge systems. Three possible systems are:

- *The single pass system* in which a badge or pass coded for authorization to enter specific areas is issued to an employee who keeps it until the authorization is changed or until leaving the company.
- *The pass exchange system* in which an employee entering a controlled area exchanges one color-coded pass for another that carries a different color code specifying the limitations of the authorization. On leaving, the employee surrenders the controlled area pass for the basic authorization identification pass. (In this system, the second pass never leaves the controlled area, thus reducing the possibility of switching, forging, or altering.)
- *The multiple pass system* is essentially the same as the exchange system, but it provides an extra measure of security by requiring that exchanges take place at the entrance to each restricted area within the controlled area.

Package Control

Every facility must establish a system for the control of packages entering or leaving the premises. However desirable it might seem, it is simply unrealistic to support a blanket rule forbidding packages either in or out as a workable procedure. Such a rule would be damaging to employee morale and in many cases would actually work against the efficient operation of the facility. Therefore since the transporting of packages through the portals is a fact of life, they must be dealt with in order to prevent theft and misappropriation of company property.

If it is deemed necessary, the types of items that may be brought in or taken out may be limited. If such is the case, the fact must be publicized and clearly understood by everyone.

Packages brought in should be checked for content. If possible where they are not to be used during work, they should be checked with the guard to be picked up at the end of the day. In most cases, spot checking will suffice.

Whatever the policy concerning packages—whether they are to be checked or inspected—that policy must be widely publicized in advance. This is to avoid the appearance of discrimination against those whose packages are opened and examined or those that are denied entrance in conformity with company policy.

Files, Safes, and Vaults

The final line of defense at any facility is in the high-security storage areas where papers, records, plans, cashable instruments, precious metals, or other especially valuable assets are protected. These security containers will be of a size and quantity that the nature of the business dictates.

Every facility will have its own particular needs, but certain general observations apply. The choice of the proper security container for specific applications is influenced largely by the value and the vulnerability of the items to be stored in them. Irreplaceable papers or original documents may not have any intrinsic or marketable value so they may not be a likely target for a thief, but since they do have great value to the owners, they must be protected against fire. On the other hand, uncut precious stones or even recorded negotiable papers that can be replaced may not be in danger from fire, but they would surely be attractive to a thief. They must therefore be protected against theft.

In protecting property, it is essential to recognize that generally speaking protective containers are designed to secure against burglary or fire. Each type of equipment has a specialized function and provides only minimal protection against the other risk. There are containers designed with a burglary-resistant chest within a fire-resistant container that are useful in many instances, but these too must be evaluated in terms of the mission.

Whatever the equipment, the staff must be educated and reminded of the different roles played by the two types of containers. It is all too common for company personnel to assume that a fire-resistant safe is also burglary-resistant and vice versa.

Files

Burglary-resistant files are secure against most surreptitious attacks. On the other hand, they can be pried open in less than half an hour if the burglar is permitted to work undisturbed and is not concerned with the noise created in the operation. Such files are suitable for nonnegotiable papers or even proprietary information since these items are normally only targeted by surreptitious assault.

Filing cabinets with a fire rating of one hour and further fitted with a combination lock will probably be suitable for all uses but the storage of government classified documents.[1]

Safes

Safes are expensive, but if they are selected wisely, they can be very important investments in security. Emphatically safes are not simply safes. They are each designed to perform a particular job to provide a particular level of protection. The two types of safes of most interest to the security professional are the record safe (fire-resistant) and the money safe (burglary-resistant). To use fire-resistant safes for the storage of valuables—an all too common practice—is to invite disaster. At the same time, it would be equally careless to use a burglary-resistant safe for the storage of valuable papers or records since, if a fire were to occur, the contents of such a safe would be reduced to ashes.

Safes are rated to describe the degree of protection they afford. Naturally, the more protection provided, the more expensive the safe will be. In selecting the best one for the requirements of the facility, a number of questions must be considered: How great is the threat of fire or burglary? What is the value of the safe's contents? How much protection time is required in the event of a fire or of a burglary attempt? Only after these questions have been answered can a reasonable, permissible capital outlay for their protection be determined.

Record Safes

Fire-resistant containers are classified according to the maximum interior temperature permitted after exposure to heat for varying periods of time. A record safe with a UL rating of 350–4 (formerly designated "A") can withstand exterior temperatures building to 2000°F for four hours without permitting the interior temperature to rise above 350°F.

The UL tests that result in the classifications are conducted to simulate a major fire with its gradual build-up of heat to 2000°F, including circumstances where the safe might fall several stories through the fire-damaged building. In addition, an explosion test simulates a cold safe dropping into a fire that has already reached 2000°F.

The actual procedure for the 350–4 rating involves the safe staying four hours in a furnace temperature that reaches 2000°F. The furnace is turned off after four hours but the safe remains inside until it is cool. The interior temperature must remain below 350°F during heating and cooling off periods. This interior temperature is determined by sensors sealed inside the safe in six specified locations to provide a continuous record of the temperatures during the test. Papers are also placed in the safe to simulate records. The explosion impact test is conducted with another safe of the same model that is placed for one-half hour in a furnace preheated to 2000°F. If no explosion occurs, the furnace is set at 1550°F and raised to 1700°F over a half-hour period. After this hour in the explosion test, the safe is removed and dropped 30 feet onto rubble. The safe is then returned to the furnace and reheated for one hour at 1700°F. The furnace and safe then are allowed to cool after which the papers inside must be legible and uncharred.

Computer media storage classifications are for containers that do not allow the internal temperature to go above 150°F. This is critical since computer media begins to distort at 150°F and diskettes at 125°F.[2]

Insulated vault-door classifications are much the same as they are for safes except that the vault doors are not subjected to explosion/impact tests.

In some businesses, a combination fire-resistant/burglary-resistant safe welded inside may serve as a double protection for different kinds of assets, but in no event must the purposes of these two kinds of safes be confused if there is one of each on the premises. Most record safes have combination locks, relocking devices, and hardened steel lockplates to provide a measure of burglar resistance. It must be reemphasized that record safes are designed to protect documents and other similar flammables against destruction by fire. They provide only slight deterrence to the attack of even unskilled burglars. Similarly the resistance provided by burglar-resistant safes is powerless to protect contents in a fire of any significance.

Money Safes

Burglary-resistant safes are nothing more than very heavy metal boxes without wheels, which offer varying degrees of protection against many forms of attack. A safe with a UL rating of TL-15, for instance, weighs at least 750 pounds, and its front face can resist attack by common hand and electric tools for at least 15 minutes. Other safes will resist not only attack with tools but also attack with torches and explosives.

Since burglary-resistant safes have a limited holding capacity, it is always advisable to study the volume of the items to be secured. If the volume is sufficiently large, it might be advisable to consider the installation of a burglary-resistant vault, which, although considerably more expensive, can have an enormous holding capacity.

Securing the Safe

Whatever safe is selected must be securely fastened to the structure of its surroundings. Police reports are filled with cases where un-attached safes, some as heavy as a ton, have been stolen in their entirety—safe *and* contents—to be worked on in uninterrupted concentration. A study of safe burglars in California showed that the largest group (37.3 percent) removed safes from the premises to be opened elsewhere.[3]

A convicted criminal told investigators how he and an accomplice had watched a supermarket to determine the cash flow and the manager's banking habits. They noted that he accumulated cash in a small, wheeled safe until Saturday morning when he banked it. Presumably he felt secure in this practice since he lived in an apartment above the store and perhaps felt that he was very much on top of the situation in every way. One Friday night, the thief and his friend rolled the safe into their station wagon. They pried it open at their leisure to get the $15,000 inside.

Pleased with their success, the thieves were even more pleased when they found that the manager replaced the stolen safe with one exactly like it and continued with the same banking routine. Two weeks later, our man went back alone and picked up another $12,000 in exactly the same way as before.

It is becoming a common practice to install the safe in a concrete floor where it offers great resistance to attack. In this kind of installation only the door and its combination are exposed. Since the door is the strongest part of a modern safe, the chances of successful robbery are considerably reduced.

Vaults

Vaults are essentially enlarged safes. As such, they are subject to the same kinds of attack and fall under the same basic principles of protection as do safes.

Since it would be prohibitively expensive to build a vault out of shaped and welded steel and special alloys, the construction, except for the door, is usually of high quality, reinforced concrete. There are many ways in which such a vault can be constructed, but however it is done, it will always be extremely heavy and at best a difficult architectural problem.

Typically vaults are situated at or below ground level so they do not add to the stresses of the structure housing them. If a vault must be built on the upper stories of a building, it must be supported by independent members that do not provide support for other parts of the building. And it must be strong enough to withstand the weight imposed on it if the building should collapse from under it as the result of fire or explosion.

The doors of such vaults are normally 6 inches thick, and they may be as much as 24 inches thick in the largest installations. Since these doors present a formidable obstacle to any criminal, an attack will usually be directed at the walls, ceiling, or floor, which must for that reason match the strength of the door. As a rule, these surfaces should be twice as thick as the door and never less than 12 inches thick.

If it is at all possible, a vault should be surrounded by narrow corridors that will permit inspection of the exterior but that will be sufficiently confined to discourage the use of heavy drilling or cutting equipment by attackers. It is important that there be no power outlets anywhere in the vicinity of the vault; such outlets could provide criminals with energy to drive their tools.

Container Protection

Since no container can resist assault indefinitely, it must be supported by alarm systems and frequent inspections. Capacitance and vibration alarms are the types most generally used to protect safes and file cabinets. Ideally any container should be inspected at least once within the period of its rated resistance. Closed circuit television (CCTV) surveillance can, of course, provide constant inspection and, if the expense is warranted, is highly recommended.

By the same token, safes have a greater degree of security if they are well lighted and located where they can be seen readily. Any safe located where it can be seen from a well-policed street will be much less likely to be attacked than one that sits in a darkened back office on an upper floor.[4]

Continuing Evaluation

Security containers are the last line of defense, but in many situations, they should be the first choice in establishing a sound security system. The containers must be selected with care after an exhaustive evaluation of the needs of the facility under examination. They must also be reviewed regularly for their suitability to the job they are to perform.

Just as the safe manufacturers are continually improving the design, construction, and materials used in safes, so is the criminal world improving its technology and techniques of successful attack. Because of the considerable capital outlay involved in providing the firm with adequate security containers, many businesspeople are reluctant to entertain the notion that these containers may someday become outmoded—not because they wear out or cease to function but rather because new tools and techniques have nullified their effectiveness. In 1990, a series of attacks on financial institutions in a major west coast city where the burglars used drainage tunnels to enter vaults from beneath the facilities points out that vaults are not impregnable.

In selecting security containers, it is important that the equipment conform to the needs of the risk, that it be regularly reevaluated, and that, if necessary, it be brought up to date however unwelcome the additional outlay may be.

Inspections

In spite of all defensive devices, the possibility of an intrusion always exists. The highest fence can be scaled, and the stoutest lock can be compromised. Even highly sophisticated alarm systems can be contravened by a knowledgeable professional. The most efficient system of physical protection can eventually be foiled.

It is necessary, therefore, to support each element of the system continually with another element—remember the concept of defense in depth. The ultimate backup surveillance must never let down.

Guard Patrols

Visual inspections by irregular patrols through office spaces or an industrial complex or constant CCTV surveillance of these same areas are vital to the success of the security program.

It is equally important to "sweep" the facility after closing time. "Hide-ins" are common in offices or retail establishments. These are thieves who conceal themselves in a closet or utility room and wait for the establishment to close and for everybody to go home. After hide-ins take what they are looking for, the only challenge is to break out. The chances of catching such thieves in a premise protected only by perimeter alarms is remote indeed. They must be picked up on the sweep when guards go through the entire facility from top to bottom or from east to west to see that everyone required to do so has left.

Specific duties of guards on patrol are discussed elsewhere, but in general, it should be noted that patrols should be made at least once each hour, more often if the area and the size of the guard force permit.

Particular attention must be paid to any signs of tampering with locks, gates, fences, doors, or windows. The presence of piles of rubbish or materials should be noted for the possibility of concealment—particularly if they are near the perimeter barrier or in the vicinity of storage areas.

In the patrol of office buildings, it is wise to stop occasionally for a long enough period of time to listen for any sounds that might indicate the presence of an intruder.

It is equally important that patrols in any facility be alert to any condition that might prove hazardous. These might be anything from an oil slick in a typically trafficked area to a heater left on and unattended. Those conditions presenting an immediate danger must be corrected immediately; others must be reported for correction. All of them must be noted in the log and on the appropriate form.

Alarms

In order to balance the cost factors in the consideration of any security system, it is necessary to evaluate the security needs and then determine how that security can, or more importantly should, be provided. Since the employment of security personnel can be costly, methods must be sought to improve their efficient use and to extend the coverage they can reasonably provide.

Protection provided by physical barriers is usually the first area to be stretched to its optimum point before looking for other protective devices. Fences, locks, grilles, vaults, safes, and similar means of preventing entry or unauthorized use are employed to their fullest capacity. Since such methods can only delay intrusion rather than prevent it, security personnel are engaged to inspect the premises thoroughly and frequently enough to interrupt or prevent intrusion within the time span of the deterrent capability of the physical barriers. In order to further protect against entry should both barrier and guard be circumvented, alarm systems are frequently employed.

Such systems permit more economical use of security personnel, and they may also substitute for costly construction of barriers. They do not act as substitutes for barriers as such. But they can support barriers of lesser impregnability and expense, and they can warn of movement in areas where barriers are impractical, undesirable, or impossible.

In determining whether a facility actually needs an alarm system, a review and evaluation of past experience of robbery, burglary, or other crimes involving unauthorized entry should be part of the survey preparatory to the formulation of the ultimate security plan. Such experience, viewed in relation to national figures and the experience of neighboring occupancies and businesses of like operation, may well serve as a guide for determining the need for alarms.

Kinds of Alarm Protection

There are three basic types of alarm system providing protection for a security system:

1. *Intrusion alarms* signal the entry of persons into a facility or an area while the system is in operation.
2. *Fire alarms* operate in a number of ways to warn of fire dangers in various stages of development of a fire or respond protectively by announcing the flow of water in a sprinkler system, indicating either that the sprinklers have been activated by the heat of a fire or that they are malfunctioning. (Fire alarms will be discussed in detail in the following chapter.)
3. *Special use alarms* warn of a process reaching a dangerous temperature (either too high or too low), of the presence of toxic fumes, or that a machine is running too fast. Although such alarms are not, strictly speaking, security devices, they may require the immediate reaction of security personnel for remedial action, and thus deserve mention at this point.

Alarms do not, in most cases, initiate any counter action. They serve only to alert the world at large or, more usually, specific reactive forces to the fact that a condition exists for which the facility was filled with alarms. Alarm systems are of many types, but all have three common elements:

1. *An alarm sensor:* a device that is designed to respond to a certain change in conditions such as the opening of a door, movement within a room, or rapid rise in heat
2. *A circuit or sending device:* a device that sends a signal about whatever is sensed to some other location. This may be done via an electrical circuit that transmits the alarm signal over a telephone, fiber optic lines, or through air waves.
3. *An enunciator or sounding device:* a sounding device, which is used to alert someone that the sensor has detected a change in conditions. The device may be a light, a bell, a horn, a self-dialing phone, or a punch tape.

The questions that must be answered in setting up any alarm system are:

1. Who can respond to an alarm fastest and most effectively?
2. What are the costs of such response as opposed to response of somewhat lesser efficiency?
3. What is the comparable predicted loss factor between these alternatives?

Alarm Sensors

The selection of the sensor or triggering device is dependent on many factors. The object, space, or perimeter to be protected is the first consideration. Beyond that, the incidence of outside noise, movement, or interference must be considered before deciding on the type of sensor that will do the best job.

A brief examination of the kinds of devices available will serve as an introduction to a further study of this field.

Electromechanical Devices

These are the simplest alarm devices used. They are nothing more than switches that are turned on by some change in their attitude. For example, an electromechanical device in a door or a window, their most common application, is held in the open, or noncontact, position by a plunger on a spring when the door or window is closed (see Figure 10.1). Opening either of these entrances releases the plunger, which, under the action of the spring, moves forward, engaging the contacts in the device and thus activating the alarm.

Such devices operate on the principle of breaking the circuit. Since these devices are simply switches in a circuit, they are normally used to cover several windows and doors in a room or along a corridor. Opening any of these entrances opens the circuit and activates the alarm. They are easy to circumvent in most installations by jumping the circuit, or they can be defeated from within by tying back the plungers with string or rubber bands.

Pressure Devices

These are also switches, activated by pressure applied to them. This same principle is in regular use in buildings with automatic door openers. In security applications, they are usually in the form of mats. These are sometimes concealed under carpeting, or, when they logically fit the existing decor, are placed in a strategic spot without concealment. Wires leading to them are naturally hidden in some way.

Photoelectric Devices

These use a beam of light, transmitted for as much as 500 feet away, to a receiver. As long as this beam is directed into the receiver, the circuit is inactive. As soon as this contact is broken however briefly, the alarm is activated. These devices are also used as door openers.

In security applications, the beam is modulated so that the device cannot be circumvented by a flashlight or some other light source as can be done in

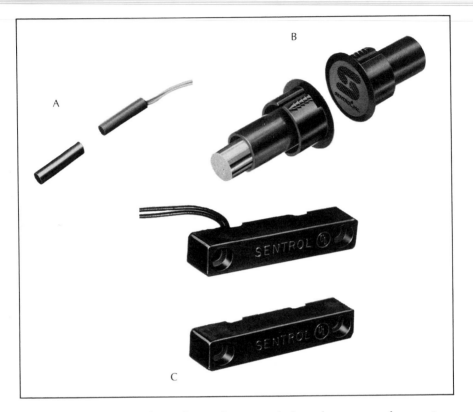

Figure 10.1 (A) Recessed switches and magnets help make a neat and attractive installation. Because they are concealed, they are more tamper-resistant. (Photo courtesy of Ademco) (B) Larger switches are sometimes easier to install. Since they are recess mounted, they are hidden from view, and their size is not noticeable. (C) Surface-mounted switches, although visible, are the least expensive and easiest to install.

nonsecurity applications. For greater security, ultraviolet or infrared light is used—although even these can be spotted by an experienced intruder unless an electronic flicker device is incorporated into the device. Obviously the device must be undetectable since, once the beam is located, it is an easy matter to step over, or crawl under, it.

In some applications, a single transmitter and receiver installation can be used—even when they are not in a line of sight—by a mirror system reflecting the transmitted beam around corners or to different levels. Such a system is difficult to maintain, however, since the slightest movement of any of the mirrors will disturb the alignment, and the system will cease operating.

Motion Detection Alarms

These operate by radio frequency or ultrasonic wave transmission.

The radio frequency (or microwave) motion detector transmits waves throughout the protected area from a transmitting to a receiving antenna. The receiving antenna is set or adjusted to a specific level of emission. Any disturbance of this level by absorption or alteration of the wave pattern will activate the alarm.

The false alarm rate with this device can be high since the radio waves will penetrate the walls and respond to motion outside the designated area unless the walls are shielded. Some such devices on the market permit an adjustment whereby the emissions can be tuned in such a way to cover only a single area without leaking into outside areas, but these require considerable skill to tune them properly.

The ultrasonic motion detector operates in much the same way as does the radio frequency unit, except that it consists of a transceiver that both transmits and receives ultrasonic waves (see Figure 10.2). One of these units can be used to cover an area. Or they may be used in multiples where such

Figure 10.2 Ultrasonic motion detector. (From Robert Barnard, *Intrusion Detection Systems* [Stoneham, Mass.: Butterworth Publishers, 1981], p. 125.)

use is indicated (see Figure 10.3). They can be adjusted to cover a single, limited area (see Figure 10.4) or broadened to provide area protection.

The alarm is activated when any motion disturbs the pattern of the sound waves. Some units come with special circuits that distinguish between inconsequential movement (such as flying moths or moving drapes) and an intruder.

Ultrasonic waves do not penetrate walls and are therefore unaffected by outside movement. They are not affected by audible noise in itself, but such noises can sometimes disturb the wave pattern of the protective ultrasonic transmission and create false alarms.

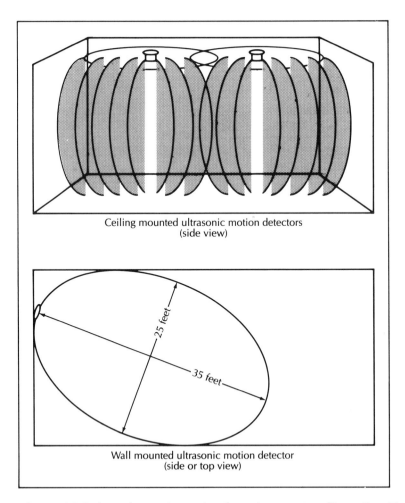

Ceiling mounted ultrasonic motion detectors
(side view)

25 feet

35 feet

Wall mounted ultrasonic motion detector
(side or top view)

Figure 10.3 Indoor ultrasonic motion detection patterns. (From Don T. Cherry, *Total Facility Control* [Stoneham, Mass.: Butterworth Publishers, 1986], p. 134.)

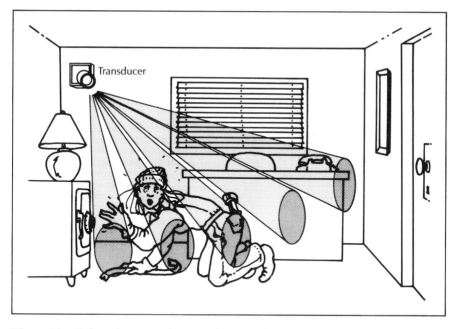

Figure 10.4 Infrared motion detector. (From Robert Barnard, *Intrusion Detection Systems* [Stoneham, Mass.: Butterworth Publishers, 1981], p. 152.)

Passive infrared motion detectors do not transmit a signal for an intruder to disturb. Rather, moving infrared radiation is detected against the radiation environment of the room (see Figures 10.5 through 10.7). This detector is designed to sense the radiation from a human body. Sunlight, auto headlights, heaters, and air conditioning units can trigger false alarms.

Dual-tech motion sensors combine the traits of passive infrared detectors with either microwave or ultasonic technology.

Capacitance Alarm Systems

Also referred to as proximity alarms, these are used to protect metal containers of all kinds. This alarm's most common use is to protect a high-security storage area within a fenced enclosure. To set the system in operation, an ungrounded metal object (such as the safe, file, or fence mentioned above) is wired to two oscillator circuits that are set in balance. An electromagnetic field is thus created around the object to be protected. Whenever this field is entered, the circuits are thrown out of balance, and the alarm is initiated. The electromagnetic field may project several feet from the object, but it can be adjusted to operate only a few inches from it where traffic in the vicinity of the object is such that false alarms would be triggered if the field extended too far.

Figure 10.5 (A) Some passive infrared detectors have decorator-styled cases, making them attractive as well as functional. (Courtesy of Aritech Corporation) (B) To make them even less noticeable, some manufacturers disguise their passive infrared detectors. This unit, once it is installed, looks like an air vent (Courtesy of Raytek, Inc.) (C) Disguised as an electrical outlet, this passive infrared detector provides protection without detracting from a room's decor. (Courtesy of Detection Systems, Inc.)

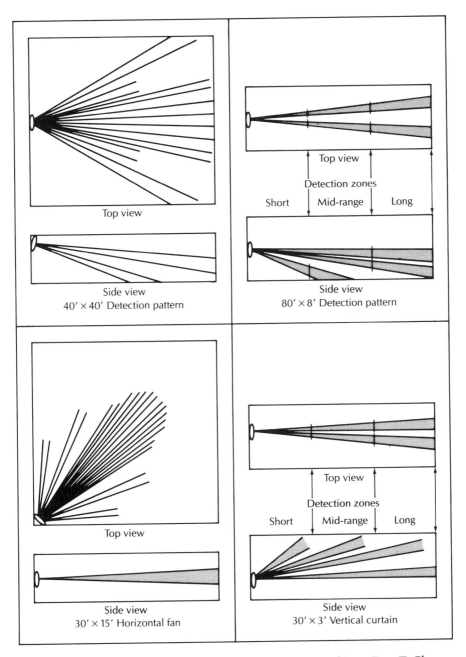

Figure 10.6 Indoor infrared (IR) motion detection patterns. (From Don T. Cherry, *Total Facility Control* [Stoneham, Mass.: Butterworth Publishers, 1986], p. 135.)

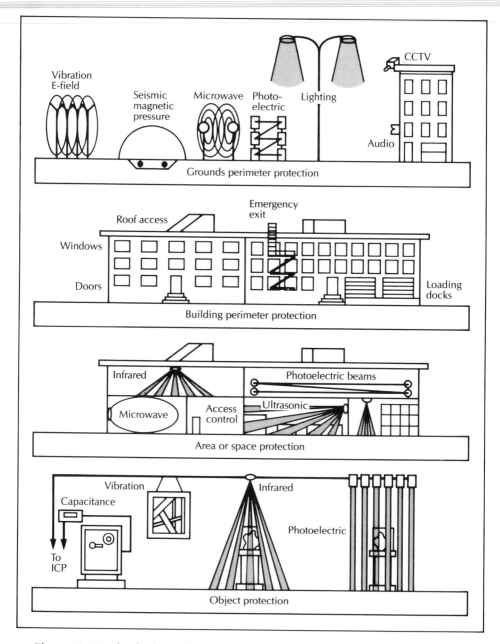

Figure 10.7 In-depth physical security. (From Don T. Cherry, *Total Facility Control* [Stoneham, Mass.: Butterworth Publishers, 1986], p. 148.)

Sonic Alarm Systems

Known variously as noise detection, sound, or audio alarms, these operate on the principle that an intruder will make enough noise in a protected area to be picked up by microphones that will in turn activate an alarm. This system has a wide variety of uses, limited only by the problems of ambient noise levels in a given area. The system consists simply of a microphone set in the protected area that is connected to an alarm signal and receiver. When a noise activates the alarm, a monitoring guard turns on the receiver and listens in on the prowler.

Such a system must be carefully adjusted to avoid setting off the alarm at every noise. Usually adjustment is set to sound the alarm at sounds above the general level common to the protected area. The system is not useful in areas where background noise levels are so high that they will drown out the anticipated sounds of surreptitious entry. This device may also come with a sound discriminator that evaluates sounds to eliminate false alarms.

Vibration Detectors

These provide a high level of protection against attack in specific areas or on specific objects. In this system, a specialized type of contact microphone is attached to objects such as works of art, safes, or files or to surfaces such as walls or ceilings. Any attack on, or movement of, these objects or surfaces causes some vibration. This vibration is picked up by microphones, which in turn activate alarms. These units may be adjusted for sensitivity, which will be set according to their application and environment. Here again, discriminator units are available to screen out harmless vibrations. These units are very useful in specific applications since their false alarm rates are very low.

Certain additional alarm devices are currently in use as perimeter protection as discussed in Chapter 8.

Some of the alarm sensors discussed in the preceding paragraphs can be defined as providing point protection. Electromechanical devices, capacitance alarms, and pressure devices, for instance, will be activated only when a specific area (point of entry) has been crossed, a door or window has been opened, or an object has been moved. On the other hand, ultrasonic, microwave, and passive infrared alarm systems protect large spaces, even entire rooms, against intrusion. These "volumetric" alarms, however, can be triggered by any number of environmental factors normally present in the protected space. Each alarm system has different strengths and weaknesses, and to assure effective performance, the total environment should be analyzed before selecting the specific system. Table 10.1 briefly summarizes the factors which affect these systems.

Table 10.1 What Detector to Select: Space Protection Guide

Environmental and Other Variables	Ultrasonic	Passive Infrared	Microwave
Vibration	No problem with balanced processing, some problem with unbalanced	Very few problems	Can be a major problem
Effect of temperature change on range	A little	A lot	None
Effect of humidity change on range	Some	None	None
Reflection of area of coverage by large metal objects	Very little	None unless metal is highly polished	Can be a major problem
Reduction of range by drapes, carpets	Some	None	None
Sensitivity to movement of overhead doors	Needs careful placement	Very few problems	Can be a major problem
Sensitivity to small animals	Problem if animals close	Problem if animals close but can be aimed so beams are well above floor	Problem if animals close
Water movement in plastic storm drain pipes	No problem	No problem	Can be problem if very close
Water noise from faulty valves	Can be a problem Very rare	No problem	No problem
Movement through thin walls or glass	No problem	No problem	Needs careful placement
Drafts, air movement	Needs careful placement	No problem	No problem

Sun, moving headlights through windows	No problem	Needs careful placement	No problem
Ultrasonic noise	Bells, hissing, some inaudible noises can cause problems	No problem	No problem
Heaters	Problem only in extreme cases	Needs careful placement	No problem
Moving machinery, fan blades	Needs careful placement	Very little problem	Needs careful placement
Radio interference, AC line transients	Can be problem in severe cases	Can be problem in severe cases	Can be problem in severe cases
Piping of detection field to unexpected areas by AC ducting	No problem	No problem	Occasional problem where beam is directed at duct outlet
Radar interference	Very few problems	Very few problems	Can be problem when radar is close and sensor pointed at it
Cost per square foot large open areas	In between	Most expensive	Least expensive
Cost per square foot divided areas, multiple rooms	Least expensive	Most expensive	In between
Range adjustment required	Yes	No	Yes
Current consumption (size of battery required for extended standby power)	In between	Smallest	Largest
Interference between two or more sensors	Must be crystal controlled and/or synchronized	No problem	Must be different frequencies

This list is intended as a guide only, and does not represent absolutes but suggests areas for consideration. (Courtesy of Aritech Corp.)

Alarm Monitoring Systems

Monitoring systems currently available are:

1. *The central station:* This is a facility set up to monitor alarms indicating fire, intrusion, and problems in industrial processes. Such facilities are set up in a location as central as possible to a number of clients, all of whom are serviced simultaneously. On the sounding of an alarm, a team of security officers is dispatched to the scene and the local police or fire department is notified. Depending on the nature of the alarm, on-duty plant or office protection is notified as well. Such a service is as effective as its response time, its alertness to alarms, and the thoroughness of inspection of premises fitted with alarms.

2. *Proprietary system:* This functions in the same way as does a central station system except that it is owned and operated by the facility and is located inside that facility. Response to all alarms is by the facility's own security or fire personnel. Since this system is monitored locally, the response time to an alarm is considerably reduced.

3. *Local alarm system:* In this case, the sensor activates a circuit that in turn activates a horn, a siren, or even a flashing light located in the immediate vicinity of the area fitted with alarms. Only guards within sound or hearing can respond to such alarms so their use is restricted to situations where guards are so located that their immediate response is assured. Such systems are most useful for fire alarm systems since they can alert personnel to evacuate the endangered area. In such cases, the system can also be connected to local fire departments to serve the dual purpose of alerting personnel and the company fire brigade to the danger as well as calling for assistance from public firefighting forces.

4. *Auxiliary system:* In this system, installation circuits are led into local police or fire departments by leased telephone lines. The dual responsibility for circuits and the high incidence of false alarms have made this system unpopular with public fire and police personnel. In a growing number of cities, such installations are no longer permitted as a matter of public policy.

5. *Local alarm-by-chance system:* This is a local alarm system in which a bell or siren is sounded with no predictable response. These systems are used in residences or small retail establishments that cannot afford a response system. The hope is that a neighbor or a passing patrol car will react to the alarm and call for police assistance, but such a call is purely a matter of chance.

6. *Dial alarm system:* This system is set to dial a predetermined tele-

phone number or numbers when the alarm is activated. The number(s) selected might be the police, the subscriber's home number, or both. When the phone is answered, a recording states that an intrusion is in progress at the location so fitted with alarms. This system is relatively inexpensive to install and operate, but since it is dependent on general phone circuits, it could fail if the line(s) being called were busy or if the phone connections were cut.

Cost Considerations

The costs involved in setting up even a fairly simple alarm system can be substantial, and the great part of this outlay is nonrecoverable should the system prove inadequate or unwarranted. Its installation should be predicated on exposure, concomitant need, and on the manner of its integration into the existing, or planned, security program.

This last point is important to consider because the effectiveness of any alarm procedure lies in the response it commands. As elementary as it may sound, it is worth repeating that an alarm takes no action; it only notifies that action should be taken. There must therefore be some entity near at hand that can take that action. Too often otherwise effective alarm systems are set up without adequate supportive or responding personnel. This is at best wasteful and at worst dangerous.

In many instances, alarm installations are made in order to reduce the size of the guard force. This is sometimes possible. At least if the current guard force cannot be reduced in number, those additional guards needed to cover areas now fitted with alarms will no longer be required.

Good business practice demands that the expense of alarm installations be undertaken only after a carefully considered cost and effectiveness analysis of all the elements. If the existing security personnel can cover the security requirements of the facility, no alarm system is needed. If they can cover the ground but not in a way that will satisfy security standards, more guards are needed, or the existing force must be augmented by an alarm system to extend their coverage and their protective ability. The costs and effectiveness must be studied together with an eye toward the efficient achievement of stated objectives.

Conclusion

Almost all sources of the security equipment industry predict growth, indicating that there is a growing use of equipment to supplement security staffs. Much equipment is available to the security manager today. Some of it is useful, some not, but none of it is better than the use to which it is put or the system into which it is integrated. No equipment can stand on its own. It can be used only if it is employed properly, fully, and effectively, and to be effective, all the components of the security system must work together. Figure 9.1 in the previous chapter illustrates the concept of lines of protection. Figure 10.7 expands on this idea by showing what security devices and types of barrier protection are commonly used for each line of defense.

A reasonable level of security cannot necessarily be assured with a single line of defense. Depending on the level of security desired, several layers of protection in an integrated system may be required.

Review Questions

1. What are the elements necessary for an effective visitor access control system?
2. Explain the characteristics of each of the common types of alarm systems.
3. Give an example of a situation where a motion detection alarm might be deployed effectively. Under what circumstances would an ultrasonic system be chosen over a radio frequency system?
4. Describe how passive infrared detectors operate. What environmental variables must be considered to assure proper operation?

References

1. Specification of government requirements can be obtained from the *Industrial Security Manual for Safeguarding Government Classified Information* (Washington, D.C.: GPO).
2. *Deibold Direct Security Catalog* (Canton, Ohio: Diebold 1990), p. 10.
3. J. Dumbauld and H. Porter, *Safe Burglars, Part III, A Study of Selected Offenders* (Sacramento, Calif.: Department of Justice, Division of Law Enforcement, 1971).
4. C. R. Jeffery, R. D. Hunter, and J. Griswold, "Crime Prevention and Computer Analysis of Convenience Store Robberies in Tallahassee, Florida," *Florida Police Journal* (1987): 65–69.

11 ⬜⬜⬜ ⬜⬜⬜ ⬜⬜⬜

Fire Protection, Safety, and Emergency Planning

No facility protection program is complete without clear, well-defined policies and programs confronting the possible threat of fire or any other natural or manmade disaster. While planning for such contingencies is a top management responsibility, unfortunately in most situations the task of carrying out the emergency response falls specifically on security. In the best of all possible worlds the responsibility is assigned to a fire department and a safety department allowing security to focus on security-related matters. Regardless of the functional placement of responsibility, security, fire, and safety personnel must work together when they are confronted with disasters.

According to Dennis F. Sigwart,

> Current and future security professionals should be aware of the absolute essentiality of disaster planning and preparedness as a viable component of the many facets [fire, earthquake, explosions, flooding, and so forth] of which they will have to perform as a practitioner. Those assigned disaster preparedness tasks must continually play the "what happens if game."[1]

Fire safety and emergency planning is designed first to anticipate what might happen to endanger people or physical property and to take the necessary preventive measures; and second to make provision—through appropriate hardware and/or personnel response—for prompt and effective action when an emergency does occur.

While the emphasis in this chapter (as in most actual practice) is on physical safeguards, it is important to emphasize the human aspect of fire safety and emergency protection. Disastrous losses often occur not from the failure or absence of physical safeguards, but from human error—the failure to close a fire door, to maintain existing protection systems in good working condition, to inspect or to report hazards, and at the management level to ensure through continuous employee education and training that the organization remains prepared at any time for any emergency. The Occupational Safety and Health Act (OSHA), National Fire Protection Association (NFPA), and Life Safety Codes dictate certain safety requirements for all businesses.

In addition, the NFPA, Factory Mutual, and Underwriters Laboratories (UL) have established standards for fire and safety that have been adopted by many state and local governments. These standards have been important in helping various insurance companies establish their rating systems.

Fire Prevention and Protection

Although a variety of special perils might be of particular concern in a given situation, the threat of fire is universal. Because it is also one of the most damaging and demoralizing hazards, fire prevention and control must be a cornerstone of any comprehensive loss-prevention program.

It should be noted here that any defense against fire must be viewed in two parts. First fire prevention, which is usually the major preoccupation, embodies the control of the sources of heat and the elimination or isolation of the more obviously dangerous fuels. This commendable effort to prevent fire must not, however, be undertaken at the expense of an equal effort for the second part of defense, fire protection.

Fire protection includes not only the equipment to control or extinguish fire, but also those devices that will protect the building, its contents, and particularly its occupants in the event of fire. Fire doors, fire walls, smokeproof towers, fireproof safes, nonflammable rugs and furnishings, fire detector systems—all are fire protection matters and are essential to any fire safety program.

Vulnerability to Fire

There are no fireproof buildings, however frequently the term may be misapplied. There are fire-resistant buildings. But since even these are filled with tons of combustible materials such as furnishings, panelling, stored flammable materials, and so on, they can become ovens that do not themselves burn but that can generate heat of sufficient intensity to destroy everything inside them. Eventually such heat can even soften the structural steel to such an extent that part or all of a building may collapse. By this time, however, the collapse of the building may endanger only outside elements since many things inside, with the possible exception of certain fire-resistant containeas and other metal or fire resistant items and their contents, may already have been destroyed.

The particular danger of this situation is that, while wooden or wood frame construction can be recognized for the fire hazard it represents, many otherwise knowledgeable people are oblivious to the potential dangers from fire in steel and concrete construction. And the danger can be largely unrecognized because the danger may grow slowly through a gradual accumulation of flammable materials in the form of office furnishings, stored inventory, or production materials.

The degree of fire exposure in any fire-resistant building is dependent on its fire loading—the amount of combustible materials that occupies its interior spaces. In the case of multiple occupancies such as large office buildings, no one office manager can control the fire loading. Hence the risk since the safety of anyone's premises is dependent on the fire load throughout the entire building. In such an environment, new furniture, decorative pieces, drapes, carpeting, unprotected insulated cables, or even volatile fluids for cleaning or lubricating are brought in every day. And the "classic triangle" of fire grows larger with each such addition.

The Nature of Fire

The classic triangle frequently referred to in describing the nature of fire consists of heat, fuel, and oxygen. This triangle has been augmented by the fire tetrahedron theory—the fire triangle making up three of the vital components in this theory. The tetrahedron theory adds a fourth element—a chemical reaction of material called pyrolosis, simply the decomposition of solids to the point where they give off enough flammable vapors and gases to form an ignitable mixture. In liquid fuels the process is called evaporation. Flammable gases require no pyrolosis since they are already in a form capable of combining with oxygen. If all four components exist, there will be a fire; remove or reduce any one, and the fire will be reduced or extinguished (see Figure 11.1).[2]

Certainly fuel and oxygen are always present. It would be difficult to imagine any facility that had no combustible items exposed, and air most certainly will be present. Only sufficient heat and the chemical breakdown associated with it are missing, and these factors can be readily supplied by a careless cigarette or faulty wiring, two of the most common causative factors.

There are, in fact, an almost infinite number of heat sources that can complete the deadly tetrahedron and start a fire raging in virtually any facility.

Every fire prevention program begins with the education of staff and visitors since it is nearly impossible to change existing fire-load problems over-

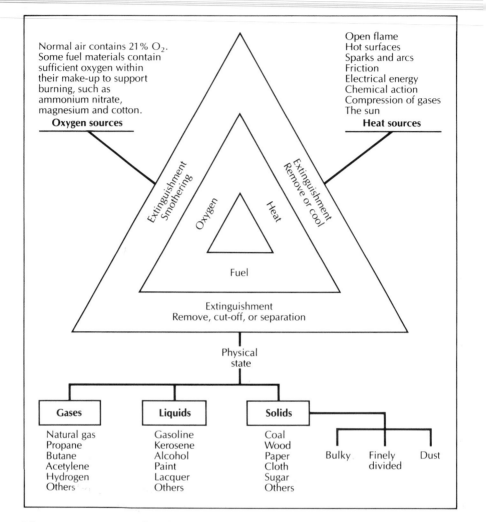

Figure 11.1 Fire triangle.

night. Yet every fire prevention program must also work to control the amount and nature of the fire load or fuel, and by instituting programs to prevent the occurrence of any heat build-up whether from careless smoking or from sparks from a welding torch.

Byproducts of Fire

Contrary to popular opinion, flame or visible fire is rarely the killer in the deaths from fire that occur in this country. Death is usually caused by smoke or heat or from toxic gas, explosion, or panic. Several such byproducts accompany every fire; all must be considered when defenses are being planned.

Smoke will blind and asphyxiate in an astonishingly short time. Tests have been conducted in which smoke in a corridor reduced the visibility to zero in two minutes from the time of ignition. A stairway two feet from a subject in the test was totally obscured.

Gas, which is largely carbon dioxide and carbon monoxide, collects under pressure in pockets in the upper floors of the building. As the heat rises and the pressure increases, explosions can occur.

Expanded air created by the heat creates fantastic pressure, which will shatter doors and windows and travel with crushing force and speed down every corridor and through every duct in the building.

All of these elements move upward and therefore permit some control over the direction of the fire—if the construction of the building has been planned with proper fire measures in mind.

Classes of Fire

All fires are classified in one of four groups. It is important that these groups and their designation be widely known since the use of various kinds of extinguishers is dependent on the type of fire to be fought (see Figure 11.2).

Class A. Fires of ordinary combustible materials such as waste paper, rags, drapes, and furniture. These fires are most effectively extinguished by water or water fog. It is important to cool the entire mass of burning material to below the ignition point to prevent rekindling.

Class B. Fires fueled by substances such as gasoline, grease, oil, or volatile fluids. The latter fluids are used in many ways and may be present in virtually any facility. Here a smothering effect such as carbon dioxide (CO_2) is used. A stream of water on such fires would simply serve to spread the substances with disastrous results. Water fog, however, is excellent since it cools without spreading the fuel.

Class C. Fires in live electrical equipment such as transformers, generators, or electric motors. The extinguishing agent is nonconductive to avoid danger to the firefighter. Electrical power should be disconnected before beginning extinguishing efforts.

Class D. Fires involving certain combustible metals such as magnesium, sodium, and potassium. Dry powder is usually the most, and in some cases the only, effective extinguishing agent. Because these fires can occur only where such combustible metals are in use, they are fortunately rare.

Kind of fire	Approved type of extinguisher						
Decide the class of fire you are fighting . . .	Foam Solution of Aluminum Sulphate and Bicarbonate of Soda	Carbon Dioxide Carbon Dioxide Gas under pressure	Pump Tank Plain water	Gas Cartridge Water expelled by Carbon Dioxide Gas	Multi-Purpose Dry Chemical	Ordinary Dry Chemical	Dry Powder
A **Class A Fires** Ordinary combustibles • Wood • Paper • Cloth etc.	●		●	●	●		
B **Class B Fires** Flammable liquids, grease • Gasoline • Paints • Oils, etc.	●	●			●	●	
C **Class C Fires** Electrical equipment • Motors • Switches etc.		●			●	●	
D **Class D Fires** Combustible metals • Magnesium • Sodium • Potassium etc.							●

How to Operate

Foam: Don't spray stream into the burning liquid. Allow foam to fall lightly on fire.

Carbon Dioxide: Direct discharge as close to fire as possible, first at edge of flames and gradually forward and upward.

Pump Tank: Place foot on footrest and direct stream at base of flames.

Dry Chemical: Direct at the base of the flames. In the case of Class A fires, follow up by directing the dry chemicals at the material that is burning.

Figure 11.2 Use of fire extinguishers.

Extinguishers

The security department must evaluate the fire risk for each facility or department and determine the types of fires most likely to occur. Although the potential for all types of fires exists and should be planned for, certain production areas are more likely to have a specific type of fire than are others. This condition should be considered when assigning extinguishers to the department or facility. Every operation is probably potentially subject to Class A and C fires, and most are also threatened by Class B fires to some degree.

Having made such a determination, security must then select the types of fire extinguishers most likely to be useful. The choice of extinguisher is not difficult, but it can only be made after the nature of the risks is determined. Extinguisher manufacturers can supply all pertinent data on the equipment they supply, but the types in general use should be known. It is important to know, for example, that over the past 10 years the soda/acid and carbon tetrachloride extinguishers have been prohibited. They are no longer manufactured. An extinguisher that must be inverted to be activated is no longer legal.

Dry Chemical

These were originally designed for Class B and C fires. The new models now in general use are also effective on Class A fires since the chemicals are flame-interrupting and in some cases act as a coolant.

Dry Powder

This is used on Class D fires. It smothers and coats.

Foam Extinguishers

These are effective for Class A and B fires where blanketing is desirable.

CO_2

Generally used on Class B or C fires, it can be useful on Class A fires as well though the CO_2 has no lasting cooling effect.

Water Fog

Fog is one of the most effective extinguishing devices known for dealing with Class A and B fires. It can be created by a special nozzle on the hose or by the adjustment of an all-purpose nozzle similar to that found on a garden hose.

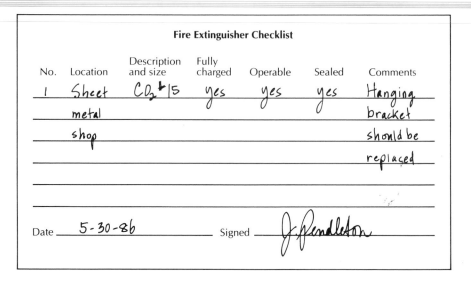

Figure 11.3 Fire extinguisher safety checklist.

It might be useful here to look briefly at the advantages fog has over a solid stream of water.

1. It cools the fuel more quickly.
2. It uses less water for the same effect so water damage is reduced.
3. Because fog reduces more heat more rapidly, atmospheric temperatures are quickly reduced. Persons trapped beyond a fire can be brought out through fog.
4. The rapid cooling draws in fresh air.
5. Fog reduces smoke by precipitating out particulate matter as well as by actually driving the smoke away from the fog.

After extinguishers have been installed, a regular program of inspection and maintenance must be established. A good policy is for security personnel to check all devices visually once a month and to have the extinguisher service company inspect them twice a year. In this process, the serviceman should retag and if necessary recharge the extinguishers and replace defective equipment (see Figure 11.3).

Fire Alarm Signaling Systems

Fire alarm systems, like intrusion alarms, can be viewed as consisting of the signaling device and the sensor. The sensor warns of fire or its dangers by activating a circuit, whereas the signaling device notifies those concerned of the danger.

The signaling system is activated by a sensor—a water-flow switch, a smoke or heat detector, or a manual alarm. The signal so activated is transmitted to an alarm receiver at a monitoring panel, which activates appropriate alarms and at the same time notifies fire protection personnel of the location of the alarm.

Manual fire alarm stations are of two different types:

1. *Local alarms* are clearly identified at the pull box as such. These alarms are designed to alert personnel in the building or in the area where such alarms sound, that a fire (or in some cases a drill) is in progress. Depending on the prescribed procedures, personnel so alerted stand by for further instructions or immediately evacuate the building. It is important to remember, however, that such alarms sound locally only. They do not notify anyone beyond the sound of the alarm of the fire threat. Unless someone notifies the fire department by phone, there will be no response by firefighters to the alarm. It will be necessary, as part of procedure, to designate the person responsible for notifying the fire department.

2. *Remote signal stations* transmit a signal directly to a monitoring panel located within security operations or at a local fire station. Typically a local signal is sounded at the same time a signal is being transmitted to the remote receiver.

Fire Alarm Sensors

A fire goes through four stages of development, each stage more dangerous than is its predecessor.

1. *The germinal or incipient stage:* Invisible products of combustion are given off. No smoke or flame is visible. There is no detectable heat at this point.
2. *Smoldering stage:* Smoke is now visible. No flame or appreciable heat is evident.
3. *Flame stage:* An actual visible fire is born. Flame and smoke are visible. Heat is still low at this point but only for a brief moment.
4. *Heat stage:* At this stage, heat is intense and growing, and the air is expanding rapidly and dangerously.

Four types of sensors are designed to be activated at each of the four stages of a fire. Since each sensor performs a different function, each one has a place in an effective fire protection system.

1. The *ionization detector* operates when it is exposed to those invisible products of combustion that are emitted by a fire in its earliest stage of development. Since a fire may be in progress for as much as

two or three hours before it gives any otherwise detectable evidence of its presence, this sensor is extremely useful in giving early warning of a fire. Invisible products of combustion—largely hydrocarbons—interfere with a current passing between two plates in this device and activate an alarm.

2. The *photoelectric smoke detector* operates on the basic principle of all photoelectric devices; a beam of light is transmitted to a cell that is in balance as long as the light source is constant. When that source is in any way interrupted, the balance is disturbed, and the unit sounds an alarm. These detectors will sound an alarm on a concentration of smoke of 2–4 percent.

3. The *infrared flame detector*, as its name suggests, reacts to the infrared emissions from flame.

4. *Thermal detectors* sense the temperature in the protected area. Some are set to sound an alarm when the temperature reaches a predetermined level; others respond to a rapid climb in the temperature. This latter type, known as a *"rate-of-rise" detector*, cannot be used in any areas where the temperature normally fluctuates strongly.

Some detectors combine the features of both the fixed temperature and rate-of-rise units and are generally considered to be more useful than is either unit alone.

Automatic Sprinkler Systems

A second level of alarm is activated by the flow of extinguishing agents (wet or dry extinguishing-agent systems) in an automatic sprinkler system. Such an alarm is important in that areas covered by sprinkler systems are rarely otherwise fitted with alarms. When the heat level in such areas rises sufficiently, the sprinkler system is activated by the melting of a fusible link (metal seal), and the extinguishing agent flows through the system on the release of sprinkler-head valves. In some systems, this activates an alarm that indicates the flow of the extinguishing agents. There are many other types of sprinkler systems. For further information on these systems seek help from your local fire department.

Education in Fire Prevention and Safety

Educating employees about fire prevention, fire protection, and evacuation procedures should be a continuous program. Ignorance and carelessness are the causes of most fires and of much loss of life. An ongoing fire-safety program will inform all employees and help keep them aware of the everpresent, very real danger of fire.

Such a program would ideally include fire and evacuation drills. Since such exercises require shutting down operations for a period of time and lead to the loss of expensive productive effort time, management is frequently cool toward them.

Indoctrination sessions for new employees and regular review sessions for all personnel, however, are essential. Such sessions should be brief and involve only small groups. They should include the following activities and subjects as well as any others that may have particular application to the specific facility.

1. Walk to primary and secondary fire exits, and demonstrate how such exits are opened. Emphasize the importance of closing exit stairwells. If possible, employees should walk down the exit stairs.
2. Explain how to report a fire. Emphasize the need to report first before trying to put the fire out.
3. Distribute a simple plan of action in the event of fire.
4. Explain the alarm system.
5. Explain the need to react quickly, and emphasize the need to remain calm and avoid panic.
6. Explain that elevators are never to be used as emergency exits.
7. Point out the danger of opening doors. Explain that doors must be felt before being opened. Opening a hot door is usually fatal.
8. Demonstrate available firefighting equipment, or show manufacturers' or fire department films on similar equipment.
9. Describe what should be done if escape is cut off by smoke or fire:
   a. Move as far from the fire as possible.
   b. Move into the building perimeter area with a solid door between you and the fire.
   c. Remove readily flammable material from that area if possible.
   d. Since expanded air exerts enormous pressures, barricade the door with heavy, noncombustible materials.
   e. Open the tops and bottoms of windows. Fire elements will be exhausted through the tops while cool air will enter through the bottoms.
   f. Stay near the floor.
   g. Hang something from windows to attract the attention of firefighters.

In many businesses visitors and guests should also be made aware of fire and evacuation plans. Pamphlets describing plans should be available as well as placards that indicate the location of fire exits in relation to the placards.

In the case of hotels and other facilities that have resident clientele, the law demands such actions.

Employees in Firefighting

Since the danger of fire with its concomitant risk to life and property affects every employee, many experts feel that the responsibility in case of fire is a shared one. The exception to this rule is when the firm has a well-trained fire unit. Few experts would disagree that everyone must be educated in the principles of fire prevention and protection, including indoctrination in evacuation procedures and into reporting a fire. But beyond this, there is little agreement on what employees should be asked to do.

Some business offices set up a system of floor wardens whose job it is to pass the word for evacuation and who then sweep their area of responsibility to see that it is clear of personnel, that papers are deposited in fireproof containers, and that high-value, portable assets are removed from the premises.

Others take the view that their employees were not hired to act as emergency supervisors. Many firms of this latter persuasion ask that certain minimal functions be performed by those persons who are on hand but do not assign roles to specific people. Examples might be a policy of returning tapes to a fireproof container in the computer area or securing fire-resistant safes in the accounting or cashier's office before evacuation. This responsibility would fall on the personnel in these areas at the time of an alarm and would or should take little time to accomplish. When the signal for evacuation is given, no time should be lost in vacating the building.

Many professionals feel that office employees should never be asked to do more than see to their own safety by beating an orderly retreat along predetermined escape routes. Only in the most extreme emergency—and then only if they are otherwise trapped—should employees engage in fighting a fire of any magnitude. They can be expected as a normal reaction to make an effort to put out a wastebasket fire or a small blaze in a broom closet, but even in these cases the alarm must be given as first priority. Any fire that threatens to involve a major part of an office or other parts of the building should be left to professionals (company fire units, security personnel, or the fire department).

Obviously all such situations are matters of on-the-spot judgment. Policies covering every situation are difficult, if not impossible, to predetermine.

The situation is quite different in industrial fire operations. In such facilities, the formation of a fire brigade composed of a few selected and trained employees is a fairly general practice. There is general agreement that the nature of their employment in industrial areas makes these employees more competent to handle firefighting assignments, which are in many cases not that far removed from their regular work.

The exact size of each fire-protection organization will vary according to the size and function of each facility. Very large facilities or those whose fire risks are high because of the nature of the operations may have a full-time fire department. In smaller or less hazardous facilities, regular employees are organized into fire brigades that are broken down, usually by departments or areas, into fire companies. These companies are assigned to given areas for purposes of fire protection, fire prevention, and firefighting. They are also available as part of the fire brigades in any other area of the plant if a fire occurs that requires more personnel than the assigned company can handle.

The size of the brigade will depend on the size of the plant and on the nature of the risk involved. It will also be affected by the general availability, size, competence, and response capability of the public firefighting facilities in the neighboring areas. Whatever the size, however, it must consist of people sufficiently well trained and familiar with the plant operation and layout to fight fires effectively in any part of the facility if such a need arises.

The plant engineer and the maintenance crew should certainly be included in the brigade. Their knowledge in servicing valves, pumps, and other machinery is invaluable in emergency situations.

Evacuation

Evacuating Industrial Facilities

Evacuation plans for an industrial facility are relatively simple to design since most buildings within the perimeter are one-, two-, or in rare cases three-story buildings. Fire exits can be readily identified for such a plan of action. Because they are occupied by personnel of a single company or under that company's jurisdiction, a single plan involving all personnel can be drawn up. And because in most cases aesthetic considerations are not a prime concern in the design of the industrial building, fire escapes can be constructed in any way for the greatest safety.

Although many of these buildings have elevators most of which serve the dual purpose of hauling freight and personnel, these elevators are not necessarily the prime means of moving to and from the upper level as they are in high-rise office buildings.

Generally, these buildings can be cleared in minutes. This is not to say that an evacuation plan is not needed. It is, and it must be widely distributed and clearly understood. Most industrial buildings are more open, the exits are more visible—more a part of the unconscious orientation of the employees and, therefore, more a part of the natural traffic flow—than these elements are in many other types of construction.

Evacuating High-Rise Buildings

Evacuation from high-rise urban buildings is quite a different story. In this situation, employees come to work and leave regularly by elevator. Yet if there should be a fire, they are told they must not use the only means of entrance and exit they really know.

In most cases, they have never been on the fire stairs. They may have only a vague idea where those stairs are located, but in a time of emergency—a time of anxiety bordering on panic when instinctual behavior is the most natural—they are asked to vacate the premises in a way that to them is very unnatural indeed.

Even in wide-open industrial facilities where orientation is quick and easy, there will always be some people who will pass a clearly marked exit to get to the employee door they are used to using. This is much more likely to happen in buildings with windowless corridors and fire exits—however clearly lighted and marked they are—well off the normal traffic pattern used by employees! A good emergency lighting system can do much to reduce this potentially life-threatening problem.

To overcome this problem, which must be overcome until such time as elevators are made safe to use in the case of fire, it is advisable to walk all employees as a drill from their desks to the nearest fire exit and to the nearest secondary exit they would use in case their first escape route was cut off by fire or smoke. In addition, the use of "You Are Here" placards can assist those, who become disoriented in a building, to find the nearest safe exist.

This could be done over a period of time with small groups at each drill. It is important that the drill actually start at the desk or office of the employee so that the route as well as the location of the exit is made clear.

Planning and Training

Evacuation plans must be based on a well-considered system and on thorough and continuing education. They should also be based on indoctrinating employees in the principles of fire safety, stressing that they are to make their own way to the proper exit and leave as quickly and as calmly as possible.

Adults do not respond to being lined up like children at a fire drill and marched down the fire stairs. Though they might be inclined to follow a leader under many circumstances, when it comes to a concept as simple as vacating the premises, a leader has no purpose or place. They will rebel or even panic if they feel restrained or regimented in their movements toward the exit.

In setting up plans for evacuation, it might be well to review and evaluate the circumstances of a given facility and then ask a few questions.

1. Are routes to exits well lighted, fairly direct, and free of obstacles?
2. Are elevators posted to warn against their use in case of fire? Do these signs point out the direction of fire exits?
3. Are handicapped persons provided for?
4. Do corridors have emergency lighting in the event of power failure?
5. Who makes the decision to evacuate? How will personnel be notified?
6. Who will operate the communication system? What provisions have been made in case the primary communication system breaks down? Who is assigned to provide and receive information on the state of the emergency and the progress of the evacuation? By what means?

Safety and Loss Control

Safety consciousness in business and industry did not begin with the passage of the Occupational Safety and Health Act (OSHA) in 1970, but it is largely a product of the twentieth century. Prior to the Industrial Revolution early in the nineteenth century, workers were independent craftspeople. If they suffered economic loss because of accident or illness rising out of prolonged exposure to a particular work environment, the problem was the craftsperson's, not the employer's. This attitude generally prevailed during the rapid expansion of the factory system in America throughout the nineteenth century. Only toward the latter part of the nineteenth century did it begin to become obvious that factories were far superior in terms of production capability to the small handicraft shops, yet they were often inferior in terms of human values, health, and safety.

The atmosphere of reform that gained impetus after the turn of the century resulted in, among other new laws, the first effective Workmen's Compensation Act—in Wisconsin in 1911. Compulsory laws on workmen's compensation followed in many states after the U.S. Supreme Court upheld their constitutionality in 1916. Even the most hard-headed employers found that their costs dictated compliance with the spirit of the law.

As a result of this growing concern for industrial safety, there followed a long downward curve in work-connected accidents and injuries that lasted through the period between the two world wars and continued into the 1950s. By 1958, this trend had leveled off, and by 1968 for the first time in over 50 years, the curve began to rise again.

Fourteen thousand occupational fatalities and over 2,000,000 disabling, work-connected injuries each year seemed to be considerably more than the number that might one day be arrived at as the irreducible minimum. The result throughout the 1960s was increasing federal concern with establishing standards of occupational safety and health. Prior to that decade, only a few federal laws, such as the Walsh-Healey Public Contracts Act, had been enacted with most legislation in this area being left to the states. During the 1960s, a number of laws were passed—the McNamara-O'Hara Service Contracts Act, the Federal Construction Safety Act, and the Federal Coal Mine Health and Safety Act among others—all dealing with safety and health standards in specific fields and under specific circumstances. Public Law 91-596, known as OSHA, which was signed into law on December 29, 1970, was the first legislation that attempted to apply standards to virtually every employer and employee in the country.

OSHA Standards

Generally speaking, OSHA requires that an employer provide a safe and healthful place for employees to work. This is spelled out in great detail in the act to avoid leaving the thrust of the legislation in any doubt.

Though much of the language in the act is technical in nature and largely couched in legalese, the thrust of the legislation is absolutely clear and unambiguous in what is known as the "General Duty" clause that states that each employer "shall furnish to each of his employees a place of employment free from recognized hazards that are causing or likely to cause death or serious physical harm to his employees" and that further he "shall comply with all occupational safety and health standards promulgated under this Act."[3] Much of the rest of the act deals with procedures and standards of safety and is in places difficult to follow.

It speaks of free and accessible means of egress, of aisles and working areas free of debris, of floors free from hazards. It gives specific requirements for machines and equipment, materials, and power sources. It specifies fire protection by fixed or portable systems, clean lunch rooms, environmental health controls, and adequate sanitation facilities. Whereas in past years, employers might contend in all sincerity that their facilities met community standards for safety and cleanliness, with the enactment of OSHA these standards have been formalized to describe minimum levels of acceptability. They might also contend that some specific demands of the act are unclear, but there is no mistaking what the act is getting at. "The Congress declares to be its purpose and policy to assure so far as possible every working man and woman in the nation safe and healthful working conditions and to preserve our human resources."

Perhaps the strongest resistance to OSHA in its first years was the complaint that some of the basic standards went too far or were unnecessary. In May 1978, the U.S. Supreme Court ruled that the agency could not conduct surprise workplace inspections without a proper warrant.[4] And with growing criticism from that time period, the OSHA administration has continually sought the elimination of "Mickey Mouse" standards that have no direct bearing on improving safety in the workplace.

In 1988, OSHA issued the Hazard Communication Standard that states that all employees have the right know what hazards exist in their place of employment and what to do to protect themselves from the hazards. Simple labels and warnings on containers are not enough. Employers must have a program to communicate more detail on all hazards including a Material Safety Data Sheet (MSDS) that must be available for each chemical at the worksite. Each MSDS contains seven sections:

1. Product identification and emergency notification instructions
2. Hazardous ingredients list and exposure limits
3. Physical and chemical characteristics
4. Physical hazards and how to handle them (that is, fire, explosion).
5. Reactivity—what the product might react with and whether it is stable
6. Health hazards—how the product can enter the body, signs and symptoms of problems, and emergency first-aid steps
7. Safe handling procedures

Setting Up the Safety Program

H.W. Heinrich, an outstanding pioneer in safety studies, held that unsafe acts caused 85 percent of all accidents and that unsafe conditions caused the remaining 15 percent.[5] Therefore if these acts could be modified, the accidents would be sharply reduced. Today safety supervisors agree that unsafe acts are the principal villain and that the system's approach to safety is the only real way to control losses. It is necessary, however, for management to get the system together and implement a strong, active program so that it is effective. Safety problems are caused, they do not just happen, and each problem can be identified and controlled.[6]

Accidents, by our definition, refer to property damage as well and in aggregate can amount to substantial cost for the company that fails to keep them under control. In fact, an effective loss-control program can be an organization's best moneymaker when it can be shown that the actual cost of accidents may be anywhere from 6 to 50 times as much as the money recovered from insurance. Uninsured costs in building damage, production damage, wages to the injured for lost time, clerical costs, cost of training new workers and supervisors, and extra time all mount up. By controlling such incidents through careful study of hazards and the introduction of safety programs to deal with the hazards, the profit picture will be immeasurably improved. In a company operating at a 4 percent profit margin, the sales department would have to generate sales of $1,250,000 just to compensate for an annual loss of $50,000 in incidents.

Assessment of the Safety Program

In order to set up for acceptable performance or to take action to bring a facility up to an acceptable level of loss-control effectiveness, an assessment of the situation is necessary. This can be done in two parts and preferably by one well-qualified person. The team approach may be used, but it is usually not as effective in the long run as is the individual approach.

The first order of business is an attitude survey. This consists of a private, one-on-one interview with all line supervisors from the facility manager to various first-line supervisors or foremen. Questions directed at each individual should elicit attitudes about current safety conditions, the need for a safety program, and safety management generally and feelings about some of the techniques (or absence of techniques) in the loss-control effort. Questions might be:

1. Who do you think is responsible for safety?
2. Does a sloppy loss-control program affect your job? How?
3. How would you improve the safety record of this facility?
4. How can top management inprove the safety record of this facility?
5. Have you done anything in the past six months to improve the safety of the facility? Your crew?
6. How much authority do you have to correct unsafe conditions?
7. What supervisory safety training have you had?

After the questionnaire has been drawn up and the interviews have been conducted with supervisors, a tabulation of responses should be very revealing. They should indicate the management levels where deficiencies exist and point out existing problems both in plant safety and in the program in general.

After the attitude survey, the assessment should undertake a review of all accident/incident records of the past three years. This should be classified by type such as burns, bruises, broken bones. From this, it will be easy to see the types of accidents that have been occurring and perhaps to pinpoint an area, process, or condition that is particularly unsafe. When this list has been drawn up, it will be necessary to assign cause and responsibility to each accident. There will usually be several causes in each case. In developing the accident-case correlation chart, assign causes as management or supervisor responsibility, employee error, mechanical design, or mechanical failure.

The next step in the assessment is to determine those accidents caused by lack of personal protective equipment—eye and foot injuries. It must be determined whether the problems arise from lack of protective equipment or from an unwillingness to use it, and corrective action must be taken.

Next determine accidents by job title, and finally list accidents under each supervisor. These last two categories should immediately suggest corrective action, whether it be changing job specifications or educating supervisors.

Finding the Causes of Accidents

The causes of accidents should be determined before they occur. Since accidents are caused, the conditions that cause them can be known and controlled. It is therefore of the greatest importance that management deal vigorously with what can cause an accident. Unsafe acts and unsafe conditions will ultimately cause accidents if they are allowed to continue.

Unsafe acts will be discovered and corrected only when immediate supervisors are alert to the problems. They must set up systems for observing all workers closely while they are performing their jobs, especially those in hazardous jobs. To do this, they must have a job-safety analysis at their disposal. This analysis divides each job into component parts, and each part is studied for the hazards it may present.

Unsafe conditions are uncovered by constant inspection. Such conditions do not disappear entirely because they have once been taken care of. Unsafe conditions are continuously created by the operation of the facility. Normal wear and tear, careless housekeeping, initial bad design, or simply the deterioration that results from inadequate maintenance caused by a cost-cutting management—all create unsafe conditions that have high potential loss factors. Early discovery of unsafe conditions is essential to good loss control, and the procedure is simply inspection, inspection, inspection.

Identification and Control of Hazards

OSHA standards (or equivalent state standards) provide the base line for a company's safety program. A bewildering catalog of standards has already developed, and new ones are constantly being added. Checklists (available from OSHA, the National Safety Council, and other sources) can provide the starting point for detailed inspections to identify hazards. The confusion that might accompany a consideration of all the standards begins to sort itself out when inspections zero in only on those standards that apply to specific operations and conditions.

A safety program should include periodic inspections scheduled at regular intervals. Figure 11.4 is an example of a monthly checklist for inspection, In addition, looking for safety hazards and violations should be part of the

Monthly Safety Check

Dept. _____ Date _____

Supervisor _____

Indicate discrepancy by ☒

General area	
Floor condition	
Special purpose flooring	
Aisle, clearance/markings	
Floor openings, require safeguards	
Railings, stairs temp./perm.	
Dock board (bridge plates)	
Piping (water-steam-air)	
Wall damage	
Ventilation	
Other	
Illumination—wiring	
Unnecessary/improper use	
Lights on during shutdown	
Frayed/defective wiring	
Overloading circuits	
Machinery not grounded	
Hazardous location	
Other	
Housekeeping	
Floors	
Machines	
Break area/latrines	
Waste disposal	
Vending machines/food protection	
Rodent, insect, vermin control	
Vehicles	
Unauthorized use	
Operating defective vehicle	
Reckless/speeding operation	
Failure to obey traffic rules	
Other	
Tools	
Power tool wiring	
Condition of hand tools	
Safe storage	
Other	

First aid	
First aid kits	
Stretchers, fire blankets, oxygen	
Fire protection	
Fire hoses hung properly	
Extinguisher charged/proper location	
Access to fire equipment	
Exit lights/doors/signs	
Other	
Security	
Doors/windows, etc. secured when required	
Alarm operation	
Department shut down security	
Equipment secured	
Unauthorized personnel	
Other	
Machinery	
Unattended machines operating	
Emergency stops not operational	
Platforms/ladders/catwalks	
Instructions to operate/stop posted	
Maintenance being performed on machines in operation	
Guards in place	
Pinch points	
Material storage	
Hazardous & flammable material not stored properly	
Improper stacking/loading/securing	
Improper lighting, warning signs, ventilation	
Other	

Figure 11.4 Monthly safety checklist.

day-to-day activity of both safety professionals and security personnel, Some hazards that might be present in any business facility are shown in Table 11.1.

A Hazardous Materials Program

In addition to the seven steps in safety planning, particular types of businesses dealing with hazardous substances should have a hazardous materials program. As a minimum, it is necessary to:

1. Identify what hazardous materials you have and where they are
2. Know how to respond to an accident involving hazardous materials
3. Know how to deal with spills
4. Set up appropriate safeguards
5. Train employees in dealing with hazardous materials

As has been discussed earlier, MSDSs are designed specifically to help identify the nature of potential hazards. These data sheets are obtainable from vendors of hazardous materials or equipment.

Table 11.1 Common Safety Hazards

1. Floors, aisles, stairs, and walkways

Oil spills or other slippery substances which might result in an injury-producing fall.

Litter, obscuring hazards such as electrical floor plugs, projecting material, or material which might contribute to the fueling of a fire.

Electrical wire, cable, pipes, or other objects, crossing aisles which are not clearly marked or properly covered.

Stairways which are too steep, have no nonskid floor covering, inadequate or nonexistent railings, or those which are in a poor state of repair.

Overhead walkways which have inadequate railings, are not covered with nonskid material, or which are in a poor state of repair.

Walks and aisles which are exposed to the elements and have not been cleared of snow or ice, which are slippery when wet or which are in a poor state of repair.

2. Doors and emergency exits

Doors that are ill-fitting, stick, and which might cause a slowdown during emergency evacuation.

Panic-type hardware which is inoperative or in a poor state of repair.

Doors which have been designated for emergency exit but which are locked and not equipped with panic-type hardware.

Doors which have been designated for emergency exit but which are blocked by equipment or by debris.

Missing or burned-out emergency exit lights.

Table 11.1 *(Cont.)*

Nonexistent or poorly marked routes leading to emergency exit doors.

3. Flammable and other dangerous materials
Flammable gases and liquids which are uncontrolled, in areas in which they might constitute a serious threat.

Radioactive material not properly stored or handled.

Paint or painting areas which are not properly secured or which are in areas that are poorly ventilated.

Gasoline pumping areas located dangerously close to operations which are spark producing or in which open flame is being used.

4. Protective equipment or clothing
Workmen in areas where toxic fumes are present who are not equipped with or who are not using respiratory protective apparatus.

Workmen involved in welding, drilling, sawing, and other eye-endangering occupations who have not been provided or who are not wearing protective eye covering.

Workmen in areas requiring the wearing of protective clothing, due to exposure to radiation or toxic chemicals, who are not using such protection.

Workmen engaged in the movement of heavy equipment or materials who are not wearing protective footwear.

Workmen who require prescription eyeglasses who are not provided or are not wearing safety lenses.

5. Vehicle operation and parking
Forklifts which are not equipped with audible and visual warning devices when backing.

Trucks which are not provided with a guide when backing into a dock or which are not properly chocked while parking.

Speed violations by cars, trucks, lifts, and other vehicles being operated within the protected area.

Vehicles which are operated with broken, insufficient, or nonexistent lights during the hours of darkness.

Vehicles which constitute a hazard due to poor maintenance procedures on brakes and other safety-related equipment.

Vehicles which are parked in fire lanes, blocking fire lanes, or blocking emergency exits.

6. Machinery maintenance and operation
Frayed electrical wiring which might result in a short circuit or malfunction of the equipment.

Workers who operate presses, work near or on belts, conveyors, and other moving equipment who are wearing loose fitting clothing which might be caught and drag them into the equipment.

Presses and other dangerous machinery which are not equipped with the required hand guards or with automatic shut-off devices or dead man controls.

7. Welding and other flame- or spark-producing equipment
Welding torches and spark-producing equipment being used near flammable liquid or gas storage areas or being used in the vicinity where such products are dispensed or are part of the productive process.

The use of flame- or spark-producing equipment near wood shavings, oily machinery, or where they might damage electrical wiring.

8. Miscellaneous hazards
Medical and first aid supplies not properly stored, marked, or maintained.

Color coding of hazardous areas or materials not being accomplished or which is not uniform.

Broken or unsafe equipment and machinery not being properly tagged with a warning of its condition.

Electrical boxes and wiring not properly inspected or maintained, permitting them to become a hazard.

Emergency evacuation routes and staging areas not properly marked or identified.

Adapted from Eugene Finneran, *Security Supervision: A Handbook for Supervisors and Managers* (Stoneham, Mass.: Butterworth Publishers, 1981).

Managing the Safety Operation

Whatever the overall integration of safety and the security operation, the safety function can operate in any one of three modes. The safety department:

1. Can act in a staff capacity, where its experts offer advice, make recommendations to upper echelon management, and develop policy for management approval. Line supervisors bear full responsibility for safety in their areas.
2. Is both staff and line in that it performs all staff functions as described above and will also help out on especially hazardous jobs. It will hold some safety meetings and training sessions.
3. Holds all safety meetings, training sessions, and accident investigations, and actively performs in all areas of safety.

A good case can be made for operating in any of the three methods, though it would appear that the combination of staff and line method is generally the most effective.

Management Leadership

Management's attitude toward safety filters down through the entire company. Top management's concern will be reflected in that of the supervisors; in turn, the supervisor's attention to safety will affect the individual employee's attitude. Management is responsible not only for a basic policy for providing a work environment free of hazards, which should be embodied in an executive policy statement, but also for active leadership. This can be expressed by holding subordinates responsible for accident prevention and in such visible ways as plant tours, letters to employees, safety meetings, posters, prompt accident investigations, and personal example. (In a hard hat area, for example, the president of the company should also put on a hard hat.)

General safety rules must be established and published in the employee handbook or manual. Safety rules should be continually reviewed and updated.

Assignment of Responsibility

Responsibility for the safety program should be clear and personal. In the small company, it may rest on the owner. Or it will generally be an added responsibility of the supervisors in companies with fewer than 100 employees.

In larger companies, safety should be a responsibility assigned to a ranking member of management who may delegate the authority to oversee the program to a safety director (who may be called the safety professional, safety engineer, or safety supervisor, depending on the qualifications and the nature of the operation). In many companies, safety is a responsibility of the security director who will often have a safety specialist as a subordinate. (In virtually all circumstances, there is a close relationship between safety and security.)

Training

All employees must be initially and periodically trained both in general safety principles and in safe work practices in their specific jobs. Safety rules such as the wearing of protective clothing (gloves, headgear, respirators, shoes, eye protection and such) should be clearly explained and promptly enforced. The importance the company attaches to safety should particularly be emphasized in new employee training, but it is also important to pay attention to regular employees including the "old timers" who did not grow up with safety awareness as part of their conditioning. Certificates for completion of classes should be given to employees at the work place to show the importance of the program.

In addition to the above, there are specific training requirements in the OSHA standards (such as those involving the operation of certain types of equipment). Employers and employees should be aware of those standards that apply in the specific workplace.

Emergency Care

Under OSHA, all businesses are required, in the absence of an infirmary or hospital in the immediate vicinity, to have a person or persons trained in first aid available along with first aid supplies. Where employees are exposed to corrosive materials, procedures for drenching or flushing the eyes and body should be provided in the work area.

Procedures should be established for handling injury accidents without confusion or delay. The extent of these preparations will, of course, depend on the nature of the business and the types of hazards.

Employee Awareness and Participation

Developing safety and health awareness is one of the primary goals of OSHA. Active steps by management, such as those suggested above, are essential to involve all employees in the need to create a safe work environment.

Safety awareness has an added benefit for both the employer and employees in that it tends to carry over into a concern for off-the-job safety. Accidents away from the work environment account for more than half of all injuries, and the ratio of deaths is three-to-one higher in off-the-job accidents. Carrying safety practices from the job to activities away from the job is an aspect of safety training that is receiving increasing emphasis from today's safety professionals.

Emergency Planning

The first thing that must be said about emergency planning is that there must be a plan, a detailed set of policies and procedures that take into account any reasonably foreseeable emergency or disaster that would affect the safety of people and the assets of an organization. The plan should be in writing, and it should spell out, in as detailed a manner as possible, the steps to be taken in a given emergency and by whom. If there is no plan, it is the security or safety manager's responsibility to see that one is developed. Such a plan will involve many different departments (fire, police, utility companies, and so on) and their key personnel. The ultimate responsibility for the completed plan rests, however, with the security or safety manager.

Note that there are two key elements in any contingency plan: (1) what is to be done and (2) who is to do it.

Having a detailed plan of action ensures that the right people, equipment, and facilities will be available in a crisis, and that everyone—management and employees—will know what to expect, what to do, and who is in charge. In a serious crisis, response must be swift and sure. Confusion and panic are all too common. If the twin objectives of preventing or minimizing injury or accident to people and preventing or minimizing the loss of assets are to be achieved in an emergency, key people in the organization must be able to act quickly and responsibly.

Advance planning has other advantages. It makes it possible to enlist the thinking of those who will be involved in the crisis situation. Table 11.2 provides a listing of typical problems and where to look to assistance. Since all facets of the organization will typically be affected, all should have some input in the planning. The committee approach in fact is most commonly used in developing emergency plans. This cooperative effort enables the organization to anticipate problems in different areas of a facility and to prepare for them.

Types of Emergencies

While it is impossible to predict all emergencies that might occur, it is possible to make reasonable estimates of vulnerabilities for a given facility in a particular geographical location. During the past decade the most common emergencies have been fire, bomb threat, and labor dispute with the result that most organizations have specific contingency plans for these haz-

Table 11.2 Typical Human Problems as a Result of Disaster and Potential Agencies for Assistance

Shelter	Civil defense and Red Cross
Food	Red Cross and civic groups
Water	Civil government
Emergency care	Hospitals and clinics
Medical evaluations	Hospitals and health agencies
Personal protection	Police and national guard
Illumination	Public utilities
Communications	Citizen band radio and national guard
Transportation	National guard, local trucking, and bus companies
Property protection	Police, auxiliary police, and national guard

From Dennis Sigwart, "Disaster Planning Considerations for the Security Safety Professional: A Historical Interface," in *Suggested Preparation Careers in Security/Loss Prevention*, John Chuvala III and Robert Fischer, eds. (Dubuque, Iowa: Kendall/Hunt 1991), p. 151.

ards (which have already been discussed). Other threats may be relatively predictable for a given site such as the possibility of explosion, a spill, or a leak in a chemical plant. In developing emergency and disaster plans, priority should naturally be given to those areas of most immediate concern.

The types of emergencies for which plans should be drawn up might include:

1. Airplane crash
2. Bomb or bomb threat
3. Building collapse
4. Civil disturbance
5. Earthquake
6. Fire
7. Flood
8. Riot
9. Sabotage
10. Strikes and pickets
11. Utility failure
12. Windstorm

While game plans should exist for each emergency, possible standard procedures should be adopted since there are many common elements in the emergency response to any crisis. Wherever possible, the same chain of command should exist and the same communications, the same command post and control center, and the same first aid center. Evacuation routes and exits should be identical for a bomb threat or a fire. An important rule in all such planning is keep it simple. Employing common elements in all plans helps to eliminate confusion and uncertainty during the frantic first moments of a disaster.

Emergency Personnel and Equipment Records

We have already said that the emergency plans should be in writing, preferably in an emergency planning manual, copies of which should be immediately available to designated members of management, the emergency team, security, finance, and other key employees with specific responsibilities in an emergency response. Plans should be reviewed periodically and kept up to date.

Permanent records, kept in a secure location (such as the security office), should include:

1. Names and phone numbers of management personnel to be notified

2. Names of emergency forces (assignments, location, phone numbers)
3. Names of backup emergency forces
4. List of emergency equipment and supplies, including type, location, quantity, backup, and outside support
5. Building plans
6. Mutual aid agreements
7. Outside organizations (police, fire, hospital, and ambulance), locations, and phone numbers
8. Emergency planning manual

Where a permanent location for the emergency command post exists, copies of all emergency personnel and equipment records, building plans, and other relevant documents should be stored at that location. Where this is a site other than the security office, an additional backup file should be maintained by security.

Elements of the Emergency Plan

Development of an emergency plan will in effect create the organization necessary to carry it out. It should provide for:

1. Designating authority to declare an emergency and to order shutdown and evacuation—total or partial
2. Establishing an emergency chain of command
3. Establishing reporting responsibilities and channels
4. Designating an emergency headquarters or command post
5. Establishing and training emergency teams for each shift
6. Establishing specific asset-protection and life-saving steps
7. Designating equipment, facilities, and locations to be used in an emergency
8. Communicating necessary elements of the emergency response plan to all affected personnel
9. Communication with outside agencies
10. Public relations and release of information

While authority to declare an emergency and to order shutdown and/or evacuation normally rests with someone in higher management, this sometimes is exercised by a plant manager in an industrial facility, for example, or by the designated emergency plan chairman or administrator. Whoever is so designated in the plan must be someone who is available or on call at all times.

Someone must also be in charge of executing the plan in an emergency—with backup to ensure coverage around the clock. This person will be responsible for initiating action according to the plan in an emergency, ordering and directing shutdown and evacuation when so authorized, making emergency announcements, and coordinating emergency responses. Often this emergency plan administrator or chief is the plant or facility manager who will take advantage of existing organizational chains of command with orders and directions filtering down through department heads to supervisors, foremen, and working personnel.

As indicated above, specific responsibilities in the plan will depend on the nature of the facility and the threat. Advantage should be taken of special skills and knowledge (of electricians, engineers, and maintenance crew). The important factor is to have reponsibilities spelled out in advance in the emergency plan.

Continuity in planning is essential. Provision should be made for alternates for each individual given responsibility in the emergency plan. In addition, since an emergency can occur at any hour of the day, the plan should designate emergency responsibilities for each shift or for open and closed hours, depending on the situation.

Security Responsibilities

While it is not possible in this generalized review to specify the duties of all those involved in the emergency response, the commonly accepted responsibilities of the security department in an emergency are essentially an expansion of normal security functions, including the preservation of order, protection of life and property, and vehicle and pedestrian control. These duties, however, should not simply be understood but, as with all aspects of emergency planning, should be designated in the plan.

1. Establishment of communication with police
2. Activation of emergency steps to protect people, property, and valuable information or other assets
3. Mobilization of an emergency guard force
4. Control of movement of personnel and others
5. Control of entrances and exits
6. Control of classified and dangerous areas
7. Control of evacuation as ordered

In some circumstances, depending on the size of the emergency team, security may also be involved in firefighting and rescue, first aid, and other necessary assistance. The security director should always be a member of any emergency planning committee as well as of the emergency team. Emergency and disaster planning is a total management responsibility, but by its very nature, security will always play an active and prominent role.

Conclusion

With the advent of OSHA, the attention focused on safety in the workplace created many new attitudes about the place of loss control within the organization. Many companies that had at best paid lip service to concepts of safety that are commonplace today came to see that safety, like security, is good business, and that a well-managed loss-control program would produce gratifying savings in a potentially costly area of company operations. But it must be noted that a well-managed safety program goes well beyond simply complying with OSHA standards.

For all of its progressiveness in mandating safety conditions that extended into tens of thousands of companies previously untouched by a safety regulation, OSHA has in some respect taken safety administration a step backward in that its focus is almost exclusively on unsafe or unsanitary conditions. For some years, the safety professionals have agreed that unsafe acts are the major cause of accidents or incidents.

In addition to recognizing OSHA standards, many companies have also placed more emphasis on fire prevention and protection. Some companies have even established their own fire departments, which are often better equipped than some municipal departments. Although there is some recognition of the importance of crisis planning, far too few firms have anything beyond a crisis management plan. Even in those companies with crisis management teams, the members often do not meet to discuss how the team would function in an actual situation.

The most progressive firms offer the team members, fire brigades, and employees an opportunity to preplan through mock exercises that replicate industrial disasters, explosions, fires, or tornado alerts. The end result is a better-prepared team of employees. Unfortunately many firms have not gone this far.

Review Questions

1. What are the classes of fire, the fuels needed to ignite each, and the extinguishing agents that can be used in each class?
2. In what ways is an ionization detector different from a smoke, infrared, or thermal detector?
3. What are the key elements of any emergency plan?
4. What should be the role of security in the emergency response?
5. When management is developing a plan for emergency evacuations, what things need to be considered?
6. What is OSHA, and what effect has it had on company safety operations?

References

1. Dennis F. Sigwart, "Diasaster Planning Considerations For The Security/Safety Professional: A Historical Interface," in *Suggested Preparation for Careers in Security Loss Prevention*, John Chuvala III and Robert Fischer, eds. (Dubuque, Iowa: Kendall/Hunt, 1991), p. 147.
2. John L. Bryan, *Fire Suppression and Detection Systems* (New York: Macmillan, 1982), pp. 11–12.
3. *General Industry: Safety and Health Regulations, Part 1910* (U.S. Department of Labor, OSHA, 1974).
4. Marshall v. Barlow's, 98 Sct. Rptr. 1816 (1978).
5. H. W. Heinrich, *Industrial Accident Prevention* (New York: McGraw-Hill, 1959).
6. Ibid.

12 □ □ □
□ □ □
□ □ □

Internal Theft Controls

It is sad but true that virtually every company will suffer losses from internal theft—and these losses can be enormous. *Security* in its *third quarterly telephone survey* (1990) of security decisionmakers reports that employee theft rose significantly over the 1988 figures. In 1988, only 14 percent of the respondents reported employee-theft problems of more than 40 incidents. In 1990, 38 percent reported between 21 and 1000 incidents. Figure 12.1 provides a comparison of the 1988 and 1990 data.[1] The significance of the employee-theft problem is shown in a study by Loss Prevention Consultants "The Silent Partner—How Many Do You Have?" This study, based on confessions of 345 employee thieves, documents a combined shrinkage of over $1 million over a four-year period. The study notes that employee theft is not seasonal and that accessibility rather than need triggers the desire to steal. The report notes, however, that 51 percent of the thieves over 41 years of age reported that they stole to satisfy financial needs. Younger employees tend to steal gadgets while older thieves take money. Figure 12.2 shows the relationship of age and type of theft.[2]

Based on past projects undertaken to evaluate the cost of economic crime in 1980, *Hallcrest I* estimated employee theft to be at least $100 billion. *Hallcrest II* begins its comments on economic crime with a review of various reported statistics and concludes that there needs to be a coordinated effort to collect data on all types of economic crime. *Hallcrest II* reports that employee-theft estimates range from $130 billion to $320 billion annually.[3] The significance of employee theft is pointed out in the January 1991 issue of *Security*, which reports that employee theft has reasserted itself as the number one security concern for 1991.[4] In addition, *Security* reports that up to 75 percent of all employees steal from their company once, and about 40 steal at least twice.

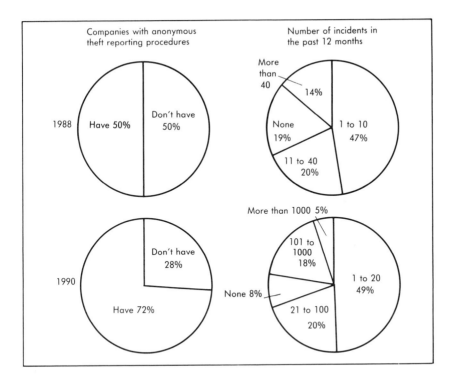

Figure 12.1 Employee theft: Reporting, incidents increase. (From *Security* magazine, Oct. 1990, p. 11. Published by Cahners Publishing Co., a division of Reed Publishing USA.)

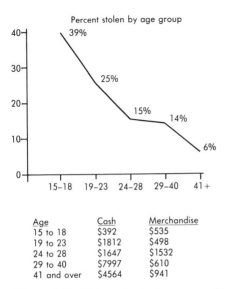

Age	Cash	Merchandise
15 to 18	$392	$535
19 to 23	$1812	$498
24 to 28	$1647	$1532
29 to 40	$7997	$610
41 and over	$4564	$941

Figure 12.2 Thieves' take-home pay. (Loss Prevention Consultants, Inc.)

What Is Honesty?

Before considering the issue of dishonest employees, it is helpful to understand the concept of honesty, which is difficult to define. Webster says that honesty is "fairness and straight forwardness of conduct, speech, etc.; integrity; truthfulness; freedom; freedom from fraud." In simple terms, honesty is respect for others and for their property. The concept, however, is relative. According to Charles Carson, "Security must be based on a controlled degree of relative honesty" since no one fulfills the ideal of total honesty. Carson explores relative honesty by asking the following questions:

1. If an error is made in your favor in computing the price of something you buy, do you report it?
2. If a cashier gives you too much change, do you return it?
3. If you found a purse containing money and the owner's identification, would you return the money to the owner if the amount was $1? $10? $100? $1,000?[5]

Honesty is a controllable variable, and how much control is necessary depends on the degree of honesty of each individual. The individual's honesty can be evaluated by assessing the degree of two types of honesty—moral and conditioned. Moral honesty is a feeling of responsibility and respect that develops during an individual's formative years; this type of honesty is subconscious. Conditioned honesty results from fearing the consequences of being caught; it is a product of reasoning. If an honest act is made without a conscious decision, it is because of moral honesty, but if the act is based on the conscious consideration of consequences, the act results from conditioned honesty.

It is vital to understand these principles because the role of security is to hire employees who have good moral honesty and to condition employees to greater honesty. The major concern is that the job should not tempt an employee into dishonesty.

Unfortunately there is no sure way by which potentially dishonest employees can be recognized. Proper screening procedures can eliminate applicants with unsavory pasts or those who seem unstable and therefore possibly untrustworthy. There are even tests that purport to measure an applicant's honesty index. But tests and employee screening can only indicate potential difficulties. They can screen out the most obvious risks, but they can never truly vouch for the performance of any prospective employee under circumstances of new employment or under changes that may come about in life apart from the job.

The need to carefully screen employees has continued to increase. In today's market, there are many individuals who have been called the "I desire it!" generation. According to a study by the Josephson Institute for the Advanced Study of Ethics, "An unprecedented proportion of today's youth lack commitment to core moral values like honesty, personal responsibility, respect for others and civic duty." The institute, which conducts nonpartisan ethics programs for the Internal Revenue Service, the Pentagon, and several major media organizations and educators, states that their findings show "a meaningful, demonstrable . . . discernible disintegration" in moral standards. To support the research, the institute notes that during the 1980s the majority of college freshman surveyed admitted to cheating in high school. In addition, approximately 25 percent of applicants under 30 falsify their resumes.[6]

The Dishonest Employee

Since there is no fail-safe technique for recognizing the potentially dishonest employee on sight, it is important to try to gain some insight into the reasons employees may steal. If some rule of thumb can be developed that will help to identify the patterns of the potential thief, it would provide some warning for an alert manager.

There is no simple answer to the question of why heretofore honest people suddenly start to steal from their employers. The mental and emotional process that leads to this is complex, and motivation may come from any number of sources.

Some employees steal because of resentment over real or imagined injustice that they blame on management indifference or malevolence. Some feel that they must maintain status and steal to augment their incomes because of financial problems. Some may steal simply to tide themselves over in a genuine emergency. They rationalize the theft by assuring themselves that they will return the money after the current problem is solved. Some simply want to indulge themselves, and many, strangely enough, steal to help others. Or employees may steal because no one cares, because no one is looking, or because absent or inadequate theft controls eliminate the fear of being caught. Still others may steal simply for excitement.

The Theft Triangle

A simplified answer to the question of why employees steal is the theft triangle. According to this concept, theft—much like fire—occurs when three elements are present: 1) motive, 2) desire, and 3) opportunity.

In simple terms, motive is a reason to steal. Motives might be the resentment of an employee who feels underpaid or the vengefulness of an employee who has been passed over for promotion. Desire builds on motive by imagining the satisfaction or gratification that would come from a potential action. "Taking a stereo system would make me feel good, because I always wanted a good stereo system." Opportunity is the absence of barriers that prevent someone from taking an item. Desire and motive are beyond the scope of the loss-prevention manager; opportunity, however, is the responsibility of security.

A high percentage of employee thefts begin with opportunities that are regularly presented to them. If security systems are lax or supervision is indifferent, the temptation to steal items that are improperly secured or unaccountable may be too much to resist by any but the most resolute employee.

Many experts agree that the fear of discovery is the most important deterrent to internal theft. When the potential for discovery is eliminated, theft is bound to follow. Threats of dismissal or prosecution of any employee found stealing are never as effective as the belief that any theft will be discovered by management supervision.

Danger Signs

The root causes of theft are many and varied, but certain signs can indicate that a hazard exists. The conspicuous consumer presents perhaps the most easily identified risk. Employees who habitually or suddenly acquire expensive cars and/or clothes and who generally seem to live beyond their means should be watched. Such persons are visibly extravagant and appear indifferent to the value of money. Even though employees may not be stealing to support expensive tastes, they are likely to run into financial difficulties through reckless spending. Employees may then be tempted to look beyond their salary checks for ways to support an extravagant lifestyle.

Employees who show a pattern of financial irresponsibility are also a potential risk. Many people are incapable of handling their money. They may do their job with great skill and efficiency, but they are in constant difficulty in their private lives. These people are not necessarily compulsive spenders, nor do they necessarily have expensive tastes. (They probably live quite modestly since they have never been able to manage their affairs effectively enough to live otherwise.) They are simply people unable to come to grips with their own economic realities.

Garnishments or inquiries by creditors may identify such employees. If there seems a reason to make one, a credit check might reveal the tangled state of affairs.

Employees caught in a genuine financial squeeze are also possible problems. If they have been hit with financial demands from illnesses in the family or possibly heavy tax liens, they may find the pressures too great to bear. If such a situation comes to the attention of management, counseling is in order. Many companies maintain funds that are designated to make low-interest loans in such cases. Alternatively some arrangement might be worked out through a credit union. In any event, employees in such extremities need help fast. They should get that help both as a humane response to the needs and as a means of protecting company assets.

In addition to these general categories, there are specific danger signals which should be noted:

- Gambling on or off premises
- Excessive drinking or signs of other drug use
- Obvious extravagance
- Persistent borrowing
- Requests for advances
- Bouncing personal checks or post-dated checks

What Employees Steal

The employee thief will take anything that may be useful or that has resale value. The thief can get at the company funds in many ways—directly or indirectly—through collusion with vendors, collusion with outside thieves or hijackers, fake invoices, receipting for goods never received, falsifying inventories, payroll padding, false certification of overtime, padded expense accounts, computer records manipulation, overcharging, undercharging, or simply by gaining access to a cashbox.

This is only a sample of the kinds of attack that can be made on company assets using the systems set up for the operation of the business. It is in these areas that the greatest losses can occur since they are frequently based on a systematic looting of the goods and services in which the company deals and the attendant operational cash flow.

Significant losses do occur, however, in other, sometimes unexpected areas. Furnishings frequently disappear. In some firms with indifferent traffic control procedures, this kind of theft can be a very real problem. Desks, chairs, computers and other office equipment, paintings, rugs—all can be carried away by the enterprising employee thief.

Office supplies can be another problem if they are not properly supervised. Beyond the anticipated attrition in pencils, paper clips, note pads, and rubber bands, sometimes these materials are often stolen in case lots. Many firms that buy their supplies at discount are in fact receiving stolen property. The market in stolen office supplies is a brisk one and is becoming more so as the prices for this merchandise soar.

The office equipment market is another active one, and the inside thief is quick to respond to its needs. Computers always bring a good price, as well as calculators and equipment used to support the microcomputer.

Personal property is also vulnerable. Office thieves do not make fine distinctions between company property and that of their fellow workers. The company has a very real stake in this kind of theft since personal tragedy and decline in morale follow in its wake.

Although security personnel cannot assume responsibility for losses of this nature since they are not in a position to know about the property involved or to control its handling (and they should so inform all employees), they should make every effort to apprise all employees of the threat. They should further note from time to time the degree of carelessness the staff displays in handling of personal property and send out reminders of the potential dangers of loss.

Methods of Theft

Various studies estimate that 7–30 percent of business failures are the result of some form of employee dishonesty.[7] Therefore there is a very real need to examine the shapes the dishonesty frequently takes. There is no way to describe every kind of theft, but some examples may serve to give some idea of the dimensions of the problem.

1. Payroll and personnel employees collaborating to falsify records by the use of nonexistent employees or by retaining terminated employees on the payroll
2. Padding overtime reports, part of which extra unearned pay is kicked back to the authorizing supervisor
3. Pocketing unclaimed wages
4. Splitting increased payroll that has been raised on signed, blank checks for use in the authorized signer's absence
5. Maintenance personnel and contract servicemen in collusion to steal and sell office equipment
6. Receiving clerks and truck drivers in collusion on falsification of merchandise count (Extra unaccounted merchandise is fenced.)
7. Purchasing agents in collusion with vendors to falsify purchase and payment documents (The purchasing agent issues authorization for payment on goods never shipped after forging receipts of shipment.)
8. Purchasing agent in collusion with vendor to pay inflated price
9. Mailroom and supply personnel packing and mailing merchandise to themselves for resale
10. Accounts payable personnel paying fictitious bills to an account set up for their own use
11. Taking incoming cash without crediting the customer's account
12. Paying creditors twice and pocketing the second check

13. Appropriating checks made out to cash
14. Raising the amount of checks after voucher approval or raising the amount of vouchers after their approval
15. Pocketing small amounts from incoming payments and applying later payments on other accounts to cover shortages
16. Removal of equipment or merchandise with the trash
17. Invoicing goods below regular price and getting a kickback from the purchaser
18. Manipulation of accounting software packages to credit personal accounts with electronic account overages
19. Issuing (and cashing) checks on returned merchandise not actually returned
20. Forging checks, destroying them when they are returned with the statement from the bank, and changing cash account records accordingly

Management Responsibility in Loss Prevention

Many security specialists have speculated that the enormous losses in internal theft come largely from firms that have refused to believe that their employees would steal from them. As a result, their loss-prevention systems are weak and ineffective.

Managers of such companies are not naive. They are aware that criminally inclined employees exist—and in great numbers—but they exist in other companies. Such managers are truly shocked when they discover how extensive employee theft can be. This does not mean that a high percentage of the employees are involved (though they may be). Two or three employees, given the right opportunities, can create havoc in any business in a very short time, and the majority of them go undetected.

National crime figures do not necessarily concern each manager. These figures can be shrugged off as an enormous problem that someone else must deal with, one that has no effect on the operation, and hopefully this is correct. But managers cannot afford to close their eyes to the potential damage. They must be convinced that one of their employees might steal. Managers must be persuaded that there is at least a possibility of embezzlement and that maybe sooner or later someone will be unable to resist the temptation to take what is so alluringly available.

It may be surprising to find that there are shrewd business people who are still willing to ignore the threat of internal theft and who are therefore unwilling to take defensive steps against it. But the fact is the possibility of internal theft does indeed exist. Many security people report that the biggest problem is in convincing management that the problem is there and that steps must be taken for the protection of employer and employee alike.

There is some evidence and even more speculation that these managers are reluctant in effect to declare themselves as suspicious of the employees—to overtly imply distrust of employees, many of whom are perhaps old and trusted members of the corporate family. Such an attitude does the manager honor, but it is somewhat distorted. It fails to take into account the dynamics of all our lives. The employee who today would stand firm against the most persuasive temptation may be in different circumstances tomorrow—perhaps with different resultant attitudes. Whereas today the thought of embezzlement is repugnant, tomorrow the notion might be viewed differently. Remember the projections for the "I deserve it!" generation.

The Contagion of Theft

Theft of any kind is a contagious disorder. Petty, relatively innocent pilferage by a few spreads through the facility. As more people participate, others will follow until even the most rigid break down and join in. Pilferage becomes acceptable—even respectable. It gains general social acceptance that is reinforced by almost total peer participation. Few people make independent ethical judgments under such circumstances. In this microcosm, the act of petty pilferage is no longer viewed as unacceptable conduct. It has become not a permissible sin but instead a right.

The docks of New York City were an example of this progression. Forgetting for the moment the depredations of organized crime and the climate of dishonesty that characterized that operation for so many years, even longshoremen not involved in organized theft had worked out a system all their own. For every so many cases of whisky unloaded, for example, one case went to the men. Little or no attempt was made to conceal this. It was a tradition, a right. When efforts were made to curtail the practice, labor difficulties arose. It soon became evident that certain pilferage would have to be accepted as an unwritten part of the union contract under the existing circumstances.

This is not a unique situation. The progression from limited pilferage through its acceptance as normal conduct to the status of an unwritten right has been repeated time and again. The problem is, it does not stop there. Ultimately pilferage becomes serious theft, and then the real trouble starts. Even before pilferage expands into larger operations, it presents a difficult problem to any business. Even where the amount of goods taken by any one individual is small, the aggregate can represent a significant expense. With the costs of materials, manufacture, administration, and distribution rising as they are, there is simply no room for added, avoidable expenses in today's competitive markets. The business that can operate the most efficiently and offer quality goods at the lowest prices because of the efficiency of its operation, will have a huge advantage in the marketplace. When so many companies are fighting for their economic life, there is simply no room for waste—and pilferage is just that.

Moral Obligation to Control Theft

When we consider that internal theft accounts for at least twice the loss from external theft (that is, from burglars and armed robbers combined), we must be impressed with the scope of the problem facing today's businesspeople. Businesses have a financial obligation to stockholders to earn a profit on their investments. Fortunately there are steps that can be taken to control internal theft. Losses can be cut to relatively insignificant amounts by setting up a program of education and control that is vigorously administered and supervised.

It is also important to observe that management has a moral obligation to its employees to protect their integrity by taking every possible step to avoid presenting open opportunities for pilferage and theft that would tempt even the most honest people to take advantage of the opportunity for gain by theft.

This is not to suggest that each company should assume a paternal role toward its employees and undertake their responsibilities for them. It is to suggest strongly that the company should keep its house sufficiently in order to avoid enticing employees to acts that could result in great personal tragedy as well as in damage to the company.

Program for Internal Security

As for all security problems, the first requirement before setting up protective systems for internal security is to survey every area in the company to determine the extent and nature of the risks. If such a survey is conducted energetically and exhaustively and if its recommendations for action are acted on intelligently significant losses from internal theft will be a matter of history. Security surveys and their companions the operational audit have been discussed in detail in Chapter 7.

Need for Management Support

Once concerns have been identified, it is especially important that the strong support of top management be secured. In order to implement needed security controls, certain operational procedures may have to be changed. This will require cooperation at every level, and cooperation is sometimes hard to get in situations where department managers feel their authority has been diminished in areas within their sphere of responsibility.

The problem is compounded when those changes determined to be necessary cut across departmental lines, and even serve to some degree to alter intradepartmental relationships. Effecting systems under such circumstances will require the greatest tact, salesmanship, and executive ability. Failing that, it may be necessary to fall back on the ultimate authority vested in the security operation by top management. Any hesitation or equivocation on the part of either management or security at this point could damage the program before it has been initiated.

This does not, of course, mean that management must give security *carte blanche*. Reasonable and legitimate disagreements will inevitably arise. It does mean that proposed security programs based on broadly stated policy must be given the highest possible priority. In those cases where conflict of procedures exists, some compromise may be necessary, but the integrity of the security program as a whole must be preserved intact.

Communicating the Program

The next step is to communicate necessary details of the program to all employees. Many aspects of the system may be proprietary or on a need-to-know basis, but since part of it will involve procedures engaged in by most or all of company personnel, they will need to know those details in order to comply. This can be handled by an ongoing education program or by a series of meetings explaining the need for security and the damaging effects of internal theft to jobs, benefits, profit sharing, and the future of the company. Such meetings can additionally serve to notify all employees that management is taking action against criminal acts of all kinds at every level and that dishonesty will not be tolerated.

Such a forceful statement of position in this matter can be very beneficial. Most employees are honest people who disapprove of those who are criminally inclined. They are apprehensive and uncomfortable in a criminal environment, especially if it is widespread. The longer such conduct is condoned by the company, the more they lose respect for it, and a vicious cycle begins. As they lose respect, they lose a sense of purpose. Their work suffers, morale declines, and at best effectiveness is seriously diminished. At worst they reluctantly join the thieves. A clear, uncompromising policy of theft prevention is usually welcomed with visible relief.

Continuing Supervision

Once a system is installed, it must be constantly supervised if it is to become and remain effective. Left to their own devices, employees will soon find short cuts, and security controls will be abandoned in the process. Old employees must be reminded regularly of what is expected of them, and new employees must be adequately indoctrinated in the system they will be expected to follow.

There must be a continuing program of education if expected results are to be achieved. With a high turnover within the white-collar workforce, it can be expected that the office force, which handles key paperwork, will be replaced at a fairly consistent rate. This means that the company will have a regular influx of new people who must be trained in the procedures to be followed and in the reasons for these procedures.

Program Changes

In some situations, reasonable controls will create duplication of effort, cross-checking, and additional paperwork. Since each time such additional effort is required there is an added expense, procedural innovations requiring it must be avoided wherever possible, but most control systems aim for increased efficiency. Often this is the key to their effectiveness.

Many operational procedures, for a variety of reasons, fall into ponderous routines involving too many people and excessive paper shuffling. This may serve to increase the possibility of fraud, forgery, or falsification of documents. When the same operational result can be achieved by streamlining the system and incorporating adequate security control, it should be done immediately.

Virtually every system can be improved and should be evaluated constantly with an eye for such improvement, but these changes should never be undertaken arbitrarily. Procedures must be changed only after the changes have been considered in the light of their operational and security impact, and such considerations should further be undertaken in the light of their effect on the total system.

No changes should be permitted by unilateral employee action. Management should make random spot checks to determine if the system is being followed exactly. Internal auditors and/or security personnel should make regular checks on the control systems.

Violations

Violations should be dealt with immediately. Management indifference to security procedures is a signal that they are not important, and where work-saving methods can be found to circumvent such procedures, they will be. As soon as any procedural untidiness appears and is allowed to continue, the deterioration of the system begins.

It is well to note that, while efforts to circumvent the system are frequently the result of the ignorance or laziness of the offender, a significant number of such instances are the result of employees probing for ways to subvert the controls in order to divert company assets to their own use.

Procedural Controls

Auditing Assets

Periodic personal audits by outside auditors are essential to any well-run security program. Such an examination will discover theft only after the fact, but it will presumably discover any regular scheme of embezzlement in time to prevent serious damage. If these audits, which are normally conducted once a year, are augmented by one or more surprise audits, even the most reckless criminal would hesitate to try to set up even a short-term scheme of theft.

These audits will normally cover an examination of inventory schedules, prices, footings, and extensions. They should also verify current company assets by sampling physical inventory, accounts receivable, accounts payable (including payroll), deposits, plant, and outstanding liabilities through an ongoing financial audit. In all these cases, a spot check beyond the books themselves can help to establish the existence of legitimate assets and liabilities, not empty entries created by a clever embezzler.

Cash

Any business handling relatively few cash payments in and out is fortunate indeed. Such a business is able to avoid much of the difficulty in this security-sensitive area since cash handling is certainly the operation most vulnerable and the most sought after by larcenous staff.

Cash by Mail

If cash is received by mail—a practice almost unheard of in most businesses—its receipt and handling must be undertaken by a responsible, bonded supervisor or supervisors. This administrator should be responsible for no other cash handling or bookkeeping functions and should personally see to it that all cash received is recorded by listing the amount, the payer, and such other pertinent information as established procedures have indicated. There is clearly a danger here at the very outset. If cash is diverted before it is entered into the accounting system, there is no record of its existence. Until it is channeled into company ledgers in some way and begins its life as a company asset, there is no guarantee that it will not serve some more private interest. This requires supervision of the supervisor. In the case of a firm doing a large catalogue business that receives large amounts of cash in spite of pleas for checks, credit card puchases, or money orders, it has sometimes been felt that the operation should be conducted in a special room reserved for the purpose.

Daily Receipts

All cash accounting entries must be checked against cash on hand at the end of each day. Spot checks on an irregular basis should be conducted.

Cash receipts should be deposited in the bank, and each day's receipts should be balanced with the daily deposit. Petty cash as needed should be reimbursed by check.

All bank deposits should be accompanied by three deposit slips. One will be receipted by the bank and returned by the cashier to the person making the deposit; the second should be mailed to the office accounting department; and the third is the bank's copy.

Each day's deposit slips should be balanced with the day's receipts.

Bank Statements

Bank statements should be received and reconciled by someone who is not authorized to deposit or withdraw funds or to make a final accounting of receipts or disbursements. When bank statements are reconciled, cancelled checks should be checked against vouchers for any possible alterations and for proper endorsement by the payee. Any irregularities in the endorsements should be promptly investigated. If the statement itself seems out of order by way of erasure or possible alteration, the bank should be asked to submit a new statement to the reconciling official's special personal attention.

Petty Cash

A petty cash fund set aside for that purpose only should be established. The amount to be carried in such a fund will be based on past experience. These funds must never be commingled with other funds of any kind and should be drawn from the bank by check only. They should never be drawn from cash receipts. No disbursements of any kind should be made from petty cash without an authorized voucher signed by the employee receiving the cash and countersigned by an authorized employee. No voucher should be cashed that shows signs of erasure or alteration. All such vouchers should be drawn up in ink or typed. In cases of typographical error, new vouchers should be prepared rather than correcting the error. If there is any reason for using a voucher on which an erasure or correction has been made, the authorizing official should initial the change or place of erasure.

Receipts substantiating the voucher should accompany it and should wherever possible be stapled or otherwise attached to it.

The petty cash fund should be brought up to the specified amount required by a check to the amount of its depletion. The vouchers on which disbursements were made should always be verified by an employee other than the one in charge of the fund. All vouchers submitted and paid should be cancelled in order to avoid reuse.

Petty cash should be balanced occasionally by management at which time vouchers should be examined for irregularities.

Separation of Responsibility

The principle of separation of responsibility and authority in matters concerning the company's finances is of prime importance in management. This situation must always be sought out in the survey of every department. It is not always easy to locate. Sometimes even the employee who has such power is unaware of the dual role. But the security specialist must be knowledgeable about its existence and suggest an immediate change or correction in such operational procedures whenever they appear.

An employee who is in the position of both ordering and receiving merchandise or a cashier who authorizes and disburses expenditures are examples of this double-ended function in operation. All situations of this nature are potentially damaging and should be eliminated. Such procedures are manifestly unfair to company and employee alike. They are unfair to the company because of the loss that they might incur; they are unfair to the employee because of the temptation and ready opportunity they present. Good business practice demands that such invitations to embezzlement be studiously avoided.

It is equally important that cash handling be separated from the record-keeping function. Cashiers who become their own auditors and bookkeepers have a free rein with that part of company funds. The chances are that cashiers will not steal, but they could and might. They might also make mathematical mistakes unless someone else double checks the arithmetic.

In some smaller companies, this division of function is not always practical. In such concerns, it is common for the bookkeeper to act also as cashier. If this is the case, a system of countersignatures, approvals, and management audits should be set up to help divide the responsibility of handling company funds from that of accounting for them.

Promotion and Rotation

Most embezzlement is the product of a scheme operating over an extended period of time. Many embezzlers prefer to divert small sums on a systematic basis, feeling that the individual thefts will not be noticed and that therefore the total loss is unlikely to come to management's attention.

These schemes are sometimes frustrated either by some accident that uncovers the system or by the greed of the embezzlers, who are so carried away with success that they step up the ante. But while the theft is working, it is usually difficult to detect. Frequently the thief is in a position to alter or manipulate records in such a way that the theft escapes the attention of both internal and external auditors. This can sometimes be countered by upward or lateral movement of employees.

Promotion from within, wherever possible, is always good business practice, and lateral transfers can be effective in countering possible boredom or the danger of reducing a function to rote and thus diminishing its effectiveness.

Such movement also frustrates embezzlers. When they lose control of the books governing some aspect of the operation, they lose the opportunity to cover their thefts. Discovery inevitably follows careful audits of books they can no longer manipulate. If regular transfers were a matter of company policy, no rational embezzler would set up a long-term plan of embezzlement unless a scheme was found that was audit-proof—and such an eventuality is highly unlikely.

To be effective as a security measure, such transfers need not involve all personnel since every change in operating personnel brings with it changes in operation. In some cases, even subtle changes may be enough to alter the situation sufficiently to reduce the totality of control an embezzler has over the books. If such is the case, the swindle is over. The embezzler may avoid discovery of the previous looting, but cannot continue without danger of being unmasked.

In the same sense, embezzlers dislike vacations. They are aware of the danger if someone else should handle their accounts, if only for the two or three weeks of vacation. So they make every effort to pass up holidays.

Any manager who has a reluctant vacationer should recognize that this is a potential problem. Vacations are designed to refresh the outlook of everyone. No matter how tired they may be when they return to work, vacationers have been refreshed emotionally and intellectually. Their effectiveness in their job has probably improved, and they are, generally speaking, better employees for the time off. The company benefits from vacations as much as the employees do. No one should be permitted to pass up authorized vacations, especially one whose position involves control over company assets.

Access to Records

Many papers, documents and records are proprietary or at least available to only a limited number of people who need such papers in order to function. All other persons are deemed off limits. They have no apparent need for the information. Such records should be secured under lock and key or through access control in the case of electronically stored data and, depending on their value or reconstructability, in a fire-resistant container.

Forms

Certain company forms are often extremely valuable to the inside as well as the outside thief. They should be secured and accounted for at all times. They should be sequentially numbered and recorded regularly so that any loss can be detected at a glance.

Blank checks, order forms, payment authorizations, vouchers, receipt forms, and all papers that authorize or verify transactions are prime targets for thieves and should therefore be accounted for.

Since there are many effective operational systems in use for the ordering, shipping, or receiving of goods as well as the means by which all manner of payments from petty cash to regular debt discharge are authorized, no one security system to protect against illegal manipulation within such systems would apply universally. It can be said, however, that, since every business has some means of authorizing transactions of goods or money, the means by which such authorizations are made must be considered in the security program. Security of such means must be considered an important element in any company's defense against theft.

Generally speaking, all forms should be prenumbered and wherever possible used in numerical order. Any voided or damaged forms should be filed and recorded, and forms reported lost must be accounted for and explained. All such numbered forms of every kind should be inventoried and accounted for periodically.

In cases where purchase orders are issued in blocks to various people who have the need for such authority, such issuance must be recorded and disposition of their use should be audited regularly. In such cases, it is customary for one copy of the numbered purchase order to be sent to the vendor, who will use that number in all further dealings on that particular order; another copy will be sent to accounting for purposes of payment authorization and accrual if necessary; and one copy will be retained by the issuing authority. Each block issued should be used sequentially although, since some areas may have more purchasing activity than others, purchasing order copies as they are forwarded to accounting may not be in overall sequence.

Computer Records/Electronic Mail, Funds Transfer/FAX

The computer has become perhaps the most powerful tool for recordkeeping, research and development, funds transfer, electronic mail, and management within most companies today. It is essential that the computer and its support equipment and records be adequately protected from the internal thief. This is such an important area of security that a full chapter has been devoted to the subject (see Chapter 17).

Besides the computer, the transfer of information via FAX has become an everyday occurrence. Approximately 30 billion pages were transmitted via FAX in 1989. Some industry analysts believe that 10 percent of all FAX traffic is important enough to be coded, yet less than .5 percent of it is presently secured. FAX encryptors are available at relatively low costs.[8]

Purchasing

Centralized Responsibility

Where purchasing is centralized in a department, controls will always be more effective. Localizing responsibility as well as authority reduces the opportunity for fraud accordingly. This is not always possible or practical, but in areas where purchasing is permitted by departments needing certain materials and supplies, there can be confusion occasioned by somewhat different purchasing procedures. Cases have been reported of different departments paying different prices for the same goods and services and thus bidding up the price the company is paying. Centralization of purchasing would overcome this problem. The use of computers and networking has allowed for centralized control with decentralized operations.

Purchasing should not, however, be involved in any aspect of accounts payable or of the receipt of merchandise other than informationally.

Competitive Bids

Competitive bids should be sought wherever possible. This, however, raises an interesting point that must be dealt with as a matter of company policy. Seeking competitive bids is always good practice, both to get a view of the market and to provide alternatives in the ordering of goods and materials, but it does not follow that the lowest bidder is always the vendor to do business with.

Such a bidder may lack adequate experience in providing the services bid for or may have a reputation of supplying goods of questionable quality even though they may meet the technical standard prescribed in the order. A firm may also underbid the competition in a desperate effort to get the business, but then find it cannot deliver materials at that price, no matter what it has agreed to in its contract.

In order to function wisely and to be able to exercise good judgment in its area of expertise, purchasing must be permitted some flexibility in its selection of vendors. This means that it will not always be the low bidder who wins the contract.

Since competitive bidding provides some security control in reducing favoritism, collusion, and kickbacks between the purchasing agent and the vendor, these controls would appear to be weakened or compromised in situations where the purchasing department is permitted to select the vendor on considerations other than cost. This can be true to some degree, but this is a situation in which business or operational needs may be in some conflict with tight security standards and in which security should revise its position to accommodate the larger demands of efficiency and ultimate economy. After all, cheap is not necessarily economical.

Controls in this case could be applied by requiring that in all cases where the lowest bid was not accepted, a brief explanation in outline form be attached to the file along with all bids submitted. Periodic audits of such files could establish if any pattern of fraud seems likely. Investigation of the analysis or assumptions made by purchasing in assigning contracts might be indicated in some situations to check the validity of the stated reasoning in the matter.

Other Controls

Copies of orders containing the amount of merchandise purchased should not be sent to receiving clerks. These clerks should simply state the quantity actually received with no preconception of the amount accepted. Payment should be authorized only for the amount actually received.

Vendor invoices and receipts supporting such vouchers should be cancelled to avoid the possibility of their resubmission in collusion with the vendor.

Purchasing should be audited periodically, and documents should be examined for any irregularities.

Payroll

It is important that the payroll be prepared by persons who will not be involved in its distribution. This is consistent with the effort to separate the various elements of a particular function into its component parts and then distribute the responsibility for those parts to two or more persons or departments.

Every effort should be made to distribute the payroll in the form of checks rather than cash, and such checks should be of a color different from those used in any other aspect of the business. They should also be drawn on an account set aside exclusively for payroll purposes. It is important that this account be maintained in an orderly fashion. Avoid using current cash receipts for payroll purposes.

Personnel Records

Initial payroll information should be prepared from personnel records, which in turn have come from personnel as each employee is hired. Such records should contain basic data such as name, address, attached W-2 form, title, salary, and any other information that the payroll department may need. The record should be countersigned by a responsible executive verifying the accuracy of the information forwarded.

This same procedure should be followed when an employee terminates employment with the company. All such notifications should be consolidated into a master payroll list, which should be checked frequently to make sure that payroll's list corresponds to the current personnel employment records.

Unclaimed Payroll Checks

Unclaimed paychecks should be returned to the treasurer or controller after a reasonable period of time for redeposit in the payroll account. Certainly such cases should be investigated to determine why the checks were returned or why they were issued in the first place. All checks so returned should be cancelled to prevent any reuse and filed for reference. Since payrolls reflect straight time, overtime, and other payments, such payments should be supported by time sheets authorized by supervisors or department heads. Time sheets of this nature should be verified periodically to prevent overtime padding and kickbacks.

Time cards should be marked to prevent reuse.

Payroll Audits

The payroll should be audited periodically by external auditors for any irregularities, especially if there has been an abnormal increase in personnel or net labor costs.

To further guard against the fraudulent introduction of names into the payroll, distribution of paychecks should periodically be undertaken by the internal auditor, the treasurer, or some other responsible official. In large this can be done on a percentage basis, thus providing at least a spot check of the validity of the rolls.

Accounts Payable

As in the case of purchasing, accounts payable should be centralized to handle all disbursements on adequate verification of receipt and proper authorization for payment.

These disbursements should always be by checks that are consecutively numbered and used in consecutive order. Checks that are damaged, incorrectly drawn, or for any reason unusable must be marked as cancelled and filed for audit. All checks issued for payment should be accompanied by appropriate supporting data, including payment authorizations, before they are signed by the signing authority. It is advisable to draw the checks on a check-writing machine that uses permanent ink and is as identifiable to an expert as is handwriting or a particular typewriter. Checks should be printed on safety paper that will show almost any attempted alteration.

Here as in order departments periodic audits must be conducted to examine the records for any sign of nonexistent vendors, irregularities in receipts or payment authorizations, forgeries, frauds, or unbusinesslike procedures that could lead to embezzlement.

General Merchandise

Merchandise is always subject to pilferage, particularly when it is in a transfer stage, as when it is being shipped or received. The dangers of loss at these stages are increased in operations where controls over inventory are lax or improperly supervised.

Separation of Functions

To control sensitive aspects of any operation involving the handling of merchandise, it is desirable to separate three functions: receiving, warehousing, and shipping. These functions should be the responsibility of three different areas. Movement of merchandise from one mode to another should be accompanied by appropriate documents that clearly establish the responsibility for specific amounts of merchandise passing from one sphere of authority to another.

Receipting for a shipment places responsibility for a correct count and for the security of the shipment on the receiving dock. This responsibility remains there until it is transferred and receives a proper receipt from the warehouse supervisor. The warehouse supervisor must verify and store the shipment, which is then the warehouse supervisor's responsibility until it is called for (by the sales department, for example) or directed to be shipped by an authorized document. The warehouse supervisor ensures that the goods are assembled and passed along as ordered and receives a receipt for those goods when they are delivered.

In this process, responsibility is fixed from point to point. Various departments or functions take on and are relieved of responsibility by use of the receipts. In this way, a perpetual inventory is maintained as well as a record of responsibility for the merchandise.

Requisitions must be numbered to avoid the destruction of records or the introduction of unauthorized transfers into the system. In addition, merchandise stock numbers should accompany all of that merchandise's movement to describe the goods and thus aid in maintaining perpetual inventory records.

In small firms where this separation of duties is impractical, and receiving, shipping, and warehousing are combined in one person, the perpetual inventory is essential for security, but it must be maintained by someone other than the person actually handling the merchandise. The shipper-receiver-warehouser should not have access to these inventory records at any time.

Inventories

Inventories will always be an important aspect of merchandise control, no matter what operations are in effect. Such inventories must be conducted by someone other than the person in charge of that particular stock. In the case of department stores, for purposes of inventory, personnel should be moved to a department other than their regularly assigned one.

In firms where a perpetual inventory record is kept, physical counts on a selective basis can be undertaken monthly or even weekly. In this procedure, a limited number of certain items randomly selected can be counted and the count compared with current inventory record cards. Any discrepancy can be traced back to attempt to determine the cause of the loss.

Physical Security

It is important to remember that personnel charged with the responsibility of goods, materials, and merchandise must be provided the means of properly discharging that responsibility. Warehouses and other storage space must be equipped with adequate physical protection to secure the goods stored within. Authorizations to enter such storage areas must be strictly limited, and the responsible employees must have means to further restrict access in situations where they feel that the security of goods is endangered (see Chapter 10 for a discussion of pass systems).

Receiving clerks must have adequate facilities for storage or supervision of goods until they can be passed on for storage or other use. Shipping clerks must also have the ability to secure goods in dock areas until they are received and loaded by truckers. Without the proper means of securing merchandise during every phase of its handling, assigned personnel cannot be held responsible for merchandise intended for their control, and the entire system will break down. Unreasonable demands, such as requiring shipping clerks to handle the movement of merchandise in such a way that they are required to leave unprotected goods on the dock while filling out the rest of the order, lead to the very reasonable refusal of personnel to assume responsibility for such merchandise. And when responsibility cannot be fixed, theft can result.

The Mailroom

The mailroom can be a rich field for a company thief. Not only can it be used to mail out company property to an ally or to a prearranged address, but it also deals in stamps—and stamps are money. Any office with a heavy mailing operation must conduct regular audits of the mailroom.

Some firms have taken the view that the mailroom represents such a small exposure that close supervision is unnecessary. Yet the head of the mailroom in a fair-sized eastern firm got away with over $100,000 in less than three years through manipulation of the postal meter. Only a firm that can afford to lose $100,000 in less than three years should think of its mailroom as inconsequential in its security plan.

Trash Removal

Trash removal presents many problems. Employees have hidden office equipment or merchandise in trash cans and have then picked up the loot far from the premises in cooperation with the driver of the trash collecting vehicle. Some firms have had a problem when they put trash on the loading dock to facilitate pick-up. Trash collectors made their calls during the day and often picked up unattended merchandise along with the trash. On-premises trash compaction is one way to end the use of trash containers as a safe and convenient vehicle for removing loot from the premises.

Every firm has areas that are vulnerable to attack. What and where they are can only be determined by thorough surveys and regular reevaluation of the entire operation. There are no shortcuts. The important thing is to locate the areas of risk and set up procedures to reduce or eliminate them.

When Controls Fail

There are occasions when a company is so beset by internal theft that problems seem to have gotten totally out of hand. In such cases, it is often difficult to localize the problem sufficiently to set up specific countermeasures in those areas affected. The company seems simply to "come up short."

Management is at a loss to identify the weak link in its security, much less to identify how theft is accomplished after security has been compromised.

Undercover Investigation

In such cases, many firms similarly at a loss in every sense of the word have found it advisable to engage the services of a security firm that can provide undercover agents to infiltrate the organization and observe the operation from within.

Such agents may be asked to get into the organization on their own initiative. The fewer people who know of the agents' presence, the greater the protection, and the more likely they are to succeed in investigations. It is also true that when large-scale thefts take place over a period of time, almost anyone in the company could be involved. Even one or more top executives could be involved in serious operations of this kind. Therefore secrecy is of great importance. Since several agents may be used in a single investigation and since they may be required to find employment in the company at various levels, they must have, or very convincingly seem to have, proper qualifications for the level of employment they are seeking. Over- or under-qualification in pursuit of a specific area of employment can be a problem so they must plan their entry carefully. Several agents may have to apply for the same job before one is accepted.

Having gotten into the firm's employ, agents must work alone. They must conduct the investigation and make reports with the greatest discretion to avoid discovery. But they are in the best possible position to get to the center of the problem, and such agents have been successful in a number of cases of internal theft in the past.

These investigators are not inexpensive, but they earn their fee many times over in breaking up a clever ring of thieves. It is important to remember, however, that such agents are trained professionals. Most of them have had years of experience in undercover work of this type. Under no circumstances should a manager think of saving money by using employees or well-meaning amateurs for this work. Such a practice could be dangerous to the inexperienced investigator and would almost certainly warn the thieves, who would simply withdraw from their illegal operation temporarily until things had cooled down after which they could return to the business of theft.

Prosecution

Every firm has been faced with the problem of establishing policy regarding the disposal of a case involving proven or admitted employee theft. They are faced with three alternatives: to prosecute, to discharge, or to retain the thief as an employee. The policy they have established has always been difficult to arrive at because there is no ready answer. There are many proponents of each alternative as the solution to problems of internal theft.

However difficult it may be, every firm must establish a policy governing matters of this kind. And the decision about that policy must be arrived at with a view to the greatest benefits to the employees, the company, and society as a whole. An enlightened management would also consider the position of the as-yet-to-be-discovered thief in establishing such policy.

Discharging the Thief

Most firms have found that discharge of the offender is the simplest solution. Experts estimate that most of those employees discovered stealing are simply dismissed. Most of those are carried in the company records as having been discharged for "inefficiency" or "failure to perform duties adequately."

This policy is defended on many grounds, but the most common are:

1. Discharge is a severe punishment, and the offender will learn from the punishment.
2. Prosecution is expensive.
3. Prosecution would create an unfavorable public relations atmosphere for the company.
4. Reinstating the offender in the company—no matter what conditions are placed on the reinstatement—will appear to be condoning theft.
5. If the offender is prosecuted and found not guilty, the company will be open to civil action for false arrest, slander, libel, defamation of character, and other damages.

There is some validity in all of these views, but each one bears some scrutiny.

As to learning (and presumably reforming) as a result of discharge, experience does not bear out this contention. A security organization found that 80 percent of the known employee thieves they questioned with polygraph substantiation admitted to thefts from previous employers. Now it might well be argued that, since they had not been caught and discharged as a result of these prior thefts, the proposition that discharge can be therapeutic still holds or at least has not been refuted. That may be true, and it should be considered.

Prosecution is unquestionably expensive. Personnel called as witnesses may spend days appearing in court. Additional funds may be expended investigating and establishing a case against the accused. Legal fees may be involved. But can a company afford to appear so indifferent to significant theft that it refuses to take strong action when it occurs?

As to public relations, many experienced managers have found that they have not suffered any decline in esteem. On the contrary, in cases where they have taken strong, positive action, they have been applauded by employees and public alike. This is not always the case, but apparently a positive reaction is usually the result of vigorous prosecution in the wake of substantial theft.

Reinstatement is sometimes justified by the circumstances. There is always, of course, a real danger of adverse reaction by the employees, but if reinstatement is to a position not vulnerable to theft, the message may get across. This is a most delicate matter that can be determined only on the scene.

As far as civil action is concerned, that possibility must be discussed with counsel. In any event, it is to be hoped that no responsible businessperson would decide to prosecute unless the case was a very strong one.

Borderline Cases

Even beyond the difficulty of arriving at a satisfactory policy governing the disposition of cases involving employee theft, there are the cases that are particularly hard to adjudicate. Most of these involve the pilferer, the long-time employee, or the obviously upright employee in financial difficulty who steals out of desperation. In each case, the offender freely admits guilt and pleads being overcome by temptation.

What should be done in such cases? Many companies continue to employ such employees, provided they make restitution. They are often grateful, and they continue to be effective in their jobs.

In the last analysis, individual managers must make the determination of policy in these matters. Only they can determine the mix of toughness and compassion that will guide the application of policy throughout.

Hopefully every manager will decide to avoid the decision by making employee theft so difficult, so unthinkable that it will never occur. That goal may never be reached, but it is a goal to strive for.

Review Questions

1. What are some of the common danger signals of employee dishonesty?
2. Discuss procedural controls for decreasing the incidence of employee theft in specific departments.
3. What should be management's role in effecting internal security?
4. Should employees be prosecuted for stealing? Why?

References

1. "Employee Theft Tab Grows, Reporting a Factor," *Security*, October 1990: 11.
2. "Weak Awareness Secures Sky-High Theft Figures," *Security*, August 1990: 13.
3. William C. Cunningham, John J. Strauchs, Clifford W. VanMeter, *The Hallcrest Report II: Private Security Trends 1970–2000* (Boston: Butterworth-Heinemann, 1990), p. 29.
4. Bill Zalud, "Tough Times—Hard Choices," *Security*, January 1991: 26–27.
5. Charles P. Carson, *Managing Employee Honesty* (Boston: Butterworths, 1977).
6. "Study Reports Youth Lack Commitment," *Macomb Journal* 12 October 1990: 14.
7. Richard C. Hollinger and John P. Clark, *Theft by Employees* (Lexington, Mass.: Lexington Books, 1983), p. 4.
8. *Diebold Direct Security Catalog* (Canton, Ohio: Diebold, 1990), pp. 22–23.

13

□ □ □
□ □ □
□ □ □

Personnel Policies for Internal Security

Personnel Screening

The objective of a program encompassing internal security is to prevent theft by employees. If all the employees were of such character that they could not bring themselves to steal, the security personnel would have little to do. If, on the other hand, thieves predominate in the mix of employees, the system will be sorely tried if indeed it can be effective at all. Basic to its effectiveness is the cooperation of that majority of honest personnel who perform as assigned and in so performing refuse to initiate or collaborate in conspiracies to steal. Without this dominant group, the system is in trouble from the start.

The best place to start then is in the personnel office where bad risks can be screened out on the basis of reasonable security procedures. Screening is the process of finding the person best qualified for the job in terms of both skills and personal integrity. The process may or may not involve a background check (which will be discussed later), but it must include at least a basic check of the applicant's references and job history.

In some industries, especially those with high technical requirements, screening can be a problem since qualified personnel may be difficult to find. There can be resistance from the employment office to the disqualification of an otherwise qualified applicant on marginal grounds of security. Here a job of education must be undertaken to convince the objectors that a person who may later embezzle from the company is a poor risk from many viewpoints, no matter how highly qualified that person may be in the specific skills required.

Rejection of bad risks must be on the basis of standards that have been carefully established in cooperation with the personnel director. Once they have been established, these standards must be met in every particular, just as proficiency standards must be met. Obviously the standards must be reviewed from time to time to avoid dealing with applicants unjustly and placing the company at a competitive disadvantage in the labor market by demanding more than is available. Even here, however, a bottom line must be drawn. After a certain point, compromises and concessions can no longer be made without inviting damage to the company.

Such a careful, selective program will add some expense to the employment procedure, but it can pay for itself in reduced losses, better people, and lower turnover. And the savings in crimes that never happened, though unknowable, could be thought of as enormous.

Employment History and Reference Checking

The key to reducing internal theft lies in the quality of employees employed by the facility. The problem will not be stamped out in the hiring process, no matter how carefully and expertly the selection may be. The system of theft prevention and the program of employee motivation are ongoing efforts that must recognize that the elements of availability, susceptibility, and opportunity are dynamic and in a constant state of flux. The point at which the problem must be taken in hand, however, is at the beginning—in the very process of selecting personnel who will work in the facility. And in this process, an immense amount of vital information about the prospective employee can be developed by a knowledgeable screener simply by knowing what to look for in the employment application or résumé. The answers are not as obvious as they once were, and the ability to perceive and evaluate what is on the application or résumé is more important than ever now that the forms are more circumstantial than they were in the past.

Privacy legislation of the 1970s together with fair employment laws has drastically changed the employment application forms in businesses across the country. What was once considered reasonable and appropriate to ask job applicants is now forbidden by law. The following federal legislation relates directly to hiring and dealing with employees.

Title VII of the Civil Rights Act of 1964
Pregnancy Discrimination Act of 1978
Executive Order 11246 (affirmative action)
Age Discrimination in Employment Act
National Labor Relations Act
Rehabilitation Act of 1973
Vietnam Era Veterans' Readjustment Assistance Act of 1974
Fair Labor Standards Act of 1938 (The Wage and Hour Law)
The Federal Wage Garnishment Law

Occupational Safety and Health Act of 1970
Immigration Reform and Control Act of 1986
Employee Polygraph Protection Act of 1988
Consolidated Omnibus Budget Reconciliation Act of 1985
Worker Adjustment and Retraining Notification Act (Plant Closing Law)
EEOC Sexual Harassment Guidelines

Table 13.1 summarizes the protected classes covered under these and other federal acts.

In some aspects, these regulations have had a streamlining effect, by eliminating irrelevant questions and confining questions exclusively to those matters related to the job applied for. The subtler kinds of discrimination on the basis of age, sex, and national origin have been largely eliminated from the employment process. In making these changes to protect the applicant, state and federal law has created new dilemmas for employers and their security staffs.

Various federal and state laws prohibit criminal justice agencies (police departments, courts, and correctional institutions) from providing information on certain criminal cases to noncriminal justice agencies (for example, private security firms or personnel offices). The Fair Credit Reporting Act requires that a job applicant must give written consent to any credit bureau inquiry. The most far-reaching legislation was the Federal Privacy Act of 1976, which required all states to pass legislation containing certain privacy provisions before January 1, 1980.

All states have some type of privacy legislation that meets the guidelines set forth in the Federal Privacy Act of 1976.

The Privacy Act—August 1973, Public Law 93–579, Section 524(b), Implementation

All criminal history information collected, stored, or disseminated through support under this title shall contain, to the maximum extent feasible, disposition as well as arrest data where arrest data is included therein. The collection, storage, and dissemination of such information shall take place under procedures reasonably designed to insure that all such information is kept current therein; the Administration shall assure that the security and privacy of all information is adequately provided for and that information shall only be used for law enforcement and criminal justice and other lawful purposes. In addition, an individual who believes that criminal history information concerning him contained in an automated system is inaccurate, incomplete, or maintained in violation of this title, shall upon satisfactory verification of his iden-

Table 13.1 Who is Protected/Who is Affected

Legislation	Federally Covered Employers and Protected Classes							Covered Employers	Federal Agency
	Race/Color	National Origin/Ancestry	Sex	Religion	Age	Handicapped	Union		
Title VII Civil Rights Act	X	X	X	X				Employers with 15 + EEs; unions, employment agencies	EEOC
Equal Pay Act (EPA) as amended			X					Minimum wage law coverage ("administrative employees" not exempted)	EEOC
†Age. Discrimination in Employment Act (ADEA)					X 40 +			20 + EEs (unions with 25 + members) Employment agencies	EEOC
*Age Discrimination: Act of 75 (ADA)					X 40 −			Receives federal money	EEOC
*Executive Order 11246. 11141	X	X	X	X	X			All federal contractors and subcontractors	OFCCP
*Title VI Civil Rights Act	X	X	X	X				Federally-assisted program or activity—public schools and colleges also covered by Title IX	Funding Agency and EEOC
*Rehabilitation Act of '73						X		Receives federal money: federal contractor, $2,500+	OFCCP
National Labor Relation Act	X	X	X	X			X	ER in interstate commerce	NLRB

						All employers	Courts
Civil Rights Act of 1866	X					All employers	Courts
Civil Rights Act of 1871	X	X	X			Private employers usually not covered	EEOC
Revenue Sharing Act of 1972	X	X	X	X	X	State and local governments that receive federal revenue sharing funds	OFCCP
Education Amendments of 1972 Title IX		X			X	Educational institutions receiving federal financial assistance	Dept. of Education
Vietnam Era Vets Readjustment Act—1974					X	Government contractors—$10,000+	OFCCP
Pregnancy Discrimination Act of 1978		X				All employers 15 + EEs	EEOC-OFCCP
Fair Labor Standards Act						Includes minimum wage law and equal pay act with complex method of coverage	DOL
Federal Privacy Act of '74						Federal agencies only	
Freedom of Information Act						Federal agencies only	
Family Educational Rights & Privacy Act						Schools, colleges, and universities; federally assisted	
Immigration Reform Act of 1986						All employers	INS

*Applies to Federal Agencies Contractors or Assisted Programs only.

†Mandatory Retirement Eliminated Except in Special Circumstances.

EE = Employee.

ER = Employer.

tity, be entitled to review such information and to obtain a copy of it for purposes of challenge or correction.

The most controversial portion of the preceding quote is "that information shall only be used for law enforcement and criminal justice and other lawful purposes." The key is the way that "other lawful purposes" is defined. Does the meaning include personnel offices and private security operations? The verdict is mixed. Personnel, security, and loss-prevention operations must be aware of the interpretation of the privacy legislation in each state in which they operate.

Understandably there is some confusion with regard to the rules governing employment screening. In spite of such confusion, the preemployment inquiry is one of the most useful security tools available employers can use against employee dishonesty and continued profit drains. Therefore they should consult legal counsel to determine the laws that relate to the locality and establish firm and precise policies regarding employment applications and hiring practices.

Generally speaking, look for, and be wary of, applicants who:

1. Show signs of instability in personal relations
2. Lack job stability. The grasshopper does not make a good job candidate.
3. Show a declining salary history or are taking a cut in pay from the previous job
4. Show unexplained gaps in employment history
5. Are clearly overqualified
6. Are unable to recall or are hazy about names of supervisors in the recent past or who forget their address in the recent past.

If the job applied for is one involving the handling of funds, it would be advisable to get the applicant's consent to make financial inquiry through a credit bureau. Be wary if such an inquiry turns up a history of irresponsibility in financial affairs such as living beyond one's means.

It is important that the application form ask for a chronological listing of all previous employers in order to provide a list of firms to be contacted for information on the applicant as well as to show continuity of career. Any gaps could indicate a jail term that was overlooked in filling out the application. When checking with previous employers, dates on which employment started and terminated should be verified.

References submitted by the applicant must be contacted, but they are apt to be biased. After all, they were names submitted by the person to be investigated; they are not likely to be negative or hostile. It is important to contact someone—preferably an immediate supervisor—at each previous employer, and such contact should be made by phone or in person.

The usual and easiest system of contact is by letter, but this leaves much to be desired. The relative impersonality of a letter, especially one in which a form or evaluation is to be filled out, leads to impersonal and, essentially, uncommunicative answers. Since many companies as a matter of policy, stated or implied, are reluctant to give someone a bad reference except in the most extreme circumstances, a written reply to a letter will sometimes be misleading.

On the other hand, phone or personal contacts may become considerably more discursive and provide shadings in the tone of voice that can be important. Even when no further information is forthcoming, this method may indicate that a more exhaustive investigation is required.

Backgrounding

It may be desirable to get a more complete history of a prospective employee—especially in cases where sensitive financial or supervisory positions are under consideration. Professional services providing this kind of investigation involve extra expense, but in many cases it can be well worthwhile. This backgrounding, which involves a discreet investigation into the past and present activities of the applicant, can be most informative.

It is estimated that approximately 90 percent of all persons known to have stolen from their employers are not prosecuted. A thorough investigation is certainly justified—into the background of anyone being considered for a job who will be responsible for significant amounts of cash or goods or who will be in a management position responsible for shipping, receiving, purchasing, or paying.

It is also significant to note that there is agreement among personnel and security experts that 20 percent of a given workforce is responsible for 80 percent of the personnel problems of all kinds. If backgrounding can turn up this kind of record, it is well worth the expense.

Backgrounding is also employed to investigate employees being considered for promotion to positions of considerable sensitivity and responsibility. Such persons may have been the very model of rectitude at the time of employment but may since have had financial reverses that threaten their lifestyles. If a background investigation uncovers such information, a company is in a position to offer assistance if it so desires, thus relieving strain and need, both of which can lead to embezzlement. Such action can boost company morale as well as reduce the potential for theft out of desperation.

Integrity/Lie Detection

Another approach to a full background investigation is the use of various integrity/lie-detection tests. In states where their use is legal, these tests, according to some experts, can be useful tools in determining the past and current records of candidates for employment or promotion to positions of considerable sensitivity.

This practice is controversial as is the discussion among practitioners about the relative merits of different types of tests. Many security people look on integrity tests as invaluable tools, however, and generally agree that their use in the hands of competent, trained professionals can be most constructive.

The three main categories of integrity/lie-detection tests are: (1) the polygraph, (2) the Psychological Stress Evaluator (PSE), and (3) the Personal Security Inventory (PSI). The first two are machines that operate on the same basic principle. The third is a psychological pencil-and-paper test.

The polygraph and the PSE operate on the premise that lying creates conflict. Conflict causes anxiety that leads to stress reactions. Stress reactions typically include increased respiration, increased pulse rate, higher blood pressure, digestive disorders, perspiration, temperature change, muscle tension, and pupil dilation. The polygraph and the PSE measure some of these changes. Most polygraphs measure galvanic skin response, blood pressure, and respiration. The PSE measures changes in voice quality from tension in the vocal cords. The readouts of both devices are recorded on paper tape and the responses to various questions are analyzed in terms of the charted reactions, which are compared with reactions to simple test questions that establish an individual's normal response to lying.

Do these machines really work? The controversy over this question continues to draw much attention in professional publications. For the present, however, the continuing debate has resulted in the Employee Polygraph Protection Act of 1988. This act severely limits the use of the polygraph to certain industries and for specific purposes. It prohibits preemployment polygraphs by all private employers except those whose primary business is providing security personnel for the protection of currency, negotiable securities, precious commodities or instruments, or proprietary information. Companies who manufacture, distribute, or dispense controlled substances may use the polygraph for an employee who would have direct access to the manufacture, storage, distribution, or sale of these controlled substances.

To determine whether the polygraph or PSE is worth using in a security operation various factors need to be considered such as: What is a lie? According to *The American Heritage Dictionary of the English Language*, a lie is making a statement or statements that one knows to be false, especially with the intent to deceive. Because a lie is really a subjective evaluation, these machines record what a person believes to be a lie. In addition, since the machines measure only stress, the subject must believe that the machine works so that enough stress is present to measure.

Since these machines simply measure the physiological symptoms of stress, other stressors may also be recorded. For example, a question concerning drug history may evoke a dramatic response from a subject who has lost a close relative to drug abuse. The subject's physical condition at the time of the test can also influence the tracings. Fatigue, drugs, and alcohol are the biggest culprits in this category, but even simple things like needing to use the bathroom or suppressing a cough can affect the tracings.

Can someone beat the machine? The answer is both simple and complex. Although the machine registers only physiological changes and thus cannot be beaten, the accuracy of the machine is solely determined by the quality of the examiner. A subject can affect the tracing of the machine by saying prayers or counting holes in acoustic tiles, but a good examiner will note these changes. The accuracy of the machines relies on the quality of the examiner.

Yet the training of examiners ranges from as little as six weeks to as long as six months. As early as 1974, authorities on the polygraph indicated in testimony before the U.S. Congress that 80 percent of the examiners were substandard and that in 38 states anyone who purchased a machine could claim to be a professional examiner.

What is the role of these devices if such doubts can be cast on their accuracy and on the skill of examiners? Jerome Skolnick, noted criminologist, suggests that they should be used "to open up leads to further investigation of information rather than being itself prima facie evidence."[1]

Today the polygraph is covered by much case law in addition to the 1988 Polygraph Act. Still its advocates are striving for national recognition through the improvement of standards for operators. In Illinois, polygraph operators must possess at least a baccalaureate degree and attend a licensed school before they can operate a machine. Even so, Illinois will not allow polygraph evidence into its courts.

As for the PSE, whether it will be able to ride on the polygraph case law is still a matter of speculation But since both machines operate on the same principles, it is likely that much of the case law related to the polygraph can be applied to the PSE. Over the past five years, however, little has changed in reference to the use of the PSE as the polygraph struggles to survive under fire.

As was noted earlier, the PSI is a psychological pencil-and-paper exam. Many variations of this test exist throughout the United States (for example, the California Personality Inventory [CPI], the Minnesota Multiphasic Personality Inventory [MMPI], Inwald Personality Inventory [IPI], Wonderlic), but they all have common traits. The tests are designed to evaluate prospective employees for honesty and integrity, drug or alcohol abuse, and violence or emotional instability. Most of these tests can be administered on company property and are thus relatively inexpensive. The test questions are designed to provide checks on each other and to provide clues for the psychologist who evaluates the personality of the person tested. For example, a typical question might be:

> You are riding on a bus. A sign indicates "No Smoking."
> A person sits down next to you and lights a cigarette. What would you do?
>
> 1. Inform them that they are not to smoke
> 2. Point out the "No Smoking" sign
> 3. Move to another seat
> 4. Get off the bus
> 5. Say or do nothing

Adherents of both systems claim a high degree of accuracy for such tests when they are conducted by properly trained personnel. Table 13.2 provides a list of pointers that can be used in evaluating pencil-and-paper tests.

It is important to determine the limitations on the use of such instruments in the various states. Some states forbid their use as a requirement for employment but permit them to be used on a voluntary basis. Other states forbid their use in any circumstances.

Generally speaking, organized labor has lobbied diligently for legislation banning the use of so-called integrity testing/lie detectors in all industrial or commercial applications, and their efforts proved successful with the passage of the 1988 Polygraph Act. The American Polygraph Association, while opposed to the use of the PSE essentially on the grounds that it has not yet proved itself, has endorsed much legislation setting stricter standards for polygraph operators but has, of course, fought labor's stand on the matter.

Many firms, despite the 1988 Polygraph Act prohibiting preemployment usage, continue to make use of the polygraph in investigations of various kinds. Those firms that do use these machines have, in general, found them useful.

According to the 1988 Polygraph Act, the polygraph may be used on existing employees under the following circumstances:

1. In connection with an ongoing investigation involving economic loss or injury to the employer's business (that is, theft, embezzlement, or misappropriation)
2. If the employee has access to the property that is the subject of an investigation

Table 13.2 Scrutinizing Vendor Pencil-and-Paper Tests: Twelve Pointers in Evaluating a Test's Relevance for Meeting Your Hiring Goals

1. Beware of tests for which little or no validation research exists.
2. Beware of tests that claim they "only replace the polygraph."
3. Beware of studies that are not based on the predication model of validation.
4. Beware of studies that do not tell you how many people were incorrectly predicted to have job problems.
5. Beware of tests that claim to predict dangerous or violent behavior or tendencies.
6. Beware of studies that report "significant" correlations as evidence of their validity.
7. Beware of studies that use small numbers of people to predict important job-performance outcomes.
8. Beware of studies that have not been cross-validated.
9. Beware of claims that tests are valid for use with occupational groups for which validation studies have not yet been conducted.
10. Beware of studies based on questionnaires or tests filled out anonymously.
11. Beware of studies that have not used real job candidates as subjects in their validation efforts.
12. Beware of tests whose validation studies have been designed, conducted, and published only by the test developer or publishing company without replication by other, totally independent, psychologists or agencies.

From materials developed by Dr. Robin Inwald, Hilson Research Inc., Feb. 1988.

3. If the employer has reasonable suspicion that the employee was involved in the accident or activity under investigation
4. If the employer provides to the employee *before* the test the specifics of the inquiry—what incident is being investigated and the reason the employee is being tested

Even if the employer meets the above criteria, the employee cannot be disciplined or discharged either on the basis on the polygraph or for refusal to take the polygraph test without additional supporting evidence.

Since such examinations cost from $50 to $150, depending on the length of the test, not every firm will find them practical. Even those firms that do find the expense acceptable usually limit their application to particularly sensitive investigations and then only after they have decided whether the risk is such that the expense is warranted and whether they can be satisfied by an evaluation based on other, cheaper methods.

Whatever the decision, the security manager would be well advised to consult a reputable firm handling integrity testing to learn about what such examinations involve.

Drug Screening

There are few areas of preemployment screening that evoke such strong sentiment as does drug screening. The two major issues in this type of testing revolve around invasion-of-privacy arguments and the problem of the risk of false-positives. The issues related to drug screening will be dealt with in more detail in Chapter 18.

Other Screening Options

In addition to the tools that have already been discussed, other sources of information provide details of the applicant's background that might be of value in making a hiring decision.

Credit reports not only reflect the applicant's financial situation and stability but also provide other useful information such as past addresses and previous employers. The legal restrictions of the Federal Fair Reporting Act must be complied with if a person is denied employment as the result of information requested through this source.

Motor vehicle records are easily obtained and can help identify high-risk employees by noting the number of violations and type.

Civil litigation records provide detailed, documented records of the applicant's personal history, background, and financial relationships. They also document previous injury complaints. They may also provide indications of other employment problems not filed as criminal charges such as theft, fraud, or serious misconduct.

There are many other possible sources of information, but time and space considerations do not allow for total coverage in an introductory text. The *National Employment Screening Directory: A Guide to Background Investigations*, however, is an excellent source on information and can be purchased through Financial Control Publishing, 1820 S. Boulder Pl., Tulsa, OK 74119.

Hiring Exconvicts and Parolees

It should be strongly noted here that rigid exclusionary standards should never be applied to exconvicts or parolees who openly acknowledge their past records. Such a policy would be at best unjust and at worst irresponsible. These people have served their sentences. Their records are available in situations where employment is being sought. To turn them away simply on the basis of their past mistakes would be to force them back into a criminal pattern of life in order to survive.

Some such people might well be unacceptable in certain companies but a rigid policy denying all of them employment would be to deny the company many potentially good employees who deserve a chance to show that they have rehabilitated themselves. Experience has shown that these employees, knowingly hired in the right positions and properly supervised, are not only acceptable but are frequently highly responsible and trustworthy. They should be given an opportunity to reestablish themselves in society.

Morale

In any organization that exists by the cooperative efforts of all its members, it is important that each member feels like an important part of the operation both as a contributor and as an individual.

This dual role is important to recognize. Each employee must feel like a significant, integrated part of the whole and identify with it while still maintaining and protecting a personal identity as an individual apart from the structure. If employees are denied reinforcement in either of these views, their sense of personal worth suffers. Anger, anxiety, frustration, or feelings of inadequacy may follow. Any of these attitudes is damaging both to the individual and to the organization as a whole, and they must be headed off.

The best way to do that is to recognize that each employee is in fact an important member of the organization. A function must be performed as a part of the larger function, and the employee is the one performing it—unique and unduplicatable. Reinforcement comes from management, supervisors, and peers. The employee is a vital, irreplaceable organ of the greater body. Of such recognition and respect is high morale created and maintained, and everyone benefits from it.

Every supervisor must be indoctrinated in the importance of morale in every business. Just as no business can operate without employees, none can operate efficiently with a workforce whose morale has been damaged and who responds with listlessness and disinterest. Threats and coercion will not restore the optimum level of morale any more than will directives and public notices. This is a condition that comes from human nature. It must be dealt with in those terms.

Additional factors are also important in this regard. Physical surroundings and appropriate rewards are part of the message that tells employees what the organization thinks of them.

In an atmosphere of concern, fairness, and mutual respect, few people will be tempted to steal. It would be like stealing from themselves. It is important that such an atmosphere be developed and maintained for the good of all.

A program aimed at improving or maintaining employee morale might contain:

1. Clear statements of company policy consistently and fairly administered
2. Regular review of wages and wage policy—updated to assure equitable wage levels
3. House organ or newsletter and bulletin boards kept current
4. Open, two-way avenues of communication between management and all employees
5. Clear procedures, formal and informal, for airing grievances and personal problems with supervisors
6. Vigorous training programs to improve job skills and pave the way for advancement
7. Physical surroundings—decor, cleanliness, sound and temperature control, and general housekeeping—at a high level.

Employee Assistance Programs

The latest innovation in coping with employee problems relating to, among other things, honesty, alcohol/drug problems, and depression has been the advent of the employee assistance program (EAP). "At a time when substance abuse, mental health problems, and other stresses beset the American work force, an effective employee assistance program (EAP) can be a wise investment."[2] By the late 1980s, 80 percent of the *Fortune* 500 had introduced EAPs. The programs vary with the type and size of company. Some companies provide full service, in-house operations while smaller firms may restrict the type of service and contract with professional EAP firms.

The fact is that EAPs are working for some firms. McDonnell-Douglas reports a 34 percent reduction in absences compared to their counterparts. In the area of attrition of drug users, they reported a drop from 40 percent in their control group to 7.5 percent in the EAP. Other firms also report success: Chicago Bell, General Motors, HARTline, and so forth. There is a belief among many of these employers that improving family life will reflect positively on the workplace.[3]

Continuity of the Program

When a company has made a systematic and conscientious effort to screen out dishonest, troublesome, incompetent, and unstable employees, it has taken a first and significant step toward reducing internal theft. It is important then that the program continue on a permanent basis.

Care must be taken to avoid relaxing standards or becoming more superficial in checking applicants. There is a tendency to lose sight of the full dimensions of the problem if the security program makes substantial inroads into the loss factor. The past is too soon forgotten, and carelessness follows close behind. Active supervision is always necessary to maintain the integrity of this important aspect of every security program.

References

1. *The Use of Polygraphs and Similar Devices by Federal Agencies, Hearing Before A Subcommittee on Government Operations, House of Representative* (Washington, D.C.: GPO, 1974), p. 29.
2. Tom Pope, "An Eye on EAP's," *Security Management*, October 1990: 81.
3. Ibid.

14 ☐ ☐ ☐
☐ ☐ ☐
☐ ☐ ☐

Insurance

As has been noted earlier, one means of handling risks is risk transfer. Insurance is an option that is regularly pursued in the area of transfer. Yet far too many managers still cling to the notion that the most effective means of guarding against unforeseen business losses is insurance, and all too many still use insurance as a substitute for a comprehensive security program. The fallacy in this attitude is twofold.

In the first place, almost all casualty insurance companies have suffered losses in underwriting crime insurance. Most insurance companies have taken drastic steps to counter this trend. They have cancelled or refused to renew policies of insurees who have suffered losses from criminal activity, limited allowable coverage to a point well below replacement or even cash value of goods or property, limited the extent of coverage, set up limitations that exclude businesses in high crime areas or in high risk enterprises from any coverage at all, and lastly increased premium rates.

In the second place, it is virtually impossible to insure against all the losses that could be incurred. Hidden damages in loss of company morale and customer confidence and in interruption of vigorous participation in a highly competitive market—all are serious if not fatal blows to any business and can never be recompensed.

Clearly insurance can never be a substitute for a security program. In many cases, the very fact that assets are insured to some degree tends to reduce the interest of the proprietor in instituting reasonable security procedures beyond those minimums specified in a policy. As an aspect of the overall picture, insurance tends also to reduce any interest the insured may have in capturing or prosecuting perpetrators of crimes, thus in effect encouraging the proliferation of like crimes.

The Value of Insurance in a Total Loss-Prevention Program

Insurance is certainly important. It is clearly necessary for any business that wishes to be protected against loss—to spread the risk—but it must be thought of as a supportive, rather than the principal, defense against losses from crime. It is equally important to realize that insurance carriers provide coverage on the basis that the "estimated value" (EV) of loss is always less than is the total of the premiums paid.

Types of Insurance

There are many types of insurance. For the purposes of this discussion, however, the focus will be on only those types of insurance that play a prominent role in security/loss prevention.

Fidelity Bonds

Commonly referred to as honesty insurance, this coverage provides remuneration for losses due to employee dishonesty. There are those who believe that bonds are not insurance because

1. Bonding always involves three parties—insurance, two parties.
2. The bond principal is in full control whereas the insured really has no control over the event causing the loss.
3. Losses are not expected in surety bonding. Premiums are service fees for the use of the surety's name—in insurance, losses are expected and reflected in the premiums.
4. In bonding, the principal is liable to the surety for losses paid—in insurance, the insured does not agree to reimburse the insurer.

These arguments are worth noting, but they have no effect on the discussion presented here as most authorities agree that fidelity bonding resembles insurance.

While "blanket bonds" are in general use because they cover categories of employees that allow automatic coverage of new employees, the name or position bonds are also popular because of the lower premium costs. The name bond covers only certain specifically named individuals while the position bond covers only those persons who hold a specific position within the company.

This type of coverage is frequently badly underestimated. In effect, the bonding company is guaranteeing the insured that bonded employees will perform in good faith, that they will not commit any dishonest acts against their employer. If any so bonded employees violate this trust, the guarantor—the bonding company—will stand the loss up to the amount insured.

The investigation by the bonding company is valuable in that it provides a further check on the background of employees in sensitive positions in addition to underwriting possible losses resulting from a violation of trust. Any employee with a past criminal history is excluded.

Most companies require that employees handling cash or high-value merchandise be bonded, but too many of these companies go along on a program calling for $5000, $10,000, or $25,000 bonds, failing to consider that, if bonding is deemed necessary, it must provide for protection against potential damage that such an employee can cause. In situations where there is no system providing a regular, foolproof audit of cash and valuable merchandise, for example, an employee might steal enormous sums over a period of time even if the daily amount is relatively small.

The Surety Association of America publishes a list of losses from various kinds of businesses caused by bonded employees and the extent of fidelity coverage. The losses from underbonding of employees are dramatic.

The association report clearly indicates the problem faced by business today. It also indicates that many businesses are not handling the problem with a coordinated systems approach. It may appear to be hindsight to point out that adequate bonding would have cost these companies the merest fraction of their ultimate losses. Yet we can assume that in most of these cases a more realistic evaluation of the exposure, risk, and insurance costs would have prevented these substantial losses.

With losses attributable to internal theft estimated in the billions of dollars, it is easy to see why fidelity bonds are thought of as high-priority coverage, especially since it provides particular protection in areas where exposure is generally the greatest. As important as this form of coverage is, it is essential that it be handled properly to provide the full protection it is capable of providing.

It is important in cases involving bonded employees discovered in theft that no arrangement concerning restitution be made with them without consulting the bonding company. Case files are filled with situations where an employee agreed to pay back the value of stolen merchandise over a period of time. Typically a few payments are made and then the employee disappeared. At that point, there is little or no likelihood that the bonding company will make good the loss. There may be good reasons to give an otherwise trusted employee a chance to make good on the larceny, but if restitution is the sole or at least the prime consideration, the entire matter should be left to the insurer who is obliged to make good the loss to its extent or to the amount of the bond. Determination of the disposition of the perpetrator's case will be in the insurer's hands.

Another matter requiring some familiarity is the confusing exclusionary clause that states: "The insuring clause does not cover any loss, or that part of any loss, as the case may be, the proof of which, either to its factual existence or as to its amount, is dependent upon an inventory computation at a profit and loss computation." What insurance companies have maintained in this clause is that, if an employee should confess to taking merchandise and selling it over a period of time, the amount of merchandise so appropriated may not be established simply by checking out what seems to be missing from stock. This, of course, assumes that the employee does not recall precisely how many items were stolen over the period of time, which is usually the case. The fact that records indicate there should be 200 items in stock and an inventory can only find 80 does not, according to a strict interpretation of the exclusionary clause, serve to establish a claim for 120 items on the bond. In fact, courts until fairly recently held that inventory records were only useful to corroborate the fact of employee theft, not its extent. In the hypothetical case above, each of the 120 missing items would have to be accounted for with convincing independent proof of theft by a bonded employee. As a result, full restitution for such losses would be difficult to obtain in spite of confessions or other proof of employee dishonesty.

The 1970s, however, ushered in a more liberal, consumer-oriented attitude in the courts, and this limiting exclusionary clause in bonding policies began to be viewed more flexibly than it had been viewed in the past. The Alabama supreme court allowed inventory records to be introduced.[1] An Ohio court, on the admission of theft by an employee, allowed the total of the inventory shortage to be insured.[2] An earlier case in New Jersey perhaps heralded this new attitude toward interpretation by carefully outlining the conditions of acceptance of inventory records as proof not of the fact of loss, but of the extent of loss, provided that proof of employee theft be arrived at independently or as corroborated by any observed shortage in inventory.

The judgment stated in part:

Such accommodation, in our judgment, should preclude recovery by the insureds under this bond: if they had no proof whatsoever of an employee connected loss other than inventory profit and loss computations, no matter how reliable in the particular case. On the other hand, inventory records may by their very nature constitute inherently indispensable proof of an allowable claim under a fidelity bond in one or the other or both of two respects:

(A) as the only available proof of the full amount of a loss, there being some appreciable proof from other facts or circumstances of a loss caused by employee dishonesty.

(B) as corroboration sufficient to make a case for the fact finder of the fact of an employee-connected loss where independent proof whereof considered alone, might be considered insubstantial.[3]

Subsequent rulings have generally followed these cases. For example, in 1983 in *Ace Wire & Cable Co., Inc., et al. v. AETNA Casualty & Surety Company*,[4] the court found in favor of Ace in a case where the Ace brought action against AETNA for failure to pay on a comprehensive dishonesty policy for the loss of 116 reels of wire and cable from their warehouse. The trial and appellate courts both held that lack of comprehensive inventory records "did not preclude proof of fact or amount of loss through records detailing actual physical count of individually identifiable units" and that affidavits to the effect that records of physical inventories of the warehouse revealed that reels were missing and could only be accounted for by employee theft were in fact admissible.

The court here states clearly that not only may inventory records be used to establish the extent of loss after independent evidence establishes employee theft but also it proceeds in (B) to allow such records to be part of the evidence establishing the fact of employee theft. Though there are few instances of other courts reiterating this viewpoint, many courts have since concurred in (A) of this decision.

In any claim in which inventory records play a role, it is very important that such records be well kept. The better they are maintained, the more powerful will be any case in which their accuracy, perhaps even their failsafe quality, is at issue.

Generally speaking, few insurance carriers will allow use of inventory records in the initial stages of the claim to describe the amount of loss. Inventory shortages can be from clerical errors, poor recordkeeping or shoplifting as well as from employee dishonesty. There is sufficient case law, however, to establish such records as a valid part of the claim in spite of the exclusionary clause. Insurance companies will ultimately deal with the issue and arrive at a mutually satisfactory settlement.

Insurance companies are not anxious to go to court in those states where precedent has established the use of inventory records as valid in establishing the extent of claims, and they are reluctant to go to court and possibly establish such precedent in those states where it does not already exist.

Surety Bonds

Also called performance bonds, this coverage provides protection for failure to live up to contractual obligations.

Storekeepers' Burglary and Robbery Policies and Mercantile Open-Stock Burglary Policies

Insurance in these categories is streamlined for the particular establishment, thus premiums vary with the opted coverage.

Federal Crime Insurance

The Small Business Administration indicates that a substantial number of businesses in this country have had some kind of problem with property insurance in any 12-month period. These problems include cancelled policies, refusal to issue or renew insurance, prohibitive rates, and limiting coverage to well below the cash value of insured property.

In inner-city locations or in certain types of businesses, policies, when they are issued, substantially limit the insurer's liability—frequently to the point where the policy is virtually useless as support protection. These actions by the insurance industry have created enough concern in the small business community to call for some kind of remedial action on the part of the federal government. Effective August 1, 1971, the Federal Crime Insurance Program came into being. This program, which requires the participation of individual states, provides for federally funded crime insurance at reasonable rates, based on the size and accepted risk of the insured property.

In order to qualify for protection under this program, however, a business must establish certain minimum protective devices and procedures. The business must, in short, recognize that it can get the supportive protection insurance offers provided it makes at least minimal efforts to protect itself.

The program prescribes locks, safes, alarm systems, and other protective devices, and establishes the kind of protection that various kinds of business must provide for themselves in order to qualify for this insurance. For example, gun stores, wholesale liquor and fur stores, jewelry firms, and drugstores must all have a central station alarm system; service stations must have a local alarm system; and so on. Small loan and finance companies, theaters, and bars—businesses rated as high risk—are also eligible for insurance under the program.

The program still has a long way to go before it covers firms in every state, but its appearance on the scene is encouraging. Not only does it provide for insurance coverage of premises otherwise difficult or impossible to insure adequately or reasonably, but it also focuses attention on the very real need for the insured to take positive steps to provide protection of the premises to prevent loss and to use insurance to defray those losses that do occur only when security measures fail.

In short, it takes insurance from the front line of crime prevention—where it clearly cannot perform—and puts it into the reserve or backup position where it can.

3-D Policies

Comprehensive dishonesty, destruction, and disappearance coverage is extremely flexible. Policies will vary in coverage and premiums based on the needs of the firm. Possible areas covered may include: burglary, robbery, employee theft, and counterfeit currency. These policies are designed to provide the widest possible coverage in cases of criminal attack of various kinds. The standard form is set up to offer five different kinds of coverage. The insured has the option of selecting any or all of the insuring agreements offered and of specifying the amount of coverage on each one selected. In addition to the coverage options in the standard form, 12 endorsements are also available to the manager having a need for any or all of them.

The coverages available on the standard form consist of:

1. Employee dishonesty bond
2. Money and securities coverage on the premises
3. Money and securities coverage off the premises
4. Money order and counterfeit paper currency coverage
5. Depositors' forgery coverage

Additional endorsements available are:

1. Incoming check forgery
2. Burglary coverage on merchandise
3. Paymaster robbery coverage on and off premises
4. Paymaster robbery coverage on premises only
5. Broad-form payroll on and off premises
6. Broad-form payroll on premises only
7. Burglary and theft coverage on merchandise
8. Forgery of warehouse receipts
9. Securities of lessees of safe-deposit box coverage
10. Burglary coverage on office equipment
11. Theft coverage on office equipment
12. Credit card forgery

Obviously, the premium on this coverage will vary according to the number of options selected and the amount of coverage desired for each.

Insurance against Loss of Use and Extra Expense Coverage

Most standard policies do not provide loss of use (the business or some suboperation ceases production resulting in losses) or extra expense coverage (the business cannot afford to be down and therefore must pay for rental space and the like to continue operations). Since both these matters can represent a very substantial loss to most companies, consideration must be given to expanding the provisions of the coverage to include one or the other. Both of these losses can be covered either by endorsement or by additional policies that will provide that coverage on a broad basis.

Even a small fire in an office may render it inoperable from smoke and water damage or damaged equipment for a substantial period of time. Even though all the damage is covered and will be cared for, the interim period during which revenues may be lost and new facilities are being occupied may be as expensive as the fire itself. In this scenario, loss of use or business interruption coverage would be suitable.

Here, too, there are options. A business interruption policy can be drawn up on a comprehensive basis, which means that it will cover a broad base of situations that might create a stoppage. Such a policy must, of course, be examined for types of incidents specifically excluded from coverage. On the other hand, such a contract might be drawn up in which the incidents covered are specified and perhaps limited to just a few potential hazards.

The amount of coverage and the nature of recovery in business interruption contracts can be complicated. If recovery is on an actual loss basis, a careful audit of actual demonstrable losses must be presented to the insurer in order to collect. If the policy is drawn as a valued loss contract, an accountant must certify the daily amount that would be lost if an interruption were to occur. This amount is entered as part of the contract. The premium and recovery are based on this amount, computed on the specified number of days to be covered for each interruption.

Extra expense coverage would be called for in a situation where the operation must immediately be transferred to another location and equipment rented until the damaged facility is back in operation. A good example would be a newspaper where the operation must continue in order to retain readership. If the business ceased operation even temporarily, subcribers would look elsewhere for their news.

Kidnap and Ransom Insurance

With the increase in international terrorism and the accompanying increase in kidnapping that went along with it, the demand for insurance for executives against such incidents also increased. These policies generally cover all costs associated with the recovery of a kidnapped executive or relative including costs of information and loss of ransom money. Some policies also cover the cost of law suits filed against the firm for inadequate protection and insufficient efforts to win release.

Such coverage requires that companies insure certain basic security measures.

1. Executives must maintain secrecy about the existence of coverage.
2. Every effort must be made to contact the police, FBI, and insurance company before payment is made.
3. Serial numbers on ransom money must be recorded.
4. A plan of action for dealing with kidnapping must be in place.

Fire Insurance

While fire insurance is a must for homeowners, the use of these once popular policies for business purposes has to a great extent been supplanted by broad coverage policies.

Business Property Insurance

These special multiperil policies (SMP) generally offer coverage against a multitude of losses including crime, property, liability, and machinery.

Liability Insurance

With the growth in the number of lawsuits filed against businesses each year for various negligent acts, the popularity of these insurance policies has grown. Coverages may include employer-employee, customer-employer, contracts, and professional services.

Workers' Compensation Insurance

This basic insurance provides for medical costs, lost wages, and rehabilitation of workers injured on the job. There are also death benefits available. In most states, this coverage is required by law.

Portfolio Commercial Crime Coverages

This form of coverage is replacing some of the individual policies listed above. The policy is composed of standard modules and allows for up to 14 endorsements.

1. Employee dishonesty
2. Forgery or alteration
3. Theft, disappearance, and destruction
4. Robbery and safe burglary
5. Premises burglary
6. Computer fraud
7. Extortion
8. Premises theft and robbery outside the premises
9. Lessees of safe deposit boxes
10. Securities deposited with others
11. Liability for guests' property—safe deposit box
12. Liability for guests' property—premises
13. Safe depository liability
14. Safe depository direct loss

Insuring against Crime

While as noted above there are various types of crime insurance that may cover the insured in the event of loss from robbery, theft, forgery, burglary, embezzlement, and other criminal acts, it is important to know the specific coverage involved in any such policy and the circumstances under which recovery of losses is allowed. For example, burglary is generally meant to refer to felonious entry and theft by force. In order to collect insurance after such an attack, there must be evidence of forced entry such as broken locks or windows, tool marks, or other clear evidence that burglary was committed. The mere fact that items are missing will in no way establish the fact that the insured has been the victim of a burglary. Theft or larceny coverage must be included in the policy in order to cover such incidents.

Robbery, too, must be specifically established according to the insurer's contractual definition rather than according to state statute. Robbery can be loosely defined as the forcible taking of property by violence or the threat of violence aimed at a person or persons covered by the policy. Theft or purse snatching, for example, would not be covered under a provision covering robbery—neither would burglary.

It is therefore essential that the terms describing criminal activity be clearly understood so that the nature and the extent of the coverage conform to the needs of the insured. This is particularly important with companies that are especially vulnerable to certain kinds of hazards. The binding terms are those in the insurance policy, not state or federal statutes!

It is also extremely important to check policies for exclusionary clauses that may exempt certain crimes from coverage or that simply do not include certain crimes. This will require a careful examination since insurance con-

tracts are notoriously long winded of necessity to cover all the possible contingencies within the area of their coverage. Certain absences of coverage or
exclusion can get lost in the sea of verbiage.

Insuring Property

Insurance against criminal acts is only one of the many kinds
of insurance that must be considered in protecting any business against unforeseen eventualities. The kinds of insurance necessary and the amount of
coverage in each category will depend on the nature of the business and the
extent of its exposure to various perils.

In a general way, however, there are certain considerations that must be
taken into account before any program can be settled on. For purposes of this
discussion, we will omit consideration of liability insurance and confine our-
selves to property insurance, which covers structures, goods, equipment,
cash, papers, records, and negotiables.

The first consideration in evaluating any kind of coverage must be the
nature and extent of the losses covered. These losses could be classified as
direct—meaning loss of certain tangible benefits resulting from destruction
or damage to the element concerned—or consequential (indirect)—meaning
those costs resulting from loss or damage to the element concerned such as
the rental of office space and/or equipment after a fire has damaged the insured office and equipment.

Evaluating Risk

Determining security vulnerabilities through surveys, operational audits and programmed supervision, and risk assessment using proba-
bility/criticality analysis were discussed in Chapter 7. The exposure is calculated, and however much coverage is then deemed necessary, it is essential
that the calculations reflect a realistic appraisal of the risk factors actually
involved. Every manager dealing with protection factors must ask what the
risk really is and what would happen to the company if any of the considered
potential perils came to pass.

In the last analysis, the manager is simply spending certain amounts of
money to shift the risk that certain potentially harmful events will or are
likely to occur to the insurer. In all cases, the firm is paying premiums so
that, although such events are not likely to occur if they were to occur, they
would be so catastrophic that the amount spent on insurance would fade into
insignificance compared to the possible losses. The balance is a delicate one,
and it requires much thought and expertise to develop the most efficient insurance program.

Insurance rates, after all, are based on actuarial tables that are presumably updated regularly to reflect the experience of various industries or types of business as a whole in losses from various sources or causes. Since most insurance companies are profit-oriented enterprises themselves, the rates also reflect that factor. They must, as part of their profit structure, charge for claims handling, sales commissions, and administrative expense. This ultimately means that a manager must evaluate the risk independently of the insurance industry's evaluation of it. Remember that from the insurers' perspective the EV of loss will always be less than the amount charged by the company for coverage.

More often than not, the manager will discover that the company is underinsured, but that the exposure to loss is well below that of the particular industry as a whole. In such a case, the manager might properly elect to save on the premium payments by insuring according to a personal appraisal of the risk (on the basis of the effectiveness of the security program, for example) instead of on the basis of exposure.

These are never easy decisions to make. The underinsured are risking ruination while the overinsured are spending substantial sums to no good purpose.

Whatever the evaluation, however, every manager must be thoroughly conversant with the risks and make provisions for them accordingly. That manager's first impulse must be to minimize the risk as much as possible by instituting security devices and procedures that will reduce the possibility of loss or at least ensure prompt notification when a loss has taken place. The manager must then reevaluate the risks in the light of this tightened or alerted security system and then reevaluate the supportive system of insurance. Thus insurance as an alternative does not rule out prevention, loss control, or even a degree of risk retention, for example, the deductible.

What Is Covered

Every manager must consider the property to be insured and check to make certain that all the designated property is covered by the policy that has been issued. Because of the changing nature of casualty insurance in today's market, certain property may be excluded from coverage because of its location or because the nature of the business creates or subjects it to special hazards that are not included under the basic coverage.

In such cases, special policies or endorsements may be required to fill out the insurance program. If the rates for such coverage are deemed excessive, it might be well to reconsider the original insurance program and to provide a sharply limited coverage in these special areas while at the same time developing special programs to reduce exposure and vulnerability.

Persons Covered

Generally speaking, property insurance is recoverable only by the insured and their agents. This is extended to include heirs named in a will or receivers in a bankruptcy proceeding. If there are others who should be named such as nonequity lenders or other interested parties, they must be entered into the contract by endorsement to make certain their interests are protected. If such an endorsement is not made, such persons have no rights under the policy and they must seek relief by other means if a loss should occur.

Time Covered

The period of time covered must be checked as well. Most policies are good for a year starting at a specified time of day on the effective date of the contract, and are in force until a specified time of day one year from that date. Some policies are effective for a longer period of time so it is important to verify the precise period of coverage referred to in the policy.

Perils Covered

Property insurance may be specific or comprehensive. It may also qualify its coverage in either kind of policy.

Name policies will name the incident or incidents covered and will further specify the degree to which they are covered. For example, in a policy in which the incidence of water damage is covered, there may be some kinds of water damage that are excluded from the coverage offered in a particular contract. It is especially important for a risk manager to be aware of these exclusions and to avoid the common mistake of supposing that, simply because a policy names water damage as a specific covered incident, the company is therefore covered for all water damage from every source.

How Much Insurance?

Since the options are essentially a choice between recovery of the cash value of the property or recovery of its replacement cost, there can be little hesitation in making a decision. Few experts disagree that insuring to the amount of replacement is clearly the wiser course to follow. When property is insured for its cash value only, there will almost inevitably be a loss to the insured unless property values decline enough to make up for the extra costs involved in replacement. The latter might include demolition of the remaining structure in the event of fire, clearing the site for rebuilding, or the declining value of the dollar. History shows us that property values, or more specifically building costs, rarely decline in this manner. Protection should therefore be arranged on the basis of resuming business as it was before the damage took place. This can normally be done only by insuring for the replacement cost of the property.

Replacement cost coverage is more expensive than is cash value coverage since the insurer must set the premium sufficiently high not only to cover the estimated likelihood of a fire occurring, for example, but also to try to anticipate the rate of increase in the cost of labor and materials in the reconstruction of the building in whole or in part.

Even insuring a replacement cost will not, as a rule, cover the full cost involved in a major disaster. Business interruption, extra expenses, site clearance, intervening passage of new and more exacting building codes—all add to the already inflated costs of replacing the existing structure so that business may resume as before as rapidly as possible.

There are many endorsements available to extend coverage to fully compensate for all expenses involved in replacement. They should all be considered in the light of individual needs. Obviously the greater the coverage, the higher the cost of coverage; but this cost must be weighed against the risk and its consequences.

Review Questions

1. Do you agree with the statement that "insurance must be thought of as a supportive rather than the principal defense against losses due to crime?" Why?
2. Why is it important for the insured to clearly understand the terms describing criminal activity (for example, burglary or robbery)?
3. In terms of property insurance, define direct loss, loss of use, and extra expense losses.
4. What are the differences between specific and comprehensive property insurance policies? If you were a business executive, which would you prefer if you had to give priority to cost effectiveness?
5. What were the problems that led to the establishment of the Federal Crime Insurance Program? What are some of the crime-prevention measures prescribed by the program?

References

1. *American Fire and Casualty Co. v. Burchfield*, 232 So.2d 606 (Ala., 1970).
2. *Sommer v. General Insurance Co. of America*, 259 N.E.2d 142 (Ohio, 1970).
3. *Hoboken Camera Center, Inc. v. Hartford Accident and Indemnity Co.*, 226 A2d 439, 448 [N.J. App., 1967].)
4. *Ace Wire & Cable Co., Inc., et al. v. AETNA Casualty & Surety Company*, 457 N.E.2d 761 (N.Y. 1983).

15

Retail Security

At the retail end of the distribution chain, merchants are beset on all sides by assaults on their profit-and-loss positions. The very nature of retailing demands that quantities of merchandise be attractively displayed in easily accessible areas. The public can roam at will and handle much of the merchandise. Every effort is made to create a desire to possess the displaced merchandise and to make the possession as effortless as possible. Of course, the merchant expects payment for the goods. Others—customers and employees alike—sometimes overlook that aspect of the transaction, and the merchant takes a loss. Generally each such loss is relatively small, but the aggregate damage to the business from such erosion of inventory can be enormous.

As in the past the employee contributes more to losses than does the shoplifter. The International Mass Retail Association reports that the loss from employees is seven times that of loss from shoplifting.[1] Drugs have become associated with both shoplifters and employees to the extent that 46 percent of the customers and 55 percent of the employees when apprehended showed evidence of drug use.[2]

Most businesses are subject to problems of inventory shortages, but few feel the problem as acutely as do retailers. They necessarily deal in merchandise that must be received, stored, and moved from warehouse or storage rooms to display areas on the selling floor. All of these operations pose a risk of loss from breakage or other damage, pilferage, or quantity theft. Even inadequate or careless recordkeeping can effectively "lose" merchandise that fails to show up on proper inventory records. According to one regional retail security manager, the inventory problem, coupled with computer records, has become his major concern. Merchandise on display is fair game for shoplifters during the day, and when the day is over, the whole cycle begins again.

The three principal sources of loss to the retailer are external losses from theft, internal losses from employee dishonesty, and losses that come from carelessness or mismanagement. In the aggregate these losses are referred to as shrinkage. Every area of loss must be counteracted in some way or retailers may find that, while gross business is booming, they are barely able to break even. Figure 15.1 presents the shrinkage costs for 1989 and the expenditures for loss-prevention retailers allocated to help prevent theft.

The arithmetic is as simple as it is familiar, but it bears repeating. Convenience store "C" sustains a $5000 shrinkage loss. If that shortage is viewed as lost net profit and the store is operating on a 3 percent profit margin, sales must increase by $166,666.66 just to recoup the $5000 loss.[3] The International Mass Retail Association reports in its *Twelfth Annual Survey of Loss Prevention in the Retail Industry* that the 1989 figures for shrinkage reached an all time high of $2.2 billion despite the $363.5 million spent to prevent theft. The average retail company spent $2.5 million to battle shrinkage—up 20 percent from the 1988 figure. The greatest spenders are department stores, which spend three times more annually than do specialty, hardline stores and twice that of drug chains and supermarkets.[4] While retailers attempt to make up for a portion of the shrinkage by passing the cost along to the customer, the end result may be reduced sales and thus reduced profits. Recent estimates are that the customer pays approximately $220 per year in added costs of merchandise to offset retail shrinkage.[5]

Generally shortage control procedures apply to retailers of every kind—from all-night restaurants to department stores. Legal considerations, surveillance techniques, cash register control, and the many other factors involved in a security program for a retailing facility are much the same. The

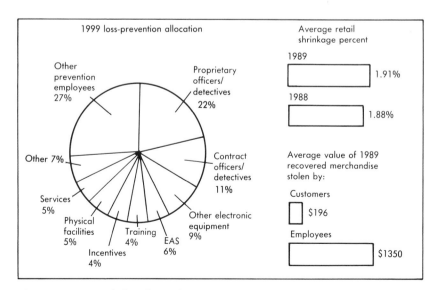

Figure 15.1 Retail shrinkage. (From *Security* magazine, April, 1991, p. 10. Published by Cahners Publishing Co., a division of Reed Publishing USA.)

details vary, and every establishment must ultimately make its own determination of what is best for its own application, but the basics are much the same throughout the trade.

Shoplifting

Retailing today demands that merchandise be prominently displayed and exposed so that customers can see it, touch it, pick it up, and examine it. Because displaying merchandise is such a successful sales technique, there is little likelihood that merchandise will ever go back behind the counter in the great majority of stores that now display it so invitingly. Some stores, however, are finding ways to make it more difficult to steal openly displayed items. These techniques and procedures will be discussed later in the chapter in the section entitled "Preventive Measures." Displaying merchandise in this way is hardly a theft-proof practice, but theft must be controlled if profit margins are to be maintained. Shortages from shoplifting are not likely to be eliminated, but they must and can be reduced by a thoughtful and energetic security program.

Extent of Shoplifting

It is difficult to assess the full dimension of the shoplifting problem accurately. Few shoplifters are apprehended and of those who are even fewer are referred to the police. In fact, the most optimistic studies of retail effectiveness in spotting shoplifters indicate that stores that do a good security job apprehend no more than 1 out of every 35 shoplifters. (Another report estimates that the figure is only 1 in 200.) Stores with vigilant personnel will report a relatively high level of shoplifting, while analogous concerns (in terms of store type, location, and size) with indifferent antishoplifting programs report few such incidents.

Information provided by one major retailer from its midwestern region provides an excellent profile of shoplifting activity. The number of shoplifting stops is consistent between April and September. Beginning in October the number of apprehensions climbs until it reaches a peak level in December. In contrast January provides the lowest number of apprehensions that increases gradually until April. Shoplifting apprehensions by day are consistent with the exception of Saturdays when apprehensions are approximately 50 percent higher than they are during the week. Sundays are the slow days. Most shoplifting apprehensions are made between 1:00 PM and 7:00 PM with the period between 4:00 PM and 7:00 PM contributing the greatest amount of activity. Of the items recovered cosmetics leads all departments followed by jewelry, ladies wear, electronics, sporting goods, men's wear, and shoes. This pattern of experience has been frequently reported. It appears that, where the vulnerability remains constant, the potential for shoplifting remains constant ultimately varying only with the effectiveness of the security measures. The unhappy lesson is simple: If you look for a shoplifter, you will find one.

Methods of Shoplifting

Shoplifting is conducted in every imaginable way; the ingenuity of the shoplifter is legendary. By and large, the great majority of thefts are simple and direct, involving nothing more sophisticated than putting the stolen merchandise into a handbag or a pocket. But there are certain methods beyond the simple taking of items that are in general use and should be anticipated, including:

1. The "bloomer" technique—using large, baggy clothes like bloomers or pantyhose that can be filled like shopping bags
2. The clothing technique—slit pockets in coats or jackets, or hiding merchandise inside a coat or up a sleeve
3. The fitting room technique—wearing stolen clothes under the thief's own clothing
4. Hiding items in purses or umbrellas
5. Palming—placing small items in the palm of the hand
6. The bag technique—using shopping bags, sometimes even using the store's own bags.
7. The packaging technique— hiding items with other prepackaged items, for instance, placing jewelry (cotton and all) into toothpaste boxes. In other situations, merchandise such as an infant car seat is removed from its box and replaced with several CD players. The package is retaped and taken through the checkout.
8. Wearing the item in plain view and walking out with large items
9. Grabbing an item and running
10. Booster boxes and cages—boxes designed with special spring lids where merchandise can be concealed or cages that are worn by women to make them appear pregnant
11. Hiding items in books, newspapers, or magazines
12. Crotch— a female technique where an item is held in place by the thighs under a skirt or dress.
13. Ticket switching or destruction

According to ongoing research by Commercial Service Systems, Inc., the techniques used vary with individual preference and type of establishment. For example, purses are most commonly used for concealment of merchandise in supermarkets followed by the use of pockets and carrying items under clothes. It is estimated that the purse is used 26–33 percent of the time, pockets 17–30 percent, and clothing 12–24 percent. One must keep in mind, however, the self-fulfilling prophecy: What one looks for most, one finds most often!

Who Shoplifts

Shoplifters come in all sizes and ages and are of either sex. Generally they are broken down by type into professional, amateur, drug user, and thrill seeker. Of these the amateur is by far the largest in number.

Amateurs come from every economic group and represent every level of education. Their thefts are generally impulsive although a significant number of them find some kind of economic or more often emotional satisfaction in their action, and they become virtually undistinguishable from professionals. The rest of them have no particular pattern of theft and may only steal once or, at most, a handful of times. Individually they do not represent a severe threat to the retailer, but the cumulative effect of such thefts, however motivated, can be very damaging.

The frequent repeaters ultimately become more methodical in their thefts and soon become a real problem. Among this group are those compulsive thieves known as kleptomaniacs—people who are unable to overcome their desire to steal. Such driven souls are very rare and do not make up a significant number or dollar loss to the retailing community.

Professional shoplifters are a very real danger. Their methods are well planned and practical; often they work with partners. "This is My Job" is the appropriate title of a video tape prepared by a professional shoplifter. The professional approaches shoplifting just as a dancer studies dance or a ballplayer plays ball. They appear in every way as ordinary shoppers, carefully fitting into the environment of the stores they single out. They select merchandise with high resale value and a ready market. They are well connected with fences and lawyers. They are in every sense suppliers in the subsystem of illegal merchandising. They are the first people in the chain of underworld retailing and their activities are damaging in a number of ways to the legal storekeeper. Not only do they create severe losses for the legitimate retailer, but they set up a system whereby they are effectively in competition with their victims' own goods.

Drug users, trapped by their addiction, must find a regular source of funds to supply their needs. They turn to many sources for the insatiable demands, but shoplifting is often the easiest.

Thefts of $500 a day and more may be required to supply an individual's habit. Typically, merchandise is stolen for fencing at between 10 and 20 percent of its retail value. In other cases it may be stolen and returned for refund. Either way, the store suffers substantial losses.

Thrill seekers are more often than not teenagers who shoplift as a gesture of defiance or under peer pressure to do something daring. Shoplifting lists are still used to initiate new members into certain gangs or groups.

Over the years, various reports have found that approximately 50 percent of the people apprehended for shoplifting are adults, 60 percent are under 30 years of age, and 80 percent are under 40. Females account for at least 50 percent of shoplifting incidents. Nevertheless, the statistics are contradictory: Females dominate the overall statistics, but males account for the majority of juvenile shoplifters. The main difference seems to be that females outnumber males in the adult shoplifting segment. Once again, the self-fulfilling prophecy may have some effect on these statistics: The housewife has been stereotyped by security professionals as a major shoplifting threat. In addition, females are in the stores more often than males, and therefore may be over-represented in the apprehension statistics. All socioeconomic classes are represented in shoplifting; unlike most criminal activity, the lower socioeconomic classes do not predominate. Rather, shoplifting is a crime of the working- and middle-classes, who are not generally motivated by need. Instead shoplifting is often a crime of greed. This contention is supported by the fact that many items recovered from shoplifters are luxuries.

Detecting the Shoplifter

Professional shoplifters will not be deterred by the normal means that would discourage the great bulk of amateurs from stealing. Only a well-trained security staff can apprehend them. Such detectives must learn to blend in with the normal routine of the average customer in a given store at a given time of day. They must learn the different patterns of a secretary on a lunch hour, a bored matron who shops to kill time, and the energetic early morning customer with a specific mission in mind. They must observe the difference in pace of customers in the 10 AM crowd and the hurry-to-get home 5:30 PM shoppers. After learning the techniques of anonymity, the detective must learn what to look for—how to spot a potential shoplifter.

A list of some of the signs to look for was developed by a large midwestern store and includes the following:

1. *Packages.* A great many packages; empty or open paper bags; clumsy, crumpled, homemade, untidy, obviously used-before, poorly-tied packages; unusual packages—freak boxes; knitting bags; hat boxes; zipper bags; newspapers; magazines; school books; folded tissue paper; briefcases; and brown bags with no store name on them

2. *Clothing.* Coat or cape worn over the shoulder or arm; coat with slit pockets; ill-fitting, loose, bulging, unreasonable, and unseasonable clothing

3. *Actions.* Unusual actions of any kind: extreme nervousness; strained look; aimless walking up and down the aisles; leaving the store but returning in a few minutes; walking around holding merchandise; handling many articles in a short time; dropping articles on the floor; making rapid purchases; securing empty bags or boxes; entering elevators at the last moment or changing one's mind and letting the elevator go; excessive inspection of packages; examining merchandise in nooks and corners; concealing merchandise behind purse or package; placing packages, coat, or purse over merchandise; using stairways; loitering in vestibules

4. *Eyes.* Glancing without moving the head, looking beneath the hat brim, studying customers instead of merchandise, looking in mirrors, glancing up from merchandise quickly from time to time, glancing from left to right in cross aisles.

5. *Hands.* Closing hands completely over merchandise, palming, removing ticket and concealing or destroying it, folding merchandise, holding identical pieces for comparison, working merchandise up sleeve and lowering arm into pocket, placing merchandise in pocket; stuffing hands in pocket; concealing ticket while trying on merchandise, trying on jewelry and leaving it on, crumpling merchandise (gloves and merchandise).

6. *At counters.* Taking merchandise from counter but returning repeatedly, taking merchandise to another counter or giving it to a minor, standing behind crowd and taking merchandise from counters by reaching through the crowd, placing merchandise near exit counter, starting to examine merchandise then leaving the counter and returning to it, holding merchandise below counter level, taking merchandise and turning back to counter, handling a lot of merchandise at different counters, standing a long time at counter.

7. *In fitting rooms.* Entering with merchandise but no salesperson, using room before it has been cleared, removing hangers before entering, entering with packages, taking in two or more identical items, taking in items of various sizes or of obviously wrong sizes, gathering merchandise hastily without examining it and going into fitting room.

8. *In departments.* Sending clerks away for more merchandise, standing too close to dress racks or cases, placing shopping bag on floor between racks, refusing a salesperson's help.

9. *Miscellaneous.* Requesting questionable refunds; acting in concert— separating and meeting, setting up lookouts, interchanging packages, following companion into fitting room independently.[6]

Obviously, many of these are the actions of a perfectly well-intentioned person, but they may indicate a shoplifter, especially if several such indications appear in the actions of one person. In such cases surveillance is essential.

Preventive Measures

Surveillance

The key to successful shoplifting prevention is surveillance. Impulse theft, which comprises 95 percent of shoplifting incidents, is motivated by availability, desire, and opportunity. Availability is a basic fact of life in modern retailing. Desire is not just a private matter, individual in character, but it is actively cultivated by the merchant aggressively selling his wares. Neither of these factors can be controlled to a significant degree, nor should they be in retailing. But opportunity can be controlled.

Shoplifters characteristically snatch loot when they think they are alone—when they are not being observed. An attentive sales staff occasionally asking if they can help or rearranging merchandise in the vicinity of a customer acting in any unusual manner can discourage most amateurs. Supervisors moving about the floor can also be effective in making known to potential shoplifters that they may be observed at any time. Obviously such store personnel are primarily concerned with serving customers. But they can be effective deterrents to shoplifting as well if they are aware of the problem and alert to any signs that might indicate a problem. In short, any method that increases the would-be shoplifter's fear of being caught will significantly decrease the temptation to steal. The public address system call, "security to department five," whether real or false, brings terror to the shoplifter since there is no way of knowing where department five is located or if the would-be shoplifter has been spotted. A professional shoplifter has indicated that when he hears this call he always ditches the merchandise and leaves the store immediately. The last thing a potential shoplifter wants to hear from store staff is, "I am sure I'll see you if you need me."

Closed-Circuit Television (CCTV)

As was noted in an earlier chapter, CCTV can either catch someone in an illegal act or prevent the act. It may have a place in retail security, but is it for deterrence or apprehension? Most merchants prefer to prevent theft rather than deal with the trouble and cost of prosecution.

Systems designed to prevent shoplifting must be obvious to shoppers. In most cases, the cameras are placed in observable locations with signs noting their presence. Some systems use flashing lights on the cameras throughout the store, to show shoppers that the system is operating.

To be effective, the system must make shoppers believe that they are being watched all of the time. In addition, however, the shoplifter must know that apprehension is likely and will result in prosecution.

The use of CCTV for apprehension of shoplifters may be a greater burden than most retail managers wish to assume. Not only is it troublesome and costly to be constantly in court for prosecution, but CCTVs that are designed for apprehension are more expensive than those designed for deterrence. The cost of the apprehension type is greater since the quality of the images must be good enough for recognition of individuals. These images should also be recorded to show shoplifters that they were caught in the act. While the deterrence systems can get by using dummy cameras, a system for apprehension needs full coverage. In addition, apprehension systems require additional personnel to monitor the system, while deterrent systems do not require constant monitoring. For all of these reasons, most CCTV systems in retail stores are primarily deterrents, but also serve as an aid to apprehension.

Electronic Article Surveillance (EAS)

The current state-of-the-art technology in retail security is EAS. The first systems were sold in 1971, and their growth has been steady ever since. According to *Hallcrest II*, the current $370 million dollar field will grow to $1.1 billion by 2000.[7] These systems have at least three components: tags, sensors, and alarm.

Tags are of various types, but two systems and their tags presently dominate the industry. The first is a VHF/microwave system. In this system, the tag contains a semiconductor that, when radiated by the transmitter frequency, reradiates or reflects a signal at the receiver. The second system uses a magnetic field rather than radio waves. Here the tag contains a magnetized strip that is sensed by a magnetometer. Most tags are designed to be reused, but newer systems have tags that can be desensitized and thrown away. The most familiar system uses a large plastic tag which is attached to clothing with a metal pin. The device can be removed only with a special tool and can be reused. These tags not only aid apprehension but also serve as prevention devices. The systems serve as a deterrent by decreasing the opportunity to steal.

Although the tagging system has been valuable in reducing shoplifting losses, it is not possible to tag every item in the store. Perhaps the deterrent value of the system is greater than the apprehension value, however. Recent developments allow the placement of EAS targets next to bar codes where they can be deactivated as the bar code is read. One manufacturer of EAS is working with manufacturers to include the EAS target in the package in an inactive state. The retailer who purchases the item will then have the option of activating the target for use with the EAS system. This will save retailers time and money in placing targets on merchandise.

In its *Electronic Article Surveillance Industry Report*, the Home Center Institute reports that EAS is 75 percent effective against the average shopper but that it only deters 15 percent of "social misfits" and 10 percent of professional shoplifters.[8]

Mirrors

Convex mirrors, which are in wide use throughout the country, may be useful in avoiding collisions of people or shopping carts rounding corners, but they have a limited use in the detection of shoplifters and may even hurt the program by creating an atmosphere of unwarranted confidence. Such mirrors distort the reflected scene in such a way that it is virtually impossible to see the details of action—and in shoplifting it is the detail of merchandise concealment that is of prime importance. Without a clear, precise image of what was taken and how it was concealed or where, it would be foolhardy, and possibly costly in legal fees, to confront a customer as a shoplifter.

On the other hand, flat mirrors of a decorative design might be built into the decor of the store at strategic spots that might otherwise be difficult to observe or keep under surveillance. Such mirrors, presenting a clear, undistorted image, can be very useful in the security effort.

Signs

There is considerable controversy over the use of signs warning of the results of shoplifting as a deterrent. Many merchants take the view that such signs are an insult to the great majority of honest shoppers who may become incensed and take their business elsewhere. Other merchants subscribe to the theory that such signs have no effect on honest people since they clearly are not those to whom the message is addressed but that they will remind those with larceny in mind of the gravity of their offense and thus deter them. There does not seem to be a clearcut resolution of these viewpoints except to say that there is no evidence anywhere that the posting of such warnings has ever had any effect on the incidence of shoplifting.

Displays of Merchandise

Merchandise displays must be appealing to attract customers, but they can also be secure to prevent theft. Symmetry in certain kinds of items displayed can be important in enabling the clerk or floor personnel to tell at a glance if any of the items are missing. Thin, almost invisible wires that in no way detract from the display can secure small items to the display rack. Dummy items look exactly like the actual merchandise and should be used when possible. Fountain pens can be displayed in a closed case, with two or three different models on counter chains outside for handling and testing. A recent addition to the display strategy is called the "bullpen." A specific type of high vulnerability merchandise such as electronic equipment is situated within the store in such a manner that customers can enter in only one or two locations which are staffed at all times. A sales representative will also be present in the bullpen to assist with customer questions. There are thousands of items and countless ways to display them to catch the customer's attention. Each such display must accommodate some means to provide security for the goods it presents.

Check-out Clerks

These clerks should check all merchandise for signs of switched or altered price tags.

Customers should never be permitted to carry out unwrapped or unbagged merchandise. All purchases should be wrapped or bagged, and if the additional precaution of stapling is taken, the receipt should be stapled to the package.

Checkers in supermarkets must check shopping carts for merchandise on the bottom shelf. They should further check all merchandise purchased for possible concealment of other goods. This includes paper bags holding purchases of produce. Other items may be concealed beneath the apples or potatoes they contain.

Refunds

Refunds should be issued on the return of merchandise with the original sales slip. Since these are frequently misplaced if the customer insists on a cash refund, full particulars including the name and address of the customer should be entered on the appropriate refund form. The original of the form, which has been signed by the clerk making out the form, the customer, and the authorizing supervisor, should be presented to the customer for cashing at a refund window or other location handling such matters. Cashing of refunds should never be permitted at cash registers on the floor since this practice could invite embezzlement by the operator of the register. Unfortunately, this last practice is not applied in all operations, as customer relations is more important than is the irriation caused by "red tape." A copy of the refund authorization should be turned in at the end of the day's business by the clerk who handled the transaction. All such refund forms should be numbered and accounted for, including damaged ones.

All customers must cash their own refunds, to avoid the possibility of forged slips supposedly being cashed by store personnel as a service to a non-existent customer.

The refund system should be further checked by periodic audits of all refund forms used and unused and by contact with the customer so refunded.

Letters should be sent out regularly to a certain percentage of customers who have received refunds asking if the service was adequate, and if their request for refund was promptly and courteously complied with. If such letters are returned as undeliverable or if the customer denies having received a refund, an investigation of refund procedures is indicated.

Arrest

There are many problems involved in making an arrest of a shoplifter. Chief among them, after considerations of justice and fair play, is the everpresent possibility of liability for false arrest or imprisonment, slander, or unreasonable detainment. Since the laws pertaining to shoplifting vary from state to state and since they are still subject to changes to conform to an equitable balance between the needs of the merchant and the protection of the general public, it is essential that legal advice be sought to guide company policy in such matters.

Every store management team should develop a specific set of instructions, and these instructions should be taught in such a way that adherence to them will be automatic in every covered instance. Any variation from approved procedure in dealing with shoplifting incidents can subject the store to severe financial reverses and damaging public relations consequences. All personnel must conform to the established policy. Since the owner is liable for all acts of employees while they are on the job under the doctrine of *respondeat superior*, the term "merchant" will be used in this discussion even though most of the acts herein dealt with are usually performed by employees.

Under common law, merchants operate in a most dangerous legal minefield. Although tort law allows property owners the privilege of defending their property against theft and even allows them to repossess their goods if they have been wrongfully removed from the premises, this privilege is not absolute and is limited in scope. The privilege is entirely dependent on the fact of wrongful taking. If the suspicion of theft turns out to be groundless, the privilege vanishes and the merchant is vulnerable to a tort action that can result in substantial damages—both compensatory and punitive.

The basis for such actions may be one or more of five torts that were discussed in Chapter 6.

The complexities of the legal climate governing the war against shoplifting require a sensitive understanding and a thorough briefing by an attorney experienced in the field.

Store policies on procedure of arrest and detainment must be predicated on legal advice and must then be followed to the letter. As a general rule, it should be noted that, in cases of detainment where neither a confession of guilt nor a form releasing the store from any liability has been signed, it will be necessary to prosecute to avoid the suit for false arrest that would be likely to ensue.

Prosecution

The argument over when and who to prosecute shows no sign of abating; certainly there appears to be little agreement among security professionals. The skew is probably more toward a tough attitude than otherwise, but every shade of opinion has its adherents.

Every study undertaken on the subject has shown that the rate of recidivism is enormous. The FBI has published figures indicating that *83.4 percent of those arrested for larceny in 1969 had been arrested before for the same crime.* Such a figure suggests that neither arrest nor the fear of arrest is a very effective deterrent.

Checks

The boom in private checking accounts that has been a part of the American economic scene for the past 40 years has led us to the point where business analysts and economists continue to predict a cashless economy within the foreseeable future. At that time, they suggest, even checks will become passe, and all transactions will be based on debits and credits handled through instant recording of the exchange of goods or services by centralized computers. Such computers would register a credit to an employee's account, credits where appropriate to various government agencies, and debit the account of the employer in the amount specified on payroll information. This process is presently available through electronic filing of IRS tax returns and through various credit card companies in cooperation with some major retail chains.

All obligations of the employee from mortgage payments to the expenses of a vacation trip would be handled in the same manner by a simple series of ledger entries in an interlocking central computer system. The automatic debit systems for checking accounts on mortgages, car loans, and insurance payments are with us now. Personal bank checks in use today are a crude and primitive version of this predicted, streamlined system.

With personal checking accounts the rule rather than the exception, it would appear that the physical handling of cash has been delegated to the banks. That day has not, of course, arrived, but it seems close. Even today almost 90 percent of all business transactions are handled by check or credit accounts.

Nature of a Check

A check is nothing more than an authorization to the holder of funds or the bank to debit the account of the authorizer and to credit the named person or the bearer in the amount specified. Provided that sufficient funds are available in the debited account, the exchange is made either in cash or by crediting the account of the payee. This system is really only a version of the most rudimentary kind of bookkeeping accomplished by the exchange of tons of paper in a neverending chain of authorizations.

Checks can and have been written on almost anything and in every conceivable form. Their legality as a negotiable instrument is in no way dependent on the usual check form in common use today. As a practical matter, many banks refuse checks other than those written on the forms they provide simply because their procedure for processing the enormous volume they are called on to record does not allow for personal eccentricities. The day when a Robert Benchley, a popular humorist of the 1930s and 1940s, could write checks in the form of risqué poems on wrapping paper is gone, not because such a check duly signed and clear in intent is not a legal instrument for transferring funds but because few people would cash it.

Checks are in such wide use today because they are safe and convenient. Since cash can almost never be identified if it is lost or stolen, once gone it is gone forever. Checks, on the other hand, have no negotiable value except as they are drawn and signed by the payor. Forgery is, of course, a problem, but that is considerably less of a risk than is loss of cash, which requires no criminal expertise of any level for its disposal.

Checks are invaluable as receipts of payments made and for recording an individual's accounts for tax and other purposes.

Checks can theoretically be used only by the designated payee. Therefore if a drawn check is lost or mutilated, payment can be stopped by notification to the bank and a new check can be drawn. Checks lost or stolen in the mail can be handled in the same way, whereas mailed cash is always at considerable risk of nondelivery because of theft, loss, or destruction.

Checks are a ready source of cash at any time. Many people are cautious about carrying substantial amounts of cash for fear of loss or theft. In the event a situation requiring funds arises, a check can provide the money necessary.

From the retailer's point of view, checks are a boon since customers will buy what appeals to them at the moment and handle the transaction with the stroke of a pen. People who buy only with cash tend to be considerably more restrained in their buying habits. They are limited by the amount of cash they are carrying, and the psychological restraints imposed by the actual doling out of cash are considerably more persuasive than are those involved in check transactions. People are cautious when handling cash, which has a reality that is automatically translated into food and doctor bills, car payments, and the like. On the other hand, check cashers are usually bigger buyers who allow their impulses to have greater sway in retail situations.

Checks and the Retailer

It has been variously estimated that somewhere between 70 and 80 percent of all bank checks are cashed in retail stores. Retailers are standing in for banks as the major supplier of cash in the country. Banks are in no way relieved of their heavy burden of accounting or of their responsibility as the ultimate repository of the funds drawn on by these documents, but they are no longer the primary source or supply of funds to the consumer. They have, in effect, thousands of agents or branch offices that perform line functions for them.

This means that retailers must keep huge supplies of cash on hand to service check-cashing customers. This not only raises the risks of internal and external theft but it also serves to increase the cost of goods, since cash that might otherwise be invested in additional merchandise or other income-producing ventures must be held in reserve to handle the demands of customers.

Some economists take the view that this situation has its bright side in that it forces many enterprises that might otherwise overcommit their funds to maintain a position of sufficient liquidity to protect against reverses. Nonetheless, many major retailers feel that their options are limited. Whatever the state of the economy, they must keep large supplies of cash available to provide what is traditionally a banking service.

Bad checks of various kinds add to the cost of doing business. Forgeries or fraudulent checks are a direct loss of both merchandise and cash. Checks that are ultimately collectable but that are returned by the bank for any number of reasons present a huge administrative headache in making the collection. Even though a majority of such checks are soon made good—often after a single letter or phone call, the cost of such follow-up and double handling, as well as the additional cost of collection agencies if such are required, may bring the cost of each returned check to between $10 and $25. The charge for any returned check is usually added onto the eventual collection, but most retailers feel that they do not collect the full amount. Such returns actually cost them in direct and indirect losses.

Types of Checks

There are many kinds of checks representing different types of transactions that may be presented to a retailer for cashing. Since the store must establish a check cashing policy eventually that will involve the kinds of checks it is willing to cash, a brief list of check types is in order.

The bank check is that most commonly in use. It is normally a rectangular piece of tamper-resistant paper that will reveal any attempts at erasure or alteration. On it are lines for date, the amount (in both script and numerals), the name of the payee, and the signature of the payor. Most checks are personalized by the imprint of the name and address of the account holder, and they carry the name and address of the bank in which the account is held. These checks also have a space in which the check can be numbered by the payee for accounting convenience, or they may be prenumbered by the bank. They will usually also have a certain amount of computerized information (such as account number) for the bank's convenience in processing. These checks are precisely as good as the credit or the account of the person drawing them, assuming that that person is legitimately the account owner.

Blank checks are simply forms that can be filled out as above, but they contain no information such as bank name, payor name, or account information. They must be filled out to designate the bank on which they are drawn as well as other pertinent information. Bank counter checks contain only the name of the bank. They must be hand processed by the bank and are, therefore, unpopular or frequently unacceptable to many banks. These types of checks should not be accepted by the retailer under any circumstances.

Traveler's checks are checks drawn to a certain designated amount and purchased from banks and other agencies. At the time of purchase each check is signed by the purchaser. When one is cashed, it must be signed again in the presence of the casher to allow the signatures to be compared. Since these checks are serialized, they may be recovered in the event of loss or destruction, provided a record of the numbers has been retained.

Payroll checks are simply bank checks drawn to an employee. Since they are issued on the account of a reputable firm, they are usually acceptable in retail establishments although they can be, and frequently are, forgeries.

A third-party check is one issued by one person to another. The merchant may cash such checks provided the designated payee endorses it as having been paid.

Government checks, whether for social security, tax rebates, salary, or any of the many uses to which they are put, are essentially cash except that the cash is assigned to a specific named person. Because the solvency of the payor is never a question, these checks have always had a lively traffic among thieves and forgers. It is particularly important that the identity of the payee be established and that these checks be examined for any signs of tampering.

Returned Checks

Generally speaking, checks are returned because there are not sufficient funds (NSF) to cover the check, the account has been closed, or there is no account in the bank on which they were drawn. Other problems such as a damaged check, illegible signature or amount, or improperly or incompletely drawn checks may cause the bank to return them for clarification, but this latter group represents a small minority of the returns.

NSF returns are in the majority. Usually they indicate that issuers are bad bookkeepers, but the issuer may also have in mind a loan from the store. The check will be covered eventually, but in the meantime the issuer has the cash to get by with.

No account and closed account returns are almost invariably fraudulent checks. It is possible that such checks were issued in error (such as transferring a bank account before all outstanding checks have cleared), but it is unlikely.

Check Approval

The two most important and relatively simple steps that can and must be taken in approving checks are a thorough examination of the check itself and a positive identification of the check casher (see Figures 15.2 and 15.3). Neither of these steps will screen out the accomplished forger or the skilled bank check artist; nor will they eliminate the problem of the checks issued by honest but careless people that are returned because of NSF. But they will reduce, or possibly eliminate a great deal of, the most persistent losses.

Retailers are not obliged to cash checks. They do so in their own interests as a service. If a check of the casher looks dubious, the check should be refused.

Since retailers will cash most checks presented, however, they must know what to look for. They must examine the check to verify the date, the amount drawn both numerically and in script, the name and address of the customer, the name of the bank, the signature of the customer, and the endorsement if it is a third-party check of any kind, including payroll or government checks.

They must also reassure themselves that the customer is properly identified. Generally any official document that describes the holder and bears a signature can be accepted as adequate identification. One that also includes

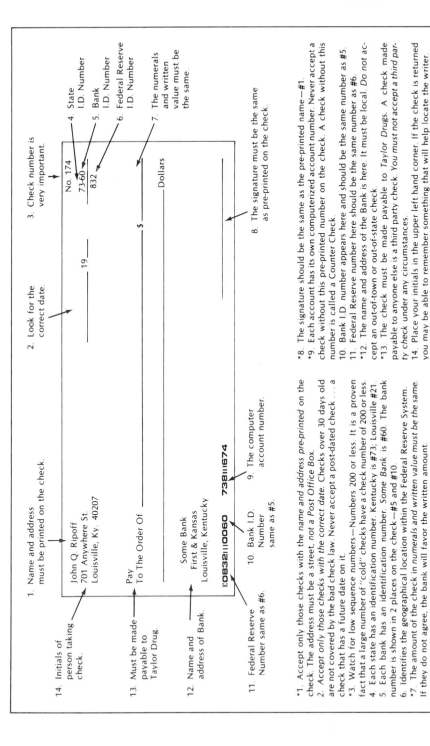

Figure 15.2 Check procedure—accepting a check. (Courtesy of Taylor Drug Stores.)

(Back of Check)

(on front)

Address _____

Telephone No. _____

Driver's License _____

Employed By _____

Credit Cards

Pay To The Order Of

First National Bank
Taylor Drug Stores #14

1. Must be pre-printed on the front of the check.

2. List residence phone.

3. The first letter of the Driver's License (In Kentucky) is the same as the first letter of the last name.

4. If not employed list employer of spouse. (Note on check).

5. List name of company but not the account number.

*Place the store check stamp on the back of the check *immediately.* This is exactly like an endorsement for *Taylor Drug Stores,* Inc. If the check was stolen it could not be cashed.

1. Be certain a complete address is pre-printed on the front of the check.
2. Copy the residence phone number here. The exchange (first three numbers) should be familiar to you. Think of your store phone number. Is this number in your area?
3. Copy the driver's license number carefully. The first letter of the number should be the same as the first letter of the last name of the check writer (Kentucky). Look at the photo on the driver's license. Is it the same person who is writing the check?
4. List here the name of the company where the writer is employed. If not employed list spouse's employer.
5. Request a credit card. List the name of the company but do not copy the account number. If the account is *not* in the name of the check writer, note the name of account on the check.

Important General Information Regarding the Handing of Checks

1. A check is exactly *like cash.* Protect the check the same way you protect cash.

2. Accept a check only for the amount of the purchase.
3. Refer any check over $25.00 to the Manager-on-Duty for approval. If it is the policy of the store to have all checks approved, you must adhere to this policy.
4. Never accept a third party check. This is a check that was written by someone (a person, company, etc.), other than the person who is presenting the check to you.
5. Never accept an altered check. This is a check that has been changed in some way, the amount may have been written over, an erasure may have been made, etc.
6. Never accept a money order. *Exception:* A money order bought at your store and returned because it was not used for the purpose intended may be accepted.
7. You may accept a Traveler's Cheque in denominations under $25.00. You must be sure the writer signs the Traveler's Cheque in your presence. Compare the two signatures on the cheque carefully. Both signatures must have been made by the same person.
8. Willful violation of the Standard Procedure for accepting and protecting a check will result in *immediate dismissal.*

Check procedures on accepting, protecting a check. (Courtesy of Taylor Drug Stores.)

a suitably laminated (or otherwise affixed) photograph is even better. Such documents can be fabricated by an artful forger, but since forging of this kind requires some equipment and skill, it is not in wide or general use.

Driver's licenses, passports, national (major) credit cards, birth certificates, and motor vehicle registrations are all acceptable identifications. Club or organization membership cards, Social Security cards, hunting licenses, and employee passes are not valid as dependable pieces of identification since they are easily obtained or duplicated.

The best identification is by an authorization system established by the store itself. Credit cards or check cashing cards issued by the store provide a running record of the customer's account and serve as nearly positive identification for check-cashing purposes. The cost of establishing such a system can be well worth it in stores suffering from substantial losses due to fraudulent or other uncollectable checks.

The information used to identify a customer should, in all cases, be entered on the back of the check for future reference. If, for example, a vehicle registration is accepted, its number should be entered on the check along with such other information as may be relevant.

ID Equipment and Systems

Equipment to record any check casher exists to help the retailer. Camera devices that photograph the customer simultaneously with the check can be used to record the transactions. Instruments to record thumbprints on the check without the use of ink also serve in this capacity. With the introduction of the automatic fingerprint identification systems (AFIS) in many states the ability to identify individuals from only a thumb print has improved greatly.

These devices are as effective as the system established for their use. If they are used carefully in accordance with a designated procedure, they can provide a useful record for the storekeeper. They tend to discourage by their very presence check passing by thieves although they will by no means eliminate it.

Electronic check verification systems, using computer interlink capabilities, also allow some establishments the ability to check individual checks against lists of problem check writers; in some cases, this technology even allows for verification of the solvency of the account on which the check is drawn.

Store Policy

Every store must set and maintain its own policy for handling checks. Certainly the policy should be reviewed and adjusted as necessary, but it must be strictly adhered to as long as it is in force. Employee indoctrination and continuing education is essential to the success of any program of check control.

As a guide, though certainly not as a rigid rule, certain limitations should be considered. The retailer should accept:

1. Absolutely NO third party checks. Payment can be stopped on such checks and the retailer's recourse is only to the customer, not to the payor.
2. No checks on out-of-town banks. Such checks are difficult to verify, and the time involved in clearance is such that, if it is fraudulent, the customer has long disappeared before the check is returned.
3. No checks over a certain amount above purchase
4. No checks for cashing other than government or payroll checks
5. No checks for cashing without adequate predetermined documents of identification
6. No checks for cashing drawn on other than personal checks imprinted with the name and address of the customer.

If such rules are followed, the loss from bad checks should be small, provided all checks are themselves carefully examined by the cashiers.

It is generally agreed that a retailer should never suffer losses greater than .05 percent of the face value of checks cashed although some do in fact have losses as high as 1 percent. Such a drain on the resources of any company is clearly intolerable. It must be corrected by the establishment of reasonable controls and a program of employee education.

Internal Theft

Methods of Theft

The list of ingenious techniques employed by dishonest employees in stealing is endless. Whatever systems are installed to control inventory shrinkage from internal theft, some clever employee will find a way around them. Theft is limited only by the imagination of the perpetrator. The problem is very real. According to *Hallcrest I*, employee theft was the only crime consistently investigated on a weekly or even a daily basis. The significance of this problem was also shown by Leonard E. Dobrin and Donald H. Smith, professors at Old Dominion University in Norfolk, Virginia. They report that, in a recent survey of students employed in the retail business, 81 percent reported stealing from their employer while the remaining 19 percent indicated that they had witnessed others stealing.[9]

It is important for managers to familiarize themselves with some of the ways employees steal in order to better understand the scope and nature of the problem. Familiarity alone will not serve to stamp out this problem, but it will aid in focusing on those areas of greatest danger and help to establish some countermeasures. Some of the most common methods of employee theft are listed below.

Cash Registers

One of the methods of theft involves some kind of juggling with the cash register. Since cashiers and managers both have access to customer cash to be deposited in registers that record the transaction, there are literally thousands of opportunities to manipulate the accounting before individual sales or even the receipts of the day are posted. Cash never recorded as received is clearly much harder to locate or identify as missing than is cash or merchandise that has been entered and later stolen. Methods used with the register usually involve the regular theft of small sums by underringing the amount received. This involves ringing $9 for a $10 purchase, for example, and pocketing the difference at the end of the day before checking in. An even cruder method is to ring up "no sale" or "void" instead of the amount paid from time to time and to pocket the cash received at the sale. The assignment of one till for each cashier rather than having several cashiers operating out of the same drawer has reduced the opportunities to steal as the cashier is responsible for balancing the drawer at the end of the day, and the use of CCTV to monitor cashier stations randomly can help to reduce underringing and no sales problems.

From time to time, employees are found who have an opportunity to remove the tape from their registers shortly before the end of the day. They put in a fresh tape and ring up all sales accurately. When they check in, they pocket all the proceeds on the new tape, destroy it and hand in the prematurely removed old tape as their record of the day's receipts. They have effectively gone into business for themselves on company time.

Several cases of such private enterprises have involved managers buying their own registers and, either alone or in collusion with another employee, setting up an additional check-out lane during a few hours of heavy traffic.

The Giveaway

According to several regional discount store security managers this is the largest employee theft problem because it is extremely difficult to detect. Checkers in supermarkets have been discovered giving away large amounts of merchandise to fellow employees when they check out by ringing up only a small fraction of the value of the merchandise. In other cases, they have similarly accommodated friends or family members.

Many cases are reported where various store clerks set themselves up as traders, exchanging stockings for another clerk's shoes or blouses for costume jewelry. In a somewhat similar approach, employees have been found who, after selling an item for its regular price, enter it as having been sold to an employee at the regular discount price. The seller then pockets the difference.

Price Changing

Every kind of store must be alert to price changing by employees and customers alike. Employees can alter price tags and buy the merchandise on their own or in collusion with an outside confederate. The growing use of the uniform product code (UPC) as a part of the prepackaged merchandise has reduced the opportunity for customer ticket switching on some merchandise. The ability of employees to change the price in the computer so that it is scanned at a lower price, however, is still possible. One retail security manager has indicated that employees have been caught changing the UPC price entry toward the end of the day, indicating that the item is going on sale, so that a confederate might purchase that item at a lower price. The next morning the employee changes the UPC back to the original price indicating that the sale was a mistake.

Vendor Kickbacks

Collusion with vendor in receipting more merchandise than is delivered is common in every business and particularly cannot be overlooked in retail establishments.

Refunds

In cases where refund controls are inadequate, it is a simple matter for employees to write up refund tickets and submit them for cash, either in person or through a confederate.

Merchandise Theft

It is common for employees to transport items of merchandise to their cars in the course of the day. This is often done in several trips or perhaps by accumulating items in one package to be removed just after the store opens or before it closes. If package control procedures are in operation, such employees may purchase an inexpensive item or two and pass out the package with the legitimate sales slip for authorization.

Stocking

Stocking crews have an excellent opportunity to steal enormous amounts of merchandise during the off-hours when they are typically working. The "box and buy" technique is one that provides stock crews with great opportunities. A large item of relatively low cost is removed from the box and placed on the shelf as a display. High-priced items are then placed into the box, and the box is resealed. The next morning the employee or confederate enters the store and purchases the box supposedly containing the lower-priced item.

Embezzlement

Embezzlement in retail establishments takes the same forms as those discussed in Chapter 12, and the same precautions must be exercised to prevent it.

The first and most important countermeasure that every store should establish is a firm employment policy that includes a careful screening of every job applicant. These procedures, which have been discussed in another chapter, may seem burdensome and even more costly than is the more cursory checking used by too many stores, but in the long run, they will pay for themselves many times over.

The other basic countermeasure is enlightened supervision. Supervision to confirm that all established procedures are being followed, as well as regular audits of their effectiveness, is vital to the success of any retail security program. No system of controls can be effective if it is not adhered to, and unless it is supervised, it may soon fall into disuse.

Controls

Shopping Services

Auditing the efficiency, effectiveness, and honesty of salespeople by shopping service investigation has long been used by retail firms as one of the most accurate methods of determining the conduct of their operation. Such an audit is not inexpensive but has established itself as sufficiently effective in the reduction of theft and the improvement in the performance of personnel to pay for itself many times over.

The tests conducted by shopping services or their shoppers usually take note of the employee's appearance, manner, helpfulness, and salespersonship as well as checking for any signs of dishonesty.

Dishonesty testing consists of the creation of situations where the employee could easily steal or fail to ring up cash. The employee is then observed or audited to check on performance under these circumstances. The situations created are in no way construed as entrapment or enticement, but represent recreations of normal situations that could be anticipated in the regular course of business. Since shoppers making these tests are unknown to the employees, employee reactions to the tests can be taken as indications of their performance in similar situations with any customer. A full report is submitted after each such test for the manager's reference and review.

Most stores contract for such services on a yearly basis at a set fee with the understanding that inspections will be made with a certain prescribed frequency. In this way, store management has some confidence that an ongoing audit made by objective outside investigators will help uncover inadequate or dishonest performance by sales employees and cashiers.

Security Audit or Survey

The store manager and security representative should conduct at a minimum an annual audit of operations. The security survey is discussed in Chapter 7.

Shipping-Receiving Controls

As in other types of business, the receiving and shipping area of any retail operation is particularly sensitive. Since the life blood of the business flows across these areas many times in the course of a year, it is essential that there must be full accountability for all movement of merchandise, that a perpetual inventory be an integral part of the system, and that the area be restricted to those persons specifically authorized to be there.

All merchandise loaded or unloaded should be subject to periodic spot checks, including a complete unloading and recounting of merchandise already loaded from time to time. Cargo seals should be secured and inventoried regularly. All broken shipments should be investigated and secured. All loading and unloading procedures should be supervised.

Maintain a restroom and lounge area for drivers that is separate from the facilities used by stockroom, warehouse, or dock personnel, and insist on maintaining this separation. Do not permit drivers to enter storage or merchandise handling areas.

The effectiveness of procedures should be audited from time to time by introducing errors into various operations. For example, the number of cases to be shipped might be invoiced incorrectly to see if the checker catches the error; truck seals might be logged and noted on invoices incorrectly to verify the alertness of the personnel involved.

Trash Removal

Trash removal has always been a problem because it provides an efficient means of removing merchandise from the premises without detection. It is important to have a supervisor on hand when trash is loaded for removal, and it is especially important that trash collection for removal be conducted in a separate area from loading or receiving dock areas. In some instances, it would be wise to inspect the dumpsters after hours. The use of clear plastic bags has reduced the potential for removal of some articles as they are clearly visible through the plastic.

Package Control

It is important that some kind of control procedure be established to inspect packages removed from the premises by employees. Retail outlets have a particularly difficult time with this problem, since employees have regular access to large amounts of merchandise, much of it small enough to be easily portable. Receipts must accompany every purchase removed, and all packages should be subject to full inspection by security personnel.

Employee Morale

The state of employee morale is the key factor in any store security program. If employees are totally familiar with all store rules and policies, if they feel that they are appreciated as human beings as well as store employees, if they feel they are an important functioning part of the organization, they will respond with increased efficiency, and the problem of dishonesty will diminish. It is essential that management bear in mind that, along with its desire to receive reports up the ladder, it must reciprocate by communicating back down the same ladder. Communication must be a two-way path.

Employees should be motivated to perform, not compelled to do so. Tom Peters refers to ownership of the job. The employees should feel that the job is truly important and that they contribute to the profitability of the firm. This can be accomplished only by clear statements of policy, supervision insisting on compliance to those policies, and intelligent leadership.[10] In this atmosphere, morale should grow, and the company should prosper.

Civil Recovery

One means of reducing the shrinkage figure is through the recovery of losses in the courts. This option was little used during the 1970s or 1980s as merchandise sales were good. Civil recovery is not a new idea. In

Table 15.1   States with Civil Recovery Statutes

Alaska	Nevada
Arizona	New Hampshire
California	New Jersey
Colorado	New Mexico
Connecticut	North Carolina
Florida	North Dakota
Georgia	Ohio
Hawaii	Oregon
Idaho	Rhode Island
Illinois	South Dakota
Indiana	Tennessee
Iowa	Texas
Louisiana	Utah
Massachusetts	Virginia
Michigan	Washington
Minnesota	West Virginia
Montana	Wisconsin
Nebraska	

Source: Read Hayes, "Winning the Civil Recovery War," *Security Management,* March 1990; 83.

fact, the concept goes back to common law. What is new are the statutes that make it easier for merchants to collect for damages resulting from theft. The first such act was passed in 1973 by the state of Nevada. The statutes have passed the test of time and the courts. In 1986 in the case of *Payless Drug Store v. Brown,*[11] the court found that the statute did not violate civil rights or due process.

In 35 states, retailers can now file civil actions as well as criminal charges against a customer or employee who steals. Table 15.1 lists the states where civil recovery statutes exist.[12]

Review Questions

1. Describe some of the common shoplifting techniques.
2. What are common preventive measures that can be used in a retail store to help reduce the incidence of shoplifting? How effective is each of these measures?

3. What are the legal implications that accompany the arrest of a shop-lifter?

4. Identify check-cashing policies a retail store might set up to reduce its losses from bad checks.

5. Discuss this statement: "The state of employee morale is the key factor in any store's security program."

References

1. "1989 Shrinkage Tab Reaches $2.2 Billion; Prevention Effort Costs Retailers Millions," *Security*, April 1991: 10.

2. "Substance Abuse Linked to Increased Problems on the Job," *Security*, April 1991: 10–11.

3. Edward M. Parker, "An Inconvenient Problem," *Security Management*, July 1990: 26.

4. "Substance Abuse," April 1991: 10.

5. Thomas W. Wathen, "Welcome to the 1990s: A Security Industry CEO Takes a Look at the Future," *Security*, April 1991: 19.

6. Bob Curtis, *Security Control: External Theft* (New York: Chain Store Publishing Corporation, 1971), pp. 75–77.

7. William C. Cunningham, John J. Straucus, Clifford W. VanMeter, *The Hallcrest Report II: Private Security Trends 1970–2000* (Boston: Butterworth-Heinemann, 1990), p. 202.

8. "EAS Effectiveness Varies With Industry and Thief," *Security*, September 1990: 15.

9. Leonard E. Dobrin and Donald Hugh Smith, "Stealing From the Store," *Security Management*, August 1990: 48.

10. Tom Peters, *Thriving on Chaos: Handbook for a Management Revolution* (New York: Harper & Row Publishers, 1987).

11. *Payless Drug Store v. Brown*, Oregon Supreme Court, 1986.

12. Read Hayes, "Winning the Civil Recovery War," *Security Management*, March 1990: 83.

16 □ □ □
□ □ □
□ □ □

Cargo Security

Cargo security has been a growing security problem since 1970 when the Senate Select Committee on Small Business[1] estimated that almost $1.5 billion in direct loss was attributable to cargo theft. By 1975, the figure had reached $2.3 billion; by 1990 it had climbed to $13.3 billion according to FBI figures. These figures do not reflect pilferage and unreported crimes that account for a minimum of 5 to 10 times the amount of the reported crimes.

The indirect costs of claims processing, capital tied up in claims and litigation, and market losses from both nondelivery and underground competition from stolen goods were estimated at between $2 and $7 for every $1 of direct loss—a $26.6 to $93.1 billion annual loss in the national economy.

The problem continues to increase in severity. In the first four months of 1985, the cost per incident of cargo theft averaged $50,000, continuing an increase that began in 1984. By 1990, the average had again increased to $75,000.

The shipment of goods is vital to the economy and ultimately to the survival of the country. Since the 1970 figures were established, the growth of international transportation systems using containers that can be transported by truck, ship, and rail has developed to the extent that land bridges, particularly in the United States, have been thoroughly established. These land routes carry millions of dollars of goods from other countries over our rail system on stack trains between the far east and European countries through the United States. The liability for the contents of these containers, moving via land bridge, is shared between a multitude of ocean carriers, rail companies, and truckers. The security concerns for the safe handling of this movement of goods are many, and include many different groups: rail police, state and local police, customs officials as well as other federal authorities.

The Role of Private Security

Since, according to an analysis made by the U.S. Department of Transportation (DoT),[2] 85 percent of goods and material stolen go out the front gates on persons and vehicles authorized to be in cargo handling areas of transportation facilities, it would appear that by far the greatest burden falls on the security apparatus of the private concerns involved. It is true that public law-enforcement agencies must make a greater effort to break up organized fencing and hijacking operations, and they must find a way to cut through their jurisdictional confusion and establish more effective means of exchanging information. But the bulk of the problem lies in the systems now employed to secure goods in transit.

There is no universally applicable solution to this problem. Every warehouse, terminal, and means of shipment has its own particular peculiarities. Each has weaknesses somewhere, but certain principles of cargo security, when they are thoughtfully applied and vigorously administered, can substantially reduce the enormous losses so prevalent in today's beleaguered transport industry.

A good loss-prevention manager must recognize that the key to good cargo security is a well-organized cargo handling system. As Louis Tyska and Lawrence Fennelly[3] note, cargo loss exists whenever the "three C's of cargo theft" are present. The three Cs are confusion, conspiracy, and the common denominator (the dishonest employee). Confusion is a primary ingredient and represents the loss-prevention specialist's opportunity to reduce theft. Confusion arises when an adequate policy does not exist or, if it does exist, when it is not followed. Tyska and Fennelly identify the following activities as great contributors to the confusion variable:

1. Personnel entering and exiting the specific facility. These people include everyone from repair people to regular employees.
2. Movement of various types of equipment, for example, trucks, rail cars, and lift trucks.
3. The proliferation of various forms of paper—freight bills, bills of lading, manifests, and so on.

Conspiracy builds on confusion. Two or more people take advantage of their positions and the confusion to steal. Many major cargo security losses would not occur, however, without the common denominator, the dishonest employee. When the security manager is dealing with more than cargo pilferage, monitoring the employee is essential. The manager must be aware of the preceding variables. By eliminating any one variable, opportunities for theft are reduced.

Accountability Procedures

The paramount principle is accountability. Every shipment, whatever its nature, must be identified, accounted for, and accounted to some responsible person at every step in its movement. This is difficult in that the goods are in motion and there are frequent changes in accountability, but this is the essence of the problem. Techniques must be developed to refine the process of accountability of all merchandise in transit.

Invoice System

This accountability must start from the moment an order is received by the shipper. As an example of a typical controlled situation, we might refer to a firm that supplies its salespeople with sales slips or invoices that are numbered in order. This is very important if any control is to be maintained over these important forms. Without numbering, sales slips could be destroyed and the cash, if any, pocketed; or they could be lost so that the customer might never be billed. When these invoice forms are numbered, they can be charged out to the salespeople in which case every invoice can and should be accounted for. Even those forms that have been spoiled by erasures or physical damage should be voided and returned to the billing department.

Merchandise should only be authorized for shipment to a customer on the basis of the regular invoice form. This form is filled out by the salesperson receiving the order and sent to the warehouse or shipping department. The shipping clerk signs one copy, signifying that the order has been filled, and sends it to accounts receivable for billing purposes. The customer signs a copy of the invoice indicating receipt of the merchandise, and this copy is returned to accounts receivable. It is further advisable to have the driver sign the shipping clerk's copy as a receipt for the load. In some systems, a copy of the invoice is also sent directly to an inventory file for use in inventory and audit procedures. Returned merchandise is handled in the same way but in reverse.

In this simplified system, there is a continuing accountability for the merchandise. If anything is missing or unaccounted for at any point, the means exist whereby the responsibility can be located. Such a system can only be effective if all numbered invoices are strictly accounted for and where merchandise is assembled and shipped only on the basis of such invoicing. The temptation to circumvent the paperwork for rush orders or emergencies frequently arises, but if the company succumbs, losses in embezzlement, theft, and/or lost billing can be substantial.

Similarly transport companies and freight terminal operators must insist on full and uninterrupted accounting for the goods in their care at every phase of the operation—from shipper to customer.

The introduction of the computer, bar coding, and scanners has made the process of accounting for merchandise from the point of purchase by the wholesaler to delivery at the retail outlet a reality. Bar coding provides not only the information discussed in the previous paragraphs but also additional information that allows security to trace losses to the specific persons with responsibility for the merchandise as the time of the loss.

Separation of Functions

Yet such a system can be compromised by collusion between or among people who constitute the links in the chain leading from order to delivery unless efforts are made to establish a routine of regular, unscheduled inspection of the operations down the line and, depending on the nature of the operation, regular inventories and audits.

It is advisable, for example, for the shipper to separate the functions of selecting the merchandise from stock from those of packing and loading. This will not in itself eliminate the possibility of collusion, but it will provide an extra check on the accuracy of the shipment. And as a general rule, the more people (up to a point) charged with the responsibility and held accountable for merchandise, the more difficult and complex a collusive effort becomes.

In order to fix accountability clearly, it is advisable to require that each person who is at any time responsible for the selecting, handling, loading, or checking of goods sign or initial the shipping ticket that is passed along with the consignment. In this way, errors, which are unfortunately inevitable, can be assigned to the person responsible. Obviously any disproportionate number of errors traced to any one person or to any one aspect of the shipping operation should be investigated and dealt with promptly.

Similarly at the receiving end, the ticket should be delivered to a receiving clerk. The truck will then be unloaded by appropriate personnel who will verify the count of merchandise received without having seen the ticket in advance. In this way, each shipment can be verified without the carelessness that so frequently accompanies a perfunctory count that comes with the expectation of receiving a certain amount as specified by the ticket. It will also tend to eliminate theft in the case of an accidental, or even an intentional, overage. Since the checkers do not know what the shipment is supposed to contain, they cannot rig the count.

Driver Loading

Many companies with otherwise adequate accountability procedures permit drivers to load their own trucks when the driver is taking a shipment. This practice can defeat any system of theft prevention since drivers are accountable only to themselves when such a method of loading is in effect. The practice should never be condoned. It is worth the investment of time to have others check the cartons tendered to the driver. The potential losses in theft of merchandise by overloading or future claims of short deliveries would almost certainly exceed the costs involved in the time or personnel involved in instituting sensible supervisory procedures.

Theft and Pilferage

Targets of Theft

An analysis of claims data from the transportation industry shows that a few very specific commodities attract the attention of pilferers and thieves.

Nine commodities—clothing, camera and video equipment, automotive parts, food products, hardware, jewelry, electronic equipment, tobacco, and alcoholic beverages—make up about 80 percent of the total national losses.

Broken down by industry, clothing and textiles represent 22 percent of the losses; food 17 percent, and jewelry 10 percent. These three products alone represent approximately half of all the losses. Obviously a company, carrier, or warehouse operator would be well advised to take special precautions when handling such merchandise. An additional 12 percent of the problem is accounted for by the theft of business machines and electronic equipment including computers and computer games.

But the kinds of things stolen vary considerably, depending on the location and the nature of the merchandise. Thieves might prefer to steal part of a shipment of clothing, but if none is available, they might just as vigorously pursue a truckload of dog food as long as there is a means of disposing of it. Anything can be stolen if the thief is given an opportunity. Anything that has a market—and nothing would be shipped unless a market existed—can be considered attractive to a thief.

It is important for transportation industry managers to recognize that all merchandise is susceptible to theft but at the same time to know the high-loss items at their locations so that they can exert extra efforts to secure such goods. It is also useful to know that motor carriers are the victims of 74 percent of the theft-related losses, rail and maritime about 24 percent, and air cargo losses are below 2 percent of the total.

Pilferage

According to the DoT analysis referred to earlier in this chapter, 25 percent of the cargo theft in this country is the result of pilferage or thefts of less than a case. The exact amount, however, cannot be established because of extensive nonreporting of these crimes. Thefts of this nature are generally held to be impulsive acts, committed by persons operating alone who pick up an item or two of merchandise that is readily available when there is small risk of detection. Typically the pilferer takes such items for personal use rather than for resale since most of those who are termed pilferers are unsystematic, uncommitted criminals and are unfamiliar with the highly organized fencing operations that could readily dispose of such loot.

Such pilferage is always difficult to detect. Because it is a crime of opportunity, it is rarely committed under controlled circumstances that can either pinpoint the culprit or gather evidence that would later lead to discovery. Generally, the items taken are small and readily concealed on the person or easy to transport and conceal in a car.

Pilferage is usually aimed at items in a freight or cargo terminal awaiting transshipment. In such instances, merchandise may be left unprotected on pallets, hand carts, or dollies awaiting the arrival of the next transport. In this mode, it is highly susceptible to pilferage as well as to a more organized plan of theft.

Broken or damaged cases offer an open invitation to pilferage if supervisory or security personnel fail to take immediate action. Accidental dropping of cases to break them open is a common device used to get at the merchandise they contain. If each such case is carefully logged—listing the name of the person responsible for the damage as well as the names of those who instantly gather at the scene—a pattern may emerge that will enable management to take appropriate action.

Whatever form pilferage takes, it can be extremely costly. Although each individual instance of such theft may be relatively unimportant, the cumulative effect can be enormous. Twenty-five percent of an estimated total direct loss of $13.3 billion adds up to a staggering bill for petty theft.

Deterring Pilferage

Here again, accountability controls can provide an important deterrent to pilferage loss. If some one person is responsible for merchandise at every stage of movement or storage, the feasibility of this kind of theft can be substantially reduced.

In cases where it does occur, a rapid and accurate account of the nature and extent of such loss can be an invaluable tool in indicating the corrective action to be taken. Properly supervised accountability controls can locate the point along the handling process where losses occurred and, even in those cases where they will not identify the culprit, these controls will underscore any weaknesses in the system and indicate trouble areas that may need more or different security application.

Movement of personnel in cargo areas must be strictly controlled. All parcels must be subject to inspection at a gate or control point at the entrance to the facility. Private automobiles must be parked outside the area immediately encompassing the facility and beyond the checkpoint. All automobiles should be subject to inspection on departure if a parking area inside the boundaries of the facility is provided.

Every effort should be made to keep employee morale high in the face of such security efforts. Though some managements have expressed an uneasiness about inspections and strict accountability procedures, fearing that they might damage company morale, it should be pointed out that educational programs aimed at acquainting employees with the problems of theft and stressing everyone's role in successful security have resulted in boosting morale and in enlisting the aid of all employees in the effort.

Here, as in other areas of security, employees should be encouraged to report losses immediately. They must never be encouraged to act as informers or asked to report on their coworkers. If they simply report the circumstances of loss, it is the job of security to carry forward further investigation or to take such action as may seem indicated.

Large-Quantity Theft

Referring again to the DoT report, we find that 60 percent of the theft of cargo consists of merchandise in quantities of one or more cases but of less than a full load. Thefts in such amounts are no longer in the category of pilferage. This becomes theft, usually engaged in by one or more persons who are in it for profit—for resale through traffickers in stolen goods.

Thieves may or may not be employees, but since in either case they need information about the nature of the merchandise on hand or expected, they will usually find accomplices inside who are in a position to have that information. They are interested in knowing what kinds of cargo are available in order to make a decision about what merchandise to hit, depending on its value and on the demands of the fencing organization with which they deal.

Dealers in stolen goods are subject to the vagaries of the marketplace in the same way legitimate businessmen are. Whereas a certain kind of merchandise may find a ready market today, it may move slowly tomorrow. Such dealers are anxious to move their goods rapidly not so much because of fear of detection (since even if they are found, mass produced goods of any nature are difficult if not impossible to identify as stolen once they find their way into other hands) but rather because they generally want to avoid the overhead and the attention created by a large warehousing operation.

Removal of Goods

Once the thieves have the information, they need to arrange to take over the merchandise and remove it from the premises. To do this, they will usually try to work with some employee of the warehouse or freight terminal.

In cases where accountability procedures are weak or inadequately supervised, thieves have few problems. In tighter operations, they may try to bribe a guard, or they might forge the papers of an employee of a customer firm. They might even create confusion—such as a fire in a waste bin or a broken water pipe—in order to divert attention in those few moments needed to accomplish the actual theft. Generally the stolen goods are taken from the facility in an authorized vehicle driven either by the thieves, who have false identification papers and forged shipping documents, or by an authorized driver who is more often than not working with the thieves.

Disposal of Stolen Goods

Disposal of the goods usually presents no problem since it is customary for thieves to steal from an order placed for any one of certain kinds of merchandise. The loot is normally presold.

It might be noted at this point that it is for this reason principally that cooperation between private security and public law enforcement is so vital in the war against cargo theft. No thief will continue to steal unless there is a ready market for the stolen goods. In the hearings of the Select Committee on Small Business, one of the most inescapable conclusions was that the fences were the kingpins behind the majority of the thefts taking place. They dictated the nature of the merchandise to be taken, the price to be paid, and the amount wanted. They directed the thefts without ever becoming involved—in many cases never even seeing the merchandise they have bought, warehoused, and sold. Without the fences—many of whom are otherwise legitimate businesspeople—the markets would shrink, the distribution networks would disappear, and losses would be dramatically reduced. Another possibility discovered by a major retailer has been the theft of merchandise by employees who either sell merchandise at local flea markets or advertise in local papers. One individual reportedly stole electronic items and developed a business through advertising in local papers for some time before getting caught.

Unfortunately only sporadic efforts have been made to break up the big fencing operations, and the business of thievery thrives. Any assistance that private security can give to public law enforcement by way of instant and full reports on thefts can help to combat these shady operations, and all private industry will benefit immeasurably in the long run.

Terminal Operations

Terminal operations are probably more vulnerable to theft than other elements of the shipping system. Truck drivers mingle freely with personnel of the facility, and associations can readily develop that lead to collusion. Receiving clerks can receipt goods that never arrive; shipping clerks can falsify invoices; checkers can overload trucks, leaving a substantial percentage of the load unaccounted for and therefore disposable at the driver's discretion.

Here again, these thefts can be controlled with a tight accountability system, but too often such facilities fail to install such a procedure or to follow up on it after it is in effect. This is poor economy, even under the most difficult situations when seasonal pressures are at their highest.

Railway employees on switching duty at a freight terminal can also divert huge amounts of goods. They can easily divert a car to a siding accessible to thieves who will unload it at an opportune time. This same device can be employed to loot trucks that have been loaded for departure the next morning. Unless these trucks are securely locked and parked where they are under surveillance by security personnel, they can be looted with ease. Drivers can park their trucks unlocked near a perimeter fence for later unloading unless the positioning and securing of the vehicle is properly supervised.

In all cases, a professional thief is someone with a mission. Such people cannot be deterred by the threat of possible detection. They recognize the possibility, accept the risk, and make it their business to circumvent detection. Only alert and active countermeasures will serve to reduce losses from their efforts.

Surveillance

There must be strict guard surveillance at entrances and exits, and there must be patrol activity at perimeters and through yards, docks, and buildings. Key control must be tight and painstakingly supervised. Cargo should be stored in controlled security areas that are enclosed, alarmed, and burglar-resistant. High-value cargo should be stored in high-security areas within the cargo area. Special locks, alarms, and procedures governing access should be employed to provide the highest possible security for these sensitive goods. The use of CCTV (closed circuit TV) and other surveillance technology is covered elsewhere in the book.

Shipments of unusual value should be confidential, and only those employees who are directly concerned with loading or unloading or transporting such shipments should be aware of their schedules. Teletype and fax information about such movements should be restricted, and trailer numbers should be covered while the vehicle is in the terminal. Employees involved in any way with such shipments should be specially selected and further indoctrinated in the need for discretion and confidentiality.

A Total Program

Adequate physical security installations supported by guard and alarm surveillance will go a long way toward protecting the facility from the thief, but these measures must be backed by proper personnel and cargo movement systems, strict accountability procedures, and continuing management supervision and presence to insure that all systems are carried out to the letter. Regular inspections of all facets of the operation followed by prompt remedial action if necessary are essential to the success of the security effort.

Planning for Security

It is important to the security of any transportation company, shipper, or freight terminal operation to draw up an effective plan of action to provide for overall protection of assets. The plan must be an integrated whole wherein all the various aspects are mutually supportive.

In the same sense in large terminal facilities occupied by a number of different companies, all individual security plans must be integrated to provide for overall security as well as for protection of individual enterprises. Without full cooperation and coordination among participating companies, much effort will be expended uselessly and the security of the entire operation could be threatened.

Such a plan should establish area security classifications. Designated parts of the building or the total yard area of the facility should be broken down into controlled, limited, and exclusion areas. These designations are useful in defining the use of specific areas and the mounting security classifications of each.

Controlled, Limited, and Exclusion Areas

Controlled areas are those restricted as to entrance or movement by all but authorized personnel and vehicles. Only part of a facility will be designated a controlled area since general offices, freight receiving, personnel, restrooms, cafeterias, and locker rooms may be used by all personnel, some of whom would be excluded if these facilities were located within an area where traffic was limited. Within this area itself, all movement should be controlled and under surveillance at all times.

It should additionally be marked by a fence or other barrier, and access to it should be limited through as few gates as possible.

Limited areas are those within the controlled area where an even greater degree of security is required. Sorting, handling of broken lots, storage, and reconstituting of cases might be vulnerable functions handled in these areas.

Exclusion areas are used only for the handling and storage of high-value cargo. They normally consist of a crib, vault, cage, or room within the limited area. The number of people authorized to enter this area should be strictly limited, and the area should be under surveillance at all times.

Since such areas should be locked whenever they are not actually in use, careful key control is of extreme importance.

Pass Systems

All employees entering or leaving should be identified, and their authorization to be there should be checked. Each employee should be identified by a badge or pass, using one of the several systems discussed in Chapter 10.

Vehicle Control

The control of the movement and checking the contents of all vehicles entering or leaving a controlled area is essential to the security plan. All facility vehicles should be logged in and out on those relatively rare occasions when it is necessary for them to leave the controlled area. They should be inspected for load and authorization.

All vehicles entering the controlled area should be logged and checked for proper documents. The fastest and most efficient means of recording necessary data is by use of a camera such as a Regiscope, which will record all of the required information on a single photograph. This should include the driver's license, truck registration, trailer or container number, company name, way bill number, delivery notice, a document used to authorize pickup or delivery, time of check, and the driver's picture if it is not on the driver's license.

The seal on inbound loaded trailers should be checked, and the driver should be issued a pass that is time-stamped on entering and leaving the area and that designates the place for pickup or delivery.

All vehicles leaving the area should surrender their passes at the gate where their seals will be checked against the shipping documents. Unsealed vehicles will be inspected as will the cabs of all carriers leaving the facility. Partial load vehicles should be returned to the dock from time to time on a random basis for unloading and checking cargo under security supervision. They should also be sealed while they are in the staging area.

Loading and unloading must be carefully and constantly supervised since it is generally agreed that the greater part of cargo loss occurs during this operation and during the daylight hours.

Other Security Planning

The security plan must also specify those persons having access to security areas, and it must specify the various components necessary for physical security such as barriers, lighting, alarm systems, fire protection systems, locks, and communications. It must detail full instructions for the guard force. These instructions must contain both general orders applicable to all guards and special orders pertaining to specific posts, patrols, and areas.

There must be provision for emergency situations. Specific plans for fire, flood, storm, or power failure should be part of the overall plan of action. Who to call in an emergency should also be specified.

After the security plan has been formulated and implemented, it must be reexamined periodically for flaws and for ways to improve it and keep it current with existing needs. Circulation of the plan should be limited and controlled. It must be remembered that such a plan, however well conceived, is doomed at the outset unless it is constantly and carefully supervised.

Security Surveys

Security managers of freight terminals or companies engaged in shipping will be continually occupied with surveys of the facility under their security supervision. Security surveys were discussed in detail in Chapter 7.

An initial survey must be made to formulate the security plan governing the premises. It should be thorough enough to detect the smallest weaknesses in the operation and to provide the information needed to prepare adequate defenses. Further surveys will be necessary to evaluate the effectiveness of the program established, and followup surveys should determine whether all regulations and procedures are being followed. Additional surveys may be necessary to reevaluate the security picture following changes in operational procedures in the facility or to make special studies of particular features of the security plan.

Inspections

In addition to these surveys, essentially designed to evaluate the security operation as a whole or to reevaluate it in the light of changing conditions, the security manager should make regular inspections of the facility to check on the performance of security personnel and to check the operating condition of the facility. Such inspections should include potential trouble areas and should not overlook a check of fire equipment and alarm systems.

Education

If the security plan is to succeed, it must have the full cooperation and support of all employees in the facility. This can only be achieved by a continuing program of education in the meaning and the importance of effective security in every phase of the business.

All personnel should be indoctrinated at the time of their employment, and a continuing program should be instituted to update the staff on current and anticipated problems. More advanced courses on procedures might be instituted for management personnel. Part of this program should be devoted to educating employees in the importance of security to each individual and job.

Security reminders are also important to keep the subject of security constantly alive in the minds of everyone. Posters, placards, and notices prominently posted are all effective devices for getting the message across. Leaflets or pamphlets covering more details can be distributed to employees in their pay envelopes.

Cargo in Transit

The Threat of Hijacking

Although the crime itself is dramatic and receives much publicity, armed hijacking of an entire tractor-trailer with a full load of merchandise represents only 1 percent of the losses suffered by the shipping industry as a whole. This is clearly not to say that it is a minor matter. On the contrary, such a crime is of extreme importance to the carrier taking the loss because the enormity of the theft represents a huge financial blow in one stroke, whatever its significance in the overall percentages.

There is, however, little that can be done by a driver who is forced over by a car carrying armed and threatening hijackers. When it comes to that point, the driver has little choice but to comply. The load is lost, but hopefully the driver is unhurt. There is little that private security can do in such cases, and it is indeed fortunate that the incidence of such crimes is as low as it is. The matter is in the hands of public law-enforcement agencies and must be handled by them.

If there is cause to believe that hijacking of a load is an imminent possibility, trucks should be scheduled for nonstop hauls and rerouted around high-risk areas. Schedules should be adjusted so that carriers do not pass through high-risk areas at night. In extreme cases, trucks might be assigned to travel in pairs or in larger convoys. Very high-value loads that are deemed especially vulnerable can be followed by company cars. Two look-alike trucks might make it more difficult to pinpoint the specific desired shipment. Such procedures constitute selective protection at best since they can be used only infrequently and are impractical for general application. The second driver, however, would be assigned the task of identifying the persons, the vehicle used, and so on and of reporting the hijacking if it occurs.

Other aspects of theft on a line haul can be dealt with, however, and it is important that procedures be established that will serve to protect the cargo.

Personnel Qualifications

The cardinal rule in the management of a transportation concern is that those assigned to line hauling duties must be of the highest integrity. Drivers and helpers must be carefully screened before they are hired, and they must be carefully evaluated by personnel and security managers before they are given this critical responsibility. An irresponsible driver can cost the company all or part of a load, and whether the loss is unintentional or the result of the driver's carelessness, the cost to the company will be the same.

Many cases have been reported where drivers set themselves up as victims of a hijack. This is difficult if not impossible to prevent unless the honesty of the driver is unquestionable—an attitude that can only be determined by a careful screening process and regular analysis of the person's behavior and performance. Any changes in a driver's demeanor or lifestyle should be noted as deterioration of morale or a basic change in attitude toward the job might lead to future problems.

Procedures on the Road

All employees should receive specific instructions about procedures to be followed in every predictable situation on the road. The vehicle should be parked in well-lighted areas where it can be observed. It should be locked at all times, even if the driver sleeps in the cab. Trailers should be padlocked as well as sealed. A high-security seal, requiring a sizable tool to remove it, should always be used on valuable shipments that are parked overnight.

Drivers must be instructed never to discuss the nature of their cargos with anyone. Thieves frequently hang out at truck stops hoping to pick up information about the nature of loads passing through. All too often, the most innocent conversations among truckers can lead to the identification of a trailer containing high-value merchandise that, when it is spotted, becomes a target.

The driver should never deviate from the preplanned route. In the case of a forced detour or a rig breakdown or if in any way the schedule cannot be met, the driver must notify the nearest terminal immediately.

Trucks should be painted on the top as well as on the sides to facilitate identification by helicopter in the event of theft.

Seals

Among the many seals available today, the one in most common use is the metal railroad boxcar type. This is a thin band of metal that is placed and secured on the trailer in such a manner that the door or doors cannot be opened without breaking it, thus revealing that the doors have been opened and a theft has, or may have, taken place. They are easy to break and must be broken when the destination has been reached and the merchandise is unloaded. They in no way secure the doors, but are placed there simply as a device to indicate whether the doors have been opened at any point between terminal stops. Each seal is numbered and should identify the organization that placed the seal (see Figure 16.1).

All doors on a trailer must be sealed. Those trucks or trailers with multiple doors may habitually load by only one, in which case those doors not in regular use may carry the same seal for months at a time with only the rear being regularly sealed and unsealed.

Seal numbers must be recorded in a permanent log as well as in the shipping papers. The dock superintendent or security personnel should be responsible for recording seal numbers and affixing seals on all trucks. The seals should be positioned in such a way that locking handles securing the door cannot be operated without actually breaking the seal. Some truck or railway

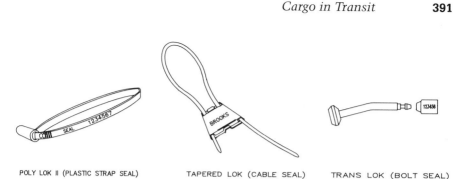

POLY LOK II (PLASTIC STRAP SEAL)   TAPERED LOK (CABLE SEAL)   TRANS LOK (BOLT SEAL)

Figure 16.1 Two security seals in common use. (Courtesy of E.J. Brooks Company.)

car locking devices are so large that several seals may have to be used in a chain to properly seal the carrier. In this case all seal numbers must be recorded.

Resealing

Trailers loaded to make several deliveries along the route must be resealed after each stop. To accomplish this, enough seals must be issued to be placed on the truck after each delivery is made. In this case, the truck is sealed at the point of origination and the seal number logged and entered in shipping documents. The additional, as yet unsealed, seals are also logged, and the numbers to be used at designated points of delivery are entered in the shipping documents. Figure 16.2 is a typical seal card showing the procedure.

When the first checkpoint is reached, the receiving clerk verifies the seal number of the truck. After the merchandise is unloaded, the next seal is affixed by the consignee, *not* the driver, as directed by the shipping documents. This procedure is followed at all stops, including the last one. There, a seal is affixed to the now-empty vehicle, which may return to the point of origin, where the seal will again be checked against the shipping documents.

Empty trailers should also be sealed immediately after being unloaded. This practice will discourage the use of empties to remove unauthorized material from dock areas, and it does not preclude the necessity of physical inspection of all vehicles leaving the controlled areas.

Seal Security

All seals must be held under the tightest possible security at all times. Previously unissued seals should be logged and secured on receipt. They should then be issued in numerical order, and the assignment of each should be duly noted in the log. The seal supply should be audited daily—a careful check to account for each seal, issued or not, should be made at the

SEAL CARD

Date: ____/____/____   From Warehouse #: _____   Trailer #: _____
Driver's Name: _____   First Store Scheduled Delivery Time: _____
Seal Verified On Departure By Security Guard: _____

		Seals On Arrival	Check If Seals Agree	Seal Change Stamp On Departure

1st. Store #: _____   Mailbag
Comments:

				Payroll
Side Door _____		☐	1st. Store Manager: _____
Rear Door _____		☐	Arrival Time _____
TR. Percent _____		☐	Departure Time _____

2nd. Store #: _____   Mailbag
Comments:

Side Door _____		☐	Payroll
		☐	2nd. Store-Manager: _____
Rear Door _____		☐	Arrival Time _____
TR. Percent _____		☐	Departure Time _____

3rd. Store #: _____   Mailbag
Comments:

Side Door _____		☐	Payroll
		☐	3rd. Store Manager: _____
Rear Door _____		☐	Arrival Time _____
TR. Percent _____		☐	Departure Time _____

4th. Store #: _____   Mailbag
Comments:

Side Door _____		☐	Payroll
		☐	4th. Store Manager: _____
Rear Door _____		☐	Arrival Time _____
TR. Percent _____		☐	Departure Time _____

5th. Store #: _____   Mailbag
Comments:

Side Door _____		☐	Payroll
		☐	5th. Store Manager: _____
Rear Door _____		☐	Arrival Time _____
TR. Percent _____		☐	Departure Time _____

Instructions: Store Manager

1. **Check** appropriate columns if seals agree. Immediately notify the Loss Prevention Manager at the servicing warehouse of any discrepancies.

2. Place seal from packet on trailer before departure.

3. Notate **arrival** and **departure** time in appropriate columns.

4. Use FULL signature (first and last name) for verification of requested information.

GP/AEA

Figure 16.2 Seal card.

same time. Without such regular inventories, the entire system can be seriously compromised. As a further part of such audit, all seals that are damaged and cannot be used as well as seals taken from incoming vehicles should be logged and secured until they can be destroyed.

Suggested Sealing System and Procedures

Introduction

The purpose of a seal is to reveal evidence of entry. The best-made seals or any other security devices are only as good as the procedures and systems used for their applications. The following report is designed to aid a seal user in developing the correct systems and procedures in order to halt pilferage and theft.

Ordering and Storage

A. Ordering
1. The responsibility of buying protective seals should belong to only one person.
2. All seal orders should originate from the home office or from a predetermined ordering location.
3. The seal manufacturer should be instructed to ship the seals to a specific person's attention at either the home office or another designated location.
4. In addition to consecutive numbering, the company name or initials should be embossed onto each seal.
5. Each terminal or transfer facility should be coded by letter, numeral, or color.
B. Storage
1. All seals and security devices should be kept in a controlled area in order to prevent unauthorized people from obtaining them for illegal use.

Outbound Recording

A. Maintain one log book for outbound seal recording and a separate log book for inbound seal recording.
B. Use hardcover books; do not use loose-leaf books.

C. The outbound log should contain the following information.
   1. The date and time the seal is applied
   2. The number of the trailer
   3. The load destination
   4. The name of the person applying the seal
   5. The name of the driver
D. If the driver is not part of the shippers' organization, the goods inventory count and the seal application should be made in the presence of the shippers' representative. The driver will note on the bill of lading or on the shipping order the seal number applied at the shippers' dock.

Application

A. In order to maintain control over the sealing system, all seals must be properly applied and checked by a security person.
B. Select a proper seal based on destination, value, and susceptibility to theft. A high-security seal may be required.
C. The following procedures for application should be used:
   1. Seal the side as well as the rear doors.
   2. Run the seal strap through the hasp once. Seals wrapped through the hasp more than once become illegible.
   3. Listen for the "click" when inserting the point of the seal into the locking sheath.
   4. In order to insure a positive seal, pull the strap and twist the section of the seal that was inserted into the locking mechanism.

Gate Procedures

A. All drivers will surrender their gate passes to the guard.
B. The guard will verify the information as presented by the driver.
C. A guard should record:
   1. Tractor number, company, and license plate number

    2. Trailer container number

    3. The seal's number, color, and coding

    4. The driver's name and driver's license number

    5. The date and time

D. In order to prevent a pattern from developing, assorted low-value shipments should also be high-security sealed.

E. The guard should have different colored seals available to permit spot checking of loads at random.

F. All spot checks should be made in the presence of another security officer.

Broken Seals

A. Should it be necessary to break a seal before its arrival at the final destination, the following information should be recorded, especially at highway weigh stations:

    1. The name of the person breaking the seal

    2. The reason for breaking the seal

    3. The time and date the seal was broken

    4. The serial number of the broken seal

    5. The serial number of the replacement seal

    6. The names of witnesses to the breaking of the seal

B. The broken seal report must be filed with the terminal manager and/or the security officer at the outbound terminal regardless of how far the driver is from the point of origin.

Seal Removal and Inbound Recording

A. In order to insure the integrity of a seal before its removal, a physical check must be made.

B. The following procedures for seal removal are recommended:

    1. Only authorized security personnel should remove seals.

    2. Enter in the inbound seal log the name, serial number, and all coding information appearing on the seal. Be sure to verify from the manifests that it is the original seal.

    3. Compare the name, serial number, and all coding

information appearing on the seal with the corresponding shipping papers.

4. Prior to removing the seal, insure that it has not been shortened or falsely sealed. Check for strange marks and tampering.

5. Pull and twist the seal to the left and right to insure that the seal head has not been violated.

6. Any discrepancy should be reported to the person(s) assigned to accept such statements as well as recorded in the inbound seal log.

7. All shipments received with a violated seal must be reported as noted in the previous section and resealed if additional transportation is required.

8. Any evidence of theft should be reported to the security department, and investigation should be begun immediately, regardless of the hour.

Supplementary Procedures

A. The following steps may be taken to reinforce the seal control program and discourage would-be pilferers:

1. Insure that the fastening devices and hinges securing the door and the locking handles cannot be removed without violating the seal.

2. Use color-coded seals to differentiate commodities, terminals, warehouses, plants, inbound or outbound shipments, and time periods.

3. Use different colored seals for trailers returning with empty loads in order to prevent drivers from privately using trailers on return trips and from transporting cargo without authority.

4. Periodically change the seal colors to prevent usage of unauthorized old seals.

5. Companies, shipping a trailer load of merchandise within a local area and making two to seven stops, may secure the trailer with a different colored seal after each stop.

High Security Seal Locks

A. Conventional metal seals or plastic seals are not always effective.

B. The development of heavy duty, self-locking, and serially numbered cable or heavy metal seal locks arose to provide physical security as well as seal integrity.
C. The use of high security seal locks is recommended for the following areas:
   1. High-security shipments
   2. Rail, ship, or air freight and intermodal shipments
   3. International shipments
   4. Shipping or storing in high-crime areas or parked vehicles
D. Either heavy-duty cable or bolt cutters should be required to remove high security locks.
   1. The use of the cutting tools should be carefully controlled.
   2. Drivers should not be allowed to carry cutters except for special occasions.

Padlocks

A. Seals function primarily to protect cargo over long distances. The padlock's basic function is to secure cargo on local deliveries.
B. The following padlock procedures should be established to ensure their effective use in your security program:
   1. A key- and padlock-control log book should be created.
   2. Use hardcover books; do not use looseleaf books.
   3. The key- and padlock-control log book should contain the following information:
      a. The date and time the key and padlock are taken
      b. The number of the trailer
      c. The load destinations
   4. All keys and padlocks must be numbered.
   5. Master keys must be restricted to two specific individuals.
   6. Locks should be fastened to the truck with a cable or chain.
   7. The padlock should incorporate heel and toe locking of the shackle.
   8. The padlock should incorporate a key-retention feature when the lock is open in order to:
      a. Prevent the loss of the key

b. Insure mandatory locking after each use
9. All locks, keys, and the key- and padlock-control logs must be kept in a secure place.
10. The additional use of a plastic or metal seal will further insure your padlock security programs.

Trailer Kingpin Locks

A. Trailer kingpin locks provide maximum protection against theft in:
1. Terminal yards
2. Road emergencies when the truck is separated from the trailer
B. A trailer kingpin lock will provide antihijacking protection if the proper procedures are followed:
1. Record in the security load register whether or not the kingpin lock has been applied and if so by whom.
2. The kingpin lock and key should be numbered.
3. Control over keys and locks must be maintained.
4. Follow all security procedures as noted in the previous section.
5. Choose a kingpin lock with a simple design in order to encourage its use by the employees.
6. Periodic maintenance and cleaning of the kingpin lock will ensure an effective locking mechanism as well as long life and continuous use.
7. Maintain a separate security load area.
8. The security load area should be readily visible to operations and/or security personnel.
9. All trailers with high-value cargo must be kingpin locked and kept in the secured area.
10. Kingpin locks should be sizable, round to prevent false hook-up on a fifth wheel, and constructed of forged, not cast, steel.
11. Place a sign on the air and electrical hook-up to forewarn drivers of the kingpin lock.

Review Questions

1. Why is it said that the greater burden in preventing cargo thefts falls on private security rather than on public law enforcement?
2. Describe the operation of an invoice system that would establish accountability for all merchandise in shipment.
3. What are some policies and procedures that would be effective in deterring pilferage?
4. Define controlled areas, limited areas, exclusion areas.
5. Offer procedures for the control of the movement of and contents in all vehicles entering or leaving a controlled area.

References

1. "Crime Against Small Business: A Report of the Small Business Administration Transmitted to the Select Committee on Small Business United States Senate" (Washington, D.C.: GPO, 1969).
2. Ibid.
3. Louis Tyska and Lawrence Fennelly, *Controlling Cargo Theft* (Stoneham, Mass.: Butterworth, 1983), pp. xxvii–xxix.

17 □□□ □□□ □□□

Computer Security

This chapter includes material from "Computer Security" by John M. Carroll[1] and "Computer Security" by Terry Magel.[2]

In the past 40 years, American business, in an almost explosive evolution, has made tremendous advances in its capacity to gather, store, and deal with vast amounts of computerized information. This ability has resulted in great improvements in the efficiency and flexibility of all financial, marketing, and design systems that can provide instant playback describing inventories, market position, and potential revenues at any given time.

There seems to be no end to the benefits to business of computerization, and the more benefits it creates, the more dependent on its magic we become. In the past decade or so, the computer has become the nerve center of our commercial activity. Indeed many modern companies frankly admit that they could not operate without the computer. In fact, "the U.S. Labor Department estimates that, by the year 2000, 80 percent of American workers will use computers and computer data on their jobs."[3]

Computer Databases

Government

The U.S. government has vast quantities of information about its citizens held in computers. The FBI maintains the National Crime Information Center (NCIC). The Bureau of the Census, the Internal Revenue Service (IRS), and the Social Security Adminstration also have extensive files on individuals.

The NCIC was established in 1967. This system connects 60,000 police agencies. There are well over 8,000,000 criminal history records contained in this file alone. Every day the NCIC system is accessed over 540,000 times with requests for information or to change information in the database.

The IRS processes over 95,000,000 tax returns each year—sorted through the use of bar codes and stored on magnetic tapes. The returns are compared with information reported from banks, employers, and insurance companies for accuracy. IRS computers can process over 30,000 returns an hour. The IRS is currently working to bring into full operation electronic tax returns and debit/credit operations with taxpayer banking accounts.

Corporate

TRW Data Systems of California maintains files on over 90,000,000 U.S. citizens, selling information on credit histories to stores and credit card companies.

Compuserve Information Service provides subscriptions to its database of news and business bulletins, banking services, and an on-line encyclopedia. Compuserve has over 500,000 members.

Computer Crime

Computer crime is defined as any action not sanctioned in law or conventional business practice that is harmful to persons or property and that is either directed against or employs high-tech information systems.

Why worry about computer crime? A recent U.S. Department of Justice study gives an analysis of computer crime (see Table 17.1).

The FBI has estimated that the average annual loss to the corporate United States due to computer crime is $600,000 based on reported incidents. This figure is low when other national estimates range from $3 to $5 billion annually.[4] Usually computer crime is nonviolent although there have been at least three murders in the New York City area that stemmed from computer crime and certainly the terrorist attacks on computer centers in France and Italy during 1979 and 1980 can scarcely be called nonviolent. In general, how-

Table 17.1 Types of Computer Crime

Type of Computer Crime	Percentage of Total	Average Loss
Physical Destruction	14	$836,000
Theft of Data/Programs	28	$3,322,000
Data Manipulation	43	$1,468,000
Unauthorized Use	15	$32,000

Source: Terry Magel, "Computer Security," in *Suggested Preparation for Careers in Security/Loss Prevention*, John Chuvala III and Robert James Fischer, eds. (Dubuque, Iowa: Kendall/Hunt Publishing Company), 1991, p. 107.

ever, computer crime involves fraud and deceit rather than stealth or violence.

The federal government has recognized the seriousness of the problem by passing the Computer Fraud and Abuse Act of 1986, which gives the federal government jurisdiction over interstate computer crimes and crimes involving computers used by the federal government. The bill makes it a crime to access classified information contained in a computer without the owner's authorization. This also includes financial records and credit histories as well as trespass into government computers. Penalities range from $5000–100,000 or imprisonment from 1 to 20 years. The act covers hackers (amateur computer operators who access systems without authorization) and their abuse of passwords and bulletin boards (computer listings of services that are available through the computer).

There are at least two reasons to view an upsurge in computer crime with alarm. First a successful computer crime can be extremely profitable to its perpetrator. Some observers have placed the average return in excess of $500,000. This can be a staggering loss to the victim; more often, it is shared broadly throughout society.

The second reason for concern is that the fabric of our society is held together by high-tech systems and the confidence of the public in the integrity of these systems is essential to the smooth functioning of society. Acts that threaten information systems strike at the heart of society.

What is so special about computer crime? Most computer crimes can ultimately be resolved in terms of theft, forgery, false pretense, and fraud. Why then should it be addressed as a special category? The answer is that successful investigation, prosecution, and prevention of computer crime require that criminal justice officials acquire technical knowledge not traditionally part of their training. There are five reasons to believe that computer crime will continue to increase.

Maturation of the Criminal Population

As criminals grow older, they tend to abandon violent crime in favor of less risky and more profitable criminal pursuits. There is no criminal endeavor more lucrative than that of computer crime and none with less risk to the perpetrator. We can expect that some of the demographic bubble that strained correctional services in the 1970s and 1980s will take to computer crime as they outgrow the 15–25 age bracket. Indeed many offenders have been trained in data processing as part of well-meaning rehabilitation programs!

Middle-Class Disaffection

It has been said that the rich get richer, the poor get welfare, and the middle class pays the shot. Inflation has pushed the good life beyond the reach of many middle-class taxpayers. Moreover the ranks of middle management are quickly filling up. Passage to upper management is becoming increasingly competitive and selective.

For all these reasons, and maybe more, we can predict a glut of highly trained and critically placed men and women increasingly frustrated by unfulfilled and unfulfillable expectations. These people, if they have access to the levers of computer power, may, if they are confronted with insoluble problems, resort to computer crime.

Rising Computer Literacy

The four 13-year-old New York schoolboys who penetrated a corporate computer in Montreal speak eloquently to the pervasive spread of computer literacy. Children growing up with an intimate knowledge of the latest computers might see nothing wrong with penetrating someone else's machine. Indeed some of them see every new security safeguard as a challenge to be answered.

Concentration of Assets in Computers

Every day a trillion dollars change hands worldwide over computerized wire funds transfer networks. Major banks turn over their capitalization that way 800 times a year. This is but a small fraction of the total flow, but it is an immense temptation to potential computer criminals. With electronic funds transfer systems now tapping every consumer's pocket, even more money is at risk. Consider that in 1978 Stanley Mark Rifkin perpetrated one of the largest electronic funds transfer scams against the Security Pacific National Bank of California. The total loss was over $10,000,000. As a computer consultant to the bank, Rifkin entered the bank's electronic funds transfer room under pretense that he was conducting an audit of the bank's wire transfer operations. He then recorded the secret authorization codes for transferring funds. After leaving the bank, he called the transfer room, identifying himself as an employee of the bank's international department. Using secret codes, he authorized the transfer of $10.2 million from Security Pacific to the Irving Trust Company of New York. In New York, he transferred these funds to Zurich.

Response of the Criminal Justice Community

The fact that the criminal justice community has thus far failed to respond to the challenge of computer crime is perhaps rooted in its non-violent, impersonal nature. There is no bleeding and battered victim crying for retribution. This is perhaps why computer criminals incur less than a one in a hundred chance of going to jail. Judges may deal leniently with computer criminals because our legal system historically has assessed the seriousness of crime by its potential for personal injury or loss of life. The fact that computer criminals seldom come to trial may derive from the extreme difficulty or futility of building cases against them.

Increasingly the onus will be on the private sector to safeguard its own computer-stored assets. The emphasis must necessarily be on security rather than on detection; it takes an average of two years to establish a computer fraud case and may require the victimized firm to produce in court its detailed corporate records with all the warts showing.

To a degree unequalled in nearly any other field, computer security is the only answer to protection of computer-stored assets.

Computer Vulnerabilities

Probably no one element in business, including catastrophic fire and the ravages of noncomputerized internal theft, presents a greater potential to wipe out an entire business as quickly and as effectively as does the computer. The dangers that can befall a computer center or can be created by it encompass virtually the entire operation of the business it serves. Viruses, embezzlement, programming fraud, program penetration, operator error, input error, program error, theft of confidential information, and plain carelessness are a few of the problems that can arise in routine operation. Add to this the potential for fire, riot, flood, and sabotage.

The points of vulnerability in computer systems are the central processors, storage devices, communication facilities, remote terminals, users, and systems personnel.

The central processor is vulnerable to failure of protection circuits and misuse of privileged instructions. Its software is vulnerable to bypassing of file protection and access control programs or falsification of user identification.

Storage devices are vulnerable to unauthorized copying of stored information, theft of removable media, and hardware or software failure that could result in compromise.

Communications facilities can be compromised by undesired signal data emanations, crosstalk between secure and insecure circuits, and technical surveillance devices.

Users may misrepresent or forge identification or authorization or seek unauthorized access to sensitive material by browsing, and they can use debugging procedures to circumvent security mechanisms.

Remote terminals can produce undesired signal data emanations, are vulnerable to technical surveillance devices, and produce compromising text as hard copy or remnant images on platens or ink ribbons.

Systems personnel have normal access to supervisor programs, accounting files, systems files, and protective features, and if these individuals are not loyal and reliable, they can become security risks.

The most probable kinds of attack fall into seven categories:

1. Subversion can result in destruction of equipment or facilities, disclosure of classified programs and data, interruption of service, improper modification of programs or data, loss of programs or data, theft of property, and misuse of resources.
2. Negligence can result in disclosure of classifed information, corruption of programs or data, interruption of service, loss of programs or data, and destruction of equipment facilities.
3. Accidents can result in interruption of service, corruption of programs or data, loss of programs or data, and destruction of equipment and facilities.
4. Covert attacks by nonemployees (stealth and deceit) can result in disclosure of classified information, interruption of service, corruption of programs or data, destruction of equipment and facilities, and theft of property.
5. Overt attacks by outsiders (force) can result in interruption of service and destruction of equipment and facilities.
6. Overt attacks by employees can result in interruption of service and destruction of equipment and facilities.
7. Input errors can result in interruption of service and corruption of data.

Classic Computer Crime Methods

Data Manipulation

Changing the data during or after input into a computer system is the simplest, safest, and most common computer crime method. Any size business is vulnerable to it. It can be performed by anyone associated with or having access to the process of creating, recording, transporting, encoding, examining, checking, converting, or transforming the data that are eventually entered. Examples include: changing credit standing in credit bureau files, deleting injurious data from one's personnel file, changing grades in student transcript files, or changing overtime hours in payroll records.

Salami Techniques

This descriptive term implies trimming off very small amounts of money from large numbers of sources and diverting the slices into one's own or into an accomplice's account. This form of crime is most common in banking environments with their large number of savings and/or checking accounts and their automated financial processing. By creating a new program or altering an existing one, an employee can randomly reduce a few thousand accounts in one- to five-cent amounts. The accumulated sums can then be withdrawn by normal methods from the receiving account.

Trojan Horse

Covertly placing a computer code that will perform an unauthorized function inside a legitimate program enables the illegal code to be protected from detection as if hidden behind a screen. The fraudulent code is not quickly discovered because it normally allows the legitimate program to perform its intended purpose. Examples of this include taking a client list from a company and selling it to a competitor and scrambling or erasing from the legitimate program data in the files.

Computer Virus

A more dangerous form of the Trojan Horse, this method uses a self-replicating code. Piggybacking into a computer's memory, this type of code causes itself to be written onto other users' files or onto the computer's operating system programs in repeated sequences until all of the computer's memory and the files connected with it are written over with the worthless code.

Logic Bombs

Like the Trojan Horse, a logic bomb or time bomb is a computer code inserted by a programmer into legitimate software. It is, however, programmed to execute only at a specific time or under certain conditions. For example, a disgruntled payroll system programmer could insert a code that would erase the entire personnel file if their own name was ever removed from the records because their employment was terminated. Software developers themselves have also used this method against companies that buy software on credit. If the company does not pay for the software on time, the program self-destructs. If the software is paid for by the agreed-on date, the software developers send the buyers instructions detailing how to "defuse" the bomb.

Time Stealing

Accessing a computer without authorization uses the computer's resources in place of an authorized user. Time stealing is like driving another person's car without their knowledge. Examples include using a company computer system to maintain private business records, playing computer games on company computers during or after working hours against company policy, and using company computers and software to produce, sell, and/or distribute another product.

Electronic Eavesdropping

This is tapping into communication lines over which digitized computer data and messages are being sent without authorization. Using technologically advanced listening devices, eavesdropping can be performed on traditional telephone circuits, local or side area networks, microwave transmission lines, and even satellite transmission networks. If data transmitted are not encoded, capturing and transforming the data is equivalent to using a clandestine tape recorder to record a standard telephone conversation.

Software Piracy

Software piracy is making unauthorized copies of copyrighted, marketable or nonmarketable computer programs. It has been estimated that for each legitimate copy of software that is sold, between 4 and 30 additional copies are made illegally. One extravagant case reported a company that legally purchased a word-processing package and copied it for its 142 secretaries. A survey by FutureComputing Inc. of Dallas revealed that piracy cost software vendors $1.3 billion between 1981 and 1984. Other estimates place the losses for the top software vendors at $100 million each year. Although most copied programs are not resold, they deny vendors and software developers profits that would have accrued legally.

The Need for Security

In the face of the risks to this sensitive machinery and to the enormous accumulation of data concentrated in a limited area as well as business's ever-increasing reliance on the computer, many firms continue to ignore the dangers. Many of them confess an uneasiness about security for the computer, but claim they cannot afford an effective protective program.

There is no question that computer security can be costly, but the stakes are too high to try to effect economies in this area. The fact is that any company involved with computers—and that includes most companies in the United States—cannot afford to have a comprehensive security program that will protect their computer operation. Since such installations can represent an investment running into the millions of dollars, a security program costing from $50,000 to $250,000 is not an unreasonable expense.

Ideally the program designed to provide computer security will be an integrated part of the company's overall loss-prevention effort. It should be administered by a specialist in computer operation, but it should report to, and be coordinated with, the larger program. It must encompass physical security, procedural or operating security, access and traffic controls, disaster planning and contingency procedures, employee education programs, and a painstaking screening procedure in the employment of computer personnel.

An effective security program is essential to any electronic data processing (EDP) operation, and it must have the vigorous support of an informed management. It is not always easy to convince chief financial officers of the need to expend substantial funds for security, but when the risks are as high as they are in computer operations, top management *must* somehow be convinced.

Physical Security

The physical security needs of a computer installation are, generally, the same as those for any business or industrial establishment. The goal is essentially to deny access to the computer area to all unauthorized persons.

In many respects, this is easier to apply to a computer installation than it is to other facilities since only a limited number of people have reason to be in the area in the first place. Whereas an industrial facility may have to make provision for the movement of employees of various trades, truckers, supervisory personnel, and others in great numbers, a computer center is not obliged to put up with any appreciable traffic of this kind to operate. It can and should be closed to all but those specifically assigned to it. Physical se-

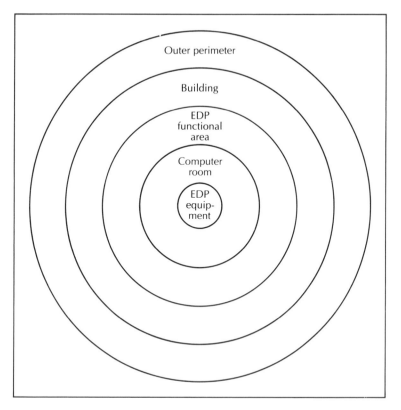

Figure 17.1 The lines-of-protection concept takes advantage of existing features so that the most sensitive asset, the computer, lies within several concentric perimeters.

curity can be based on the lines-of-protection concept of keeping one's most sensitive assets within concentric perimeters that become increasingly well-defined as one progresses inward. The lines-of-protection concept is illustrated in Figure 17.1.

Structural Barriers

To prevent surreptitious or forced entry, the facility should be housed within an area already secured against intrusion or if possible in a separate building far enough from other structures to be free from the danger of fire spreading from them. In any event, it should be protected by appropriate fencing, whether standing alone or housed within the perimeter protection of another building. It should be adequately lighted, and it should not be obstructed by ornamental plantings and landscaping that could provide concealment for an intruder. All other features of physical security design should be considered.

Site Selection

In considering location, it is important to evaluate the environmental and human factors that might affect the site as well as the services available in the area. Some of the factors that must be considered are discussed below.

Fire and Police Protection

Check response capability and general efficiency. In this same regard, the availability of central station alarm protection and its reliability must be investigated.

Surrounding Neighborhood

High-crime areas are undesirable not so much because of computer vulnerability as because they create a problem in employee morale. Such a neighborhood could have an adverse effect on employee retention and could also serve to increase insurance premiums in various areas of coverage.

Access

The site must be easily accessible to its personnel. Ideally it should be served by adequate public transporation—remembering that virtually every such installation often has a three-shift or a 24-hour schedule.

Maintenance

The response time for manufacturer maintenance and repair personnel must be considered.

Space Requirements

The equipment required for a specific operation may take more space than the headquarters building can provide. The weight of the equipment also may be such that extensive and expensive remodeling may be needed in the existing building.

Natural Phenomena

Consideration must be given to the possibility of floods, earthquakes, hurricanes, and tornadoes. Obviously such disasters cannot in themselves be anticipated, but this possibility can be anticipated in the planned site. Earthquakes can be anticipated on or near existing faults; floods can be considered a possibility in certain types of areas. Some areas suffer from tornadoes or hurricanes more than do others. All of these factors must be considered before a site is finally chosen.

This evaluation should also take into account the presence of radar and microwave installations. In the past, there have been several cases of tapes being erased by radiation as much as an eighth of a mile away.

Environment

A tape library suffered a loss of more than $75,000 from acid fumes given off by a neighboring manufacturing facility. This is as much a problem of internal climate control as of location, but the presence of such potential pollutants as well as a high incidence of particulate matter in the air must be known and dealt with.

Power Source

Check the power company's record for reliability and for efficient and speedy response to power failures. Any fluctuation in line voltage can cause inaccuracies in data transfers. While some operations are not seriously hampered by fluctuations, with others the problem can be serious. Where this is the the case, the practice is to isolate the computer from the power from the local utility by the use of batteries, constantly recharged by line voltage, which supply the computer through solid-state interrupters.

Site location must also take into account the presence of water mains and proper drainage in the computer room and library if an already existing building is under consideration. Much damage has resulted from flooding caused by broken water mains or pipes, further complicated by the lack of adequate drainage.

Access Control

Since one of the principal means of computer security is access control, it must be planned so that those employees authorized to be in the EDP center can get in with a minimum of restrictions and red tape while unauthorized persons are positively excluded. A number of systems currently in use accomplish this with a high degree of success. For further discussion of access controls see Chapter 10.

Fire Protection

EDP centers are particularly vulnerable to fire. The maze of wires and equipment under the floor and the accumulation of paper from printouts in addition to the normal fuel load characteristic of any office make for substantial quantities of combustibles to feed any fire that might get started. The losses in such a fire usually are tremendous. The equipment involved is extremely costly, and the loss of data on destroyed tapes can be many times more harmful and expensive.

Causes of Fire

The causes of fires in EDP centers is a matter of some dispute. Potentially it would appear that the principal causes should be from electrical malfunctions. The miles of wiring and the possibilities of short circuits are powerful persuasions to exercise great care and to conduct frequent inspections in those areas accessible to inspection.

Statistically, however, the major cause of fire is from adjacent occupancies either in the same or neighboring buildings. Most EDP centers have been contructed and equipped to resist fire very effectively, but they are often located in buildings that are not so well protected. Obviously the computer will go down with the rest of the building in case of fire no matter how well it is itself protected. There have been cases where the floor has collapsed in a fire and dropped the computer and its attendant equipment into the fire below.

Careless use of cigarettes around accumulated waste paper is the second most common cause of fires in EDP centers, and electrical fires are the third most common. But although it is third on the list, the threat of fire from the power system is always present.

Sensors

Since some polyester-backed tape and diskettes used in computers can be rendered unreadable at temperatures of 150°F, it is essential that a sensor system providing the earliest possible warning of a fire be installed. The most economical time for installation of such a system is during the construction of the facility, but it must be done whether the facility is already built or not. Sensors should be located on ceilings, under raised floors, inside false ceilings, in air ducts, and within the equipment itself. This same protection must be extended to the tape library as well. The earliest warning comes from ionization or products-of-combustion detectors, which respond to the earliest stages of combustion before the development of smoke or flame. These sensors must be checked regularly to be certain they are in working condition.

Sprinkler Systems

Perhaps the most effective automatic fire extinguishing system in general use is the water sprinkler system, but its use in computer installations is a matter of considerable controversy. The Factory Mutual group of insurance companies favors the use of sprinklers in computer installations—and they are experts in the field of fire protection. IBM, the world's largest manufacturer of computers, has said that they are harmful to the equipment and should never be used. There are compelling arguments for both views.

In most cases, water from a sprinkler system will run indefinitely after it has been triggered by an alarm or by heat, until it is turned off manually. This continuous stream of water cools the burning material below the point of combustion so that it will not start to burn again after the water is turned off. This cooling effect can be important in cases of smoldering combustion (as opposed to flaming combustion).

Unfortunately, there are serious side effects in a computer application. If the power to the computer is not turned off before the water hits the equipment, the effect on electronic and electromechanical parts can be ruinous. Then too, tapes (disks) can be destroyed. Tapes (disks) are not at all affected by a short immersion in water, nor are they damaged by temperatures as high as 250° in a dry environment, but some can be ruined by a combination of heat and humidity. As noted above, they will deteriorate to unusability at 150°F in a humid environment. After sprinklers discharge into a fire, they produce steam that may quickly wipe out the tapes (disks) subject to wipe out.

There are answers to these problems. One lies in the installation of a system that sounds an alarm first and provides enough of a delay before water is discharged to allow an employee time to turn off the equipment before water is discharged from the sprinklers. This procedure could also be automatic, whereby the equipment was inactivated by the alarm prior to the flow of water. In such a case, the equipment would have to be dried out before it could be used again.

In cases where the facility is shut down, all equipment should be covered to protect it from the possibility of water damage. If a fire started inside one of the machines, it would burn away the cover and become accessible to the extinguishing efforts of the sprinkler, but the other unaffected machines would still be protected by covers.

Other Extinguishing Systems

Halon 1301, an inert, odorless gas, is an efficient extinguishing agent recommended by many authorities. This gas is nonconductive, leaves no residue, and is highly effective in fighting fires. It presents problems, however. It has no cooling effect, and although it is extremely effective when used against flaming combustion in solid fuels, it is considerably less effective against smoldering combustion. Every automatic halon system is limited by the quantity of halon contained in its storage receptacle. Whereas water will continue to flow until it is turned off, the halon will be discharged only until it is exhausted. Usually this will be enough, but in some cases of stubborn smoldering fires, it may not be.

Finally whereas halon in its normal use presents no hazard to humans, it is a toxic chemical. Although the National Fire Protection Association (NFPA) has stated it has no effect on humans in concentrations up to 7 percent, it does have harmful effects in higher concentrations. They further suggest that concentrations of 20 percent might even cause death if exposure to it is prolonged.

Halon systems are also extremely expensive and generally require a second halon system as a backup.

Carbon dioxide (CO_2) systems are as effective as halon, but CO_2 is very dangerous to use since it is deadly in the concentrations needed. All personnel must be evacuated from the immediate premises before it can be discharged. If a CO_2 system is installed, all personnel must be trained in evacuation procedures and indoctrinated in the dangers of this gas.

Dry chemicals are effective in smothering a fire, but they leave behind a residue of powder on the equipment and in the air that may be more harmful to the machines than the fire itself would be.

CO_2 extinguishers should be placed throughout the facility, and all personnel should be schooled in their use. These extinguishers are not a substitute for a total extinguishing system, but they are valuable for bringing small fires under control before they become big enough to require disruptive and expensive discharge of the main fire-prevention system.

General Fire Prevention

Perhaps the most important element in the fire-prevention program is the creation of a carefully supervised fire-resistant environment. This involves a trash disposal system that will prevent the otherwise inevitable buildup of waste paper in the computer area; the establishment of no-smoking rules in and around the computer room and the tape library; frequent inspections and cleanings under the raised floor; fireproofing all rugs, drapes, wallpaper, and furniture; sealing off all holes and passages that violate the fire-resistant integrity of floors, walls, and ceilings; and installing multiple manual cutoffs of air conditioning.

System Protection

Computer system security involves measures relating to hardware, computer programs, and communications. There are five defense mechanisms for computer system security:

1. Personnel security concerns the selection, screening, clearance, and supervision of employees.
2. Encryption of sensitive information protects data communications and sensitive files by making them unintelligible to personnel other than authorized recipients.
3. Technical surveillance inspection protects against intrusion devices that might be planted within secure premises.
4. Suppression of compromising emanations may be necessary because typewriters, terminals, line printers, and visual display units produce acoustical and electromagnetic emanations that can be intercepted, analyzed, and interpreted.
5. Line security safeguards communications lines from the physical access needed to implant intrusion devices. These mechanisms will be discussed in greater detail later in this chapter.

Backup Systems

Since most companies are dependent on computers, it is vital that some contingency plan be developed for emergencies of any kind that render computers inoperable. Such a breakdown could come from any of a number of sources—machine malfunctions, power failure, natural disaster, fire, malicious destruction, or even building renovation.

It is customary in setting up such a plan to locate a computer of the same model or configuration in another business, and to enter into some kind of mutual assistance pact, in which it is agreed that, if either party should suffer from some kind of breakdown, one can continue to operate on the other's computer.

This is sensible preplanning, but it must be pursued much further than this. It is important in the first place to remember that not all machines— even of the same model—are compatible. Systems vary according to ancillary equipment and memory size. Even in cases where the equipment is identical in every detail, differences in programs may cause incompatibility.

There is no real way of knowing whether one system will operate with another's software without a trial run. Before any mutual agreement is entered into, it is essential that each company test its needs on the other's equipment. If the systems are compatible, periodic test runs should still be made to verify the continuing compatibility of the systems. Since equipment and program changes are common in computer operations, there is always the distinct possibility that what is a suitable backup system today will be unusable when it is needed most. Only regular testing can establish this. Agreements to notify the other company of any changes in the system cannot be depended on.

Another problem that arises regularly in such agreements is the change in each party's requirements for machine time. If both concerns are on a 16-hour machine use schedule, they have a basic problem to begin with. Even if they are each on an 8- or a 12-hour schedule at the time the agreement is entered into, there is no assurance that their needs will not increase to such an extent that neither can fully accommodate the other. Ideally a similar agreement should be made with several companies to assure continued operation in the face of an emergency. This complicates the problem, but it is sufficiently important to make the effort worthwhile.

Since most manufacturers can now deliver an exact copy of a customer's machine promptly, an alternative to shared backup systems is an alternate site where a duplicate system can be installed. Site preparation, however, can still require a long time. One economical approach to providing such an alternate processing site for emergency use is for several companies to share a site that affords all facilities except the computer.

Off-Premises Protection

However effective security measures may be, there is always the possibility the defenses may be penetrated. If such penetration should result in the loss or destruction of stored data, the results could be catastrophic.

Here as elsewhere it is important to remember that a company, once it has undergone the difficult process of converting its operation to computers, cannot operate manually. Therefore the loss of much of its carefully accumulated data would be ruinous. The destruction of a database carrying perpetual inventory information or a record of accounts receivable could create problems from which the company might never recover. It is therefore essential that duplicates of such data be stored in some remote location where their protection can be assured.

Data stored in this manner must, of course, be regularly updated to reflect the current status of the company. How duplicate data are created, as well as the method and frequency of updating, are matters to be determined by the cost and other factors involved. In some instances, duplicate tapes of all programs are made during processing. In the past, it has been common to provide off-site storage for as many as five generations of data or to use a three-generation system consisting of a duplicate of data up to the time of storage and journal tapes to provide the information needed to update the latest version. Today most companies use database management systems that store data on disk units and not necessarily in the form of distinct files. These databases are usually updated in real time. Therefore it is no longer possible to rely for backup on rotating the generations of tape files. Arrangements must be made for off-site storage of updated tapes and for periodic dumps of the database.

As a final note, it must be pointed out that the destruction of computer data is less often the result of criminal activity than of natural disaster, fire, or even more often, program error, machine malfunction, or input error. Whatever the cause, however, the results are the same, and some carefully supervised system of duplication must be installed to protect against the possibilities of loss.

Protecting against Unauthorized Use

One of the particularly disturbing problems faced by a company that has converted to a computer operation is the possibility that unauthorized persons might operate the system either at the installation or through remote terminals, thus gaining access to privileged data that they can then convert to their own use. This is a very real and valid concern since all the company's files and records have, in fact, been transferred to an instrument that is accessible to many people within the company or, in the case of time-sharing operations, to many people outside the company.

The key to effective security precautions is to identify, by name, persons who will be held personally responsible for each and every specified asset. Accountable persons should maintain up-to-date documentary evidence relating to the security of assets and attesting to their acquisition, deployment, movement, modification, use, disposal, and authorized destruction. The next step in organizing for security is to control access to every specified asset. The security coordinator should maintain up-to-date records to help do this. These should include:

Lists of persons holding passes or badges
Control list of keys, cards, or combinations
Passwords, lockwords, codewords, and who knows them
Logical working names for hardware devices
Unique names of all files and who can see or change them

Unique names of all programs and who can run or modify them

Security profiles of all center users—that is, what users are permitted to
do with every file or program to which they have access

Project and programmer names and numbers

Continuous custody histories of all confidential documents

Local rules regarding where and how to lock away specified assets

Passwords

The machine contains a complete and accurate data source essential to the operation of the business it serves. It will on command produce any or all of that information. It will do precisely what it is told to do. Security of data lies in concealing what the machine is told to do. This usually consists of a file system with the establishment of a password (or passwords) when the file is created. The machine is, in effect, told to release certain files only after the programmed password is used. It is further instructed never to reveal the password in readouts or system reviews.

Graduated Access

Some files are further protected by a preprogrammed permissions system in which the names of authorized system users are entered into the file on a graduated access basis. In this way, a file can be used to its fullest extent by allowing full and restricted use simultaneously to users at various levels of authority. Machines whose use is restricted to only a few special employees are seriously hampered in their effectiveness. A system of graduated access, however, opens up its potential usefulness and at the same time restricts its use to a need-to-know or need-to-use basis.

Access control requires that isolating barriers permit information to flow only in accordance with preestablished access rules. Implicit in the existence of any access-control system is a specification of what access privileges exist within the system (for example, read, write, execute, delete, append); a security profile of each user specifying exact access privileges is available to that user; and an access list specific to every information asset specifying what access privileges each authorized user has over that asset.

Two basic principles should be reflected in access rules:

1. *Minimal privilege.* Only such information or processing capability that the user absolutely must have to carry out an assigned task should be made available.
2. *Minimal exposure.* Once a user gains access to sensitive information or material, that user has the responsibility of protecting the information. The user should make sure that only persons whose duties require it obtain knowledge of this information while it is being processed or stored or is in transit.

The security manager should maintain an access-control list for every computer program and every data file. These lists should reflect the intent of access rules laid down by department heads, security statements sent along with each program or data file, and the expressed desires of the originator. Access-control lists should contain:

1. The identifier of the particular asset
2. The unique identifier of every authorized user
3. What each user is permitted to do with the asset
4. Conditions under which access may be granted.

The security manager should maintain a security profile of every authorized user. The profile should consist of:

1. The identifier of the user
2. The identifiers of all projects to which the user belongs
3. The identifiers of all categories to which the user belongs such as security clearance
4. The identifiers of specific files to which the user has access, and what can be done to each file.

No access to a computer system should be granted until the user's password has been checked against the list of valid passwords.

Remote Terminal Security

In the early stages of computer technology, information was produced only at the site of the machine itself. Protection of its information was simpler since denial of physical access to the machine denied access to its information. This is not to say that unauthorized personnel did not obtain sensitive information directly from the computer, but when this occurred, it was because of a failure in the personnel access procedures.

Today, however, thousands of concerns operate on what are referred to as management information systems. Such systems, much like airline reservation systems, locate consoles, teletypes, and other readout devices in convenient locations within the company building or in a network of locations tied in with telephone lines across the country. Many of these devices enable a user to access the computer. In the same way, smaller companies using a computer on a timesharing basis have similar terminals with which they can access the computer operated by a service bureau.

In both cases, the security problem is the same, though its focus is somewhat different. In the case of the proprietary computer, it is necessary to restrict information to those people and those locations where such information is authorized. The timesharing company must be restricted to access to its own database, and must be prevented from entering the files of other customers. How it restricts that information within itself is for the company to decide and program accordingly, but it, as well as all other customers, must be assured that its file is secure from access by any but authorized personnel.

In either system, both personnel and location authorization must be considered as part of the security system. For example, the personnel manager may be authorized to retrieve payroll information at a location within the confines of the personnel department. Although authorized to receive the data, the personnel manager would be denied the information if it were requested from any other location. This is an important precaution in areas where a visual display might well expose confidential information to any number of unauthorized people.

Checks and Audits

Examining the total process of information retrieval in a security situation, we would find that an initial check and ongoing audit of the on-line user's authority is basic to the system. The user would activate a remote station and would be asked for name, organization, and password. The software would identify the individual, verify the authority, acknowledge the password, and combine that verification with the status of the terminal in use and the access level of the user. After this initial access, the user would ask for a particular file, using such other passwords as might be indicated. On further verification, the computer would provide the data needed. Any information sought from the machine would be validated before delivery. If during this time at any stage the user attempted to retrieve unauthorized information, appropriate security alarm procedures would be initiated.

Software Protection Packages

Additional software protection can be achieved through such packages as Resource Access Control Facility (RACF) and CICS Online Protection System (COP). These packages define user groups and subgroups, maintain security profiles, update data logs, report security violations and attempted violations, guard direct-access and tape-storage units and produce written periodic reports. They operate in conjunction with the computer's operating system like an outer layer of protection restricting and controlling access to all the computer's resources.[5]

Encryption

Encryption is the transformation of data for the purpose of rendering them unintelligible to those ignorant of the transformation process. The changes may be made by transposition or substitution of characters, or by arithmetic, algebraic, and/or logical manipulation of the data. In 1976, the U.S. National Bureau of Standards adopted the Data Encryption Standard (DES). DES was developed and patented by IBM, which guaranteed it to contain no errors and to perform as it was designed. A study by Stanford University concluded that there are over 70 quadrillion possible key-bit combinations thus making breaking the code through guessing highly improbable.

The best protection for data, either when stored within a computer system or while in transit from one terminal to another, is encryption. As a result of the proliferation of the use of computers in business and because of the ability through the use of modems to tie into computers from personal units, the amount of money spent on encryption exceeded $10 million in 1982. As *Hallcrest I* noted, this increase in spending is the result of increasing losses from computer theft or fraud. Sales of encryption devices and software for computer security may reach $20.1 million in 1985.[6] *Hallcrest II* reported that the cost of protecting computer data was $3 billion in 1990.[7]

Protecting against Errors

It is important to review the operation of a computer system in order to grasp the significance of even the smallest error, whether caused by carelessness or by actual intent to compromise the machine.

In the first place, computers store information in their own language and there are many different languages available for machine use depending on the application. Printouts are frequently in direct statements easily comprehended by the uninitiated, but stored information is in the form of digits. Everything has been turned into numbers and, in order to retrieve it, the numbers must be called for. If anything has in any way compromised the integrity of a number, that information cannot be retrieved. If, for example, some item has been designated a "3" but by error has been entered into the machine as a "2," it may never be found. Since the program clearly carries it as a 3, there is no way of knowing that it has somehow found its way into the databank as a 2.

It is essential, therefore, that procedures of operation as well as programming include many methods of cross-checking, and the computer must be further programmed to notify the operator if a cross-check fails.

An insufficiently trained or unqualified operator may not recognize such problems when they arise and may continue to damage the stored information in such a way that the original error is compounded and a chain of lost information is created. Such a situation can be extremely damaging to an otherwise efficient operation.

This kind of loss of control over the information stored is one of the costliest and most frustrating problems facing EDP managers today. The damage potential from unqualified personnel, who though sincere are nonetheless quite capable of bungling a job, is a greater security hazard in most companies than are all possible criminal conspiracies combined.

It is essential that only highly qualified personnel be permitted to function in areas affecting the accuracy and efficiency of the computer operation. To operate otherwise is to invite disaster.

It is equally essential that systems be established for every part of this invaluable function. A computer is very costly to install and operate. The demands for its use grow as its usefulness becomes more evident throughout the company. Economy dictates that it be used as efficiently as possible.

Obviously priorities will be established governing the programs to be run, and explicit systems and procedures regarding the operation of these programs must be developed, communicated to all employees involved, and prominently posted in an appropriate place within the computer complex. These instructions should be reviewed regularly for update.

It is frequently the case that procedural rules are developed, distributed, posted, and then not pursued. Inevitably, operators work out shortcuts that may or may not be beneficial. It is management's responsibility to see to it that all procedures are followed as published.

It must also be remembered that some procedures can be burdensome and inefficient. If such appears to be the case after reasonable reevaluation, they must be changed. Operators will frequently find simpler and safer ways of achieving an end. Their suggestions should never be ignored. If they come up with a new way of accomplishing a job, it should be examined and, if it is feasible, adopted as a change in operating procedures. The important thing is to insist that prescribed routines be followed to the letter but at the same time to keep an open mind to suggestions for better ways.

Computer Crime Measures

Most operating routines are designed to avoid mistakes that will result in a loss of control over the retrieval of information or to avoid operational missteps that could damage or destroy data already accumulated. These are the computer professional's nightmare. But it has become increasingly evident that management controls must be established to prevent the use of the computer for criminal acts.

The computer presents a formidable challenge to security personnel. Its efficiency makes its use as an instrument of embezzlement almost impossible to detect—most instances of such use that have been uncovered have been as a result of some unforeseen accident, not from routine or even special audits. The revelations yet to come may be astonishing. A study by the Florida Department of Law Enforcement surveyed 900 businesses and law-enforcement agencies and found that 1 out of 4 businesses was victimized by computer crime.[8]

Computers are operating faster and faster and producing fewer and fewer of the printouts that auditors and financial officers need to follow the flow of dollars processed by the machines, "If auditing staffs don't get involved in designing computer systems soon, they might as well climb up on their stools, pull down their green eyeshades and pray for early retirement to come," says Joseph Wasserman of Bell Telephone Laboratories.[9]

Sophistication in computer disciplines is necessary to use the machine for one's own purposes. Fortunately this knowledge is not possessed by every thief, but the conditions are ideal for the thief educated in the ways of this technology. Computer records present a different world for the old-fashioned ledger. There are no erasures, only removals that leave no trace. No numbers or entries need to be doctored. They are simply changed, and it can be done in seconds. With most systems such a change can never be detected.

Almost none of the major embezzlements uncovered were found by audits of programs, but were discovered only when a check was accidentally returned by the post office, when an accomplice informed the police for revenge, or when an account was audited off schedule. In other words, the result of the rigged program instruction was stumbled upon—in many cases years after systematic embezzlement had begun—but neither the machine nor its software was set up to frustrate these schemes or to detect them after they were established.

Remember, a computer can do only what it is told, and it does that incredibly well. It makes no judgments and asks no questions. It simply performs as directed.

There is not, at this time, a totally embezzler-proof method. That day may come, but the state of the art today is such that, if it could be done at all, the machine would be essentially inoperable. For all practical purposes, it is a hazard to which every computer operation is heir.

Security Management Strategies

There are three management principles basic to computer security. The "never-alone" principle dictates that two or more designated persons should witness every security-relevant action and attest to it by signing a log.

The second principle—"limited tenure"—suggests that no one should ever be left in any security-related position so long that that person begins to believe that the position is permanent, or that the duties are wholly predictable. Crews should be randomly rotated among shifts; individuals should be randomly rotated among crews; and mandatory vacation periods should be enforced.

The third principle—"separation of duties"—mandates that no person should have knowledge of, be exposed to, or participate in any security related functions outside that person's own area of responsibility.

Four administrative rules are necessary to implement the separation of duties.

1. Programmers shall not operate computers.
2. Operators shall neither write nor submit programs.
3. Implementation of modifications to computer operating systems that are intended to enhance security shall be a separate, distinct duty.
4. Quality control and audit shall exist as functions separate and distinct from data-processing production.

Operating Procedures

The following are some procedures that, if they are developed and supervised, will substantially reduce the danger and make determined thieves work much harder for their loot.

First reduce or eliminate contact between the four principal categories of computer personnel—the programmers, the operators, the test and auditing personnel, and the maintenance crew. C.F. Hemphill and J.M. Hemphill, in their informative book on computer security, *Security Procedures for Computer Systems*, refer to a major Eastern banking chain that has discouraged contact between operators and programmers (whose collusion would be the most likely and the most effective from a criminal standpoint) by "requiring these two classifications of employees to enter widely separate entrance gates, to park in segregated lots, and to enter work areas through entrances on opposite sides of the building." Continuing this separation, cafeteria access, coffee breaks, and toilet facilities are provided in different areas of the building. Passing from one area to the other with a written pass is possible only during hours of controlled supervision. At other times, an alarm system and uniformed guards prevent traffic between programmer areas and operating areas.[10]

These are extreme measures, to be sure, and perhaps more stringent than is necessary or even possible, from a labor relations view, in other applications. But the point is clear. Programmers must not be permitted to be involved in machine operation—not personally or through collusion with an operator. If such a situation were permitted, any programmer who was criminally inclined could build any loophole into the system and then feed it any information necessary to accomplish a theft.

For much the same reason, though to a lesser degree, contact between programmers, operators, test and audit personnel, and maintenance personnel should be minimized. It must be remembered, however, that employees in all of these categories are professionals in a complex and exacting field.

They cannot be treated arbitrarily, simply because they probably will not put up with it. And they cannot be hampered or tied up in excessive red tape, or their usefulness and efficiency will be substantially reduced.

Second insist that all programs be documented as the program is being developed. Frequently programmers fail to record their progress or even record the details of the program after it has been completed. This can lead to some confusion and certainly loss of time when errors need correction or changes in the program need to be made. This oversight is also a handicap to new people assigned to the project who have no way of knowing what the program consists of, either up to the stage when they are assigned or in the case of a completed program in its final form.

Third insist that programmers stay out of the computer room. They rarely if ever have a function to perform there, and their presence could lead to problems for the company.

Fourth transfer programmers and operators to different programs and different machines from time to time. This may serve to discourage any plans to set up long-term embezzlement programs. More often than not, the schemes that have been discovered involved the regular issuance of checks or a regular transfer of funds rather than a single raid on company assets. Such transfers could minimize the risk of such steady drains on company funds and increase the likelihood of discovery of any plot by the newly assigned operator or programmer.

Fifth control all aspects of machine operation. The operator that has free access and control over input operations has effectively become a programmer/operator and can use the machine in a number of unauthorized and possibly criminal ways. The status of any program run should always be known and its progress supervised.

Sixth insist on careful logging of all aspects of the operation. If trouble develops in the operation, reference to such a log, if it has been well and accurately kept, can serve to locate the source of the difficulty.

Seventh separate computerized check writing from the source authorizing check issuance. This is only reasonable business practice that would be demanded in any company, computerized or not.

Eighth insist on careful audits and evaluation of machine usage. Such examinations will keep management abreast of computer needs and activities for consideration in assigning priorities of use. They will also help to discover unauthorized or unnecessary usage of this valuable instrument.

Ninth establish a routine for the regular disposal of all output information, punch cards, and program information. This material should be shredded or carried off, under supervision, to be incinerated.

Tenth check on programs periodically after adoption. Such checks can be made by comparing the original copy of the program against the copy being used by the operator. If any changes have been introduced, they should be immediately apparent. No changes should be permitted without supervisor approval.

Eleventh, test-run all new programs thoroughly before allowing them to become operational. Without such pretesting undertaken under a prescribed routine, some programs can create havoc with customer relations or damage existing data.

Personnel Considerations

In the last analysis, no system of safeguards can absolutely prevent theft by computer. There are too many people who must have access to programs and the machinery itself in order to function. Any one or group of persons could turn their expertise and virtually private knowledge of the company's systems into a criminal scheme. No company can ultimately protect itself against EDP personnel by guards, access systems, or even validation systems. Such protective devices can keep out strangers or dabblers but not authorized personnel. They create and operate the systems, and they can destroy them.

This is by no means to say that they are, as a group, inclined to damage the company. Quite the contrary, they are usually dedicated specialists whose instinct is to always improve existing operations by creating foolproof and tamper-proof programs. And they should be recognized as such. Security systems that materially reduce their efficiency will be resented although they as a group are inclined to be the first to recognize the need for reasonable security procedures.

Screening and Evaluation

Careful screening of personnel is of the highest priority in any computer security program. Exhaustive evaluation of background, previous employment experience, and level of training and competence is a must. Having satisfied these basic requirements, every new employee must be thoroughly indoctrinated into the peculiarities of the company's operation, then phased into an operational function but without undue haste. This phase-in period will permit management to further evaluate the employee's ability and attitude.

It is also important to remember that the evaluation at this phase is mutual. The new employee will be weighing the acceptability of the new position with just as much thought and concentration as the company will be determining the employee's suitability to its operation. Since recent studies have indicated that the average annual turnover in computer personnel amounts to approximately 15 percent, and since competent trained people are in short supply in this exploding market, it is important to keep this mutuality of satisfaction in mind.

A Special Breed

At this point, it would be well to consider that computer people are a special breed. They speak a different language and, generally speaking, their dedication is to the demands of the machinery and software, not to the company that owns them. They pursue challenges wherever they may arise. Encouraging company loyalty is an important consideration and should be pursued in a mature and intelligent manner. The computer room is the last place for locker room pep talks.

Management must recognize that the demands of this technology introduce different work routines and that any attempt to force nonapplicable company policies in this regard on computer personnel will be nonproductive and probably damaging. This is not to say that they need to be coddled or accorded any special privileges; it is simply to point out that they are specialists in a specialized field and that many of the standard rules and routines are irrelevant and do not apply.

Salaries

This staff must be adequately paid. This will probably adjust itself since the demands for good people in this field are so great that offers below the going market rate will be ignored. But pay scales must be regularly reviewed. If the salary range in a company is frozen at a point that is later exceeded by the computer business as a whole, large-scale resignations can be expected. Excessive turnover of such personnel, beyond the already considerable rate, is expensive and counterproductive.

If all this seems excessively conciliatory, that is unfortunate. Those are generally the facts. Computer people today are in some respects the glamor element, the stars of the business world. They are now, and will be for the immediate future, in a position to demand respect and appreciation. Any other attitude by management would be to deny the realities in today's commercial world.

The best security lies in enlightened employee relations combined with conscientious leadership. The computer staff can be the most important weapon in the fight against computerized crime.

Insurance

Since the potential for loss in a computer operation is so enormous and since no existing system can provide a guarantee against such losses, insurance coverage is essential to back up the operation after all other reasonable precautions have been taken.

Because this kind of coverage is relatively new in the field of casualty insurance, new policies are still being developed. And since data on liabilities and claims are necessarily limited at this stage, rates may vary considerably from company to company, depending on exposure and operational techniques.

At the moment, more claims are presented for damage from water damage than from any other type of loss, but this may not continue as coverage becomes more comprehensive and auditing techniques become more sophisticated.

Equipment insurance is perhaps the first consideration. It covers all equipment for a wide variety of risks from fire to accidental damage. Since such insurance may be offered with a deductible feature, savings may be effected in certain instances. In the case of leased equipment, the contract must be studied to determine the liabilities of lessee and lessor, since some agreements do not hold the lessee liable for damage while others do in certain instances.

Software can be covered under the company standard fire insurance contract, but such insurance covers only the physical material such as the tape or disk.

A separate policy or an endorsement on the standard policy will be required to cover the cost of reconstructing records destroyed by various hazards. Such a policy, however, probably will not cover operator errors that result in damage to the database.

Business interruption and extra cost insurance covering computer operations is available and recommended.

Accounts receivable insurance is available but may not be necessary if a good program of off-site storage is followed.

Errors and omissions insurance could be very important to the operator of a data processing service. This covers liability incurred by such a service making honest mistakes in the performance of a job for a client firm. Court cases, in which the defense disclaims responsibility for damages because "the computer did it," seem to indicate that the courts do not consider computer error a mitigating circumstance or a valid defense. Insurance coverage in this area is advised.

Many of the above may be covered by an all-risk policy that provides comprehensive coverage of most phases of the computer operation, but only a very careful study will determine its practical application to any given business.

Review Questions

1. Why is it safe to assume that computer crime will increase in the years ahead?
2. What are some of the vulnerabilities unique to computer systems?
3. Justify the statement that, ideally, a computer center probably should be located by itself out in the country.
4. What significance does the term "password" have in the area of computer security?
5. In computer center fire control, cite the advantages and disadvantages in using (a) sprinkler systems, (b) Halon 1301, (c) carbon dioxide, and (d) dry chemicals.
6. What special risk is involved in having a computer programmer also function as an operator?
7. What are the three management principles basic to computer security?

References

1. In Lawrence J. Fennelly, *Handbook of Loss Prevention and Crime Prevention* (Stoneham, Mass.: Butterworth, 1983).
2. Terry Magel, "Computer Security," in *Suggested Preparation for Careers in Security/Loss Prevention*, John Chuvala III and Robert James Fischer, eds. (Dubuque, Iowa: Kendall/Hunt Publishing Company), 1991.
3. Ibid., pp. 103–104.
4. Ibid., pp. 109–111.
5. Ibid., p. 118.
6. William Cunningham and Todd H. Taylor, *Private Security and Police in American: The Hallcrest Report* (Portland, Oreg.: Chancellor Press, 1985), p. 156.
7. William C. Cunningham, John J. Strauchs and Clifford W. Van Meter, *The Hallcrest Report II: Private Security Trends 1970–2000* (Stoneham, Mass.: Butterworth-Heinemann, 1990), p. 72.
8. Ibid., p. 67.
9. A. Adelson, "Embezzlement by Computer," in *Computer Security: Equipment, Personnel and Data* (Stoneham, Mass.: Butterworth Publishers, 1974), p. 43.
10. C. F. Hemphill and J. M. Hemphill, *Security Procedures for Computer Systems* (New York: Dow-Jones-Irwin, 1973).

18 ⬜⬜⬜
⬜⬜⬜
⬜⬜⬜

Specific Security Threats

The preceding chapters have highlighted the most important aspects of the security and loss-prevention field. The discussions in the past few chapters have centered on security in areas such as retailing and cargo transportation and on the devices and techniques used to reduce potential losses. This chapter examines several of the security threats common to many businesses. Although these threats are common to many businesses in the United States, they are not vulnerabilities, with one possible exception that will be faced by every firm.

Drugs in the Workplace

The one possible exception is drugs in the workplace. While many U.S. citizens view drugs as a recent problem, the use of drugs in the workplace has been a problem for many years. In fact, historically private enterprise has pioneered most of the programs in drug detection, rehabilitation, and prevention.

How great is the drug problem? No one knows for sure, but the federal government has adopted a policy that makes illegal drugs and drug usage unacceptable. According to federal figures, the annual price tag for illicit drug abuse was $59 billion in 1987, $100 billion in 1988, and $144 billion in 1989.[1] Support for the federal policy has been forthcoming from all segments of society, including federal government, state government, and business. Federal studies estimate that 10 to 20 percent of all U.S. workers use dangerous drugs, including alcohol, on the job. Others would place the figure at 25 percent since this approximates the proportion of the total population that uses illicit drugs.[2] The exact costs associated with the drug problem at work are not known, but they are known to be staggering. The Research Institute in North Carolina reports that drug abusers are three times as likely as are nonusers to injure themselves or others while at work. Horror stories abound. In 1975, 50 train accidents were the result of drug-impaired workers. In 1983, the National Transporation Safety Board identifed marijuana as the cause of the fatal crash of an aircraft, and the Exxon Valdez captain was using alcohol while on the job. Dr. Howard Frankel, former Medical Director for Rockwell International's Space Shuttle Division, estimated that 20 to 25 percent of the workers at his facility were under the influence of drugs while on the job.[3] A recent American Medical Association report finds that approximately 12 percent of the workforce is using drugs on the job.[4]

Drug usage on the job is directly linked to:

Theft. Many security administrators say that "[d]rug abuse and theft go hand in hand." Drug users often steal from employers and fellow employees to support their habits. A study commissioned by A Drug-Free Workplace finds that 96 percent of Illinois employees favor workplace drug testing with 50 percent supporting random drug testing.[5]

Productivity and quality control problems. Several years ago during a break period, one line employee for a major corporation was slipped drugs in his drink for laughs. The joke got out of control when the employee threw a bucket into a conveyor. Fifty percent of the operation was shut down. The company lost several hours of work while still paying employees who were idled by the incident. *The Journal of the American Medical Association* reports that employees who use drugs have 85% more accidents than non-users. Cocaine has the greatest effect on accident rates.[6]

Absenteeism. Alcohol is the major drug problem in this area. The North Carolina Research Triangle Institute estimated that alcoholism cost the U.S. economy $117 billion in 1983 up $30 billion from 1980. The *Journal of the American Medical Association* reports that employees who use drugs are absent 78 percent more often than are nonusers. Marijuana users have a higher turnover rate.[7] Figure 18.1 presents a comparison of drugs and their effect on turnover, accidents, and disciplinary actions.

The problem may be getting worse. According to Gregory M. Louis-Nont, President of Louis-Nont and Associates, a firm specializing in employee assessment and evaluation, a full 66 percent of the employees who are entering the job market have used illicit drugs sometime during their life, and unfortunately 44 percent have used an illegal drug within the past 12 months.[8]

One solution is drug testing and proper advertising. The words, "Must have a clean drug history" will discourage those who have drug problems from applying.

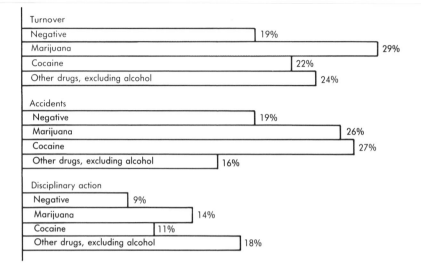

Figure 18.1 Employees and drugs. (From *Security* magazine, April, 1991, p. 10. Published by Cahners Publishing Co., a division of Reed Publishing USA.)

Drug Testing

The federal government recognized the importance of preemployment drug screening with the passage of the Drug Free Workplace Act of 1988. Table 18.1 indicates the percent of companies with drug programs in 1988.[9] Several types of drug screening are available. The most frequently discussed is urine analysis, followed by blood testing. The National Institute on Drug Abuse (NIDA) has established standards for drug-testing laboratories that should ensure quality testing. Both tests are intrusive and require that someone monitor the removal of material to be tested.

To counter the problems of intrusiveness some firms prefer to use pencil-and-paper tests. Various types of pencil-and-paper tests claim to provide an indication of previous or present drug use. Additional information on these tests can be found in Chapter 13.

A relatively new addition to the field is RIAH (radioimmunoassay of hair). This test requires that the individual provide a strand of hair that is then tested for drugs. Human hair maintains a 90-day record of materials ingested by the body. A laboratory can also determine the date within 7 days of when a drug was last used. Hair can also be matched to the owner with the exactness of fingerprints.

Unfortunately the high-profile publicity surrounding the introduction of

Table 18.1   Percent of Companies with Drug Programs 1987–1988

Size of Company (employees)	Department of Labor Survey	Gallup Survey
5000 +	50%	28%
1501 to 5000*	43%	13%
500 to 1500	N/A	10%
Less than 50	N/A	2%

*Department of Labor criterion is "more than 1000 employees."

Source: William C. Cunningham, John J. Strauchs, Clifford W. VanMeter, *The Hallcrest Report II: Private Security Trends 1970–2000* (Boston: Butterworth-Heinemann, 1990), p. 57.

drug testing has allowed the violators to develop a countereducational movement to beat the screening systems. Smuggling urine into the bathroom is widely practiced. In addition, users of cocaine know that it stays in the system for a maximum of 72 hours; thus it is possible to abstain prior to urine testing so that the test results are negative for cocaine use. RIAH testing, on the other hand, would require at least 3 months of abstinence.

Spotting Drug Use

Aside from the problems of reduced efficiency, increased absenteeism and accident proneness, supervisors should look for other signs of drug use. The following is only a sample of signs of which supervisor should be aware.

Crack Cocaine

A simple Coke can is crushed in the middle, and holes are punched in the can with a nail. Crack is placed over the holes and lighted. The user smokes the can by inhaling the smoke through the open tab end of the can. When the user is finished, the can is discarded.

Cocaine

Small vials are often placed in the employee's wallet, along with supporting paraphernalia such as a straw, a pocket mirror, and a razor blade. In addition, small safes that are made to look like soft drink cans or fire extinguishers are becoming popular hiding places.

Other Methods

Tin foil, old prescription bottles, and zip-top bags have long been used by drug users.

Drug Policies

Preemployment

When companies conduct preemployment screening they should adopt the following guidelines.

Notify the applicant of the company's policy of drug screening.
Make sure the test results are valid by using a reputable laboratory.
Ensure confidentiality.

Postemployment

As with most policies, the key is that the policy be well written and communicated to the employees in a clear manner. Expectations regarding the use of drugs and the penalities associated with that use must be clearly stated. Policies should specify under what conditions an employee will be expected to submit to drug testing—for example, after an on-the-job accident.

In addition, all policies should:

1. Be consistently administered
2. Spell out prescription drug use, including what types of drugs need to be declared to company supervisors
3. Require substantive proof of drug use

The adoption of an employee assistance program and its use should also be spelled out in the policy. Under the employee assistance program, the employer agrees to assist employees who have a substance abuse problem rather than resort to immediate termination.

Economic/White-Collar Crime

Today, the concept of white-collar/economic crime is familar to most of us. The junk-bond market and insurance scams are regularly reported in the news media. Ivan Boesky and other names are familiar for their involvement in various financial scams. The total cost of economic crime for 1990 was estimated by the *Hallcrest II* staff at $144 billion with white-collar crime comprising $57 billion of that figure.[10] Figure 18.2 shows the *Hallcrest*

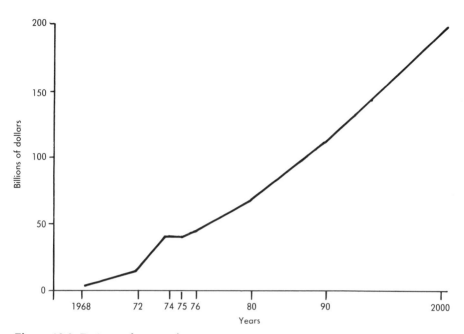

Figure 18.2 Estimated costs of economic crimes.

II estimated costs of economic crime. Table 18.2 presents various estimates of losses from different categories of economic crime. We know that white-collar crime is against the law, yet there is no legal definition for it, and it does not appear as part of the criminal code (although some of the crimes committed by white-collar criminals are codified—for example, embezzlement).

Government and the private sector keep declaring war on white-collar crime, yet they have failed to define what they are fighting. The problem is that white-collar crime is a social abstraction, not a legal concept. Morality and society's commitment to equal justice are more a part of the white-collar crime issue than is a true legal definition. While some white-collar crimes are violations of criminal laws, others are violations of regulatory statutes and general standards of moral conduct.

Definitions

The first mention of white-collar crime as a concept was made by Edwin H. Sutherland in 1939 at an American Sociological Society conference. He defined white-collar crime as "an offense committed by a person of respectability and high social status in the course of his [or her] occupation." In 1970, Herbert Edelhertz presented a newer and perhaps more descriptive

Table 18.2   Estimates of Losses from Various Categories of Economic Crime

Crime/Loss	Amount
Employee theft, "time theft," and drug abuse on the job	$320 billion annually
White-collar crime	$ Hundreds of billions annually
Computer crime	$200 billion annually
Time theft *(bogus sick days, late arrivals, early departures, excessive socializing on the job, etc.)*	$170 billion annually
Lost worker productivity due to drug use	$130 billion annually
Business property theft	$100 billion annually
Savings and loan (S&L) fraud	$100 billion
Worldwide product counterfeiting [U.S. product counterfeiting	$100 billion annually $8–20 billion annually]
Federal income tax evasion	$81.5 billion annually
Workplace drug abuse	$60–100 billion annually
Income of organized crime	$546.6 billion annually
Theft of intellectual property	$40 billion annually
Retail theft	$30 billion annually
Retail shrinkage	$16–24 billion annually
Employee theft	$15–25 billion annually
Bank crime [check fraud [loan fraud [embezzlement [credit card fraud [ATM fraud [bank robbery	$17–21 billion annually $7–10 billion annually] $6–7 billion annually] $2.1 billion annually] $1.2 billion annually] $70–100 million annually] $60–70 million annually]
Commercial bribery (kickbacks)	$3.5–10 billion annually
Telephone fraud	$500 million annually
Business failures due to economic crime	20–30%
Underwriting losses on bonds guaranteeing employee honesty	112% increase (1979–1984)

definition: an "illegal act or series of acts committed by nonphysical means and by traditional notions of deceit, deception, manipulation, concealment or guile to obtain money or properties, to avoid the payment or loss of money or property, or to obtain a business or personal advantage."[11] Edelhertz's definition has been widely accepted since it relies more on the actions of the perpetrator than it does on the economic social status. There is also no restriction to criminal offenses in his definition by including regulatory issues as well. Experience has shown that white-collar offenses are not limited to the rich and powerful and that the offenses need not arise out of the context of one's occupation.

Regardless of which of the definitions one chooses for white-collar crime, the concept today has the following common elements.

1. It is an illegal act committed in the context of a lawful occupation.
2. It generally involves deceit, deception, manipulation, and breach of trust.
3. It does not rely on physical force.
4. It has the acquisition of money, property, or power as the primary goal.

Impact

Although the crime itself may be nonviolent, the end result could be violent (an industrial plant knowingly allows carcinogenic waste to pollute water; a pharmaceutical corporation knowingly sells an anticholesterol drug that has known potentially toxic side effects). Thus the nonviolent statement is only appropriate to the means of delivery or action necessary, not to the end results. Gilbert Geis says, "corporate criminals deal death not deliberately, but through inadvertence, omission and indifference."[12]

The exact extent of white-collar and economic crime is difficult to establish. A lack of standard classifications and definitions coupled with limited reporting of workplace crime contributes to the problem of accurate measurement. Over the past 15 years five studies have identified the need for indices to measure economic crime and its true impact on society accurately. But there is still no progress! "Security executives told the Hallcrest research staff that their companies' incident or crime loss reporting system was incomplete or nonexistent." One key security executive with one of the nation's largest corporations said, "We probably know of only 1 fraud out of every 10 that is occurring or has occurred."[13]

White-collar crime will continue to be a growing problem into the twenty-first century. A recent $1.1 million loss was the result of collusion between the contracting company vice president and the security firm vice president.[14] Even security is not immune from white-collar crime problems.

Burglary and Robbery

Burglary and robbery have remained two of the greatest crime problems in the United States. All types of establishments are subject to their attack, but certain businesses are more prone to these crimes than are others. Obviously banks and retail stores have more to fear from robbery than do manufacturing firms. Before discussing these two problems, we should define them; far too often people use the terms burglary and robbery interchangeably. Burglary is committing a crime through stealth by entering a building or other structure. In most cases, the crime committed is larceny (theft), but rape and arson are also committed by burglars.

Robbery, on the other hand, is a crime of force or threat of force. While burglars do not like to confront people, robbers work by creating fear or by forcing people to give up their property. Although burglary may involve different kinds of crimes, robbery is strictly a crime comprising only two offenses—theft and assault and battery.

Recent statistics presented in the Uniform Crime Report (UCR) indicate that the growth of these two crimes has decelerated; however, both are difficult crimes to deal with. Robbery has the potential of physical harm that all firms must consider. Burglary has the problem of unsolvability since less than 2 percent of all burglary cases are solved, and the recovery rate for stolen property is less than 4 percent.

Burglary

According to the FBI's UCR, burglary currently represents almost 50 percent of all crime in the United States although its incidence has steadily decreased since 1981. Even though the number of incidents has decreased, burglary costs Americans billions of dollars annually. Because burglary is the most frequently occurring crime, it is essential that every business take particular care to protect itself against this form of crime.

The Attack

A burglary attack on a retail establishment is similar to such attacks on other types of facilities except that the job of the burglar is simplified by the ease with which the premises can be inspected before the attack. The physical layout, store routines, police patrols, and internal inspections (if any) can be easily assessed by a burglar posing as a customer. For a more exhaustive survey, the burglar might even pose as a building or fire inspector and make a minute examination of alarm installations, safe location, interior lock construction, and every other detail of the store defenses.

Assuming a weak point has been found, the burglar enters through a door or window, through the roof, or possibly from a neighboring occupancy. Most successful burglaries (and over 90 percent of detected attempts are successful) are made by forced entry. Curiously enough, the greatest number are made through the front door or main entrance.

A considerably smaller number of burglaries involve the stay-in who gathers the loot then breaks out and is gone before the guards or police can respond to an alarm.

Merchandise as Target

Most burglaries involve the theft of high-value merchandise although any goods will do in the absence of the big ticket items. Police reports repeatedly show the most astonishing variety of goods that have been targeted by enterprising thieves. Anything from unassembled cardboard cartons to bags of flour are fair game. Obviously such merchandise would hardly be considered high-risk assets, but it cannot be overlooked since possible burglars of loot come in all sexes, races, and sizes and what may seem to one as cumbersome and unprofitable may be remarkably appealing to another.

Cash as Target

Cash is naturally the most sensitive asset and the most eagerly sought, but since it is usually secured in some manner, it represents the greatest challenge to the burglar.

Stores keeping supplies of cash on hand are particularly susceptible, especially before payday. If such stores customarily cash payroll checks as a service to their employees, a burglar can assume that adequate cash must be on hand in anticipation of the next day's demands. Particular care must be taken in such cases if there is no way to handle cash needs other than to store it on the premises overnight. Every other avenue should be explored before the decision is made to keep substantial supplies of cash on hand overnight.

Since any cash will normally be held in a safe, it requires some degree of expertise to get at it. Boring, jimmying, blasting, and even carrying away the entire safe are the methods most commonly used. Few burglars are sufficiently skilled to enter a safe by manipulation of the combination, so applied violence is the normal approach. Unfortunately even in cases where an attack is unsuccessful, the damage to the container is likely to be severe enough to require its replacement. This is equally true in all areas where entry is made or attempted. The high cost of repairs of damage to buildings and equipment can be almost as harmful as the loss in cash or merchandise.

Physical Defense against Burglary

Burglary defense has been widely studied for years, and several strategies have been developed to combat this crime. The most common approach is referred to as target hardening. Simply speaking, this means that the basic security precautions outlined in the preceding chapters are applied to the facility, including attention to door construction, locks, alarms and surveillance devices.

It is always wise to let potential burglars know that the facility is well protected. In most cases, a burglar will avoid facilities where the chance of getting caught is great, and instead seek out other locations that are not as well protected.

Another defense against burglary that has met with some success is "reducing the value of merchandise." This approach usually includes marking company property with company identification tags or recording serial numbers that are easily traced. Because many fencing operations will turn away merchandise that is well marked and thus identifiable, burglars prefer merchandise that has no identifiable numbers.

In addition, some communities have developed "sting" operations, that is, fencing operations run by law-enforcement officials. These operations require large outlays of cash, but have proven effective in closing down major theft rings. Firms suffering substantial losses from theft should consider working with local officials in developing sting operations.

Alarms

Alarms of some kind can make the difference between an especially effective program and one that is providing only minimal protection. The type of alarm providing the best results is a matter of some disagreement, but there is little disagreement over the effectiveness of having some kind of system however simple. Several alarm systems are covered in Chapter 10.

Many stores report satisfaction with local alarm systems. They feel that the sound of the signaling device scares off the burglar in time to prevent the looting of the premises. Many police and security experts feel such alarms are ineffective because the response to the signal is only by chance and because such a device serves to warn the intruder rather than aid in capture. Since most managers are less interested in apprehending thieves than they are in preventing theft and since local systems are inexpensive and can be installed anywhere, they continue to be widely used. Certainly they are preferable to no alarm system at all.

Whether the outer perimeter should be fitted with alarms and whether space coverage alarms should be used is a matter peculiar to each facility. This must be carefully studied and determined by the manager. But it is always important to have the safe fitted with an alarm in some way.

Safes

The location of the safe within the premises will depend on the layout and the location of the store. Many experts agree that the safe should be located in a prominent, well-lighted position readily visible from the street where it can be seen easily by patrols or by passing city police. In some premises—especially where no surveillance by passing patrols can be expected—it is generally recommended that the safe be located in a well-secured and alarm-rigged inner room that shares no walls with the exterior of the building. Floors and ceilings should also be reinforced. The safe should be further protected by a capacitance alarm. The classification of the safe and the complexity of its alarm protection will be dictated by the amount of cash it will be expected to hold. This should be computed on the maximum amount to be deposited in the safe and the frequency with which such maximums are stored therein.

Basic Burglary Protection

Obviously the amount of protection and the investment involved in it will depend on the results of a careful analysis of the risks involved in each facility. There is no single way—no magic solution to the problem of burglary. Every system and each element of that system must be tailored to the individual premises.

Managers must evaluate the incidence of burglary in their neighborhoods as well as the efficiency and response time of the police. They must consider the nature of the construction of the building and the type of traffic in the area. Consideration must also be given to the ease with which merchandise can be carried off and by what probable routes. Managers must consider the reductions in insurance premiums provided by various security measures. The advice of city police in antiburglary measures and their experience in analogous situations should be sought out. In short, retailers owe it to themselves to learn as much as they can about coping with the problem of burglary and dealing with it as forcefully, economically, and energetically as possible.

Robbery

Although the number of robbery incidents has declined, robbery remains a serious crime because of the potential harm to its victims. Recent deaths in convenience store holdups make this point all too clear!

Aside from private individuals, retailers and banks take the brunt of these attacks. Since less than a third of all robbers are arrested, retailers are obliged to take measures to protect themselves from this most dangerous crime.

The Nature of Robbery

There are few differences in the experience with robbery due to geographical location, and the occurrence of such incidents is fairly constant throughout the week. The daily peak of robberies is at 10:30 PM. Those stores remaining open all night, however, suffer the majority of robberies between midnight and 3:00 AM. Over 90 percent of the money stolen is taken from cash registers, and 8 out of 10 robbers are armed with handguns. Eight out of 10 assailants are generally under 30, and of these, the vast majority are male. Although weapons are used (or the threat of harm), violence is generally carried out in less than 5 out of 100 cases. Eighty percent of the fatal cases occur in situations in which store personnel did nothing to motivate the attack. And while 60 percent of all robberies are carried out by a lone robber, 75 percent of the death or injury occurrences take place in situations involving two or more robbers.

We thus find that the robber is most apt to be a young man working alone, carrying a pistol, and threatening employees with bodily harm unless they hand over the money from cash registers. He rarely carries out his threats—probably because the employees wisely comply with his demands—unless he is accompanied by a partner, in which case he is very likely to cause death or injury without provocation. The recent deaths of convenience store employees during holdups with multiple assailants clearly illustrate this trend.

Robbery Targets

Robbers are typically criminals making a direct assault on people responsible for cash or jewelry. Their targets may be messengers or store employees taking cash for deposit in the bank or bringing in cash for the day's business. Robbers frequently enter stores a few minutes before closing and hold up the managers for the day's receipts, or they may break into stores before opening and wait for the first employees who they force to open safes or cash rooms. In recent cases, managers or members of their families have been kidnapped or threatened in order to coerce access to company cash.

Delivery trucks and warehouses can also be targets for robbers. These latter cases require several holdup people working together, and they are a very real threat and do occur. The majority of cases, however, are still carried out by the lone bandit attacking the cash register.

Businesses most frequently attacked are supermarkets, drug stores, jewelry stores, liquor stores, gas stations, and all-night restaurants or delicatessens.

Cash Handling

Probably the major cause of robbery is the accumulation of excessive amounts of cash. Such accumulations not only attract robbers who have noticed the amount of cash handled but they are also more damaging to business if a robbery does occur.

It is essential that only the cash needed to conduct the day's business be kept on hand, and most of that should be stored in safes. Cash should never be allowed to build up in registers, and regular hourly checks should be conducted to audit the amounts each register has on hand.

Every store should make a careful, realistic study of actual cash needs under all predictable conditions, and the manager should then see to it that only that amount plus a small reserve is on hand for the business of the day. Limits should also be set on the maximum amount permitted in each register, and cashiers should be instructed to keep cash only to that maximum. Overages should be turned in as often as necessary and as unobtrusively as possible.

In large-volume stores, a three-way safe is an invaluable safety precaution. Such safes provide a locked section for storage of two or three hours' worth of money that may be called on for check cashing or other cash outlays. The middle section has a time-lock that is not under the control of any of the store personnel and has a slot for the deposit of armored-car deliveries or cash buildups. Cash register trays are stored in the bottom compartment.

Movement of cash buildups from registers to the safes should be accomplished one at a time, and every effort should be made to conceal the transfer. This is particularly important at closing time when registers are being emptied. The sight of large amounts of cash can prove irresistibly tempting to a potential robber.

Cash-Room Protection

If the store has a cash room, it must be protected from assault. Basic considerations as to location and alarming were outlined in the discussion on antiburglary measures earlier in this chapter, but an additional precaution to protect against robbery should also be noted. The room itself must be secure against unauthorized entry during business hours. If possible, a list naming those persons authorized to enter the cash room and under what conditions should be drawn up. It should be made clear that there are to be no deviations under any circumstances from these authorizations.

The door to the room must be secure in itself and securely locked. If fire regulations indicate the need for additional doors, they should be equipped with panic locks and have alarms fitted to them. The entrance should be under the control of a designated person who, through a peephole or other viewing device, can check persons wishing to enter. In larger facilities, entrance can be controlled by an employee at a desk outside the room although this arrangement should be studied carefully before implementation since a robber could force such an employee to permit entrance unless the position is protected from the threat of attack.

Opening Routine

Since the potential for robbery is always present when opening or closing the store, it is important that a carefully prescribed routine be established to protect against that possibility.

At opening, the employee responsible for this routine should arrive accompanied by at least one other employee. The second employee should stand well away from the entrance while the manager prepares to enter. The manager should check the burglar alarm, turn it off, and enter the store. The interior, including washrooms, offices, back rooms, and other spaces that might offer concealment to robbers, should also be checked. After a specific, preestablished time, the manager should reappear in the main entrance and signal the second person with a predetermined code.

This code, which should be changed periodically, should be given both in voice and in some hand signal or gesture such as adjusting clothing or smoothing hair. One coded reply and gesture should indicate that all is clear; another should indicate trouble. It is important that this code be innocent and reasonable sounding to allay any suspicions on the part of robbers (if any are present).

If assistants get the danger sign, they should reply with something to the effect that they will return after getting a paper, checking the car, or buying a cup of coffee. The assistants should then proceed slowly and deliberately to a predetermined phone and call the police. Experienced security experts all stress the value of a card with the number of the police station typed on one side and coins to make the call taped to the back. For lack of change, stores have been robbed.

Transporting Cash

Since a basic principle in robbery protection is minimizing cash on hand, money will necessarily have to be moved off the premises to a bank from time to time. Ideally this should be done by an armored-car service. If this cannot be done because of cost or unavailability of such service, efforts should be made to get a police escort for the store employee acting as messenger.

In any event, messengers so assigned must be instructed to change their routes; they should also be sent out at different times of day and if possible on different days of the week. They should regularly change the carriers in which the money is stored. It might be anything from a brown paper bag to a tool box. They should stay on well-populated streets and move at a predetermined speed. The bank should be notified of their departure and given a close estimate of the time of arrival.

Closing Routine

Shortly before closing time, the manager should make a check of all spaces, similar to that conducted during opening. An assistant should watch unobtrusively for any unusual activity on the part of departing customers. When all registers have been emptied and the money locked up, the assistant should wait in the parking lot and watch as the manager completes the closing routine. When the manager has checked the alarm and locked up, the assistant will be free to go. If the manager signals trouble during any of this routine, the assistant should follow the same routine as at opening.

Other Routines

Since any entry into a store leads to a potential for robbery, it is important that the manager never try to handle it alone. There have been a number of instances where robbers have called managers and reported damage or a faulty alarm ringing in order to lure the managers into opening the store. They are then in a position to be coerced into opening the safe or at least into providing a bypass of the alarm system. If so notified, the manager should phone the police and/or the appropriate repair people and wait for them to arrive before getting out of the car. A manager should never try to handle the matter without some backup present.

Employee Training

A fully cooperative effort by all employees is essential to any robbery prevention program. Properly indoctrinated employees will know how to use a silent, "hands off" alarm if such an installation is deemed advisable. They will learn to question persons loitering in unauthorized areas. They will be alert to suspicious movements by customers and will know what to do and how to do it if they are aware that a holdup is in progress in some other part of the store. They will remain cool and make mental notes of the robbers' appearance for later identification. They will cooperate with the robbers' demands to an acceptable minimum. They will not under any circumstances try to fight back or resist. If possible, they will hand over the lesser of two packs of money if that choice is open, but they will never do so if there is the slightest chance that the robbers will notice. They will remain alert to the possibility of robbery, and if they are involved in one, they will make careful observations for assistance in apprehending the criminals.

Robbery Prevention

By incorporating some of the ideas already discussed in this chapter, several companies have developed robbery prevention programs. These are comprehensive plans designed to make stores less attractive targets for robbers, to protect employees, and to assist officials in apprehension.

The primary goal of these programs is to make the store less attractive to potential robbers. One successful strategy has been to publicize the fact that the store has a robbery prevention program and does not keep large amounts of money in cash registers and that employees do not have the combination to the drop safe. Today it is not unusual to see large signs stating these facts placed in plain view in many stores. This program became essential to several major convenience store and gas station chains during the early 1970s when a rash of robberies left several employees dead, and the importance of such programs has again dramatically come to public attention with the rash of slayings associated with convenience stores in 1990.

Cash register location has also been carefully studied. In general, it is advisable to locate cashiers in areas where they are visible from the street but where the register drawer and cash transactions are not easily observed by passers-by.

Robbery prevention programs also stress the wellbeing of the employee. No cash loss is worth the death of an employee. Employees should be instructed to cooperate and not do anything that would make the robber resort to violence. Although they should cooperate, employees should also be trained to be observant and to note any features and actions of the robber that might later help officials apprehend the robber. After a robbery has occurred, employees are often supplied with forms that ask for specific details about the robber's appearance and voice and show pictures of various weapon types as an aid to identification. While it may not be possible to describe a robber in the police jargon (for example, 6'2", 200 lbs., light complexion, dark brown hair), it is possible to use descriptive aids that will allow the police to develop such a description. Since many people are not practiced enough to guess someone's specific height, such information is often not reliable. Employees can be trained, however, to match a person's height to reference points in the store or to other people. For example, employees might notice how the robber's height compared to their own or might observe that the robber came up to a certain point on a doorway. Weight and build might be better described by comparing the robber with another person—perhaps the police officer or store manager. In addition, employees must realize that the best information concerning the robbery is the escape mode. Did the robber leave on foot, on a motorcycle, or in a car? Only one employee should try to follow the robber after allowing the robber the time to get far enough away so that the employee is not in jeopardy.

As in the case of burglary, there is no absolute solution to the problem of robbery, but this does not mean that firms must accept robbery as a given of business. It has been shown that robbery attempts can be reduced by careful management procedures and by certain physical security measures, for example, surveillance devices.

Bombs and Bomb Threats

Any business, industry, or institution can become the victim of a bombing or a bomb threat. Most telephone bomb threats—approximately 98 percent—turn out to be hoaxes. The target of the threat, however, has no way of knowing whether a real bomb has been planted. Contingency planning is necessary for an organization to be able to protect its personnel and property from the hazards of an explosion. In the absence of a specific response plan, the bomb threat will often cause panic. This may be the precise result the caller seeks.

Controlling access to the facility; having adequate perimeter barriers and lighting; checking all parcels and packages; locking areas such as storerooms, equipment rooms, and utility closets; and taking note of any suspicious persons or of anyone not authorized to be in an area—all these are measures that can thwart a bomb planter as well as a thief or other kind of intruder.

Contingency plans should specify who will be responsible for handling the crisis and delegating authority in the event a bomb threat is received. The officer in charge of responding to a bomb threat must be someone who will be available 24 hours a day. A control center or command post provisioned for communication with all parts of the facility and with law enforcement agencies should also be designated. All personnel who will be involved in the bomb threat response must receive training in their assignments and duties. Plans should be in writing.

Telephone Operator's Response

The telephone operator's role is critical in handling the bomb threat call. The operator should receive training in the proper response so as to elicit from the caller as much information as possible. The two most important items of information to be learned are the expected time of the explosion and the location of the bomb. The operator should remain calm and attempt to keep the caller talking as long as possible in hopes of gaining information or clues that will aid investigators. The caller's accent, tone of voice, and any background noises should be noted. Many organizations provide telephone operators with a bomb threat report form for recording all information (see Figure 18.3).

After receiving a bomb threat call, the operator must inform the designated authority within the organization (the chief of security, for example). Law-enforcement authorities, and others in the organization, will be notified in turn according to the written contingency plans.

Search Teams

A decision must be made whether to conduct a search of the premises and how extensive the search should be. If possible, the search should be conducted by employee teams rather than police or fire department officers. Employees are familiar with their work area and can recognize any out-of-place object. An explosive device may be virtually any size or shape. Any foreign object, therefore, is suspect.

Basic techniques for a two-person search team include:

1. Move slowly and listen for the ticking of a clockwork device. (It is a good idea to pause and listen before beginning to search an area to become familiar with the ordinary background noise that is always present.)
2. Divide the room to be searched into two halves. Search each half

**CHECKLIST WHEN YOU RECEIVE
A BOMB THREAT**

Time and date reported: _____

How reported: _____

Exact words of caller: _____

_____

_____

Questions to ask: _____

1. When is bomb going to explode? _____

2. Where is bomb right now? _____

3. What kind of bomb is it? _____

4. What does it look like? _____

5. Why did you place the bomb? _____

6. Where are you calling from? _____

Description of caller's voice: _____

Male _____ Female _____ Young _____ Middle age _____ Old _____ Accent _____

Tone of voice _____ Background noise _____ Is voice familiar? _____

If so, who did it sound like? _____

_____

Other voice characteristics: _____

Time caller hung up: _____ Remarks: _____

_____

_____

Name, address, telephone of recipient: _____

_____

_____

Figure 18.3 Telephone bomb threat information form.

separately in three layers: floor to waist level, waist to eye level, and eye to ceiling level.

3. Starting back-to-back and working toward each other, search around the walls at each of the three height levels; then move toward the center of the room.

If a suspicious object is found, it must not be touched. Its location and description should be reported immediately to designated authorities. A clear zone with a radius of at least 300 feet should be established around the device (including the floors above and below). Removal and disarming of explosive devices should be left to professionals.

Those assigned to search a particular area should report to the control center after completing the search.

Evacuation

Evacuating the facility for any reason, particularly in response to a bomb threat, is a drastic reaction to the potential danger. There clearly are situations when such an extreme course is indicated, but such a decision should never be undertaken lightly. It is essential that a thorough and exhaustive dialogue relative to this complex problem be undertaken at the earliest opportunity so that plans and policies may be formulated prior to any actual pressure caused by such an emergency. Many experts in the field argue that a total evacuation is rarely if ever indicated. The argument concerns the risk of exposing a great number of people to the blast when the location of the bomb is unknown. Whenever personnel are moved about in large groups, the possibility of exposure to injury is increased. Moreover the movement of large numbers under the threat of bombing can create panic—a very dangerous situation.

A bomber who has shown familiarity with the facility by placing a bomb on the premises can be assumed to be familiar with normal and perhaps even abnormal or emergency traffic patterns of that facility. The bomber has probably placed the bomb in such a way as to create the greatest possible injury and havoc. In such a situation, total evacuation might serve only to expose the greatest number of employees to injury and death.

It has also been found that hoaxers or mischief-makers may be encouraged by a mass evacuation to repeat such calls and to subject the facility to a string of bomb threats.

The decision whether to evacuate will be made by management of the threatened facility, often in conjunction with law-enforcement officials. It may be decided to evacuate the entire facility, only the areas in the vicinity of the suspected bomb, or (unless a device has actually been discovered) not to evacuate at all. Detailed plans are necessary to insure safe and orderly evacuation. Personnel should leave through designated exits and assemble in a predetermined safe area. Elevators should not be used during evacuation. Doors and windows should be left open for increased venting of the explosive force.

When authorities have determined that the bomb threat emergency has ended, all personnel who have been notified of the threat should be informed that normal operations are to resume.

Labor Disputes

If a facility is faced with a deteriorating labor-management relationship during negotiation of a new union contract, it may be necessary to review those security measures designed to protect personnel and property during unusual periods.

Security directors should review every element of these plans with their departments to ensure that the staff is totally familiar with the job to be performed and that every member of the staff is adequately trained to perform as necessary. They should be certain that all security personnel are aware that their role is to protect personnel and property only and that they are not to participate in any way in the elements of the dispute, which is strictly between management and the participating union.

In clarifying policy and getting approval of specific plans of action from responsible management, foresight is indicated. The earlier the protection system is established, the better. Many elements will require time and considerable concentration from those executives who will later be occupied with handling the labor problem and therefore may not be available for consultation.

A checklist of some possible measures is listed below as a guide to the development of a more thorough plan that will apply more specifically to a given facility.

1. Secure all doors and gates not being used during the strike and see that they remain secured.
2. Remove all combustibles from the area near the perimeter—both inside and outside.
3. Remove any trash and stones from the perimeter that could be used for missiles.
4. Change all locks and padlocks on peripheral doors of all buildings to which keys have been issued to striking employees.
5. Recover keys from employees who will go out on strike.
6. Nullify all existing identification cards for the duration and issue special cards to workers who are not striking.
7. Check all standpipe hoses, fire extinguishers, and other firefighting equipment after striking workers have walked out.
8. Test sprinkler systems and all alarms—both fire and intrusion—after striking workers have walked out.
9. Consider construction of barriers for physical protection of windows, landscaping, and lighting fixtures.
10. Move property most likely to be damaged well back from the perimeter.

11. Be certain all security personnel are familiar with the property line and stay within it at all times when they are on duty.

12. Guards are not to be armed, nor are guards to be used to photograph, tape, or report on the conduct of the strikers. The only reports will relate to injury to personnel or property.

13. Notify employees who will continue to work to keep the windows of their automobiles closed and their car doors locked when they are moving through the picket line.

14. Consider the establishment of a shuttle bus for nonstriking employees.

15. Establish, in advance, which vendors or service persons will continue to service the facility, and make arrangements to provide substitute services for those unwilling to cross the picket line.

16. Keep lines of communication open.

17. Since functional organizational lines may be radically changed during the walkout, find out who is where, and who is responsible for what.

Terrorism

Terrorism continues to be a major concern although the "hype" factor may be more significant than the actual probability of becoming a victim. In 1986, only 12 U.S. citizens were killed and 100 wounded in worldwide international terrorism. In 1987, the number killed dropped to 7 with only 40 wounded. By 1989, 16 U.S. citizens were killed and only 19 wounded.[15] However, the loss of even one life and the fear associated with becoming a victim cannot be overestimated.

The impact on the corporate United States is very significant. Twenty of the top 25 U.S. firms have been targeted by terrorists. And terrorism has had an impact on almost all international firms. The largest firms have taken security precautions.

One of the newer (but certainly not new) trends in attacking companies has been assault on executives—primarily kidnapping for ransom. This practice has been common in many foreign countries and is also increasing in the United States; the problem seems to be related to the increase in terrorism throughout the world. Figure 18.4 shows the increase in terrorism through 1989. To be able to develop adequate protection for executives, security managers must understand the terrorist problem and the strategies of various terrorist leaders.

A universal definition of terrorism is difficult to obtain because the acts are seen differently by the victim, the perpetrator, and others who are not involved in the act. For example, the Palestine Liberation Organization (PLO)

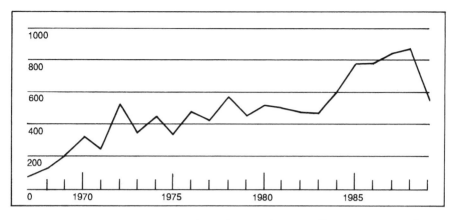

Figure 18.4 Increase in terrorism through 1989. (From William C. Cunningham, John J. Strauchs, Clifford W. VanMeter, *The Hallcrest Report II: Private Security Trends 1970–2000* (Boston: Butterworth-Heinemann, 1990), p. 81.

sees itself as a group fighting to liberate its homeland while the Israelis see the PLO as a terrorist group bent on the destruction of Israel. Outsiders might support either group. Despite these varying views, both the Private Security Advisory Council and the Task Force on Disorders and Terrorism define terrorism in terms of its actions and goals. Both groups agree that terrorism is an act of threat used to create fear for coercive purposes for political or economic objectives.[16] To complicate this definition, however, groups and individuals who do not fit into the above description are often labeled as having used terrorist tactics to accomplish their objectives. These activities can be termed "quasi-terrorism." The Private Security Advisory Council (PSAC) defines quasi-terrorism as activities incidental to the commission of crimes of violence that are similar in form and method to true terrorism but that lack its essential ingredient: creating fear for coercive purposes. Quasi-terrorist activities are taking hostages in bank robberies, skyjacking for private gain, and so on.

Although the number of terrorists may be small, their actions have a great deal of impact. Throughout the world there are over 50 major terrorist organizations, which vary in size from a few members to several hundred. In all, there are about 3000 members. Only 4 or 5 such groups have enough members and support to be transnational threats. The real problem arises from terrorist sympathizers. Most of these groups have support from various governments and thus have access to automatic weapons, surface-to-air missiles, antitank weapons and sophisticated bombs. In 1975 over Orly Airport in France, a Yugoslavian aircraft was damaged by such a missile. And in 1988, Pan Am Flight 103 was blown from the air over Scotland by a bomb.

Why does terrorism exist? Although political terrorism often appears irrational and unpredictable to victims and observers, it is very rational from the terrorist point of view. Basic to most terrorist theory is that violence will bring the uncommitted masses into the conflict on the side of right—of course, the terrorist—point of view. Terrorist actions are violent because:

1. They show the strength of the group.
2. They are provocative, causing the general population to pay attention to the group's activities.

Today terrorism is a very viable method of attracting not only local, but also national or world, attention through the mass media.

In the last few years, terrorist organizations have shifted their targets from governments to business. Since 1975, targeting of businesses has become more widespread even in the United States. Attacks on private businesses in Chicago and on the west coast are indicative of this trend. Terrorists use the rich nation/poor nation issue whereby multinational and other large companies are portrayed as exploiters of the poor. Many of these large companies are rich enough to pay enormous ransoms, and in the past, have paid the ransoms. Coupled with government target-hardening stances, companies are more attractive targets. Because of these trends, businesses are more vulnerable to terrorism than at any time in the past.

Despite this vulnerability because businesses are profit-oriented, the cost of the additional security measures must always be justified. In many cases, CEOs (chief executive officers) view the cure as worse than the disease, and many CEOs are unwilling to give up their personal liberty and freedom for protection. These same CEOs generally are unwilling to concede that their firms could be targets for terrorists. In addition, many corporations are willing to pay ransoms rather than invest in protective measures because they believe that a possible ransom will work out cheaper than constantly spending money on security.

The United States and many other countries, however, have adopted a posture of not making concessions to terrorists.

Executive Protection

Countermeasures against terrorism for businesses are not as costly as executives may believe. Of course, no program can entirely guarantee protection against attack. But a business can take action to lessen its attractiveness as a target. In general, executive protection programs include target hardening, bodyguard operations, and training sessions to teach executives how to avoid being identified as targets, and what to do if they become targets. The key to success in executive protection is preplanning for a possible attack. One successful approach has been the crisis management team (CMT).

A company's CMT is comprised of a carefully selected group of experts in a variety of fields who meet several times a year to discuss how to prevent attacks and what to do if an executive is kidnapped or another type of threat is received by the firm (for example, a bomb threat). In general these teams are composed of a senior executive, a team leader, a security executive, a police liaison, a medical consultant, a lawyer, a financial adviser, a communications expert, and a terrorist liaison. Each team member brings specific knowledge that will be crucial should a threat be received. The senior executive is responsible for making the final decisions. The security executive must coordinate security operations for the facilities involved to protect other employees or company property. The police liaison is responsible for seeing that the authorities are fully apprised of the situation and that the company cooperates with the civil authorities to its fullest ability. The medical consultant must have access to medical files on each executive so that a medical profile can be developed to help the kidnappers keep the victim in good health. The lawyer interprets what actions the company can take without violating company policy or various laws. This is particularly vital when multinational corporations are involved in negotiations with foreign countries. In the past, several firms that cooperated with terrorists in an attempt to recover kidnapped executives found that the governments involved prohibited such negotiations and subsequently confiscated the firms' assets. The financial adviser is necessary to determine how and if funds can be pulled together to meet demands. Ideally most firms do not have $1 million in cash simply laying around. Rather, firms invest their capital in equipment, stocks, and bonds. The communications expert handles any direct communications desired by the terrorists. In many cases this operation may be handled by the authorities. The terrorist liaison may be the most difficult member to recruit; this person must understand terrorist organizations and their intentions. The terrorist liaison must analyze the terrorists' demands and predict their responses to actions by the company. In general, this role is filled by a psychologist, psychiatrist, or sociologist.

Regardless of what actions a firm takes to prevent or respond to terrorist attacks, it is most important that some action be taken. The problem must be recognized, and some type of planning must follow. It is prudent to note, however, that the *Hallcrest II* researchers believe that most companies are overspending in this area. At the rate of $26 billion in counterterrorism spending overseas, the spending in 1986 is equivalent to $223 million per victim. The report states that the 1989 ratio was $714 million.[17]

Review Questions

1. What distinguishes robbery from burglary?
2. What is target hardening? List several target-hardening techniques.
3. Describe the concept of robbery prevention.
4. When someone phones to make a bomb threat, what information should be obtained from the caller?
5. Why is total evacuation of a facility a drastic reaction to a bomb threat? What potential hazards are caused by such an action?
6. List some of the measures that should be taken prior to a labor strike.
7. Briefly outline the present terrorist situation. How does terrorism relate to executive protection?

References

1. William C. Cunningham, John J. Strauchs, Clifford W. VanMeter, *The Hallcrest Report II: Private Security Trends 1970–2000* (Boston: Butterworth-Heinemann, 1990), p. 53.
2. Peyton B. Schur and James E. Broder, *Investigation of Substance Abuse in the Workplace* (Boston: Butterworth-Heinemann, 1990), p. 12.
3. Ibid., pp. 12–14.
4. "Substance Abuse Linked to Increased Problem on the Job," *Security* (April 1991): p. 11.
5. Ibid.
6. Ibid.
7. Ibid.
8. Gregory M. Louis-Nont, "Alternatives to Drug Testing,"*Security Management*, May 1990, pp. 48–50.
9. Cunningham, et al., p. 57.
10. Cunningham, et al., p. 17.
11. Herbert Edelhertz as quoted in Gary S. Green, *Occupational Crime* (Chicago: Nelson Hall, 1990), p. 11.
12. Gilbert Geis as quoted in ibid., p. 16.
13. Cunningham, et al., p. 28.
14. Thomas W. Wathen, "Welcome to the 1990s: A Security Industry CEO Takes a Look at the Future," *Security* April 1991, p. 19.
15. Cunningham, et al., p. 80.
16. William C. Cunningham and Philip J. Gross, *Prevention of Terrorism: Security Guidelines for Business and other Organizations* (McLean, Va.: Hallcrest Press, 1978), p. 3.
17. Cunningham, et al., p. 80.

19 ▫▫▫▫▫▫▫▫▫

Security: Its Problems, Its Future

The National Crime Survey (NCS) reports that the percentage of households touched by crime declined 23 percent between 1975 and 1988. Despite the efforts of law-enforcement agencies, community programs, and private security, however, the crime problem continues to be a major concern for most U.S. citizens. *Hallcrest II* researchers report that "[i]ndicators suggest strongly that fear of crime is increasing even while the statistics indicate that crime itself is stabilizing or declining."[1] Today few would deny that the criminal justice system alone has not been effective in reducing crime. In addition, declining funding for public law enforcement has forced most law-enforcement administrators to cut back on services. Many such policies forbid personnel from responding to or investigating certain types of crime. To fill this void, criminal justice administrators and scholars have called for greater involvement from the private sector. The *Hallcrest II* staff says that the "coproduction of security resources by public law enforcement, private security, and citizens is necessary to reduce the fear of crime."[2] In recent years the private sector has responded willingly.

While the overall perceptions of crime are important, the economic impact of crime on businesses is of greater significance to security management. *Hallcrest II* reports that economic crime will continue to grow at astounding rates. Part of the problem stems from the nation's inability to find a set of accurate measures. This problem coupled with others must be overcome before the nation will be effective in dealing with economic crime. To make the situation worse, *Hallcrest II* predicts that not only will the problem continue to grow in volume but it will also become increasingly sophisticated—aided by the use of computers and electronic transfer of funds. The recent scandals of insider trading and savings-and-loan failures are indicators of problems yet to come.

Private Security Resources

The *Hallcrest II* researchers estimate that the manufacturer's value of shipments for security-related products and revenues for security services will reach a combined total of $32 billion by the year 2000.[3] In addition, one market research firm predicts that revenues for security services in the private sector will exceed $53 billion in 1995. *Hallcrest II* estimates total U.S. employment in private security at 1,493,300 people in 1990 with projected growth to 1,900,000 by the year 2000.[4]

Growth in private security is shown by increases in expenditure, employment numbers, and value of equipment. In addition, many new firms have entered the business, established firms are showing strong growth, and some Fortune 500 companies as well as foreign firms are buying security firms.

In a time when public law enforcement is experiencing little or no growth, private security directors are experiencing greater demands on their resources. Still, over half of local and central station alarm firms reported annual budget increases. Private security industry will continue to grow.

To fill the gap left by public law enforcement and to help alleviate some of the fears felt by the public, private sector security has offered its services in a variety of areas, including private patrols of residential areas, security for courtrooms, correctional facilities, traffic control, and so on.

Hallcrest II made a variety of recommendations for improving the efficiency of the private sector in its quest for acceptance in the criminal justice system. The recommendations cover economic crime, business ethics, drug abuse, computer crime, terrorism, dimensions of protection, security personnel issues, security services and products, and comparisons of private security and law enforcement. These recommendations are well worth study and should be reviewed by those seriously involved in either law enforcement or private security.

The private sector has a tremendous impact on crime and the criminal justice system. Therefore, it is absolutely necessary for the private sector system to be completely understood. *Hallcrest II* indicates that in the future the private sector will bear more of the burden for crime prevention while law enforcement will narrow the focus of police services to crime control. Most of the security managers surveyed by the researchers were willing to accept this growing role.

Interaction and Cooperation

Although *Hallcrest I* rated interaction and cooperation between the public and private sector as good, it also noted (as did The Rand Report and the Private Security Advisory Council [PSAC]) that certain impediments to interaction and cooperation still existed. These impediments included role conflict, negative stereotypes, lack of mutual respect, and minimal knowledge on the part of law enforcement about private security. As was noted when these topics were discussed in earlier chapters, both private and public sector administrators are cooperating to try to overcome these problems.

Hallcrest II found that security and the police have made great strides in cooperating in a variety of areas. Some discussion of these areas was presented earlier in this text. The trend by the public sector to contract services with greater cooperation between the public and private sectors will continue into the twenty-first century. According to Robert Trojanowicz:

> One question that need not be asked is whether the trend will persist. We are already too far down the road to turn back. Therefore, the ultimate question is not whether this change is good or bad, but whether these changes will occur piecemeal and poorly or throughtfully and well.[5]

Limitations of Security

A great burden has been placed on the private sector, and some of the expectations will very likely not be met. It is impossible to be everything to everyone, especially in an area which is changing so rapidly. Consider, for example, the changes in technology. Security's main purpose is to prevent losses. Historically losses were reduced through the use of various physical security devices that served as delaying devices to would-be intruders. As the targets for theft changed, security modified its strategies and adopted new security technologies. Today security in many companies is truly a full loss-prevention operation, and within such operations, there are state-of-the-art security systems, coupled with traditional security methods.

How effective are security devices today? Security managers would be wise to remember that no system is completely effective. A determined person can find ingenious methods of defeating any system. For example, consider the progressive development of lock technology. It began with a simple doorknob lock with a spring latch. As we know today, this combination offers virtually no protection from a person who wants to gain entry. The simplest and least-destructive method of gaining access would be to card the lock. If this option is removed by installing a dead latch, the intruder will have to choose another means of access. Since the latch does not extend more than half an inch into the door frame, a burglar could spring the door or twist the doorknob off to gain access to the locking mechanism. This problem may be solved by installing a good dead bolt lock. Each step that security takes requires a burglar to use more time. But the burglar is still not stopped. The burglar chooses to either cut the dead bolt or twist the collar mechanism off the dead bolt lock. Security then responds by installing a dead bolt with a slip collar (or recessed system) and a dead bolt with a case-hardened core.

In most cases if the door and frame are of solid construction (that is, metal), burglars will not attack them. But some might want company assets enough to find another method of entry. The keying device then becomes a target; key cores can be drilled or popped. Security managers who have been thinking ahead will purchase locks with case-hardened drill plates, which will foil both drilling and popping. There is still the chance to pick the lock. But security can anticipate this and install a pick-resistant lock.

Has security now stopped the potential intruder? In reality most thieves would not bother to assault this level of protection; but if the target is sufficiently valuable, other alternatives exist. The thief's imagination is the only limiting factor.

With today's high-tech security devices, a security manager can virtually eliminate any target's probability of being attacked. The modern age has brought "Star Wars" devices such as computer-access systems based on fingerprints or voice identification, laser beam alarm systems and communication devices, sophisticated listening devices, and their counterparts—sweeping devices. Lighting technology has made it possible to illuminate areas to daylight levels with reduced costs. The list goes on, but the question remains: Why does crime continue to plague us?

The answer may lie in the fact that when thieves are sufficiently motivated, they will find a way. Or it may be because a security manager has failed to convince executives to pay for a security operation that appears to them to be an added expenditure that will not add to the profit margin.

High-tech has made the operation of most businesses much easier. The photocopier, the fax, and the computer make information transfer simpler and more efficient. The convenience has at the same time created new problems for security in the areas of increased information and physical security risks.

Trends

While the field is now over 1.1 million personnel with the majority employed in contract security, the trend will continue toward fewer and smaller proprietary security operations. Firms will hire contract security or security consultants for special purpose projects. Contract firms will continue to merge. For example, California Plant Protection and Pinkertons is now Pinkerton.

The security equipment industry will continue to grow from its $17 billion per year base at an annual rate of 15 percent. Experts predict that annual growth will slow to an average of 9–12 percent by the year 2000.

The testing industry geared to preemployment, drug, and psychological testing will continue to offer services sought after by the private sector. Advocates of privacy standards will continue to restrict the use of these types of tests.

The use of outside investigators and security specialists will increase. The trend will be toward a manager of security services using security consultants for special projects.

Technology will continue to stress integration of computers and biometrics with CCTV (closed circuit TV) and access controls. Telephone systems will be used increasingly for the connection of security systems and safety devices. Microprocessing chips dedicated to security purposes will be embedded in equipment. Robotics will continue to grow, particularly in the area of corrections and guard operations within confined areas. Miniaturization is a trend. CCTV cameras the size of cigarette packages are already on the market. EAS (electronic article surveillance) will continue to grow as prepared packaging becomes more prominent.

Liability costs, while remaining relatively high, will continue in the downward trend that began in 1986. The downward trend may be attributable to better-prepared security managers who are learning the value of risk management.

Drug testing will continue to be a major issue for corporations. Until the nation is able to control the drug problem, this issue will remain an ethical as well as a legal problem for many firms. The cost associated with screening can be prohibitive, and while the public relations aspect of the EAP (employee assistance program) cannot be disputed, there are those who are now asking whether the company can afford to spend thousands of dollars on each employee who needs rehabilitation.

In addition to its role in fighting the increase of economic crime in general, security will face an increase in computer and computer-related crime. As noted earlier in this text, estimates of the cost of computer crime range from between $1 billion to $200 billion annually. *Hallcrest II* estimated that in 1990 computer security expenditures reached $224 million or 2 percent of all security equipment expenditures. *Hallcrest II* staff predicts that these expenditures will grow at an annual rate of 17 percent and reach $864 million by the year 2000, representing 3 percent of the total expenditures on equipment.[6]

On the international scale, there is more concern about security issues. The Common Market recently mandated that security laws be reviewed and upgraded to bring commonality to the European community.

Terrorism is also a problem, especially for companies operating on an international scale. No international political terrorist incidents have occurred in the United States since 1983. *Hallcrest II* believes that security expenditures in this area are out of phase with the real threat to U.S. businesses. The recent Gulf war, however, has caused a growth in concern among most multinational companies. The key in planning antiterrorist security operations for the twenty-first century will be providing adequate protection without spending money for unnecessary security.

The Future

The future for the security field is very positive. Professionalization is being pursued; large sums of money are being spent to improve security and loss-prevention operations. For the first time since World War II, security has found its place in business. In addition, limitations of the criminal justice system have been identified, and the resultant void is being filled with some success by the private sector. The future in private security is exceptionally bright for the talented person who wishes to do something special—especially if that person has a sound educational preparation.

Technology

The future for technological advances in security is also bright. In just 40 years, the security business has seen the arrival of CCTV, microwave detection systems, small portable radios and cameras, magnetic sensors, and laser technology. Security has taken advantage of these technological improvements through necessity—the realization that for every new piece of security equipment there is a person who, given the challenge, will find a way to subvert, bypass, or defeat it.

Combinations of biometric, electronic, and computer technologies will allow security and other management personnel to follow employees from the time they enter the facility until the time they leave it.

Today's battles with criminals are far more often battles of intellect than they are of muscle. Gigliotti and Jason predict that, since security is one of the fastest-growing businesses, we will probably see security measures such as force fields, holographic security officers, and laser pistols.[7] The future is limited only by the security technician's imagination.

Management

As Tom Peters notes in his writings, the manager of the future must be able to predict and manage change.[8] In fact, Peters would probably prefer the word "leader" to "manager." The security leader of the twenty-first century will need to be flexible. As Thomas Sege, Chairman and chief executive officer (CEO) of Varian Research, notes, "You have to approach things much more flexibly. Change can come from all directions. You can't chart one course and hold to it. Course corrections are going to have to be made."[9]

All businesses will continue to stress the benefits of cost management. Profit margins must be improved and security will be expected to offer its fair share. The security manager will thus become a security program educator and saleperson.

Security managers must learn to sell security as if it was any other product. Because CEOs think in terms of profit, a good security manager must find ways of selling security as a cost-effective investment. For example, perhaps better lighting is needed in a particular place of employment. All the CEO sees is a cost for new lighting, which the security manager suggests might reduce theft, vandalism, and accidents. Will possible savings in these areas offset the cost? Probably not in the first year. But why not project the cost of the project over five or more years? Also consider the savings in electricity costs from installing more efficient fixtures and the possible reduction in insurance rates. Now the CEO is interested. All of a sudden the investment is at worst breaking even—and it might even save the company money. The "bottom line" will be more important than ever.

Security managers will find that safety, architecture, consulting and engineering, human resources, compliance, transporation, telecommunications, information processing, and marketing will demand more from the security operation, and that in order to develop future oriented security programs, they must take an interest in these areas.

Theft

The greatest threat for security managers will continue to be employee theft. Worker loyalty will decrease. Ethical issues will become important for security managers as they struggle to protect company information as well as physical property. Employee theft will continue to cost business about $40 billion annually. Worker gangs will conspire to steal and use company facilities and time to conduct their outside drug, money laundering, and mail fraud businesses.

Education/Professionalization

Experts predict that by the year 2020 the majority of new jobs will require postsecondary education. Yet today, 20 percent of the U.S. workforce reads at no better than an eighth-grade level. This means that unless something changes the workers of the future will not be able to read basic materials necessary to perform at the required level. The staff at *Security* predict that, in the future, professional organizations representing security will approach colleges, universities, and community colleges and ask for help with programs that train security officers and security professionals.[10]

Certification/Standards

The discussions presented earlier in this text point toward the need for some type of mandated minimum standards for the security industry. Recent developments may lead the way for some type of industry-imposed regulations similar to the British system. If security is to continue to take the place of law enforcement, the field must present a professional image. The image can exist only when outsiders can view the field with the respect that comes from established standards.

Conclusion

As was stated in the fourth edition of this text, the future for security is bright. The more the educated person becomes a part of the security occupation, the greater the professional development of that occupation. It is obvious that the public cannot afford to pay for all the protection needed in our modern world. The only means of providing security as defined in Chapter 1 is through the use of private resources that keep the costs of products down and provide an environment wherein our free enterprise system can prosper.

Review Questions

1. List several major trends for security in the twenty-first century. Explain their significance from a management perspective.
2. Explain the need for security management to develop into educators and salespeople for security programs. Give an example of how you might present a security program to your CEO.
3. What role should security play in the prevention of terrorism in the twenty-first century?
4. What is the future of public/private cooperation in the twenty-first century?

References

1. William C. Cunningham, John J. Strauchs, and Clifford W. Van Meter, *The Hallcrest Report II: Private Security Trends 1970–2000* (Boston: Butterworth-Heinemann, 1990), p. 312.
2. Ibid., p. 319.

3. Ibid., p. 190.
4. Ibid., p. 196.
5. Robert Trojanowicz, "Public and Private Justice: Preparing for the 21st Century," *Criminal Justice Alumni Newsletter*, Michigan State University, V, no. 1 (Fall/Winter 1989): p. 2.
6. Cunningham, et al., p. 71.
7. Richard Gigliotti and Ronald Jason, *Security Design for Maximum Protection* (Stoneham, Mass.: Butterworth Publishers, 1984).
8. Tom Peters, *Thriving on Chaos: A Handbook for a Management Revolution* (New York: Harper & Row Publishers, 1987).
9. "Exploring Security Trends...," special report *Security*, 1989, p. 2.
10. Ibid., pp. 5–6.

Index